Nancy Silverton is the co-owner of Osteria Mozza (which was awarded a Michelin Star in 2019), Pizzeria Mozza, Chi Spacca, and Mozza2Go, in Los Angeles and Newport Beach, California. She is the founder of the La Brea Bakery and is the only person ever to be awarded both the Outstanding Chef and Outstanding Pastry Chef awards from the James Beard Foundation. In 2014, Silverton was listed as one of the Most Innovative Women in Food and Drink by both *Fortune* and *Food & Wine* magazines, and in 2017, she was profiled in an episode of Netflix's award-winning docu-series *Chef's Table*. Silverton is the author of ten cookbooks, including *Mozza at Home*, *The Mozza Cookbook*, *A Twist of the Wrist*, *Nancy Silverton's Sandwich Book*, *Nancy Silverton's Pastries from the La Brea Bakery* (recipient of a 2000 *Food & Wine* Best Cookbook Award), *Nancy Silverton's Breads from the La Brea Bakery,* and *Desserts*. She is planning to open two new restaurants, an Italian steakhouse in the Hollywood Roosevelt Hotel called The Barish—named after her ancestors, who were cattle ranchers in Saskatchewan, Canada, during the early twentieth century—and Pizzette in Culver City.

Instagram: @nancysilverton
Twitter: @NancySilverton

CHI SPACCA

CHI SPACCA

A New Approach to American Cooking

Nancy Silverton

with Ryan DeNicola and Carolynn Carreño

Photographs by Ed Anderson

Alfred A. Knopf   New York   2020

THIS IS A BORZOI BOOK
PUBLISHED BY ALFRED A. KNOPF

Library of Congress Cataloging-in-Publication Data
Names: Silverton, Nancy, author. | DeNicola, Ryan, author. |
Carreño, Carolynn, author. | Anderson, Ed (Edward Charles), photographer.
Title: Chi Spacca : a new approach to American cooking / Nancy Silverton
with Ryan DeNicola and Carolynn Carreño ; photographs by Ed Anderson.
Description: First edition. | New York : Alfred A. Knopf, [2020] | Includes index.
Identifiers: LCCN 2019021142 | ISBN 9780525654650 (hardcover : alk. paper) |
ISBN 9780525654667 (ebook)
Subjects: LCSH: Cooking, Italian. | Cooking—United States. |
Chi Spacca (Restaurant)
Classification: LCC TX723 .S48377 2020 | DDC 641.5945—dc23
LC record available at https://lccn.loc.gov/2019021142

Some of the recipes in this book include uncooked or unwashed ingredients.
When these foods are consumed, there is always a risk that bacteria may
be present. For this reason, always buy from a reliable grocer and consult
a healthcare professional before serving infants, small children, pregnant
women, the elderly, or any persons who may be immunocompromised.
The author and publisher expressly disclaim responsibility for any
adverse effects that may result from the use or application of the
recipes and information contained in this book.

Jacket photograph by Ed Anderson
Jacket design by Kelly Blair

Book design by Cassandra J. Pappas

Manufactured in Germany
First Edition

Alla mie famiglie Italiane:

Dario Cecchini, my brother, and his wife, Kim Wicks,
for showing me generosity, hospitality, and, most important,
respect for the animal.

And Faith Willinger and Massimo Tarli
for inviting me year after year into their kitchen
to experience the joys of the Italian table.

—N.S.

Contents

INTRODUCTION 3

THE SPACCA PANTRY 16

CHI SPACCA GRILLING CLASS
by Ryan DeNicola 27

SPUNTINI 34

INSALATE 74

CARNE 128
Ryan's Meat Tutorial 130
Beef and Veal 133
Pork 168
Lamb 189
Duck, Rabbit, and Chicken 207

PESCE 218

CONTORNI 260

DOLCI 316

Sources 357
Acknowledgments 359
Index 361

CHI SPACCA

Introduction

This book is a collection of recipes that we serve at Chi Spacca, one of three restaurants (along with Pizzeria Mozza and Osteria Mozza) on the corner of Melrose and Highland in Los Angeles. Pronounced "key-SPA-kah," the name literally translates to "she (or he) who cleaves," and is another way of saying "the butcher" in Italian. It is a small, intimate restaurant with forty seats plus twelve at the counter, where everything, from the stretching of our famous Focaccia di Recco (page 39) to the plating of our salads and a three-pound Bistecca Fiorentina (page 134) resting on the grill, is done at the front of the dining room and within arm's reach of those seated at the counter.

The food at Chi Spacca is inspired by how an Italian butcher might cook—and eat—or, it would be more accurate to say: how *I* would cook and eat if I were a butcher. In addition to luxurious grilled steaks and chops and lesser-known, less expensive cuts of meat, we offer boldly seasoned fish dishes; an ever-changing array of caramelized farmers' market vegetables, many of them served whole or in ways that show off their distinct shapes, accompanied by unctuous, herby condiments; a long list of beautiful salads built with unusual lettuce varieties and layered with complementing flavors and textures; and simple, seasonally based, not-too-sweet desserts.

Despite the name, Chi Spacca is not an Italian restaurant. We are definitely more influenced by Italy than by any other country, but we draw inspiration from all over the map in a way that I believe truly reflects our time. In the 1970s when I started cooking, we cooks were influenced mostly by French techniques and traditions. That changed as Italy became the primary outside inspiration. Then Asian-fusion cooking came along, although I never really played with those flavors. And then we were back to Italy. But today, with the Internet and Instagram (and the habit of photographing and "sharing" everything we eat), the world is a smaller place, and the way we eat and cook naturally has changed, too. The components that comprise once-exotic cuisines such as Japanese, Persian, and Mexican have become part of our culinary vocabularies—and pantries. The unique style and ingredients of Israeli cuisine have come into our lives thanks to the beautiful books of Yotam Ottolenghi, as did the eye-opening practice of roasting eggplants whole. Over the last decade, those and other global influences have worked their way into my repertoire and this book. A Milk-Braised Veal Breast with Hazelnuts (page 163) could only be Piedmontese, while the Lacquered Duck with Honey-Balsamic Glaze and Crispy Black Rice (page 208) has its roots in Peking duck. The idea for Roasted Amberjack Collars with Labneh, Zhug, and Radish Salad (page 221) came from Ryan's and my experiences eating them in Japanese restaurants here in Los Angeles (though it is plated with Middle Eastern condiments), but a dish of Fideus a la Catalana with Sweet Sherry and Garlic Aioli (page 236) is undeniably Spanish. I use dried Persian lime in one recipe and chipotle chile powder in others. We make our own riffs on the Middle Eastern "dry pesto" called dukkah, swoosh yogurt under platters of roasted whole vegetables, a style I adopted after seeing it beautifully done on two recent trips to Israel. But I am firm in my conviction that this is not fusion food. It's a sign of the times. We are a country whose population is in constant evolution, and our national cuisine, naturally, has changed, and will continue to change, to reflect that. This beautiful, delicious, global palette of ingredients, techniques, and dishes is American food today.

I didn't intend to open a restaurant that was such a departure from my usual Italian or Cal-Ital style. In fact, I didn't mean to open another restaurant at all. Chi Spacca is a restaurant that found itself. It evolved out of customer demand and the creative thinking of a whole team of chefs, partners, and managers, and it is all the better for that. When the space next to Osteria Mozza came up for rent, our then general manager, David Rosoff, told me: "If we don't rent it, somebody else will." (Which is sort of obvious, but I got the point.) At the time, what we needed more than anything was a place to make pizza; the ovens in Pizzeria Mozza couldn't accommodate the demand for takeout during prime hours. Even when guests having lunch or dinner in the Pizzeria asked for more pizzas to take home, we had to turn them down. So we decided to take the space. It solved the problem of not having enough ovens, but it simultaneously created another problem: the space was too large for just a pizza takeout. Now we had to figure out what to do with this big room. We created a small jewel box of a retail store in front, the purpose of which essentially was eye candy. I didn't want people to walk into an empty cube to pick up their pizza; I wanted them to walk in and be dazzled. We designed the room to look like the small shops and pharmacies in Italy—with marble counters and floor-to-ceiling shelves painted shiny black and filled

with a selection of highly curated artisanal (mostly) Italian products, including pastas, tomatoes, anchovies, olive oil, vinegar, and wine, among other treats. But then we still had more real estate alongside the store to work with. After a lot of brainstorming, we added a third concept: a cooking school. We hung a sign, SCUOLA DI PIZZA, and offered a couple of pizza classes and a couple of pasta classes each week. They were great, and the people who took the classes loved them. But it was a big room with a lot of hours to fill, and we soon began to think about more uses for it.

One of my favorite experiences eating in Italy is at Officina della Bistecca, one of three restaurants owned and operated by my friend Dario Cecchini, the famous Tuscan butcher, located in the idyllic hillside town of Panzano in Chianti. At the Officina, upstairs from the butcher

shop, Dario serves a fixed-price meal, family style at long communal tables, utilizing all parts of the cow. It's a great feast and a lot of fun, and in looking for uses for the Scuola, I thought about the Officina and realized that the Scuola was the perfect place to host such a dinner. We set up one long table in the middle of the room and created a multi-course menu—a collaboration between me, Mozza's founding executive chef Matt Molina, and Chad Colby, who at the time was a cook at Osteria Mozza and would go on to be the founding executive chef at Chi Spacca. The meal was, like at Dario's, a celebration of the cow, starting with carne cruda (Italy's version of beef tartare) and progressing through braised oxtails, grilled short ribs, and a giant bistecca Fiorentina. It was a huge hit. People loved the communal table and the informality that goes with family-style eating; they enjoyed the set menu and not having to make choices; and they loved the food. Even though it was a success, Chad and Matt and I weren't completely satisfied; there was something missing. For Dario, those dinners allow him to showcase the ways in which he uses the whole animal, which is at the core of his philosophy as a butcher. Using all parts of the cow is Dario's way of honoring the life and the death of the animal. But we couldn't use the whole cow. It was too large, the room was too small, and, more important, we weren't a butcher shop.

I thought back to the annual pig dinners that Paul Bertolli used to host when he was chef at the Berkeley restaurant Oliveto. I loved those dinners and used to make the trip to the Bay Area every year to attend. Chad had already started to buy whole hogs for his charcuterie, which meant that with a pork dinner, unlike with a beef dinner, we *would* be able to use the entire animal. So we gave it a try and hosted a family-style meal like the beef dinner but using pork. The pig dinner kicked off with Chad's salumi and pâtés and continued with various preparations from different parts of the hog—pork belly sausage, pork leg ragù, and roasted pork shoulder—and ended with cookies made with pork fat. People went *hog wild* for it! (Pardon the pun.) Soon, we made the pig dinners a regular Saturday-night occasion.

Riding the wave of the success of the pig nights, my partner Joe Bastianich came up with the idea of doing the same type of family-style, multi-course feasts, each celebrating a different seasonal ingredient—citrus, corn, tomatoes, you name it. Usually when restaurants decide to do a special dinner, it involves focusing on a region or highlighting a wine producer, but Joe's idea was something I'd never seen, and the dinners turned out great. We started offering our ingredient-based dinners on Fridays, in addition to the pig dinners on Saturdays, and we sold out every dinner, every week.

By this time, Chad had his charcuterie program in full swing and he decided to start a weekly salumi bar in the Scuola on Thursday nights. His idea was that people might stop in for a glass of wine and a plate of salumi or drop in while waiting for a table at the Osteria next door. I was skeptical, to say the least. Through all of our brainstorming and all of the different incarnations, I had never envisioned the Scuola space as a traditional à la carte restaurant. Boy, was I wrong. When I walked into the room on Chad's first Salumi Night and saw it so crowded and lively, everyone having a good time, I said to Chad, "Wow! I never thought it would work!" Even though the menu on those nights was limited to a short, salumi-based list of appetizers and snacks, people stayed for hours. We added Salumi Nights to our weekly schedule and got a glowing review in *LA Weekly*. The next step was obvious. It was time to grow up and become a full-blown restaurant.

Since Chi Spacca started its life as a cooking school, the kitchen is designed like an open-format fantasy home kitchen with a long counter that has a wood-fired grill and plancha (flat top) on it, and a four-burner stove and a wood-burning oven behind it. The limited kitchen (both in terms of the size and the equipment) dictated our menu: we would focus on wood-fired cooking both on the grill and in the wood-burning oven. To make room for a salad station, we covered the burners with cutting boards so we don't even have a stove! In keeping with the tradition of our dinners, we would continue to butcher whole hogs, honor seasonal ingredients, and also continue to honor the spirit of the Italian butcher who inspired those first dinners. I decided on the cleaver logo, and with that as our guide, we landed on the name Chi Spacca.

Considering the logo, it's no surprise that we are known for our meats—and no doubt about it, our three-pound Bistecca Fiorentina (page 134) and the Flintstone-like Grilled Tomahawk Pork Chop with Fennel Pollen (page 169) are showstoppers, as is the Beef Cheek and Bone Marrow Pie (page 149). But I cannot emphasize enough to you, nor to the non–meat eaters who dine with us and those I hope will be cooking from this book, that we are not a steak house. In fact, one of the greatest compliments that I receive at Chi Spacca is when someone who doesn't eat meat tells me how much he or she loved their meal.

In addition to a healthy selection of meat and seafood, we have a long, ever-changing list of seasonal salads; some are comprised of whole vegetables shaved on a mandoline to reveal their unique shapes. Others are built using unsung heroes of the lettuce world, such as escarole, Castelfranco, and puntarella. All are so bold fla-

vored, layered, and satisfying, you could make a meal of them. (I often do!) Likewise, we offer a revolving selection of seasonal side dishes that are reflected here in the Contorni (side dish) chapter (page 260).

We keep a short, sweet menu of desserts at Chi Spacca, all seasonally inspired, simply plated, and meant to be served as I imagine a butcher would do: in the center of the table with a knife or a big spoon, so guests can slice or scoop for themselves. The desserts also make larger portions than the rest of the recipes in this book, but tell me: What butcher wouldn't want a slice of yesterday's pie with her (or his) morning coffee?

These recipes, like a meal at Chi Spacca, are meant to be served family style, and the meat, fish, vegetable, and salad recipes, with a few exceptions, serve four. I suggest you approach cooking from this book in the same way we advise our customers to order dinner: pick your protein first (if you're having one) and then choose from the Spuntini (Snacks) (page 34), Insalate (Salads) (page 74), and Contorni (page 260), as well as an optional dessert (see Dolci, page 316) to go with them.

My Recipes

A lot of times people who cook from books think that the chef or cookbook author leaves something out, some secret that they're holding back that makes the reader's food turn out inferior to the version they see in the picture, or that they've had at the chef's restaurants. I can tell you that I have held nothing back—not in the recipes themselves nor in the way they're served. This cookbook is a record of how I do things, scaled and interpreted for the home cook, but by no means dumbed down. Each and every one of the steps, the choices, the specific ingredients, and the little tricks that we use to get our food where it is, is here.

Where many cookbooks separate their recipes into subrecipes, I choose to put the recipes for all of the components that make up a dish—the marinades, sauces, rubs, and condiments—into one recipe. For that reason, there are a few recipes, such as salsa verde, or pie dough, that occur in the book more than once. I personally don't love having to flip back and forth between recipes in a book and don't want to make you have to do that very often. In addition, I want to be able to take you through the recipe from beginning to end. If one recipe is built as a subrecipe, then you have to guess as to the order in which to do things. The oven might already be occupied with a giant braising pot and then you find yourself needing it to toast pistachios. As I have written these recipes, I take the guesswork out and walk you through each recipe from beginning to end.

Every chef has his or her own plating style, and you'll notice that I communicate mine in my recipes. I don't just tell you to make a dish and then leave you on your own. I tell you how to put the food on the plate because the plating is part of the recipe. How a dish is presented—the layering of a salad, the swirling of a sauce, the way lemon zest or fried sage leaves fall onto a platter—creates the final experience. I even specify the vessel you will need for serving, or if you will be serving a dish in the pot or pan you cooked it in.

Because these recipes are served family style, the majority go on large (11 × 7 inches of surface area) or extra-large (14 × 9 inches of surface area) platters. Others can be served on a large cutting board; sauces and other condiments are served in small bowls, while many of the side dishes are served in larger, deeper bowls; and some of the salads can go in large wide-mouth bowls.

Know Your Butcher, Fishmonger, and Farmer

We encourage you to shop for these recipes (and in general) from butchers, fishmongers, and farmers. The products they sell are thought-out, researched, and curated based on quality and flavor. They are also very knowledgeable, so they will understand what you are asking for, and may even point you in the direction of alternatives when needed.

There are essentially two kinds of butchers: old-school butchers that have been around for decades, even generations, watching trends come and go, and the new wave of butchers, many of which specialize in grass-fed meats, heritage breeds, and whole animal butchery. Both are great, and both have their place. For those instances when your butcher doesn't have exactly what you want, Ryan has also provided a list of online sources (see Sources, page 357) where you can get the cuts and quality of meats we recommend.

Seafood shops and specialty food stores with a good fish counter promise the freshest product and the most knowledgeable assistance. Several of the recipes in the seafood chapter give an option of which fish to use; a good fishmonger will point you toward the best choice based on what is available locally, what is in season, and what is the freshest that they have on hand. Additionally, many of these recipes call for more unusual varieties or cuts of fish, such as salmon steaks (versus fillets), skate wing, and butterflied branzino, that require some fishmongering skill and that you likely won't find in a regular grocery store.

Farmers' market fruits and vegetables are so far superior in taste that buying them or not could make or break a dish. One of the reasons the farmers' market's product is so much better is that small farmers who sell at a farmers' market generally choose what varieties to grow based on flavor, whereas agribusiness farmers who sell at grocery stores (even the best grocery stores) choose what to grow based on how it looks, how long it lasts, and how well it travels. Grocery store fruits (including tomatoes) are picked unripe so they won't get bruised while bouncing around in a truck. But no matter how long they sit on your counter, these fruits and vegetables will never have the flavor of those ripened on the tree or vine. Also, by shopping at a farmers' market, the question of what is in season is answered for you because farmers sell only what they harvest and usually within days, even hours, of picking.

A Few Tools Worth Mentioning

I was ambivalent about including a list of tools in this book because I thought: Who wants to have to go out shopping for a tool just to use a cookbook? In the end, I decided to include a few tools or gadgets. I'm going to assume that if you have this book in your hand, you also have saucepans, skillets, sharp knives of various sizes (including a serrated knife for slicing bread), mixing bowls, a salad spinner, a stand mixer, and more than one baking sheet. Below is a list of a few more tools that you may *not* have, and that I have come to rely on or that I get pleasure in using, and think you might, too.

MICROPLANE

About ten years ago, I gave up mincing garlic when I discovered how easy it was to grate it instead on a rasp-like kitchen tool called a Microplane. This is a brand name, and while I don't normally recommend brands, this is a worthwhile exception. These recipes call for a fine Microplane to grate garlic, ginger, citrus zest, and hard cheese such as Parmesan. We call for a coarse Microplane when grating fresh horseradish and hard-cooked eggs, and an extra-coarse Microplane to grate larger grates of cheese. Last, a large shaver Microplane makes easy work of shaving very thin shards of hard cheese.

MORTAR AND PESTLE

One of the most obvious symbols of how relaxed I am in Italy is that I break out my mortar and pestle and use it for everything from grinding spices and cracking peppercorns to making pesto and salsa verde. In this book, I give you the option of using a mortar and pestle for the same purposes. When buying a mortar and pestle, the first consideration is that you buy one large enough to make sauces such as Salsa Verde (page 142), Zhug (page 222), and pesto, and other sauces. My favorite mortar and pestle also happens to be one of the first pieces of cooking equipment that I bought when I was at the Cordon Bleu in London, in 1977: a 12-inch Milton Brook ceramic mortar with a ceramic and wood pestle that originated as a pharmaceutical tool in England. It won't break unless you drop it, and that's a good quality in a piece of equipment used for pounding. I remember doing a cooking demonstration at a cooking store—they brought out a beautiful white porcelain mortar and pestle, I started pounding away to make pesto . . . and the mortar cracked! The Milton Brook won't do that. You can order it from one of the original online (or mail-order) sources, Fantes Kitchen Shop (see Sources, page 357). Once you get used to the feel of grinding spices or fresh herbs for sauces using a mortar and pestle, there's nothing like it.

SPICE GRINDER

As much as I love to use my mortar and pestle, there are some ingredients that are too tough to grind by hand, including cinnamon sticks, whole cloves, star anise, and dried porcini mushrooms. For that, an electric spice grinder is invaluable. A spice grinder looks like an old-school coffee grinder, and if there is a difference, it's minimal. (In fact, these days, many of them are called coffee and spice grinders.) Look at online reviews to find the best one within your budget.

MANDOLINE

Even the best of chefs with the sharpest of knives can't slice things as thin as we sometimes want them, such as vegetables for salads, potatoes, shavings of Parmesan, and even very thinly sliced bread for cracker-like toasts. For occasions such as these, we use a mandoline, a plane-like tool with a sharp blade that you slide ingredients on to shave or very thinly slice them. There are many types of mandoline, some very pricey, but you don't have to spend a lot of money: a Benriner mandoline (available at cookware stores or through online sources) works great and is both affordable and widely available. Mandolines have a knob for adjusting the blade to determine how thick it will slice. In recipes where the precise thickness really makes a difference, I instruct you to slice a couple of slices, take a look at them, and adjust the blade to slice thicker or thinner as needed. In general, when slicing vegetables for a salad, I call for you to slice them just thin enough that they hold their shape even when dressed, but not so thin that they wilt or fall apart. Using your hand to slide something back and forth against a sharp blade can be scary or intimidating and you should use a mandoline cautiously. Some come with a plastic safety guard that you can use instead of your hand to slide, but I find these awkward, and use my hand. If you're slicing something large, extend your palm out and use the heel of your hand to slide whatever you're slicing along the blade. If you're slicing something small, such as garlic, you will have to use your fingers. In either case, stop just before you feel your hands or fingers are getting dangerously close to the blade. Alternatively, you may want to wear a stainless-steel mesh glove—just in case! (See Sources, page 357.)

MEAT THERMOMETER

There is no shame in using a meat thermometer to check the temperature of your meats, and for large cuts, there is no other way. Our cooks use them constantly, and if you want perfectly cooked steaks, chops, chicken, and other meats, you should, too. Meat thermometers are easy to find and not nearly as expensive as the meat you will ruin if you don't use one. Our favorite meat thermometer is ThermoWorks; it's available at cookware stores or online sources.

DEEP-FRY THERMOMETER

We fry a number of things in this book, from herbs to grains to main dishes, such as calamari and whole fish. Frying at home can be intimidating, but a deep-fry thermometer takes the guesswork out of the equation and makes the process much less daunting. With the oil at the correct temperature, deep-frying is easy.

MINI FOOD PROCESSOR

Although I prefer to make aioli (garlic mayonnaise) by hand, I've found that the home cook is more comfortable making it in a mini food processor; in these recipes, that is how I instruct you to do it. The reason I specify a mini is that, when making a small, one-egg batch of aioli, the amounts are not sufficient for a full-size food processor; the blade would whir around and never touch the egg. That said, for those who want to try their hand at making aioli the old-fashioned way, there's this: Making Aioli by Hand (page 104).

CITRUS ZESTER

A citrus zester is a small hand-held tool with five or six (depending on the brand) small, sharp-edged holes on the end that, when dragged across the outside of citrus, produces long, thin threads of zest. Back then, if we wanted smaller pieces, we would mince the threads. A citrus zester was the only tool cooks had to remove the bright-colored outer layer of rind that's wanted when zesting citrus, but the Microplane, which grates the rind, has killed the citrus zester. But I still like those long, thin threads that you get from a zester. We use them as a garnish in several places in these recipes. If you don't have a citrus zester, you can peel the outer zest with a vegetable peeler and then slice the peels into thin threads. My favorite brand is a Victorinox; the blade is riveted into the handle, so it doesn't break off when you're zesting.

Trick of the Book

I am going to continue a tradition that I started in my last book, *Mozza at Home,* of introducing one new trick in every cookbook. There I introduced readers to a trick I had recently learned: that of using the oven floor to replicate the intense heat we get from our wood-burning pizza ovens. By preheating the oven to 500°F and putting a baking sheet on the oven floor (or the lowest rack, if you have an oven that doesn't allow you to put something on the oven floor), we created an environment where food is being roasted by means of "conductive heat," which means the heat is transferred directly from the hot surface, not through hot air (that is, "radiant heat"). Cooking this way, you are able to caramelize vegetables without softening them. This method works great, but I'm happy to report that I have evolved.

My new thing is to put a cast-iron skillet on the oven floor—the same idea, taken to the next level. The skillet is preheated along with the oven, so rather than starting with a cold pan, which of course has to heat up before anything like caramelization can happen, the vegetables go directly into a hot pan, where they start caramelizing immediately. At Chi Spacca, we always have cast-iron skillets in the wood-burning oven. When we get an order for Roasted Cauliflower Wedges (page 278), Roasted Parsnips (page 281), or Charred Sugar Snap Peas (page 287), we pull the skillet out and put the vegetables in. You could do the same with a two-burner cast-iron griddle/grill pan. The only issue is that this griddle is very heavy and difficult to pull out of the oven, especially when it is scorching hot. If you do use the two-burner griddle, rather than removing the griddle, leave it in the oven and remove the vegetables from it.

The Spacca Pantry

Many of the recipes in these pages use spice blends specific to that dish, but what follows on pages 19 to 25 are some of the rubs and spice blends that we use repeatedly, or that you might like to keep in your pantry. When buying spices or blends, seek out sources that specialize in them; these products are likely to be better quality and/or fresher than bottled grocery store versions. Another good option is bulk spices, which are likely to be fresher than bottled spices. There is also less waste involved in packaging.

Additionally, I want to mention three ingredients that are essential to these recipes, and that you will see repeatedly throughout this book: black pepper, flaky sea salt, and olive oil.

BLACK PEPPER

I have always preferred Tellicherry peppercorns, but only recently did I discover that they are not a distinct variety; Tellicherry peppercorns, named for the Indian city in the province of Kerala, where peppercorns originated, are simply the biggest peppercorns. After being picked, the peppercorns are graded by size and the largest peppercorns are labeled Tellicherry. The peppercorns lose some of their heat as they grow, but their flavor and aroma become more complex.

I call for two "grinds" of pepper in these recipes: "fresh coarsely ground black pepper" refers to the sort of coarse grind you'd get from your pepper grinder. I use this to season vinaigrettes, vegetables, and salads. In other recipes, I call for you to very coarsely grind whole peppercorns in a mortar or spice grinder. (I consider "very coarsely ground" to mean cracking the peppercorns to about one-fourth their original size.) This is sometimes referred to as "butcher's grind" or "butcher's cut" pepper. This is the pepper we prefer for seasoning meats, because it forms a crust on the exterior of the meats. At the restaurant, we crack the peppercorns using the back of a skillet pressed against a cutting board. This takes a bit of elbow grease and practice; a mortar and pestle or spice grinder is foolproof. Another tool I love for this job is an antique, hand-cranked wooden coffee grinder. I collect them when I'm shopping at flea markets in Italy. They're adjustable, so you can use them to produce butcher's cut pepper, or a more standard coarse grind. And to top it off: these grinders have little drawers underneath to store the pepper once it's ground.

SALT

I use three types of salt in my cooking: kosher salt, rock sea salt, and flaky sea salt. I use kosher salt to season meats and fish before cooking them, and for seasoning sauces, dressings, and condiments. I like the size of the grains and texture of kosher salt, and I like that I can keep it in a saltbox or bowl and reach into it with my hand and grab as much as I need. At my house in Italy, I have a salt grinder filled with Sicilian *sale grosso*, or rock salt; kosher salt isn't available there and fine sea salt is finer than I like for seasoning meats. (I can adjust my grinder to grind to the texture that I like.) This salt has great flavor, but unlike with kosher salt, you don't get the feel of it in your hand. Last, I use flaky sea salt as a "finishing salt," meaning when the salt is being used as an ingredient, such as for sprinkling on meats after they are grilled. Two brands to look for are Maldon, which is from England, and Jacobsen, which is harvested off the coast of Oregon. Both of these finishing salts have large, tender, shard-like flakes and a wonderful minerally flavor. To use flaky sea salt, you will generally crush it between your fingertips to fall over whatever you're salting; in the instances where you want large flakes, just drop it onto whatever you're finishing.

OLIVE OIL

We use three types of olive oil in our cooking, and in these recipes. One we refer to as "olive oil," another as "extra-virgin olive oil," and a third, "finishing-quality extra-

virgin olive oil." We call for "olive oil" to cook with; this can be your basic supermarket variety. It doesn't even have to be extra-virgin. It does, however, have to be fresh. Don't buy more than you can use in a year and keep it out of the sunlight because it will go rancid. (Look on the bottle for the date the oil was pressed.) We call for "extra-virgin olive oil" when the oil is part of the finished product. For this, look for a quality extra-virgin olive oil, but nothing too expensive, since you'll be using it in fairly large quantities to make vinaigrettes and sauces, such as Salsa Verde (page 142). Last, we call for "finishing-quality extra-virgin olive oil," which refers to the costly bottles that you see in specialty food stores. This olive oil is used not as a vehicle for cooking or in a sauce, but on its own, like a condiment or an ingredient to "finish" a dish. Although it isn't cheap, you use only a drizzle here and a drizzle there. Years ago, a local Los Angeles food writer reviewing Osteria Mozza wrote that our use of olive oil was a "lazy" way to make things taste better. I completely disagree. It would be lazy if you were pouring canola oil on the food, but this is a curated product, used very deliberately to elevate the flavors in a dish. When choosing any olive oil, but particularly one that you will use as a condiment, it's ideal to go to a store that has a "face," someone you can talk to about the olive oil and, even better, where you can taste the oil, because what you like in olive oil is a matter of taste. Sometimes I'm looking for a more aggressive olive oil, and other times I want a smoother, more mellow olive oil.

Dario Salt

Makes about 1¼ cups

My friend Dario Cecchini sells this mixture of sea salt, herbs, and spices in his butcher shop, Antica Macelleria Cecchini, in Panzano in Chianti, in Tuscany. It comes in a pretty hexagonal jar, and Dario also packs it in a flat, vacuum-sealed package that you can easily slip into your suitcase; those packets are by far the thing I am most often asked to bring back from my trips to Italy. We re-created the salt for this book to make Dario's Whipped Lardo (page 59). It's a great seasoning for any grilled meats or vegetables. The scent of it takes me to the hills of Tuscany, and to my own backyard in Umbria, where I enjoy grilling beautiful steaks and vegetables with Dario and his wife, Kim Wicks; the Italian culinary authority Faith Willinger and her husband, Massimo; and a collection of local and American friends. This is the only place in this book where you will see fine sea salt. I don't use it in my cooking, but I wanted to be true to Dario's original recipe—plus, it's the perfect texture for this blend.

Combine the juniper berries, fennel seeds, and clove in a mortar or spice grinder and finely grind them. If you're using a spice grinder, transfer the spices to a small bowl. Add the rosemary, sage, salt, ginger, and cinnamon to the mortar or bowl and stir to combine.

6 juniper berries

1 teaspoon fennel seeds

1 whole clove

1 tablespoon finely chopped fresh rosemary leaves

1 tablespoon finely chopped fresh sage leaves

1 cup fine sea salt

½ teaspoon ground ginger

¼ teaspoon ground cinnamon

Fennel Rub

Makes about ¼ cup

Fennel is a classic and foolproof seasoning for pork. We use this blend of salt, pepper, and fennel on many of our pork preparations at Chi Spacca, including the Grilled Tomahawk Pork Chop with Fennel Pollen (page 169), Pork al Latte with Fennel Pollen and Crispy Sage (page 177), and the tenderloins for Pork Tonnato with Crispy Capers (page 183).

Combine the fennel seeds, peppercorns, and salt in a spice grinder and coarsely grind them.

3 tablespoons fennel seeds

3 tablespoons black peppercorns

3 tablespoons kosher salt

Garam Masala

Makes about ½ cup

Garam masala is a classic Indian spice blend, similar to the more commonly known yellow curry, but with the addition of sweet spices including cinnamon, nutmeg, and cloves. We use it to season the Roasted Honeynut Squash with Pistachio-Hazelnut Dukkah (page 291) and Indian-Spiced Chicken Salad with Mixed Lettuces, Walnuts, and Preserved Lemon Vinaigrette (page 113).

Break the cinnamon stick in half or thirds and finely grind it in a spice grinder. Leave it in the grinder.

Toast the cumin seeds, coriander seeds, cardamom pods, peppercorns, cloves, and árbol chile in a small skillet over medium heat for 1 to 2 minutes, until the spices are toasted and fragrant, shaking the skillet often so they don't burn. Transfer the spices to the grinder. Add the bay leaves and finely grind the leaves and spices. Transfer the ground spices to a medium bowl. Add the turmeric, fenugreek, and nutmeg and stir to combine.

1 small cinnamon stick

¼ cup cumin seeds

¼ cup coriander seeds

1 tablespoon cardamom pods

1 tablespoon black peppercorns

1 teaspoon whole cloves

1 árbol chile, stem removed and discarded

2 dried bay leaves

1 teaspoon ground turmeric

1 teaspoon ground fenugreek

½ teaspoon freshly grated nutmeg (grated with a fine Microplane or a nutmeg grater from a whole nutmeg)

Porcini Rub

Makes about ⅔ cup

People ask us all the time: What makes your meat taste so good? Very often, the answer is this rub—a combination of salt, sugar, red pepper flakes, and ground porcini mushrooms—which we use on a variety of meat preparations at Chi Spacca. The sugar in the rub creates a beautiful caramelized exterior, and the ground porcini impart that crave-able, umami quality. We use it on Grilled Porcini-Rubbed Short Ribs with Salsa Verde and Scallions (page 141) and Porcini-Rubbed Double-Bone Veal Chops with Roasted Onions and Brown Butter Jus (page 166). You'll need to grind the porcini in the spice grinder in batches; a blender does not grind as finely as you want the porcini, but it will work in a pinch. Use this rub on any beef or veal preparation. It also makes a great gift for a meat-loving friend.

Working in batches, finely grind the porcini in a spice grinder and transfer the ground porcini to a medium container or bowl. Finely grind the peppercorns and red pepper flakes and add them to the container or bowl with the porcini. Add the salt and sugar and stir to combine.

1 ounce dried porcini mushrooms (about ½ cup)

1½ tablespoons black peppercorns

1½ teaspoons red pepper flakes

¼ cup kosher salt

1½ tablespoons sugar

Preserved Lemons

Makes 1 quart

Lemons preserved in salt are a signature of North African cuisine. We use a combination of salt and sugar, which is a common variation. Preserved lemons add a bright, acidic flavor to salads, vinaigrettes, and sauces. To use them, you rinse the lemons and discard the insides, using only the rinds. We use preserved lemon in the Indian-spiced Chicken Salad with Mixed Lettuces, Walnuts, and Preserved Lemon Vinaigrette (page 113) and Braised Lamb Necks with Castelvetrano Olives and Preserved Lemon (page 191).

Put the lemons in a large bowl. Add the sugar and salt and toss to coat the lemons in the sugar and salt, massaging the salt and sugar aggressively into the cut sides of the lemons until they begin to release liquid. Cover the bowl with plastic wrap and refrigerate the lemons for 2 days.

6 lemons, halved lengthwise

1½ cups sugar

1 cup kosher salt

Remove the bowl from the refrigerator, uncover it, and toss to combine the lemons with the liquid that will have collected in the bowl. Transfer the lemons and their liquid to a 1-quart container with a lid or a 1-quart mason jar, packing them in tightly. Drizzle the liquid in the bowl over the lemons to cover them. Cover and refrigerate the lemons for at least 2 weeks before using them, and for up to 5 months.

Ras el Hanout

Makes about ¾ cup

Ras el hanout is a North African spice blend. The name means "head of the shop" in Arabic, suggesting that the blend is the best that the shopkeeper has. Ryan uses it to season his Moroccan-Braised Lamb Shanks with Pistachio Gremolata and Celeriac Purée (page 204).

Toast the cumin seeds, coriander seeds, mustard seeds, allspice, cardamom pods, and cloves in a small skillet over medium heat for 1 to 2 minutes, until the spices are toasted and fragrant, shaking the skillet often so they don't burn. Transfer the spices to a spice grinder and finely grind them. Transfer the spices to a small bowl. Add the paprika, salt, sugar, turmeric, sumac, ginger, cinnamon, garlic powder, nutmeg, and cayenne and stir to combine.

2 teaspoons cumin seeds

1 teaspoon coriander seeds

1 teaspoon mustard seeds

½ teaspoon whole allspice

2 cardamom pods

4 whole cloves

3 tablespoons sweet smoked paprika

1 tablespoon kosher salt

1 tablespoon sugar

1 tablespoon ground turmeric

1 tablespoon sumac

1 tablespoon ground ginger

2 teaspoons ground cinnamon

1 teaspoon garlic powder

1 teaspoon freshly grated nutmeg (grated with a fine Microplane or a nutmeg grater from a whole nutmeg)

¼ teaspoon cayenne pepper

Za'atar

Makes about 1 cup

Za'atar is a Middle Eastern spice blend; if you go to Israel and you see a greenish spice blend sprinkled on just about everything you eat, chances are it's za'atar. Recipes vary from cook to cook, or from shop to shop, but they all contain sesame seeds and sumac, a red berry from the sumac plant with a tangy, citrusy flavor. Traditionally za'atar also contains hyssop, an herb native to the mint family, but we use thyme in its place. I add orange zest to brighten up the mix. If you don't want to make your own za'atar, buy it from a good spice store (see Sources, page 357).

Unhulled toasted sesame seeds are sold as "roasted sesame seeds" in shaker canisters in the Japanese section of supermarkets. If you can't find them, use the more widely available hulled white sesame seeds and toast them in a small skillet over medium heat for 1 to 2 minutes, until they're toasted and fragrant.

Place as many thyme sprigs as will fit with plenty of room between them on a microwave-safe plate. Cook the sprigs in the microwave on high for 2 to 3 minutes, until they are completely dried out. Remove the sprigs from the plate and place them on a separate plate to cool and dry out. Repeat drying out the remaining sprigs in batches, adding them to the cooling plate as they are done.

Pick the thyme leaves from the stems and let the leaves fall into a small bowl. Add the sesame seeds, sumac, salt, and red pepper flakes to the bowl with the thyme leaves and stir to combine. Just before using, use a fine Microplane to zest the bright orange outer layer of the orange into the bowl (reserve the orange to juice another time) and stir to combine.

2 cups fresh thyme sprigs, about 1 bunch (or ½ cup Sicilian oregano on the branch)

½ cup toasted sesame seeds

¼ cup sumac

2 teaspoons kosher salt

1 teaspoon red pepper flakes

1 orange

Chi Spacca Grilling Class

by Ryan DeNicola

Chi Spacca has a small, open kitchen with a countertop that has a wood-fired grill built into it, so grilling is front and center, literally, to Chi Spacca's cuisine. Although the vast majority of the recipes that involve grilling in this book are in the Carne chapter (page 128), Nancy and I decided to put this grilling class here, front and center of the book, to mirror the grill's place in the restaurant. I love grilling—both the act of doing it and the effects that it has on food, specifically the deeply caramelized exterior that comes from grilling foods over a very hot fire, and the flavor that cooking this way imparts.

There is no substitute for the color and flavor that cooking over fire gives to your food. With this tutorial, I hope to show you how easy it is, in order to convince any die-hard gas grillers to move over to "real fire." But I'm a realist. So in case I fail at that, I also give instructions for using a gas grill for our recipes. Let's start from the beginning.

I know I am fighting an uphill battle against the convenience of the gas grill. I teach regular grilling classes at Chi Spacca, and the first thing I ask my students is what kind of grill they use: a gas grill or one that burns wood or charcoal? The *vast* majority use gas. I get it. Using a gas grill is fast, easy, and doesn't require as much cleanup. But in many ways, it defeats the purposes of grilling. A gas grill will never give you wood-fired flavor (how could it when there's no wood!), and unless you're investing in an extremely expensive, professional-level gas grill, it won't get hot enough to even caramelize your food. It's basically like cooking on a gas range, with grates.

Seriously, if you don't want to "hassle" with wood or charcoal, a better option is to bring the "grilling" inside and use a two-burner cast-iron griddle/grill pan instead. With your stovetop burners on high heat, you'll be able to get this pan hotter than almost any gas grill on the market. The hot surface will at least give you the seared exterior you want on the meat, even if it won't give you the flavor of cooking over fire. And of course you also sacrifice the ambience of cooking outside.

What Kind of Grill to Buy

If you're transitioning from being a gas griller to being a wood- or charcoal-fired griller, the good news is that it's cheap. A basic kettle grill, such as the old-fashioned, iconic Weber, works perfectly, and you can find one for sale at any hardware store for about a hundred dollars. Sure, there are fancier grills on the market, but the kettle grill is all you truly need.

What to Burn

There are two good options for cooking over fire: hardwood and lump charcoal. Hardwood is the best option; it burns the hottest and the longest, and it will impart the most wood-fired flavor to your food. It is called hardwood because the wood is hard, which is what allows it to burn for a long time. Softwood, by contrast, which is what is often sold as firewood in bundles at grocery stores, burns very hot (*too* hot for cooking) and very fast; pine is the most common example of softwood. Depending on where you live, you will have different types of hardwood available. We use exclusively almond wood at Chi Spacca, but oak and cherry are also good options. While hickory and applewood burn well, they also produce a strong smoky flavor, which is great when you're making southern-style barbecue, but not necessarily what you want for everyday grilling. No matter what kind of wood you are using, start with quartered logs of wood, about two feet long and two to four inches wide. If the wood is thicker than that, it will be difficult to light.

Lump charcoal is also a great choice. Also referred to as "hardwood charcoal," it actually *is* wood that has been pre-burned. It burns as hot as hardwood, but not as long. It is easier to light than hardwood, which is its primary appeal. The downside of using lump charcoal as opposed to hardwood is that a lot of the flavorful compounds in the wood were burned away in the process of turning it into charcoal, so it doesn't impart quite as much wood-fired flavor as wood does. (Briquettes, which contain charcoal but are bound with fillers and chemicals, are not a good choice because they don't burn as hot as lump charcoal or wood. They are prized for being easy to light, but after you read this tutorial, you will be able to light hardwood or lump charcoal with ease.)

Cleaning Your Grill

Whether you are burning gas, charcoal, or wood, the first thing you want to do is clean your grill. If you don't clean the grill, the fat that dripped down into the grill from the previous use will ignite when you light the fire. The fuel for your fire will not be wood, charcoal, or even gas, but rather *old grease*. This is not the flavor you want to impart to your food.

To clean your grill, first remove the grill grates. If you're using a grill that burns wood or charcoal, empty it of ashes; this is important, because ashes will block the grates and vents, depriving the fire of oxygen. If your fire can't breathe properly, it will never live up to its potential. Prepare a bowl with soapy water using a grease-cutting dish soap, such as Dawn, and use the soapy water and a gentle scrubber to clean the bottom and sides of the inside of your grill. Rinse the grill with clean water. Use the soapy water and a grill brush to clean the grill grates; rinse with clean water.

Lighting a Charcoal or Wood Fire

Starting the fire is the most intimidating part of cooking with wood or lump charcoal, but it's easier than you might think. The ingredients that any fire needs in order to exist and thrive are fuel, heat, and oxygen. In the context of a fire for a grill, the fuel will be the wood, charcoal, or gas. The heat will be whatever you use to ignite the fire. And the oxygen refers to the air the fire needs in order to breathe; for a wood or charcoal fire, this is determined by the way in which wood or charcoal are piled.

My preferred means of starting a charcoal fire at home is with an electric fire starter, an inexpensive wand-like tool that you stick into a pile of charcoal to light it. I like to say that grilling satisfies my caveman sensibility, and an electric wand that you plug in is not at all primitive, it is super easy, and you're guaranteed success every time—both things that this caveman appreciates. You can buy electric fire starters from online sources or wherever grills are sold. To light a charcoal grill using an electric fire starter, lay enough lump charcoal to cover the bottom grate of the grill, leaving a few inches around the perimeter of the grill free of coals. (I like to use thick garden gloves or grill gloves to do this so my hands don't get dirty. Charcoal is very hard to clean off your hands.) After you have piled half of the charcoal to build a pyramid base, stick the metal part of the wand into the base, then pile more charcoal on top of the wand to create a mound or pyramid about 8 inches high. Plug the wand into the electric outlet and allow it to heat the coals. After about 15 minutes, the wand will turn bright red, indicating that the coals are ready to cook on.

Another fantastic, inexpensive aid for starting a fire is a capsule-shaped gadget called a chimney. The way a chimney works is that you fill the top side of the chimney with charcoal (preferably lump charcoal), put crumpled newspaper into the underside, and light the paper from below. The fire ignites the charcoal above and, because it is in such a contained space, the charcoals burn down quickly, and you have red-hot coals, which will be your "starter coals," in about 10 minutes. To start a charcoal fire using a chimney, fill the chimney with charcoal, ignite the paper from underneath, and let the charcoal burn for about 15 minutes, until the coals are red hot covered in white ash. Dump the coals out onto the bottom grill grates and use tongs to spread them out over the grate, leaving a few inches around the perimeter free of coals. The fire is now ready to cook on.

To maintain the fire, if you are grilling items that take 15 minutes or less, you will not need additional fuel. If you are grilling longer-cooking items, add several pieces of lump charcoal or lay two or three logs in the same direction on top of the coals to continue to fuel the fire.

Another great means to start a charcoal fire is to use cooking oil. We learned this method from our Brazilian friend Eduardo. It's basically a natural alternative to lighter fluid or commercial fire starter. When using this method, pile the charcoal into a pyramid about 8 inches tall, leaving a few inches around the perimeter of the grill free of charcoal. Then roll up a few paper towels or sheets of newspaper into a long "rope," leaving one end open to form a cone at the end of the rope. Pour cooking oil (such as canola oil, vegetable oil, or olive oil) into the cone. Weave the rope through the crevices between the pieces of charcoal, then light the paper. The oil burns off gradually enough to allow the charcoal to ignite. Using Eduardo's method, the cooking oil does the same thing as commercial lighter fluid and fire starters, but the advantage of using cooking oil is that the oil is pure; you know what it is and you don't mind the smell or remnants of it in your food. This is Nancy's preferred method for starting a fire because it's so pure.

Once your charcoal fire is going, if you are grilling items that take 15 minutes or less, you will not need additional fuel. If you are grilling longer-cooking items, add several pieces of lump charcoal or lay two or three logs in the same direction on top of the coals to continue to fuel the fire.

If you want to start your fire with wood rather than adding wood to a charcoal fire, lay three logs in the same direction on the bottom grate of a grill, leaving 2 to 3 inches of space between each log. Place three more logs in the opposite direction on top of the first logs, stacking them log-cabin style. Repeat until you have a pile four layers high, each layer of logs laid in the direction opposite from the one before. Light the grill using Eduardo's cooking oil method, described above. It will take about 15 minutes for the wood to ignite, and then you'll want to cook the wood down for 15 to 25 minutes, until there is fire burning from the logs, and they have burned sufficiently that you can break each log into two or three smaller chunks. At that point, use tongs to move the logs to cover the bottom of the grill. The fire is now ready to cook over.

If you are grilling items that take 15 minutes or less, you will not need additional wood. If you are grilling longer-cooking items, lay two or three logs facing the same direction on the hot logs to continue to fuel the fire.

Direct and Indirect Heat

Grilling can be broken down into two techniques: direct, or hot heat, and indirect heat, or low heat. Moving food from direct to indirect heat is a way of controlling the heat while grilling, the same way you would by turning the knobs on your stove. Direct heat is required to achieve that dark, burnished, sometimes crusty exterior to grilled foods, and that makes grilled meats look so delicious. We start with direct heat to caramelize the exterior of all cuts of meat, and we use *only* direct heat when we are cooking thinner cuts, which cook quickly, such as Grilled Porcini-Rubbed Short Ribs with Salsa Verde and Scallions (page 141).

Indirect heat is essentially a way of slow cooking on a grill. After caramelizing the exterior of larger cuts of meat, such as the Bistecca Fiorentina (page 134), Grilled Tomahawk Pork Chop with Fennel Pollen (page 169), or Coffee-Rubbed Grilled Tri-Tip (page 146), we move the meat to the indirect heat side of the grill, where the meat cooks more slowly. This ensures that the inside of these cuts will be cooked evenly all the way through without the outside getting charred as it would if you were to cook these large cuts over direct heat the whole time.

To create direct and indirect heat sources using a hardwood- or lump charcoal–fired grill, once the embers are ready, move them all to one side, so you have a pile of embers on one side of the grill and an empty space, free of embers, on the other. The side of the grill with the embers is the direct heat source, and the area with no embers is the indirect heat source.

To create indirect and direct heat sources using a gas grill, put the lid of the grill down and turn all of the burners on as high as they go. This will let your grill get as hot as it possibly can. Turn off the burners on one side of the grill and leave the lid down on that side. Keep the other side burning as high as possible and open the lid. The side of the grill with the heat on high and the lid open is your direct heat source. The side with the burners off and lid closed is your indirect heat source. (If your grill doesn't give you the option of closing the lid on only one side, open the lid and turn off the heat on one side.)

A Few Helpful Tips

Many of the tips below are also spelled out in the recipes, but I wanted to include them here because they are part of the big picture of how we grill at Chi Spacca.

Bring meat to room temperature before grilling. This ensures that it will cook evenly all the way through. If you start with a cold piece of meat, particularly when cooking larger cuts, the meat will be heating up before it is cooking, and it will cook unevenly.

Season meats before grilling them. We season all of our meats at Chi Spacca with a teaspoon of salt for every pound of meat. If you are seasoning the meat with cracked black pepper or other cracked spices, press the spice or spice blends into the meat so it adheres.

Use a meat thermometer to check for doneness. Even professionals do this. We give you the desired temperatures to cook the meats to in the individual recipes. With those temperatures and a meat thermometer (my favorite brand is ThermoWorks, available wherever cooking supplies are sold), you have everything you need to cook your meat perfectly. Keep in mind that meat will continue to cook another ten to twenty degrees after you take it off the heat. See page 13 for more information.

Rest grilled meat before cutting into it. Resting refers to taking the meat off the grill and letting it rest. When meat has just come off the grill, the muscle fibers are tightly wound. By resting before cutting into the meat, you allow the muscle fibers to relax and the juices released during cooking to disperse throughout the meat, resulting in a more tender, juicy piece of meat. This is especially important with large cuts. I like to rest meat on a cutting board so I can move straight to slicing it when it's ready. If the meat has a bone, set the meat on the bone to prevent the meat from overcooking while it rests.

Controlling the flames. When grilling over direct heat, the fat that is cooked off the meat will melt and drip down onto the fire, causing the flames to flare up. You don't want the flames to make direct contact with the meat; this will burn the meat and impart a bitter, burned flavor. If the fire is flaring up, take the meat off the grill, remove the grill grates if necessary, and move some of the coals to the side to cool the fire slightly. (I don't like to use a squirt bottle of water because it pushes ashes into the air and actually puts out the fire, neither of which you want to do.)

How to Build an Antipasto Platter   37

Focaccia di Recco   39

Taralli   46

Pork Tenderloin Pistachio Pâté   49

Butcher's Pâté   52

Pane Tostato   55

Chianti "Tuna"   56

N'duja   58

Whipped Lardo   59

Pane Tostato with Bistecca Drippings   61

Cetara Anchovies and Butter on Toast   62

Marinated Olives with Garlic and Fresh Pecorino   64

Warm Dates with Sea Salt   65

Roasted Lipstick Peppers with Anchovies, Mint,
and Pecorino Toscano   66

Pickles   68

Turmeric Cauliflower Pickles   69

Pickled Fennel   70

Spicy Green Bean Pickles   71

Cucumber Pickles   72

Giardiniera   73

Spuntini

Spuntini means "snacks" in Italian, and that's what these recipes are: delicious finger foods to put out while you're waiting for guests to arrive. The recipes, from whipped lardo and pork pâtés to marinated olives and warm, salted dates, don't even require serving plates and forks. They're meant to be enjoyed with a cocktail napkin in one hand and a glass of wine in the other, as you, your family, and friends look forward to the feast ahead.

How to Build an Antipasto Platter

Enjoying charcuterie is an integral part of the Chi Spacca experience. Even though I chose not to include our cured meats in this book, you should at least know how to put together a sliced meat antipasto platter, or *tagliere*. The word *tagliere* literally means "cutting board," but in Italy it is used to describe a board (or platter) of sliced cured meats, salami, pâtés, cheeses, crackers, olives, and other finger foods. To put together an attractive and delicious *tagliere,* choose a selection of charcuterie with a variety of textures and flavors.

- Choose at least one "whole muscle" cured meat, meaning those meats that are not chopped or ground but cured whole, such as prosciutto, speck, culatello, coppa, capicola, pancetta, guanciale, segreto, bresaola, and lonza.

- Choose one ground meat cure, or salami. This includes soppressata, finocchiona, cotechino, salami Genoese, mortadella, and countless others.

- Choose at least one "fresh cure," a term for potted meats and pâtés that are salted for one day and emulsified with fat, so they are rich, creamy, and spreadable. We included recipes for three such cures, Pork Tenderloin Pistachio Pâté (page 49), Butcher's Pâté (page 52), and Duck Rillettes (page 93).

- Serve a fatty option, such as sliced lardo, Whipped Lardo (page 59), or N'duja (page 58).

- Include something bready, such as Pane Tostato (page 55) or Taralli (page 46).

- Prepare a selection of olives (see Marinated Olives with Garlic and Fresh Pecorino, page 64).

- Provide a selection of hard and soft cheeses. Visit your favorite cheese store and let them help you pick out a selection.

- Finally, don't forget the Pickles (page 68).

Focaccia di Recco

Makes 2 focaccia

If you're a regular at Chi Spacca, this recipe for focaccia di Recco might be the single reason you have this book in your hands. Eighty-five percent of our customers order focaccia di Recco, and it is hands down the recipe I am most often asked for—by customers, the media, and other chefs. But if you've never been to the restaurant, you may have no idea what focaccia di Recco is. Also called *focaccia col formaggio* (focaccia with cheese), this is nothing like any other focaccia you've ever tasted. It is made from two sheets of non-yeasted dough, stretched almost to the point of tearing, like a strudel dough, with a layer of stracchino cheese melted in the middle. Baked until it is golden brown, it's a delicate, crispy, and flaky pastry drizzled with olive oil and sprinkled with salt. My friend the food writer Ruth Reichl hit the nail on the head when she broke into a piece for the first time at Chi Spacca and said it reminded her of matzoh with butter.

I discovered this rare breed of focaccia by accident. I had decided I wanted to make focaccia for Chi Spacca and was told by Italian food aficionados that I had to try the focaccia from Recco, a small town near Genoa, on the coast of Liguria in the northern part of Italy. I had recently been to Puglia, the "boot heel" of Italy, where I experienced wonderful, thick, tomato-studded focaccia, and that was what I thought focaccia was. But on my next trip to Umbria, I took a detour to Liguria to see what these experts were talking about. I made my way from the coast to the hillside town of Recco and found a local bakery where I tried their focaccia for the first time. Instead of the pillowy, yeasted bread sliced into wedges from an oil-drenched pan that I was familiar with, I experienced a thin, flaky, almost cracker-like pastry, filled with cheese. It was certainly different. But it was not spectacular; it had obviously been sitting around for a while. I have to say, I was underwhelmed.

At lunch later that day in nearby Portofino, I mentioned to my waiter that what brought me to the area was to try focaccia di Recco, and he told me that I had to try again. For the very best *focaccia col formaggio,* he said, I had to go to the place that claims to have invented it: Ristorante Manuelina. So, for my second lunch that day, I went to Manuelina. The focaccia came to the table straight from the oven and was placed tableside; it was so enormous that they had special stands just to put it on. I tore off a piece and tried it: tender, flaky pastry, with just the right amount of fruity olive oil drizzled over it, a nice amount of salt sprinkled on top, and filled with a thin layer of melted mild cheese. It was extraordinary! There was absolutely no room for improvement. All I could do was come home and hope to replicate it. And after much trial and error, I believe I have. Here is the recipe. →

This is one of the more challenging recipes in the book, but all the details are here. Even if you were to follow the instructions to a T, it might take you a few tries to get it right. It did me! The good news is: all those less-than-perfect versions you make along the way will be delicious. The reward for going to the effort is that you can use the dough scraps to make Taralli (page 46), delicious ring-shaped cracker-like snacks from the southern region of Puglia.

I don't normally like to send people shopping to execute my recipes, but to succeed at focaccia di Recco, there are three things you absolutely must invest in.

1. **An Italian copper pizza pan** (see Sources, page 357). Copper conducts heat better than any other material, and this is also a heavy-gauge pan. If you don't use this very specific pan, the focaccia won't have its characteristic crisp, flaky layers.

2. **A baking steel or baking stone.** Either will work, but if you're investing in one, I suggest you buy the steel, which conducts heat even better than the stone does. The stone or steel, which you preheat while you are preheating your oven, creates a solid heat source. When you bake the focaccia on it, the bottom gets crisp and nicely browned.

3. **The right cheese.** Focaccia di Recco is filled with crescenza (also called stracchino), a soft, young cow's milk cheese. When I first started trying to replicate focaccia di Recco, the crescenza that I found was too wet and made the focaccia watery and soggy. I worked closely with our cheese maker, Mimmo Bruno of Di Stefano Cheese in Los Angeles, to make a crescenza that was a bit dryer. Bellwether Farms and Cowgirl Creamery both sell crescenza, as does the more widely available BelGioioso, under the name Crescenza-Stracchino. All of these tend to be too wet. For best results, buy the cheese and let it sit in your refrigerator for ten days to two weeks to dry out, until it holds its shape when you cut it into cubes, but not so long that it is dry.

Now, since you've stuck with me this far, I'm going to give one more hint—and this won't cost you a thing. I've done my best to describe the process of stretching dough, but the best way to learn is the way I did: by watching a YouTube video of the baker at Manuelina making *focaccia col formaggio*. When I started working on it, first in my kitchen in Umbria immediately after having tried the focaccia for the first time, and later back home in Los Angeles, I watched this video over and over again.

You will need a 34-centimeter (approximately 14-inch) copper pizza pan to make this and an extra-large round platter or cutting board to serve it.

To make the dough, combine the olive oil with 1 cup water in the bowl of a stand mixer and dump the flour on top of the liquid. Fit the mixer with the dough hook and mix on low speed for about 5 minutes, until the dough forms a ball and pulls away from the sides of the mixer bowl. Turn off the mixer.

Lightly dust your work surface with flour and place the dough on the floured surface. Cut the dough in half and form each half into a ball. Wrap each ball in plastic wrap and set aside at room temperature to rest for 1 hour or as long as 8 hours. (This dough does not handle well if you rest it any longer than that.)

To make the focaccia, cut the cheese in half and reserve one half for the second focaccia.

Brush the bottom and sides of the pizza pan with olive oil. Set the pan aside but within arm's reach.

Lightly dust a large flat work surface with flour, unwrap one half of the dough, and place it on the floured surface.

Lightly dust the dough with flour and use your hands to press it into a roughly 8-inch oval.

With the short side of the oval parallel to you, lightly dust the dough and a rolling pin with flour. Starting with your rolling pin in the center →

For the Dough

½ cup olive oil

4 cups unbleached all-purpose flour, plus more for dusting

For the Focaccia

1 pound Bellwether Farms or Cowgirl Creamery crescenza or BelGioioso Crescenza-Stracchino

½ cup finishing-quality extra-virgin olive oil, plus more for oiling the pan

Unbleached all-purpose flour for dusting

Flaky sea salt

of the oval, roll forward and back until the oval is about 18 inches from top to bottom, lightly dusting the dough, rolling pin, and work surface as needed.

Carefully lift the dough and turn it 90 degrees, dusting underneath with flour. Dust the dough again with flour and use your fingers to spread the flour over the surface of the dough. Roll forward and back until the oval is about 10 inches from top to bottom.

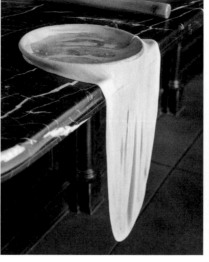

Pick up the dough with the balls of both fists and place both fists a few inches apart in the center of the dough to begin stretching it. Move your fists toward the edge of the dough and work them around the perimeter with one fist closer to the center and one closer to the edge. Continue, moving your fists around the dough to stretch it until it is about 18 inches wide and 3 feet long.

Place the pizza pan in front of you. With your hands in fists at the top of the long oval of dough, lay that end of dough down on the pan so the top edge of the dough overhangs the top edge by a generous 1 inch and the remaining dough hangs from the bottom edge of the pan off the counter.

Gently run your fingers around the perimeter of the pan to fit the dough into the crease of the pan.

Break the cheese into 2-inch chunks and place them on the dough, placing one chunk in the center of the pan and the rest around the perimeter like the numbers on a clock.

Lift the bottom edge of the dough without stretching it and flip it so it falls, with slack, over the pan. →

Working your way around the pan, lift the edges of the dough to create slack and ease the dough into the creases to lock the dough in place.

Using the fingertips of both hands, pinch the dough in opposite directions to create 9 small tears in the dough: one between each of the cheese balls around the perimeter of the focaccia and 3 near the center of the focaccia. Using your fingers, press down on the dough next to each tear. (The tears create air pockets in the dough; pressing the dough together around the pockets prevents the air pockets from getting too big and creates peaks and valleys in the baked focaccia.)

Holding the rolling pin at a 45-degree angle to the pan, press the pin against the outside edge of the rim and roll it around the rim to trim the dough. You will need to run the pin around the pan in quarters, rolling from three o'clock to six o'clock, then giving the pan a quarter turn and rolling the pin from three o'clock to six o'clock again. (By holding the pin at an angle and trimming the outside edge of the dough, you create slack in the dough, which prevents it from shrinking down into the pan when baked.) Pull the trimmings away from the pan and form them into a ball. Wrap the dough in plastic wrap and refrigerate it until you are ready to use it to make Taralli (page 46); or discard the dough.

Drizzle about 1 teaspoon finishing-quality olive oil and crush a pinch of flaky sea salt over the focaccia.

Place the focaccia on the pizza steel or stone and bake it for 8 to 10 minutes, until it is golden brown and bubbling.

Remove the focaccia from the oven and use a rolling pizza cutter to make 2 cuts about 2½ inches apart in each direction, tic-tac-toe style. Drizzle about 1 teaspoon finishing-quality olive oil and crush about 1 teaspoon flaky sea salt over the focaccia and serve the focaccia in the pan in which it was baked. If you are going to make a second focaccia right after the first one, slide the focaccia onto a large cutting board after it is cut, and serve. Make sure the pan has cooled to room temperature before making the second focaccia.

Taralli

Makes about 30 taralli

The purpose of this recipe is to make use of the scraps of dough you will have after making the Focaccia di Recco (page 39).

Taralli means "tires" in Italian, and the term also refers to the doughnut-shaped "cracker" from Puglia. Whenever you sit down for a glass of wine or an *aperitivo* there, you will probably also be served a bowl of these. Traditional taralli are made with wine, where the focaccia di Recco dough is made with water, and the flavorings, such as fennel seeds, red pepper flakes, or sesame seeds, are added to the dough, where in this recipe they are sprinkled on the dough. These taralli have the same tender consistency as those made with wine instead of water, but since the dough is already made, we sprinkle the seasonings on top of the taralli rather than mixing them in. If you want to make traditional taralli, follow the recipe for focaccia di Recco dough, substituting white wine for the water and mixing in fennel seeds, sesame seeds, and red pepper flakes in whatever combination you like.

Both black and white unhulled toasted sesame seeds are sold as "roasted sesame seeds" in shaker canisters in the Japanese section of supermarkets. If you can't find them, use the more widely available hulled white sesame seeds and toast them in a small skillet over medium heat for 1 to 2 minutes, until they're toasted and fragrant.

Fill a large saucepan with water and add kosher salt so it tastes like the ocean, adding 1 scant tablespoon per quart of water. Bring the water to a boil over high heat.

Adjust the oven rack to the center position and preheat the oven to 350°F.

Put the fennel seeds in a mortar or spice grinder and very coarsely grind them. If you're using a spice grinder, transfer the cracked seeds to a bowl. Add the red pepper flakes and sesame seeds, crush the flaky sea salt between your fingertips into the mortar or bowl, and stir to combine.

Dust a flat work surface lightly with flour, unwrap the ball of focaccia di Recco dough trimmings, and place it on the floured surface. Cut the dough into 4 equal pieces. Leave 1 piece on the floured surface and set the remaining 3 pieces aside.

Kosher salt

2 tablespoons fennel seeds

1 tablespoon red pepper flakes

2 tablespoons unhulled roasted black or white sesame seeds (or hulled white sesame seeds, lightly toasted)

1 tablespoon flaky sea salt

Unbleached all-purpose flour for dusting

Trim from Focaccia di Recco (page 39)

2 tablespoons extra-virgin olive oil

Dust your hands lightly with flour and roll the dough into a log. Place both hands side by side in the center of the log and roll the dough under your fingers, gradually working your hands outward to roll the dough into an even ½-inch-thick rope. Move the rope to the top of your work surface to get it out of the way. Roll the remaining 3 segments of dough into ropes, dusting with flour as needed.

To shape the taralli, dust a large baking sheet lightly with flour.

Put one of the ropes in front of you and pick up one end. Roll the end around the index and middle fingers of your other hand and attach it back to the rope to create a small ring, or *tarallo*. Use your fingers to pinch the dough together to both create the ring and simultaneously cut the ring from the rope. Place the ring on the floured baking sheet. Repeat until you have formed taralli of the entire rope. Repeat, forming taralli with the 3 other ropes and adding them to the baking sheet. Don't worry about making the taralli look the same. They should look handmade, each one a little different.

Have a second baking sheet and a mesh strainer handy.

Drop the taralli into the boiling water and cook for 1 to 2 minutes, until they rise to the top. Use the strainer to remove the taralli from the pot and drain them for a few seconds, then transfer them to the clean baking sheet. When you have removed all of the taralli from the water, drizzle them with the olive oil and toss to coat them with the oil.

Arrange the taralli so they're lying flat in a single layer on the baking sheet and sprinkle the spice mixture evenly over them.

Bake the taralli for 15 to 17 minutes, until they're golden brown, rotating the baking sheet from front to back halfway through that time for even browning. Remove the baking sheet from the oven and set aside until the taralli are cool enough to touch.

Serve, or store in an airtight container at room temperature for as long as 1 week.

Pork Tenderloin Pistachio Pâté

Serves 8 to 10

This pâté is wrapped in sliced bacon and has a perfectly cooked pork tenderloin running through it. It's really pretty when sliced, with the cross section of the tenderloin suspended in the pâté and the bacon "frame." The pâté itself contains pistachios, which are a classic Italian addition. Serve this by itself, or with Pane Tostato (page 55) and Pickles (page 68).

You will need a meat grinding attachment to a stand mixer to make this. You will also need a 12- × 3-inch terrine mold, a roasting pan large enough to hold the terrine mold, and a piece of cardboard cut to fit just inside the dish.

Ask your butcher for Kurobuta (or another heritage breed) pork. Seeking out heritage pork is especially beneficial with pork tenderloin, which has little fat and can tend to be dry. Pork from heritage breeds has more marbling and is moister and more flavorful.

You will need a large cutting board or platter to serve the pâté.

If your pork tenderloin is longer than 10 inches, trim it to 10 inches long, reserving the trimmings. Wrap the tenderloin in plastic wrap and refrigerate it until you're ready to use it.

Cut the pork belly into 1-inch chunks and put the chunks in a large container or a medium bowl. Add the trimmings from the pork tenderloin, if there are any. Cover and place the pork in the freezer along with the meat grinding attachment, including the smallest die and the blade, and chill for 10 to 15 minutes. (You don't want to freeze the pork; you just want to chill it so it firms up, which makes it easier to grind.)

Remove the meat grinding attachment and the meat from the freezer and fit the mixer with the grinding attachment. Place a bowl under the mixer attachment and pass the pork belly and garlic cloves through the grinder into the bowl.

Put the peppercorns, coriander seeds, and cloves in a mortar or spice grinder and finely grind them. Add them to the bowl with the pork and garlic. Add the milk, egg, shallots, pistachios, salt, sugar, cinnamon, and nutmeg and stir to combine. →

1 (about 1-pound) pork tenderloin

1 pound pork belly (or pork shoulder)

2 large garlic cloves, peeled

1 teaspoon black peppercorns

½ teaspoon coriander seeds

8 whole cloves

½ cup whole milk

1 extra-large egg, lightly beaten

2 shallots, peeled and minced

3 tablespoons shelled pistachios

2 teaspoons kosher salt

½ teaspoon sugar

⅛ teaspoon ground cinnamon

⅛ teaspoon freshly grated nutmeg (grated with a fine Microplane or a nutmeg grater from a whole nutmeg)

12 thick slices applewood-smoked bacon

Starting at the far left or right side, drape one bacon slice into the mold, with the length of the slice going across the short side of the mold, centering it. Push the bacon into the corners and against the side of the mold, letting the strip flop over the edges. Continue across the length of the mold until you have lined the mold with 8 slices of the bacon. Use the remaining 4 slices of bacon to line the dish lengthwise.

Spoon half of the pâté mixture into the mold, pressing it against the bottom. Remove the tenderloin from the refrigerator, unwrap it, and lay it in the mold on top of the pâté, nestling it gently into the pâté. Spoon the remaining pâté mixture over the tenderloin and smooth out the top.

Starting with the lengthwise strips of bacon, fold each slice over the pâté. Fold all of the strips on one of the long sides over the pâté, then fold all of the strips on the other long side over. Cover the pâté with plastic wrap and refrigerate for at least 1 hour to chill, and up to 1 day to allow the pâté to settle around and envelop the tenderloin.

Adjust the oven rack to the center position and preheat the oven to 275°F.

Remove the terrine mold from the refrigerator, unwrap it, and place it in a roasting pan that is at least 3 inches deep. Fill the pan with enough water to come halfway up the side of the terrine mold.

Place the roasting pan in the oven to cook the pâté for about 1 hour 20 minutes, until an instant-read thermometer reads 145°F when inserted into the center of the pâté. While the pâté is cooking, cut a 12- × 3-inch piece of cardboard and wrap it in aluminum foil. Remove the pan from the oven and let the pâté rest in the water for about 10 minutes, until it is cool enough to handle. Remove the terrine mold from the pan with the water and discard the water.

Place the foil-wrapped cardboard on the pâté and place a brick or a heavy can or cans on top of the cardboard to weigh it down. Place the mold inside the roasting pan to catch any juices that will release from the terrine mold when the pâté is pressed and set aside to cool to room temperature, about 30 minutes. Place the roasting pan with the terrine mold and weights in the refrigerator to press the pâté overnight or for at least 6 hours.

Remove the pan from the refrigerator and remove the terrine mold from the pan. Drain the liquid that will have collected in the pan. Remove and discard the cardboard. Fill the roasting pan half full with hot tap water (about 120°F). Place the terrine mold in the water and let it sit for 30 seconds to loosen the pâté. Remove the mold from the water and wipe it dry. Slide an offset spatula or knife around the inside of the mold to loosen the pâté from the sides.

To serve, place a large plate upside down on top of the terrine mold and quickly flip the pâté upside down onto the plate. Transfer the pâté right side up onto a cutting board or large platter. Use the length of a large knife to slice the pâté ½ inch thick in one or two deliberate motions; don't press directly on it from above or you'll squish the pâté and cause it to fall apart.

Butcher's Pâté

Serves 8 to 10

In the *Chef's Table* episode about the Tuscan butcher Dario Cecchini, Dario talks about never having eaten a steak until he was eighteen. Instead, his grandmother boiled pig snout and other parts of the animal they were less likely to sell in the family butcher shop. This pâté, made with pig's liver and heart, honors that tradition.

You'll probably have to request the heart and liver from your butcher in advance, so plan for that. Caul fat is the lining of the pig stomach; it's used to wrap foods, such as this pâté. You can find it at any butcher store. Serve this pâté by itself, or with Pane Tostato (page 55) and Pickles (page 68).

You will need a meat grinding attachment to a stand mixer to make this. You will also need a 12- × 3-inch terrine mold, a roasting pan large enough to hold the terrine mold, and a piece of cardboard cut to fit just inside the dish.

You will need a large cutting board or platter to serve the pâté.

Cut the fatback into ½-inch cubes and place the cubes in a small saucepan over medium heat to melt them. Place the pig heart in the melted fat. Add ½ cup water, plus more if needed so the heart is submerged, and heat the liquid until it starts bubbling. Reduce the heat to low and cook the heart for 30 to 35 minutes, until it is firm and rubbery to the touch. Remove the heart from the fat and set aside until cool enough to touch, about 10 minutes.

While the heart is cooking, finely grind the coriander seeds and cloves in a spice grinder and transfer them to a small bowl.

Cut the pork belly into 1-inch chunks and put the chunks in a large container or a medium bowl. Cover and place the pork in the freezer along with the pork liver and meat grinding attachment, including the smallest die and the blade, and chill for 10 to 15 minutes. (You don't want to freeze the pork; you just want to chill it so it firms up, which makes it easier to grind.)

3 cups pork fatback (or lard)

1 pig heart (about 4 ounces)

1 teaspoon coriander seeds

8 whole cloves

1 pound skinless pork belly

8 ounces pork liver

1 large garlic clove, peeled

2 teaspoons kosher salt

½ teaspoon sugar

1 tablespoon black peppercorns

¼ teaspoon ground cinnamon

⅛ teaspoon freshly grated nutmeg (grated with a fine Microplane or a nutmeg grater from a whole nutmeg)

½ cup whole milk

Remove the meat grinding attachment, pork belly, and liver from the freezer and fit the mixer with the grinding attachment. Place a bowl under the mixer attachment and pass the pork belly through the grinder into the bowl, working quickly so the pork fat doesn't melt. Add the pork liver and garlic clove to the grinder and grind into the bowl with the pork belly. Add the salt, sugar, peppercorns, cinnamon, nutmeg, and ground coriander and cloves to the bowl with the ground pork and mix to combine. Add the chopped pig heart, the milk, eggs, onion, parsley, tarragon, and chervil, and stir to combine.

Stretch the caul fat out into a long sheet and drape it over the terrine mold, centering it. Press the caul fat into the bottom and sides of the mold, pushing it into the corners and against the sides, to line the dish. Let the excess caul fat flop over the sides.

Spoon the pâté mixture into the mold and smooth out the top. Fold the overhanging caul fat over to enclose the pâté mixture, as if you're covering it with a blanket. Trim and discard any excess caul fat that is hanging over the opposite edge. Cover the mold with plastic wrap and refrigerate for at least 1 hour and up to 1 day to allow the pâté to settle and chill.

Adjust the oven rack to the center position and preheat the oven to 200°F.

Remove the terrine mold from the refrigerator, unwrap it, and place it in a roasting pan that is at least 3 inches deep. Fill the pan with enough water to come halfway up the side of the terrine mold.

Place the roasting pan in the oven to cook the pâté for about 1 hour 20 minutes, until an instant-read thermometer reads 145°F when inserted into the center of the pâté. While the pâté is cooking, cut a 12- × 3-inch piece of cardboard and wrap it in aluminum foil. Remove the pan from the oven and let the pâté rest in the water for about 10 minutes, until it is cool enough to handle. Remove the terrine mold from the pan of water and discard the water.

Place the foil-wrapped cardboard on the pâté and place a brick or a heavy can or cans on top of the cardboard to weigh it down. Place the mold inside the roasting pan to catch any juices that will release from the terrine mold when the pâté is pressed and set aside to cool to room temperature, about 30 minutes. Place the roasting pan with the terrine mold and weights in the refrigerator to press the pâté overnight or for at least 6 hours. →

2 extra-large eggs, whisked

½ small yellow onion, peeled and finely chopped

2 tablespoons finely chopped fresh Italian parsley leaves

1 tablespoon finely chopped fresh tarragon leaves

1 tablespoon finely chopped fresh chervil leaves

¼ pound caul fat

Remove the pan from the refrigerator and remove the terrine mold from the pan. Drain the liquid that will have collected in the pan. Remove and discard the cardboard. Fill the roasting pan half full with hot tap water (about 120°F). Place the terrine mold in the water and let it sit for 30 seconds to loosen the pâté. Remove the mold from the water and wipe it dry. Slide an offset spatula or knife around the inside of the mold to loosen the pâté from the sides.

To serve, place a large plate upside down on top of the terrine mold and quickly flip the pâté upside down onto the plate. Transfer the pâté right side up onto a cutting board or large platter. Use the length of a large knife to slice the pâté ½ inch thick in one or two deliberate motions; don't press directly on the knife from above or you'll squish the pâté and cause it to fall apart.

Pane Tostato

Serves 4

This thick-sliced rustic bread cooked on the grill is one of the staples at Chi Spacca. Serve it as part of your *tagliere* (antipasto platter), or with any salad or entrée. At Chi Spacca, we serve it on its own, and also topped with Whipped Lardo (page 59) or N'duja (page 58).

You will need a large platter or cutting board to serve the pane.

Adjust the oven rack to the center position and preheat the oven temperature to 350°F.

Lay the bread on a baking sheet, brush the tops with olive oil, and toast in the oven for 20 to 25 minutes, until the bread is golden brown but not crunchy, rotating the baking sheet from front to back halfway through that time for even browning. Remove the toast from the oven and transfer it to a cutting board.

To serve, crush about ½ teaspoon flaky sea salt over each piece of toast and cut each piece in half. Pile the toasts on a large platter or cutting board.

2 (2-inch-thick) slices from the center of a 1-pound loaf of rustic bread

Olive oil

Flaky sea salt

Chianti "Tuna"

Serves 6

This classic Tuscan preparation is called *tonno di Chianti,* or "Chianti tuna," because the pork is slowly poached and packed in a jar with olive oil, like tuna. The pork is so tender that it even flakes like tuna. Dario Cecchini sells it at his butcher shop. To tell the story behind this dish, I'll let Dario speak for himself:

"A long time ago, an elderly gentleman told me a story about his father, a butcher, long since dead, who deboned pork thighs and shoulders, and with an alchemy of which he was now the final keeper, boiled them in white wine. The idea struck me as curious. Never in my research on the use of meat had I heard of a similar treatment for pork. In fact, the elderly gentleman admitted that many had considered his father a little strange, but that, undaunted, he continued his entire life preparing his magical mystery recipe. Over time, thinking back on this conversation, my curiosity won, beating out the conventional idea that only ham and prosciutto could be made from a leg of pork. With much experimenting, trying and trying again, I found the formula of the old butcher. He was right! Freeing up our imagination can lead to extraordinary discoveries. 'Tuna of Chianti' was reborn. The name is actually mine, given the similarity of taste with tuna from the sea."

You will need a medium bowl or large platter to serve the pork.

Cut the pork in half and put both halves in a large baking dish. Add the salt, peppercorns, juniper berries, and bay leaves. Add the rosemary sprigs and toss to coat the pork with the salt and to distribute the seasonings. Cover the dish with plastic wrap and refrigerate overnight or for at least 6 hours.

Remove the dish from the refrigerator, uncover, and transfer the pork to a large saucepan. Add the white wine and 4 cups water, or enough to submerge the pork, and bring the liquid to a simmer over medium heat. Reduce the heat to medium-low to maintain a steady simmer and cook the pork for 2 to 3 hours, until fork-tender. To test for doneness, insert a fork into the pork and turn it slightly; if the meat pulls apart with very little effort, it's done.

For Cooking the Pork

1 (2-pound) pork shoulder

2 teaspoons kosher salt

10 black peppercorns

5 juniper berries

3 bay leaves (preferably fresh)

2 fresh rosemary sprigs

1 cup dry white wine

1½ cups finishing-quality extra-virgin olive oil, plus more as needed

Drain the pork in a colander and discard the seasonings. Transfer the pork chunks to a container just large enough to hold them comfortably and add just enough finishing-quality olive oil as needed to completely cover the pork. Cover and refrigerate the pork overnight or for as long as 2 weeks.

When you are ready to serve the pork, remove it from the refrigerator and set it aside to come to room temperature, 30 minutes to 1 hour.

Adjust a mandoline to slice ⅛ inch thick. Trim one end of the onion and place the trimmed end on the mandoline and slice 2 slices. Check their thickness; you want the slices just thick enough that they don't fall apart. If they are too thick, adjust the mandoline to slice thinner. If they are so thin that they tear or don't hold their shape, adjust the blade to slice thicker. Continue slicing the onion, stopping when your fingers get dangerously close to the blade; discard the end or reserve it for stock. Put the onion slices in a medium bowl and squeeze the juice of the lemon over them.

Drizzle 1 tablespoon of the oil the pork was packed in over the onion, sprinkle with the salt, and toss to coat the onion with the seasonings.

Remove the pork from the oil and shred it into long strands into a medium bowl or down the length of a large platter. Drop the onion slices in tangles over the pork.

For Serving
1 red onion, peeled
1 lemon, halved
1 teaspoon kosher salt

N'duja

Makes about 3 cups

Pronounced *en-DOO-ya,* this is a traditional spiced ground pork—or, rather, it's spiced ground pork *fat*—from Calabria, in southern Italy. When it first started appearing in restaurants here, we—cooks and diners—didn't know how to pronounce it, or what it was. Now it's an obsession among both. It has a unique and very intense flavor that comes from the Calabrian chiles it is spiced with. You can find the chiles chopped or whole, packed in oil, at Italian and specialty food stores. It's delicious on its own, as part of an antipasto platter or *tagliere,* or smeared on Pane Tostato (page 55) for a rich and decadent starter. Adding a little bit of n'duja to another dish is a great way to add a lot of flavor with little effort. We add it to our meatball blend (Grilled Pork-and-Veal Meatballs with Fresh Ricotta and Braised Greens, page 175) and to Baked Mussels and Clams with N'duja and Aioli, and Toast for Dipping (page 230). Plan to make this in advance, because the fat for the n'duja has to be seasoned for one to two days before it is ground.

You will need a meat grinding attachment to a stand mixer to make this.

Cut the fatback and pork belly into 1-inch chunks and put the chunks in a large container or in a medium bowl. Add the Calabrian chiles, paprika, and salt. Use a fine Microplane to grate the garlic cloves into the container or bowl and toss to coat the meat with the seasonings. Cover and refrigerate the pork for at least 24 hours and up to 2 days.

When you are ready to grind the pork, remove it from the refrigerator and transfer it to the freezer along with the meat grinding attachment, including the smallest die and the blade, and chill for 10 to 15 minutes. (You don't want to freeze the pork; you just want to chill it so it firms up, which makes it easier to grind.)

Remove the pork and meat grinding attachment from the freezer and fit the mixer with the grinding attachment. Place a bowl under the mixer attachment and pass the pork through the grinder into the bowl, working quickly so the pork fat doesn't melt.

The n'duja can be used right away, refrigerated for as long as 5 days, or frozen for as long as 3 months.

12 ounces pork fatback

10 ounces pork belly

2 tablespoons chopped Calabrian chiles in oil

1 tablespoon hot smoked paprika

2 teaspoons kosher salt

2 large garlic cloves, peeled

Whipped Lardo

Makes about 4 cups

Every summer I make at least one day trip from my house in Umbria to visit the butcher Dario Cecchini at his shop in the charming Tuscan town of Panzano. Before you have both feet in the door to his shop, one of Dario's staff has poured you a stemless bistro glass of Chianti; walk a step farther and there's a small table displaying snacks, including a big bowl of whipped lardo along with olive oil–toasted crostini. *Lardo,* in case you haven't guessed, means "lard," and Dario's whipped lardo, which he calls "Chianti butter," is uncured pork fat seasoned with his own salt blend, ground, and whipped to a luxurious spreadable consistency. The more common way of eating lardo is cured and sliced, like prosciutto. Whipped lardo is a more unusual presentation, and it's also much easier to make.

We offer whipped lardo on Pane Tostato (page 55), and we also use it to dress baked potatoes, see Dario's Baked Potatoes with Whipped Lardo (page 293), and in place of the butter in Lardo Asador Potatoes (page 301).

You will need a meat grinding attachment to a stand mixer to make this.

Cut the fatback into 1-inch chunks and put the chunks in a large container or a medium bowl. Cover and place in the freezer along with the meat grinding attachment, including the smallest die and the blade, and chill for 10 to 15 minutes. (You don't want to freeze the meat; you just want to chill it so it firms up, which makes it easier to grind.)

Remove the meat and grinding attachment from the freezer and fit the mixer with the grinding attachment. Place a bowl under the mixer attachment and pass the meat through the grinder into the bowl, working quickly so the pork fat doesn't melt. Add the salt and rosemary and fold it in. Transfer the ground lardo to the bowl of a stand mixer. Fit the mixer with the paddle attachment and whip the lardo on high speed for 3 to 4 minutes, until it is light and fluffy.

The lardo can be used right away or refrigerated for as long as 5 days.

For the Lardo

2 pounds pork fatback

2 tablespoons Dario Salt (page 19)

2 tablespoons finely chopped rosemary

Pane Tostato with Bistecca Drippings

Serves 4

This toast, topped with chopped roasted trimmings from our dry-aged meat, is the ultimate example of not letting anything go to waste. The melted fat seeps down into the bread, while the chunks of crispy fat and meat rest on top. It's essentially the experience of sopping up the fat in the bottom of the pan you cooked a roast in, only you get to eat it sitting down with a glass of wine, not standing in the kitchen when nobody's looking.

Ask your butcher for beef trimmings (preferably dry-aged), consisting of 80 percent fat and 20 percent meat.

Adjust the oven racks so one is in the top third and one is in the bottom third and preheat the oven to 400°F.

Lay the bread on a baking sheet and brush the tops with olive oil. Toast the bread on the lower rack of the oven for 20 to 25 minutes, until it is golden brown but not crunchy, rotating the baking sheet from front to back halfway through that time for even browning. Remove the toast from the oven and transfer it to a cutting board.

While the bread is toasting, spread the trimmings out in a single layer on a large baking sheet and roast them on the upper rack of the oven, along with the bread, for 12 to 15 minutes, until they are golden brown and crispy in places. Remove the trimmings from the oven and set aside until they are cool enough to touch. Chop the trimmings into ¼-inch cubes and put them in a small bowl. Pour enough of the liquid fat from the baking sheet to cover the chopped trimmings and discard any remaining fat.

To serve, spoon the beef trimmings and fat over the toasts, dividing them evenly. Using a long sharp knife, cut each slice of bread into 3 or 4 pieces. To cut the bread without losing all of the toppings, place the knife on the bread where you want to make the cut and with one hand on the handle and the other pressing on the knife blade, push directly down on the knife in one forceful motion. Crush the flaky sea salt between your fingertips and grind a few turns of pepper over the toasts. Arrange the toasts in different directions on a large platter.

2 (2-inch-thick) slices from the center of a 1-pound loaf of rustic bread

Olive oil

1 pound beef trimmings (preferably dry-aged; including meat and fat)

Flaky sea salt

Fresh coarsely ground black pepper

Cetara Anchovies and Butter on Toast

Serves 4

Just as the pairing of butter and ham is a French classic, butter and anchovies are a traditional Italian combination. These toasts offer a simple, perfect union of sweet creamy butter and salty, aggressive anchovy.

I use Cetara anchovies, a very special, flavorful oil-packed anchovy from the Amalfi coast, for these and in any application where I am serving the anchovies whole. They have all of the flavor without being overly briny. You can find them in Italian specialty stores and online. Since the butter in this recipe is part of the dish, not something to cook in, you need to use quality, European high-fat butter: Rodolphe Le Meunier is one of my favorites. It is wrapped in beautiful gold foil; it makes a great present. Le Beurre Bordier, Échiré, and Beurre d'Isigny are also good choices, as is the more widely available Plugra.

A butter curler is a simple tool, shaped a bit like a horseshoe cleaner, used for shaving butter into long curls. It's one of those things that you may not use often, but you'll be happy to have it on those occasions when you do. If you don't have a butter curler, use the edge of a large spoon.

You will need a large platter or cutting board to serve these toasts.

Line a large plate with parchment paper. Use a butter curler or the side of a spoon to shave 8 (¼-inch-thick) pieces of butter from the block. Lay the butter slices in a single layer on the plate and place them in the refrigerator to chill.

Adjust the oven rack to the center position and preheat the oven to 350°F.

Lay the bread on a baking sheet and brush the tops with olive oil. Toast the bread in the oven for about 15 minutes, until it is golden brown but not crunchy, rotating the baking sheet from front to back halfway through that time for even browning. Remove the toast from the oven and transfer it to a cutting board.

Cut each piece of toast into 4 (1½-inch-wide) "soldiers."

To serve, remove the butter from the refrigerator and place one curl on each finger of toast. Drape one anchovy fillet on each curl of butter and place the toasts in a single layer on a large platter or cutting board.

A chunk of quality, European unsalted butter, cold

2 (½-inch-thick) slices from the center of a 1-pound loaf of rustic bread

Olive oil

8 Cetara anchovy fillets (or another quality, oil-packed anchovy)

Marinated Olives with Garlic and Fresh Pecorino

Makes about 1 quart

When friends come in to Chi Spacca, I often send them this dish—a selection of different sizes and colors of olives, with ribbons of orange peel and chunks of delicious cheese, all swimming in olive oil. It's a very pretty dish, and in my opinion, these are the perfect things to nibble on while you're poring over the menu or enjoying your first glass of wine.

Fresh pecorino is a young sheep's milk cheese. It's soft, about the texture of Jack cheese. It has a mild flavor, not to be confused with pecorino Romano, which is a very pungent, hard, grating cheese, and not what you want here. I'm spoiled because in my town in Italy, they sell this cheese at little shops along what seems like every country road. In Los Angeles, we use a version from Rome called cacio di Roma. If you can't find fresh pecorino, use fresh provolone or quality Jack cheese.

You will need a small deep bowl to serve this olive and cheese mixture.

Heat the extra-virgin olive oil in a medium skillet over medium-high heat for 2 to 3 minutes, until the oil slides easily and is smoking around the edges of the pan. Add the garlic cloves, reduce the heat to medium, and cook, stirring often, until the garlic cloves are light golden brown and tender but not mushy when pierced with a small knife. Turn off the heat.

Combine the olives, rosemary, árbol chiles, bay leaves, and pepper in a large bowl and toss gently to combine. Add the garlic and its oil to the bowl and gently stir to coat the olives with the oil and combine the ingredients, being careful not to smash the garlic. Let the mixture come to room temperature, then add the cheese and refrigerate, covered, for up to several months. (Add more oil to the container as needed to keep the olives, garlic cloves, and cheese submerged while you store them.)

To serve, transfer the olives to a small deep bowl and scatter the oregano leaves over the top. Serve the olives and cheese with a tiny fork and a small bowl on the side for guests to put the pits.

1½ cups extra-virgin olive oil, plus more as needed

¾ cup large garlic cloves (about 30 cloves), peeled

4 cups mixed olives with pits (such as 1 cup each: Taggiasche, Lucques, Castelvetrano, Niçoise, and Picholine), drained

4 fresh rosemary sprigs

3 árbol chiles

4 bay leaves (preferably fresh)

½ teaspoon fresh coarsely ground black pepper

6 ounces fresh pecorino (or another young, mild white cheese, such as provolone or Jack), cut into ½-inch cubes (about 1 cup)

A few fresh oregano leaves for garnish

Warm Dates with Sea Salt

Serves 4 to 6

This is hardly a recipe, and maybe I should feel guilty including it in this book, but these warm dates are so delicious that what I am really doing is giving you a tip: How to make a crowd-pleasing appetizer with no effort whatsoever. The answer: Take plump fresh dates and warm them. The end! Warmed, the dates are totally transformed. The insides almost melt and become jam-like. We top them with flaky sea salt to contrast with their sweetness.

In order for this transformation to happen, you need to start with fresh, very moist dates. We're spoiled in Southern California to have fresh dates, harvested in the desert around Palm Springs, available all winter long at our farmers' markets. My favorite variety is Black Sphinx; Medjools, Halawi, and Honey dates are also delicious. Maybe it's time you take a trip to Palm Springs!

You will need a small plate to serve the dates.

Combine the dates and extra-virgin olive oil in a small skillet over medium heat, and cook for about 5 minutes, shaking the pan occasionally to prevent the dates from sticking, until they are warmed through.

To serve, place the dates on a small plate. Drizzle with the olive oil from the pan and crush the flaky sea salt between your fingertips over the dates.

12 large dates (with pits)

2 tablespoons extra-virgin olive oil

Flaky sea salt

Roasted Lipstick Peppers with Anchovies, Mint, and Pecorino Toscano

Serves 4

This recipe is the epitome of ingredients speaking for themselves. Lipstick peppers are a small, sweet variety; I assume they get their name from the fact that they're bright red, like the shade of Chanel lipstick I wear. This recipe calls for pecorino Toscano, a Tuscan sheep's milk cheese. It is a hard cheese with a slightly granular texture. Look for it in cheese shops, or use pecorino Romano or Parmesan. The peppers are roasted in a cast-iron skillet that is preheated while the oven is preheating; this is our way of replicating the intense heat we get from our wood-burning ovens. By adding the peppers to an already-hot skillet, you are able to caramelize them without overcooking them.

You will need a large cast-iron skillet to char the peppers for this recipe.

You will need a large platter to serve this melange on.

Adjust the oven racks so none is near the oven floor; you'll be putting the baking sheet directly on the oven floor. If you are using an electric oven or another oven where you can't put anything on the floor, place the rack as close to the floor as possible and put a pizza steel or stone, if you have one, on it. Place a large cast-iron skillet on the floor or the lowest rack or stone. Preheat the oven to 500°F.

Put the peppers in a large bowl, drizzle with the olive oil, sprinkle with the salt and black pepper, and toss the peppers with the oil and seasonings. Open the oven and, using oven mitts, carefully pull out the hot skillet. Dump the peppers into the skillet and spread them out over the surface. Return the skillet to its original position, close the oven door, and cook for 12 to 14 minutes, until the peppers have softened and are charred in places, stirring them halfway through that time so they char evenly. Remove the skillet from the oven and immediately drizzle the balsamic vinegar over the peppers; shake the baking sheet to coat the peppers. Pour the finishing-quality olive oil over the peppers and gently turn them to coat them with the oil, taking care to keep the peppers intact as much as possible. Set the peppers aside for 1 hour to marinate.

2 pounds lipstick peppers (or another small sweet pepper, such as baby Italian peppers, Jimmy Nardello peppers, or baby pimiento peppers)

¼ cup olive oil

2 teaspoons kosher salt

½ teaspoon fresh coarsely ground black pepper

½ cup balsamic vinegar

½ cup finishing-quality extra-virgin olive oil

12 Cetara anchovy fillets (or another quality, oil-packed anchovy)

½ lemon

3 ounces pecorino Toscano (or pecorino Romano or Parmesan)

¼ cup fresh mint leaves

To serve, lay the peppers evenly over the surface of a large platter and drape 1 anchovy fillet over each pepper. Drizzle any marinade left on the baking sheet and squeeze the lemon half over the peppers. Use the large holes of a box grater or an extra-coarse Microplane to grate the cheese and tear each mint leaf into 2 to 3 pieces to fall over the peppers.

Pickles

We offer a changing selection of pickles at Chi Spacca. The recipes we chose to include here call for vegetables that are available year-round. Serve the pickles with Duck Rillettes (page 93), Butcher's Pâté (page 52), Pork Tenderloin Pistachio Pâté (page 49), or as part of any *tagliere* (antipasto platter). You may notice that these recipes call for different amounts of liquid and yield different amounts of pickles; these amounts are based on the sizes and shapes of the vegetables that are being pickled.

Turmeric Cauliflower Pickles

Makes 2 quarts

You will need a small bowl to serve the pickles.

Combine the vinegar, sugar, salt, turmeric, ginger, and 2 cups water in a large saucepan.

Cut the cauliflower florets off the core into 1-inch pieces and discard the core, and add the florets to the saucepan with the pickling liquid.

Cut the onion in half, root to tip. Separate the layers of the onion, stack two or three layers on top of one another, and slice them ¼ inch thick lengthwise. Set aside.

Bring the pickling liquid to a boil over high heat, stirring occasionally to dissolve the seasonings. Turn off the heat and add the onion slices. Let the vegetables sit in the pickling liquid until the liquid cools to room temperature. Pour all the ingredients into a large container with a lid (or two 1-quart canning jars); if you have more liquid than will fit, discard it. Cover and refrigerate the pickles for at least 24 hours and up to 1 month.

To serve, remove the pickled cauliflower and onion from the refrigerator and let them come to room temperature. Remove the cauliflower and onion slices from the liquid and arrange them in a small pretty bowl; refill the bowl as desired.

3 cups champagne vinegar (or white wine vinegar)

2 tablespoons sugar

1½ tablespoons kosher salt

1 tablespoon ground turmeric

1 teaspoon ground ginger

1 medium head cauliflower (about 1½ pounds)

1 large yellow Spanish onion, peeled

Pickled Fennel

Makes 2 quarts

You will need a small bowl to serve the pickles.

Toast the coriander seeds, fennel seeds, dill seeds, and peppercorns in a small skillet over medium heat for 1 to 2 minutes, until they are toasted and fragrant, shaking the pan so they don't burn. Transfer them to a large saucepan. Add the vinegar, garlic, salt, sugar, and 2 cups water.

Cut off the fronds from the fennel bulbs if they are still attached, at the point where the bulbs start to sprout into separate stalks and discard them. (Trimming fennel this way shows off its pretty shape when sliced.) Trim the very bottom of the root end, making sure to leave enough of the core so that the bulb stays intact. Remove any brown or unappealing outer layers; use the outer layers and stalks to make stock another time or discard them.

Adjust a mandoline to slice ¼ inch thick. Lay 1 fennel bulb on its side on the mandoline and thinly slice it, stopping just before your fingers get dangerously close to the blade; snack on the end piece. Repeat with the second fennel bulb. Put the fennel slices in a large container with a lid (or two 1-quart canning jars). Add the dill sprigs.

Bring the pickling liquid to a boil over high heat, stirring occasionally to dissolve the salt and sugar. Turn off the heat and pour enough of the pickling liquid over the fennel to fill the container or jar and discard the remaining liquid. Set aside to cool to room temperature. Cover and refrigerate the pickles for at least 24 hours and up to 1 month.

To serve, remove the pickled fennel from the refrigerator and let them come to room temperature. Remove the fennel slices from the liquid and arrange them in a small pretty bowl; refill the bowl as desired.

1 teaspoon coriander seeds

1 teaspoon fennel seeds

1 teaspoon dill seeds

1 teaspoon black peppercorns

2 cups champagne vinegar (or white wine vinegar)

4 large garlic cloves, peeled and smashed with the side of a knife

1½ tablespoons kosher salt

1 teaspoon sugar

2 pounds fennel bulbs

3 fresh dill sprigs

Spicy Green Bean Pickles

Makes 1 quart

You will need a small bowl to serve the pickles.

Put the green beans in a container with a lid (or a 1-quart canning jar).

Combine the vinegar, salt, sugar, cloves, allspice berries, red pepper flakes, and 2 cups water in a large saucepan.

Use a small sharp knife to cut a slit down the length of each habanero chile to expose the seeds. Add the chiles to the saucepan and bring the liquid to a boil over high heat, stirring occasionally to dissolve the salt and sugar. Reduce the heat to medium to maintain a steady simmer and simmer for about 5 minutes to infuse the pickling liquid with the habanero and spices. Turn off the heat, remove the chiles, and add them to the container or jar with the beans. Pour enough of the pickling liquid over the beans to fill the container or jar and discard the remaining liquid. Set the green bean pickles aside to come to room temperature. Close the container and refrigerate the green bean pickles for at least 2 days and up to 1 month.

To serve, remove the pickled green beans from the refrigerator and let them come to room temperature. Remove the green beans from the liquid and arrange them in a small pretty bowl; refill the bowl as desired.

1 pound green beans (preferably haricots verts), stems removed and discarded, tails intact

2 cups red wine vinegar

2 teaspoons kosher salt

2 teaspoons sugar

5 whole cloves

1 tablespoon allspice berries

½ teaspoon red pepper flakes

3 habanero chiles

Cucumber Pickles

Makes 1 quart

You will need a small bowl to serve the pickles.

Place the cucumbers, garlic, and dill in a container with a lid (or a 1-quart canning jar) and set aside.

Toast the cumin seeds and coriander seeds in a small skillet over medium heat for 1 to 2 minutes, until they are golden brown and fragrant, shaking the pan so they don't burn. Transfer the seeds to a large saucepan.

Add the vinegar, salt, sugar, and 1 cup water to the saucepan with the spices and bring it to a boil over high heat, stirring occasionally to dissolve the salt and sugar. Reduce the heat to medium and simmer for about 5 minutes to infuse the liquid with the spices. Turn off the heat and pour enough of the pickling liquid over the cucumbers to fill the container or jar with the cucumbers, discarding the remaining liquid. Set the cucumber pickles aside to cool to room temperature. Cover and refrigerate the cucumber pickles for at least 3 days and up to 1 month.

To serve, remove the pickled cucumbers from the refrigerator and let them come to room temperature. Remove the cucumbers from the liquid and slice them 1 inch thick on an extreme bias. Arrange the slices in a small pretty bowl; refill the bowl as desired.

1 pound Persian cucumbers (preferably about 4 inches long)

5 large garlic cloves, peeled and smashed with the flat side of a knife

5 fresh dill tufts (pulled from the stems)

1 teaspoon cumin seeds

1 teaspoon coriander seeds

2 cups champagne vinegar (or white wine vinegar)

1 tablespoon kosher salt

2 teaspoons sugar

Giardiniera

Makes 2 quarts

Giardiniera is the crunchy fresh mix of pickled vegetables I associate with old-school Italian American restaurants. This recipe calls for baby bell peppers, which are the sweet bell peppers sold in bags. You can also use the small sweet peppers you find at farmers' markets during the summertime. The point is that the peppers should be sweet, not spicy, and you want to avoid green bell peppers, which aren't sweet at all.

You will need a small bowl to serve the pickles.

Combine the vinegar, salt, sugar, red pepper flakes, and 4 cups water in a large bowl and stir to dissolve the salt and sugar.

Cut off and discard the stems from the peppers and cut the peppers in half. Remove and discard the seeds and cut the peppers in half again to quarter them. Put the peppers in a large bowl. Cut the cauliflower florets off the core in 1-inch pieces and discard the core. Add the florets to the bowl with the peppers. Cut the onion in half, root to tip. Separate the layers of the onion, stack two or three layers on top of one another, and slice them ¼ inch thick lengthwise. Put them in the bowl with the other vegetables. Cut the carrot at an angle into 1-inch segments and add them to the bowl. Peel the rounded (convex) side of the celery and slice it ¼ inch thick on an extreme bias. Add the celery to the bowl with the other vegetables.

Toss to combine the vegetables and transfer them to a large container with a lid (or divide them between two 1-quart canning jars). Pour enough of the pickling liquid over the vegetables to cover them. Close the container or jars and refrigerate the vegetables for 2 days. Add the oregano and refrigerate for 1 more day before serving, or for up to 1 month.

To serve, remove the giardiniera from the refrigerator and let it come to room temperature. Remove the vegetables from the liquid and arrange them in a small pretty bowl; refill the bowl as desired.

1½ quarts (6 cups) champagne vinegar (or white wine vinegar)

3 tablespoons kosher salt

1 tablespoon sugar

1 tablespoon red pepper flakes

12 baby bell peppers

½ medium head cauliflower (about ¾ pound)

1 large yellow Spanish onion, peeled

1 medium carrot

2 celery stalks

1 tablespoon dried oregano (preferably Sicilian oregano on the branch)

Little Gems with Herb Bread Crumbs, Bacon Vinaigrette, and Grated Egg   77

Pinkerton Avocados with Pea Shoots, Toasted Pine Nuts, and Prosciutto   81

Castelfranco and Persimmon Salad with Candied Pecans, Parmesan,
and Fruit-and-Nut Toasts   83

Puntarella and Cauliflower Salad with Bagna Cauda, Anchovies,
and Soft-Cooked Eggs   87

Watercress and Avocado Salad with Pears and Gorgonzola Vinaigrette   90

Chrysanthemum Greens with Kumquats and Duck Rillettes Toasts   93

Insalata Primavera: Shaved Spring Vegetable Salad
with Roasted Artichokes and Dill   96

Insalata Inverno: Shaved Winter Vegetable Salad with Parmesan and Olio Nuovo   99

Spacca Caesar with Fried Parsley, Anchovies, Orange Zest,
and Bagna Cauda Croutons   101

Making Aioli by Hand   104

Misticanza: Shaved Vegetable Salad with Radicchio
and Sherry Dijon Vinaigrette   106

Heirloom Tomato Panzanella with Olive Bread Croutons and Feta Yogurt   108

Butter Lettuce and Herb Salad with Lemon Dijon Vinaigrette   110

Indian-Spiced Chicken Salad with Mixed Lettuces, Walnuts,
and Preserved Lemon Vinaigrette   113

Roasted Beets with Chicories, Yogurt, and Lemon Zest   115

BLTA Salad with Aioli and Herb Bread Crumbs   118

Grains and Seeds Salad with Escarole, Avocado, Bacon, Egg,
and Horseradish Dressing   121

Burrata and Stone Fruit Salad with Mizuna and Sweet Peppers   126

Insalate

At Chi Spacca, our challenge is to prove to our customers that we love vegetables as much as we love meat, and we show that through a long and ever-changing list of seasonal salads. We take our salads seriously, layering each one with contrasting flavors and textures in combinations so satisfying you can make a meal out of them. And just as our meats showcase many cuts you may never have heard of, we look beyond your usual lettuce suspects for our salads. We build our salads from varieties of "lettuces" that are often overlooked, such as puntarella, escarole, radicchio, Little Gem, watercress, and pea shoots.

Little Gems with Herb Bread Crumbs, Bacon Vinaigrette, and Grated Egg

Serves 4

In 1979, the chef Jonathan Waxman hired me for my first pastry job at the legendary Santa Monica restaurant Michael's. Jonathan is a master with vegetables and salads, and at the time, he was making a salad that was his spin on the classic French bistro frisée salad, which consists of lettuce, lardon, a poached egg, and a warm mustard dressing; I couldn't get enough of it. I make mine with a grated rather than a poached egg, Little Gem lettuce, which is a new variety of small romaine lettuce whose crunchy, sturdy leaves hold up to the thick, tangy, mustardy dressing it's tossed with. It is so satisfying and has so much flavor. As with Jonathan's salad forty years ago, I could eat this every day.

I am very specific about how I like hard-cooked eggs. If I am grating them, as I do for this salad, or making egg salad, I cook the eggs just long enough so they are cooked all the way through, but not so long that the yolks are dry and dusty or have a gray ring around them. The recipe makes more bread crumbs than you will need; store them at room temperature and use them in the week ahead on other salads, pasta, or roasted vegetables.

You will need a large platter or large wide-mouth bowl to serve this salad.

To make the vinaigrette, adjust the oven rack to the center position and preheat the oven to 350°F.

Place the bacon on a baking sheet and cook it in the oven for 16 to 20 minutes, until the bacon is cooked but not crisp, rotating the baking sheet from front to back halfway through that time so the bacon cooks evenly. Create a bed of paper towels. Remove the bacon from the oven and transfer it to the paper towels to drain and cool. Leave the oven on.

Pour the bacon fat from the baking sheet into a small saucepan. Leave one-third of the bacon on the paper towels (you will use this for the salad) and finely chop the remaining bacon. Put the chopped bacon and shallots in the saucepan with the bacon fat and cook over medium heat for 7 to 10 minutes, stirring occasionally, until the shallots are soft. While the bacon and shallots are cooking, fill a medium bowl with ice and place a small bowl in the ice. →

For the Vinaigrette

12 ounces applewood-smoked slab bacon, cut into ½-inch cubes (or thick-sliced applewood-smoked bacon)

½ cup peeled and minced shallots

½ cup sherry vinegar

2 tablespoons Dijon mustard

½ cup extra-virgin olive oil

For the Herb Bread Crumbs

Half of a 1-pound loaf of rustic bread

½ cup olive oil

Turn off the heat and transfer the bacon and shallot mixture to the bowl resting atop the ice. Add the vinegar and mustard and whisk for about 1 minute to combine and cool the ingredients. Slowly add the bacon fat and extra-virgin olive oil, whisking constantly to emulsify the vinaigrette. Let the vinaigrette rest over the ice for about 10 minutes to cool, whisking every few minutes to keep the dressing emulsified. (If it is not cooled over ice, the dressing will separate.)

To make the bread crumbs, pull the inside of the bread out of the crust in 1- to 1½-inch chunks and put the chunks on a large baking sheet. (Reserve the crusts to snack on or discard them.) Drizzle with the olive oil, sprinkle with the salt, and toss to coat the bread chunks. Spread the bread chunks out on the baking sheet and bake for 10 to 12 minutes, until the bread chunks are golden brown and crispy, stirring them and rotating the baking sheet from front to back halfway through that time for even browning. Remove the croutons from the oven and let them cool slightly. Transfer the croutons to a food processor fitted with a metal blade and pulse until they are fine bread crumbs. Transfer the bread crumbs to a medium bowl. Add the chives, tarragon, and parsley and stir to combine. Return the bread crumbs to the baking sheet and return the sheet to the oven to bake for 2 to 3 minutes, until the herbs are brown. Remove the bread crumbs from the oven and set them aside to cool to room temperature. (You will use 2 tablespoons of the bread crumbs for this salad; store the remaining bread crumbs in a covered container at room temperature for as long as 1 week.)

To cook the eggs, bring a large saucepan of water to a boil over high heat and add the salt. (The salt does not penetrate the egg shells and season the eggs; it helps the whites to solidify quickly if there is a crack in an egg.) Carefully lower the eggs into the water and reduce the heat so the water is gently simmering. Simmer the eggs for 5 minutes, turn off the heat, and let the eggs sit in the water until the water comes to room temperature. Peel the eggs under a gentle stream of running water.

1 teaspoon kosher salt

2 tablespoons finely chopped fresh chives

2 tablespoons finely chopped fresh tarragon leaves

2 tablespoons finely chopped fresh Italian parsley leaves

For the Eggs

1 tablespoon kosher salt

2 extra-large eggs

For the Salad

4 heads Little Gem lettuce (or 2 baby romaine or hearts of romaine)

2 large scallions

½ lemon

½ teaspoon kosher salt

To prepare the salad, remove and discard any unappealing outer leaves from the heads of lettuce. Tear the leaves from the cores, breaking the larger leaves in half, and drop the leaves into a large bowl. Discard the cores. Trim and discard the root ends and any wilted greens from the scallions and slice the scallions into ¼-inch-thick rounds (white and green parts). Add the scallions to the bowl. Squeeze the lemon half over the salad, sprinkle with the salt, and toss to coat the salad with the lemon and salt. Drizzle the vinaigrette over the salad and toss, massaging with your hands to coat the lettuce and scallions with the vinaigrette. Add the bacon and toss to combine.

To serve, building the salad in two layers, lift half of the lettuce leaves out of the bowl and arrange them to cover the surface of a large platter or wide-mouth bowl. Grab a handful of the bacon cubes and scallions from the bowl and scatter them evenly over the lettuce leaves. Using a coarse Microplane, grate one egg over the salad and sprinkle 1 tablespoon of the bread crumbs over the grated egg. Lay the remaining lettuces on top of the first layer and scatter any bacon and scallions that are left in the bowl over the lettuce. Grate the second egg over the salad and sprinkle with the remaining 1 tablespoon bread crumbs.

Pinkerton Avocados with Pea Shoots, Toasted Pine Nuts, and Prosciutto

Serves 4

This is more like a composed plate than a salad, made up of carefully chosen ingredients, including Sicilian pine nuts, Pinkerton avocados, and prosciutto arranged on a bed of pea shoots and dressed with a peppery Tuscan olive oil. We cure our own meats at Chi Spacca, a tradition started by one of our former chefs, Chad Colby. It takes a lot of patience to cure your own meat, and it's exciting when you finally get to enjoy it. At the start, after twelve or eighteen months of waiting, we were ready to slice into the prosciutto, and we designed this salad to celebrate the occasion. This is one of the few salads I make that isn't tossed. The simple act of picking up the salad and transferring it to your plate tosses the salad just as much as is needed. Formally tossing it would smash the more delicate ingredients.

Sicilian pine nuts, which are labeled as such, are longer than the more commonly found Chinese pine nuts. Find them at Italian specialty stores and online sources. For this salad, make sure to buy prosciutto sliced to order rather than packaged, presliced prosciutto, and ask for it sliced moderately thin. You don't want the slices so thin that they tear into shreds when you pick them up, but you don't want them thick and leathery. Having the person behind the deli counter hand you a slice to inspect (and eat!) is one of the perks of shopping for prosciutto. Pinkertons have become my favorite avocado in recent years. I like their flavor and creamy texture, and I also appreciate their elegant, slender shape. They have a thin, shiny skin that is very easy to peel off, leaving you with an avocado that looks really pretty when sliced. In Southern California, we find Pinkertons at farmers' markets from August through October. If you can't find them, use Fuerte or Hass.

You will need an extra-large platter to serve this salad.

Adjust the oven rack to the center position and preheat the oven to 325°F.

Spread the pine nuts on a baking sheet and toast them in the oven for 8 to 10 minutes, until they are fragrant and toasted, shaking the baking sheet and rotating it from front to back halfway through that time so the nuts brown evenly. Remove the pine nuts from the oven and set them aside to cool to room temperature. →

¼ cup pine nuts

8 cups pea shoots

2 ripe but firm avocados (preferably Pinkerton, Fuerte, or Hass)

Flaky sea salt

Scatter the pea shoots to cover the bottom of an extra-large platter.

Cut the avocados in half lengthwise and twist each half in opposite directions to separate them. Plunge the edge of a large knife into the pits and twist the knife to release the pit from each avocado; discard the pits. With the avocados still in their skins, slice each avocado half lengthwise into 4 equal slices, making sure not to cut through the skins.

Crush about 1 teaspoon flaky sea salt between your fingertips over the avocados. Use a large spoon to scoop the avocado slices out of the skin and lay the slices in random directions over the pea shoots. Squeeze the juice of the lemon over the avocados and pea shoots and drizzle about 3 tablespoons finishing-quality olive oil over the salad. Tear the prosciutto slices apart and drape one torn piece over each slice of avocado. Scatter the pine nuts over the salad.

1 lemon, halved

Finishing-quality extra-virgin olive oil

4 thin slices prosciutto (about 2 ounces)

Castelfranco and Persimmon Salad with Candied Pecans, Parmesan, and Fruit-and-Nut Toasts

Serves 4

Often one of my cooks will come to me with an idea for making something with a particular ingredient, and that is what happened here, in the case of persimmons. I've never been the biggest fan of persimmons; I find their flavor a little bland. But when one of the talented cooks at the Osteria, Anna Nguyen, told me she wanted to make a persimmon salad, I said, "Let's give it a try." We collaborated to create this composed salad of persimmon, candied pecans, and Castelfranco piled on top of crisp fruit-and-nut bread slices. The result is like a fruit-and-cheese platter turned into a salad.

Castelfranco is a variety of radicchio, with mottled pale green and red leaves; you find it in farmers' markets and specialty produce shops in the fall and winter months, the same time persimmons are in season. If you can't find it, use small heads of radicchio instead. There are two types of persimmon. Hachiya persimmons, when ripe, are mushy; you typically eat them with a spoon. Fuyu persimmons, which is what we use for this salad, are still firm and sliceable, even when they are ripe. At the restaurant, I make the toasts using a fruit-and-nut bread from La Brea Bakery, sliced very thin using a meat slicer. Because the bread isn't widely available and slicing that thin for the home cook isn't really possible, I call for Raincoast Crisps, crackers that are readily available. The recipe for candied pecans makes twice what you need for this salad. My thought is that if you're going to go to the effort to make them, there should be some for the cook to snack on.

You will need a large platter to serve this salad.

To make the candied pecans, put the sugar in a heavy medium saucepan. Add 2 cups water and stir to combine. Brush the sides of the pan with a wet pastry brush to remove any undissolved sugar granules. Bring the mixture to a boil over high heat without stirring, tilting and swirling the pan so the sugar dissolves. Add the pecans, reduce the heat to medium, and cook, stirring occasionally to prevent the nuts from sticking together, until the syrup boils vigorously and the liquid has →

For the Candied Pecans

2 cups sugar

2 cups pecan halves

Canola oil (or another neutral-flavored oil) for frying (about 4 cups)

1 teaspoon flaky sea salt

reduced by half, about 35 minutes. (The nuts and sugar will not brown at this point. This step is to sweeten the nuts; they will brown when they are fried in the next step.) Reduce the heat to the lowest setting to prevent the syrup from crystallizing.

While the nuts are cooking, fill a medium saucepan 3 to 4 inches deep with the canola oil and fasten a deep-fry thermometer, if you have one, to the side of the saucepan. Heat the oil over medium-high heat until the thermometer reads 350°F or a pinch of salt sizzles when dropped into the oil. Place a large baking sheet near the stove.

Use a large slotted spoon or mesh strainer to transfer half of the pecans from the syrup to the oil and fry them for 2 minutes, stirring gently to prevent the nuts from sticking together. Use the spoon to remove the pecans from the oil, transfer them to the baking sheet, and immediately sprinkle them with half of the flaky sea salt. Repeat with the remaining pecans and sprinkle them with the remaining flaky sea salt. Discard the syrup. Let the nuts cool to room temperature. Set aside 1 cup of the candied pecans for the salad and save the rest to snack on.

To make the dressing, combine the mustard, shallot, vinegar, lemon juice, kosher salt, and a few turns of pepper in a small bowl. Gradually add the extra-virgin olive oil, whisking constantly.

To prepare the salad, remove and discard any unappealing outer leaves from the heads of the Castelfranco. Remove the remaining leaves from the cores and drop them into a large wide-mouth bowl, taking care to keep the leaves whole if possible; discard the cores.

Adjust the blade of a mandoline to slice ¼ inch thick. Holding the stem end, place the bottom of the persimmon on the slicer and slice it until you get close to the stem; discard the stem. Repeat with the second persimmon. Add the persimmon slices to the bowl with the Castelfranco and drizzle with 2 tablespoons of the dressing. Toss the salad, massaging with your hands to coat each leaf and persimmon slice with the dressing; add more dressing as needed to coat them thoroughly.

For the Dressing

3 tablespoons Dijon mustard, plus more as needed

1 tablespoon peeled and minced shallot

1 tablespoon sherry vinegar

1 teaspoon fresh lemon juice

¼ teaspoon kosher salt

Fresh coarsely ground black pepper

2 tablespoons extra-virgin olive oil

For the Salad

2 heads Castelfranco (or another chicory, such as Treviso or radicchio)

3 ripe but firm Fuyu persimmons

8 Raincoast Crisps (any variety)

A chunk of Parmesan for shaving

To serve, arrange the crisps in a single layer on a large platter. Using the back of a small spoon, spread a thin layer of the dressing on each crisp. Lay 2 slices of the dressed persimmon, overlapping each other, on each crisp. Building the salad in four layers and choosing the largest leaves, arrange one-third of the Castelfranco leaves in concentric circles like the petals of a flower on top of the toasts, Lay one-third of the remaining dressed persimmon slices on the Castelfranco. Use a large shaver Microplane or a mandoline to shave 10 to 15 shavings from the chunk of Parmesan and scatter the shavings and about one-third of the candied pecans over the persimmons. Make three more layers the same as the first, using the medium leaves for the second and third layers and reserving the smallest leaves for the top layer, and making each layer smaller than the one before. The top, fourth, layer will have 2 persimmon slices with a few Parmesan shavings and a handful of candied pecans scattered over the top.

Puntarella and Cauliflower Salad with Bagna Cauda, Anchovies, and Soft-Cooked Eggs

Serves 4

Puntarella is an Italian green with long slender leaves. It is a chicory, so it has a bitter, peppery taste like radicchio or escarole. When I go to Rome in the wintertime, when puntarella is in season, I order a puntarella salad, invariably dressed in anchovy dressing, whenever I see it on a menu. In this country, I've seen puntarella only at farmers' markets, so I offer shaved fennel as an alternative.

I normally use salt-packed anchovies to cook or make a sauce with. They have more flavor than oil-packed anchovies, but they can also be too briny and intense. So when I'm serving anchovies to eat whole, I use Cetara, a special variety of oil-packed anchovies from the Amalfi coast that are plumper, with a mild complex flavor. Since this salad calls for both whole anchovies and anchovies that are "melted" into the bagna cauda, I use Cetara for both so you don't have to buy two types of anchovies to make it. If you feel inclined to buy both, use salt-packed for the bagna cauda and oil-packed in the salad. The eggs in this salad are cooked so they are still runny when you break them open, so the yolks spill out into the salad. The recipe makes more bread crumbs than you will need; store them at room temperature and use them in the week ahead on other salads, pasta, or roasted vegetables.

You will need an extra-large platter to serve this salad.

To cook the eggs, bring a large saucepan of water to a boil over high heat and add the salt. (The salt does not penetrate the egg shells and season the eggs; it helps the whites to solidify quickly if there is a crack in an egg.) Carefully lower the eggs into the water and reduce the heat so the water is gently simmering. Cook the eggs for 4 minutes, turn off the heat, and let the eggs sit in the water for 4 minutes. Prepare an ice bath in a small bowl and transfer the eggs to the ice bath to chill. Peel them under a gentle stream of running water. →

For the Eggs

1 tablespoon kosher salt

4 extra-large eggs

For the Bagna Cauda

4 tablespoons (½ stick) unsalted butter

½ cup extra-virgin olive oil

To make the bagna cauda, combine the butter and extra-virgin olive oil in a small saucepan. Finely chop the anchovies with a large knife and use the flat side of the knife to smash them into a paste; add the paste to the saucepan. Using a fine Microplane, grate the garlic into the saucepan. Heat the bagna cauda over low heat for 5 minutes, stirring occasionally, to melt the butter and meld the flavors. Turn off the heat. Set aside ½ cup of the bagna cauda to use for the bread crumbs. Use the Microplane to grate the bright yellow outer layer of the lemon into the saucepan with the remaining bagna cauda. Reserve the lemon to juice for the salad.

To make the bread crumbs, adjust the oven rack to the center position and preheat the oven to 350°F.

Pull the inside of the bread out of the crust into 1- to 1½-inch chunks and put the chunks on a large baking sheet. Drizzle the reserved ½ cup bagna cauda over the bread and toss to coat the bread with the bagna. Spread the bread chunks out on the baking sheet and bake for 10 to 12 minutes, until the bread chunks are golden brown and crispy, stirring them and rotating the baking sheet from front to back halfway through that time for even browning. Remove the croutons from the oven and set aside to cool slightly. Transfer the croutons to a food processor fitted with a metal blade and pulse until they are fine bread crumbs. Transfer the bread crumbs to a medium bowl. Use a fine Microplane to grate the zest, the bright yellow outer layer of the lemon, over the bread crumbs, add the capers, and stir to combine. Reserve the lemon segment to juice over the fennel later in this recipe. (You will use ¼ cup of the bread crumbs for this salad; store the remaining bread crumbs in a covered container at room temperature for as long as 1 week.)

To prepare the salad, trim the cauliflower and cut it into quarters, keeping the core intact. Adjust the blade of a mandoline to slice ⅛ inch thick. Slice 2 slices of cauliflower and check their thickness; you want the slices just thick enough that they don't fall apart. If they are thick, like slabs, adjust the mandoline to slice thinner. If they are so thin that they crumble into pieces, adjust the blade to slice thicker. Continue slicing the cauliflower and put the slices and the residual cauliflower crumbles into a large bowl.

10 Cetara anchovy fillets in oil (or another quality, oil-packed variety; or 5 whole salt-packed anchovies, rinsed and backbones removed)

4 large garlic cloves, peeled

1 lemon

For the Bread Crumbs

Half of a 1-pound loaf of rustic bread

1 lemon

¼ cup capers (preferably salt-packed), soaked for 15 minutes if salt-packed, rinsed, drained, and finely chopped

For the Salad

½ large head cauliflower (about ½ pound)

1 head puntarella (about 1 pound; or 1 large fennel bulb, about 12 ounces)

¼ cup finishing-quality extra-virgin olive oil

½ teaspoon kosher salt

2 tablespoons finely chopped fresh Italian parsley leaves

6 Cetara anchovy fillets (or another quality, oil-packed anchovy)

If you are using puntarella, tear the stalks from the core of the puntarella and discard the core. Slice the puntarella stalks ¼ inch thick on an extreme bias and put the slices in a large bowl. If you are using fennel, cut off the fronds from the fennel bulb, if they are still attached, at the point where the bulb starts to sprout into separate stalks and discard them. (Trimming the fennel this way shows off its pretty shape when it is sliced.) Trim the very bottom of the root end, making sure to leave enough of the core so that the bulb stays intact. Remove the brown or unappealing outer layers and reserve them for another use, such as to make stock, or discard. Cut the fennel in half lengthwise and lay the fennel, flat side down, on the mandoline and thinly slice it, checking the thickness and adjusting the mandoline as needed. Transfer the puntarella or fennel slices to the bowl with the cauliflower. Cut the reserved lemon from the bagna cauda in half, squeeze the juice of half of the lemon, and sprinkle the salt over the vegetables. Toss to coat the vegetables with the lemon and salt. (Lemon juice prevents sliced fennel from browning.)

Cut off and discard the top and bottom of the lemon you zested for the bread crumbs at the point where you can see the flesh. Place the lemon upright on a cutting board and cut down the side at the point where the pith meets the flesh, following the natural curve of the fruit to remove the pith along with the peel. Discard the pith and peels. Turn the lemon on its side and cut along one of the membranes toward the center of the fruit. Working your way around the lemon, cut along both sides of each membrane to release all the segments from the core. Add the lemon segments to the bowl with the vegetables and squeeze the core of the lemon over the bowl to extract any remaining juice; discard the core.

To serve, spoon ¼ cup of the remaining bagna cauda to pool in the center of an extra-large platter and use the back of the spoon to spread it toward the edges in an organic, uneven way. Lay the cauliflower, puntarella, and lemon segments on top of the pool of bagna cauda. Sprinkle with the bread crumbs. Break the eggs open like a book so the halves remain intact and nestle the eggs randomly on the salad. Spoon 1 tablespoon of the bagna cauda on each egg half and sprinkle the eggs with the parsley. Drape the anchovies on the salad, around the eggs.

Watercress and Avocado Salad with Pears and Gorgonzola Vinaigrette

Serves 4

Every Monday, our produce purveyor, Dragan, pulls his truck into the shared parking lot behind our restaurants to bring us fresh produce. He gets it from all parts of California, so essentially, it's like having all the best farmers' markets in the state pull up at our back door. Very often, an item we see on Dragan's truck inspires us to build a dish around it. That's how this salad came about. Dragan was selling delicate bunches of spicy watercress, and I thought of pairing the bright green watercress with the varied green shades of avocado. The rest of the salad developed as I began playing with ingredients to complement those two.

You might be surprised to see jarred cocktail onions on this salad. As many vegetables as we do pickle at our restaurants, pearl onions are not one of them. Using our bar onions was my shortcut to getting the pickled onion flavor I wanted to dress the avocados, without doing any pickling ourselves. There are a lot of artisanal pickled onions on the market; use whatever brand you like. Warren pears are my preferred pears to work with: they're creamy, juicy, and flavorful. If you can't find them, look for Comice, D'Anjou, or Bartlett. Buy gorgonzola cheese by the wedge and crumble it yourself. Pre-crumbled cheese tends to be lower quality, and also dried out.

Look for watercress from a farmers' market, which is spicier and more flavorful than upland cress, which you often find in supermarkets; upland cress is also more fragile and wilts easily.

You will need a large platter to serve this salad.

To make the vinaigrette, combine the shallot, lemon juice, pickling juice, vinegar, kosher salt, and pepper in a small bowl. Gradually add the extra-virgin olive oil, whisking constantly. Add the gorgonzola and stir gently to combine the ingredients without breaking up the chunks of cheese.

To prepare the salad, cut the avocados in half lengthwise and twist each half in opposite directions to separate them. Plunge the edge of a large knife into the pit and twist the knife to release the pit from each avocado; discard the pits. With the avocados still in their skins, slice each avocado half lengthwise into 4 equal slices, making sure not to cut through the

For the Vinaigrette

1 tablespoon peeled and minced shallot

2 tablespoons fresh lemon juice

2 tablespoons pickling juice from the jar of pickled onions (see below)

2 teaspoons champagne vinegar

½ teaspoon kosher salt

Fresh coarsely ground black pepper

skins. Scoop the slices out of their skins and transfer them to a large bowl. Crush about 1 teaspoon flaky sea salt between your fingertips over the avocados.

Place one pear on a cutting board and cut 4 slabs off the core so you are left with a straight-sided core; discard the core and repeat with the remaining pear. Slice the pears ½ inch thick lengthwise and add them to the bowl with the avocados, then add the pickled cocktail onions. Drizzle with 1 cup of the vinaigrette and toss gently to coat the ingredients with the dressing, taking care to coat the avocado and pear slices without smashing them.

Trim and discard the stems from the watercress, leaving about 2 inches of the stems intact.

To serve, building the salad in layers, lay half of the watercress to cover the surface of a large platter. Arrange half of the avocado and pear wedges over the watercress, fish a small handful of the cocktail onions from the bottom of the bowl the salad was tossed in, and scatter the onions over the avocados and pears. Reserve a handful of the watercress and lay the remaining watercress on top of the avocados and pears, making that layer slightly smaller than the one before. Arrange the remaining avocados and pears on top of the watercress and scatter the remaining pickled onions left in the bowl over them. Drop the crumbled gorgonzola on top in penny-size clumps, pile the reserved watercress in the center, and drizzle the remaining vinaigrette over the entire salad.

¼ cup extra-virgin olive oil

½ cup crumbled gorgonzola cheese (about 4 ounces)

For the Salad

2 ripe but firm avocados (preferably Pinkerton, Fuerte, or Hass)

Flaky sea salt

2 ripe but firm pears (such as Warren, Comice, D'Anjou, or Bartlett)

10 pickled cocktail (pearl) onions, halved through the stems

12 cups watercress (about 3 bunches)

½ cup crumbled gorgonzola cheese (about 4 ounces)

Chrysanthemum Greens with Kumquats and Duck Rillettes Toasts

Serves 4

We have a customer who swings by the restaurant during kumquat season, carrying bags of fruit from her trees. The kumquats usually find their way into my dessert world, but I was determined to find a place for them in a salad. While dining at Izakaya Rintaro, a wonderful Japanese restaurant in San Francisco owned by Sylvan Brackett, who worked with Alice Waters for many years, I was served a delicious duck salad with chrysanthemum leaves and kumquats. That was the inspiration I had been looking for. I took the components of Sylvan's salad and turned them into this refreshing salad of chrysanthemum greens and kumquat served with duck rillettes toasts. You can find chrysanthemum greens at farmers' markets and Asian markets.

Rillettes is a term for potted meat. Unlike pâté, it is spreadable, not molded. You can make rillettes with different meats, but because duck is so fatty and flavorful, duck rillettes is by far my favorite. This recipe makes more than you will need for the four toasts in this recipe. Serve the rest in a pretty bowl on the side or save it for another day; serve it on its own or with Pane Tostato (page 55) as part of a *tagliere* (antipasto platter). At the restaurant (and for the photograph), I decorate the toasts with fried thyme sprigs, but I didn't want to ask you to fry thyme just for this, so you have my permission to sprinkle fresh thyme leaves on the toasts instead.

You will need an extra-large platter to serve this salad.

To make the rillettes, place the duck legs in a baking dish large enough to hold them in a single layer.

Combine the salt, pepper, bay leaves, and juniper berries in a medium bowl. Use a fine Microplane to zest the bright orange outer layer of one orange half into the bowl and stir to combine. Sprinkle the spices over the duck and use your hands to massage them into the meat, so the entire surface of each leg is covered. Cover the dish with plastic wrap and refrigerate the duck for 24 to 48 hours to cure.

Adjust the oven rack to the center position and preheat the oven to 250°F.

Remove the duck from the refrigerator and uncover it. Rinse the duck legs under cool water to remove the seasonings and pat them dry. →

For the Rillettes

4 duck legs (with thighs attached; about 2½ pounds)

1 tablespoon kosher salt

½ teaspoon fresh coarsely ground black pepper

4 bay leaves (preferably fresh)

2 juniper berries, crushed (with the flat side of a knife, a mortar and pestle, or the bottom of a pan)

1 orange, halved

4 cups duck fat

Melt the duck fat in a Dutch oven just large enough to hold the duck legs in a single layer over medium heat. Turn off the heat. Lay the duck legs in the fat and scatter the garlic cloves over them. Put the lid on the Dutch oven and place the duck legs in the oven to cook for 6 to 8 hours, until fork-tender. To test for doneness, remove the lid from the Dutch oven, insert a fork into a duck leg, and turn the fork slightly; if the meat pulls apart with very little effort, it's done. Remove the duck from the oven, and let the duck legs cool in the fat for 1 hour.

Remove the duck legs from the fat, reserving the fat, and shred the meat off the bone into a large bowl, discarding the bones and cartilage that you encounter as you shred. (It is preferable to have some larger pieces rather than to shred the meat too fine, so you will have texture in your rillettes.) Add 3 tablespoons of the fat you cooked the duck in, stir to combine, and add more if needed so the rillettes are moist. Reserve the remaining duck fat for another use, such as to make Crispy Black Rice (page 208) or to use as a cooking oil in place of olive oil. Zest the bright orange outer layer from the remaining orange half into the bowl. Add the parsley and stir to combine.

To make the toasts, adjust the oven rack to the center position and preheat the oven to 350°F.

Lay the bread on a baking sheet, brush the tops with olive oil, and toast it in the oven for 20 to 25 minutes, until it is golden brown but not crunchy, rotating the baking sheet from front to back halfway through that time for even browning. Remove the toasts from the oven and rub the top of each one with the garlic clove. Drizzle about 1 teaspoon of finishing-quality olive oil over each toast.

While the bread is toasting, to make the vinaigrette, combine the shallot, lemon juice, vinegar, salt, and a few turns of pepper in a small bowl. Gradually add the extra-virgin olive oil, whisking constantly.

10 large garlic cloves, peeled

2 tablespoons finely chopped fresh parsley leaves

For the Toasts

2 (2-inch-thick) slices from the center of a 1-pound loaf of rustic bread

Olive oil

1 large garlic clove, peeled

Finishing-quality extra-virgin olive oil

1 teaspoon fresh thyme leaves

For the Vinaigrette

2 tablespoons peeled and minced shallot

2 tablespoons fresh lemon juice

2 teaspoons champagne vinegar

½ teaspoon kosher salt

Fresh coarsely ground black pepper

¼ cup extra-virgin olive oil

To make the salad, pick the chrysanthemum leaves off the stems; discard the stems and put the leaves in a large wide-mouth bowl. Slice the kumquats into ⅛-inch-thick pinwheels. Pick out and discard the seeds. Add the kumquat slices to the bowl with the greens. Squeeze the lemon half over the salad, sprinkle with the salt, and toss to coat the greens and kumquats with the lemon and salt. Drizzle the salad with the vinaigrette and gently massage with your hands to coat the greens and kumquats with the dressing.

To serve, spoon ½ cup rillettes on each piece of toast, using the back of the spoon to spread it in uneven mounds, leaving the edges of the toast visible. Sprinkle the thyme leaves evenly over the toasts and lay the toasts side by side on one side of an extra-large platter. Pile the salad on the other half of the platter, making sure the kumquat slices are distributed throughout.

For the Salad

12 cups chrysanthemum greens (about ½ pound)

12 kumquats

½ lemon

½ teaspoon kosher salt

Insalata Primavera: Shaved Spring Vegetable Salad with Roasted Artichokes and Dill

Serves 4

This salad is a celebration of two of my favorite springtime vegetables: artichokes and aspara-gus. There are four types of asparagus on the commercial market: colossal, jumbo, large, and pencil. You need either colossal or jumbo for this; the others would be impossible to shave on a mandoline. If you don't want to slice the asparagus on a mandoline, cut the tips off the spears at an extreme bias and slice the remaining spears as thinly as possible on an extreme bias. You can find baby artichokes in season at farmers' markets, specialty markets, and some supermarkets.

You will need an extra-large platter to serve this salad.

To roast the artichokes, adjust the oven rack to the center position and preheat the oven to 400°F.

Working one at a time, trim and discard ½ inch of the dry stem ends of each artichoke. Remove and discard the outer leaves from the artichokes until you reach the bright greenish-yellow leaves. Use a vegetable peeler to peel the stem until it is the same light color as the body of the artichoke you just exposed; discard the peelings. Cut the tips off of the artichokes at the point where they start to slope up, giving the artichokes a flat top. Place the artichokes on a small baking sheet or in an ovenproof skillet. Drizzle with the olive oil, sprinkle with the kosher salt, and massage the artichokes with your hands to coat them with the oil and salt.

Roast the artichokes in the oven until they are golden brown and the hearts (where the stem meets the flower) are tender when pierced with a skewer or sharp knife, about 25 minutes. Remove the artichokes from the oven and set them aside to cool slightly.

To make the salad, while the artichokes are roasting, adjust the blade of a mandoline to slice ⅛ inch thick. Snap off the ends of the asparagus at their natural breaking point and discard them. Lay the asparagus lengthwise on the mandoline and begin to slice the spear into long rib-bons, stopping just before your fingers get dangerously close to the blade; you will probably be able to slice only half of each spear. Set the unsliced

For the Artichokes

12 baby artichokes

¼ cup olive oil

1 teaspoon kosher salt

For the Salad

4 colossal or jumbo asparagus spears

1 lemon, halved

¼ cup plus 1 tablespoon finishing-quality extra-virgin olive oil

Flaky sea salt

1 small fennel bulb (about 6 ounces; or ½ large fennel bulb)

¼ cup fresh dill (tufts pulled from the stems)

portion of the spears aside. When you have sliced all of the spears as far as you can on the mandoline, lay the ribbons to cover the surface of an extra-large platter. Squeeze half of the juice of one lemon half, drizzle 2 tablespoons of the finishing-quality olive oil, and crush about ½ teaspoon flaky sea salt over the asparagus.

Place what is left of the asparagus spears on a cutting board and, one at a time, slice them as thinly as possible on an extreme bias. Place the asparagus slices in a bowl. Squeeze the remaining juice of the lemon half and drizzle 1 tablespoon of the finishing-quality olive oil over the asparagus. Crush a pinch of flaky sea salt between your fingertips over the asparagus and toss to coat the asparagus with the seasonings.

(If you prefer to cut the asparagus, snap off the ends at their natural breaking point and discard them. One at a time, cut the tip end of the asparagus on an extreme bias and cut the remainder of the spear as thinly as possible on an extreme bias. Place the tips and slices in a medium bowl. Squeeze the juice of one lemon half, drizzle 3 tablespoons of the finishing-quality olive oil, and crush a generous ½ teaspoon flaky sea salt between your fingertips over the asparagus. Toss to coat.)

Trim the tops off the fennel at the point where the bulb starts to sprout into separate stalks. (Trimming the fennel this way shows off its pretty shape when sliced.) Trim the very bottom of the root end, making sure to leave enough of the core so that the bulb stays intact. Remove any brown or unappealing outer layers; use the outer layers and stalks to make stock another time or discard them. Lay the fennel on its side on the mandoline. Slice 2 slices and check their thickness; you want the slices just thick enough that they don't fall apart. If they are thick, like slabs, adjust the mandoline to slice thinner. If they are so thin that they tear or don't hold their shape, adjust the blade to slice thicker. Continue slicing the fennel, stopping just before your fingers get dangerously close to the blade; snack on the end pieces or reserve them for stock.

To serve, lay the fennel slices over the asparagus ribbons, leaving the asparagus layer visible around the edges. Drizzle with 2 tablespoons of the finishing-quality olive oil and crush about ½ teaspoon flaky sea salt over the fennel. Scatter the hand-sliced asparagus over the top of the salad, leaving the edges of the fennel layer visible. Nestle the artichokes on top of the salad and crush a pinch of flaky sea salt over them. Scatter the dill over the top of the salad.

Insalata Inverno: Shaved Winter Vegetable Salad with Parmesan and Olio Nuovo

Serves 4

We already had the Insalata Primavera (Spring Salad) (page 96) on the menu when one of our cooks, Cameron Thollaug, came up with this winter salad as a counterpoint to that. The salad is very simple: shaved winter vegetables dressed with *olio nuovo*. Olio nuovo, or "new oil," refers to olive oil that has just been pressed and that arrives in late November or early December, the same time of year these vegetables come into season. It has a very special, green, peppery quality to it that takes this salad over the top. If you can't find it or it is not in season, use another finishing-quality olive oil. We shave the portobello over the top of the salad in the same style that truffles are shaved over a dish. This salad tastes just as good an hour after it is made since none of the ingredients wilts quickly, so it's perfect for when you're entertaining and have many dishes to prepare.

You will need an extra-large platter to serve this salad.

Trim the tops off the fennel at the point where the bulb starts to sprout into separate stalks. (Trimming the fennel this way shows off its pretty shape when sliced.) Trim the very bottom of the root end, making sure to leave enough of the core so that the bulb stays intact. Remove any brown or unappealing outer layers; use the outer layers and stalks to make stock another time or discard them.

Adjust the blade of a mandoline to slice ⅛ inch thick. Cut the fennel in half lengthwise. Lay the fennel halves, cut side down, on the mandoline. Slice 2 slices and check their thickness; you want the slices just thick enough that they don't fall apart. If they are thick, like slabs, adjust the mandoline to slice thinner. If they are so thin that they tear or don't hold their shape, adjust the blade to slice thicker. Continue slicing the fennel, stopping just before your fingers get dangerously close to the blade; snack on the end pieces or reserve them for stock. Lay the fennel slices to cover the surface of an extra-large platter and drizzle with ¼ cup of the olio nuovo. Squeeze the juice of one lemon half and crush about ½ teaspoon flaky sea salt between your fingertips over the fennel. →

1 large fennel bulb
(about 12 ounces)

¾ cup olio nuovo
(or finishing-quality extra-virgin olive oil)

1 lemon, halved

Flaky sea salt

3 large portobello mushrooms

2 bunches celery

Fresh coarsely ground black pepper

A chunk of Parmesan for shaving

Clean the outsides of the mushrooms with a damp towel and trim and discard the very ends of the stems; don't trim too much as you want to maintain the shape of the stemmed mushrooms. Place the mushrooms on their sides on the mandoline and slice them ⅛ inch thick, checking the thickness of the slices and adjusting the mandoline as needed. Scatter the mushroom slices over the fennel slices, leaving the edges of the fennel layer visible. Drizzle with ¼ cup of the olio nuovo and juice the remaining lemon half over the mushrooms. Crush about ½ teaspoon flaky sea salt over the mushrooms.

Remove the outer layers from the bunches of celery until only the small, pale green tender stalks with their leaves remain. Break the hearts of celery from the core and discard the core. Reserve the stalks for another use, such as to make Chicken Stock (page 159). Scatter the celery hearts and leaves over the mushrooms, leaving the edges of the mushroom layer visible. Drizzle the remaining ¼ cup olio nuovo and grind a few turns of pepper over the salad. Crush about ½ teaspoon flaky sea salt over all. Slice 12 shavings of Parmesan ⅛ inch thick on the mandoline and scatter the shavings over the salad, leaving the celery layer visible between the shavings of cheese. Serve.

Spacca Caesar with Fried Parsley, Anchovies, Orange Zest, and Bagna Cauda Croutons

Serves 4

The classic Caesar salad, which comes from the Hotel Caesars in Tijuana, consists of whole romaine lettuce leaves coated in a creamy, garlicky, usually anchovy-intense dressing, Parmesan cheese, and croutons. I've heard it's the most popular salad in the world and that's easy to believe; it's probably harder to find a cookbook that *doesn't* have a Caesar salad recipe in it than one that does. So although the world clearly doesn't need another Caesar salad recipe, at Chi Spacca, we came up with a version that is different enough from the others that it justifies sharing. We substitute escarole for romaine and add shaved cauliflower and fried parsley to the mix, which gives the salad more layers of flavor and texture. Then we layer it with Cetara, the special oil-packed variety of anchovies from the Amalfi coast, orange zest, and bagna cauda croutons. Although it's quite a departure from a traditional Caesar, it still captures the essence of that salad.

When shopping for escarole, look for "blanched escarole" at farmers' markets and specialty food stores. Blanched escarole is light green, almost white, in color, and sweeter and crunchier than traditional escarole. It is grown the same way white endive and white asparagus are grown, by shielding the young plants from direct sunlight so they don't go through photosynthesis, which is what gives all plants their green color. If you can't find blanched escarole, buy conventional escarole and remove the dark, floppy outer leaves as described in the recipe. I would normally use salt-packed anchovies to make Caesar dressing because they have more flavor than oil-packed. But in this recipe, I use Cetara anchovies in the dressing so you don't have to buy two types of anchovies. If you feel inclined to buy both, use salt-packed for the dressing and oil-packed in the salad.

This recipe calls for you to make the Caesar salad dressing in a mini food processor. To make it by hand, see Making Aioli by Hand (page 104).

You will need a large platter or large wide-mouth bowl to serve this salad. →

To make the bagna cauda croutons, adjust the oven rack to the center position and preheat the oven to 325°F.

Combine the butter and extra-virgin olive oil in a small saucepan. Finely chop the anchovies with a large knife and use the flat side of the knife to smash them into a paste; add the paste to the saucepan. Using a fine Microplane, grate the garlic into the saucepan. Heat over low heat for 5 minutes, stirring occasionally, to meld the flavors. Turn off the heat.

Pull the inside of the bread out of the crust into 1- to 1½-inch chunks and put the chunks on a large baking sheet. (Snack on the crusts or discard them.) Drizzle the bagna cauda over the bread and toss to coat. Spread the bread chunks out on the baking sheet and bake for 10 to 12 minutes, until golden brown and crispy, stirring them and rotating the baking sheet from front to back halfway through that time for even browning. Remove the croutons from the oven and set aside to cool to room temperature.

To fry the parsley, pour enough canola oil into a small saucepan to fill it 1½ to 2 inches deep. Fasten a deep-fry thermometer, if you have one, to the side of the pan. Heat the oil over medium-high heat until the thermometer reads 350°F or a pinch of salt sizzles when dropped into it. While the oil is heating, create a bed of paper towels. Turn off the heat and carefully add half of the parsley leaves to the pot, stepping back when you add them because the moisture in the parsley will cause the oil to splatter. Cook the parsley leaves for 5 seconds. Use a mesh strainer or slotted spoon to lift the leaves out of the oil and spread them out on the paper towels to drain. Season the fried parsley leaves with ¼ teaspoon of the salt. Add the remaining parsley leaves to the oil and fry, drain, and salt them in the same way. Let the oil cool and strain it into a container; cover and reserve the oil to cook with another time.

To make the dressing, combine the lime juice, vinegar, Tabasco, and Worcestershire sauce in a small measuring cup or bowl. Combine the extra-virgin olive oil and canola oil in a measuring cup with a spout.

Combine the egg yolk and salt in the bowl of a mini food processor fitted with a metal blade. Finely chop the anchovies with a large knife and use the flat side of the knife to smash them into a paste. Put the paste in the bowl of the mini food processor. Using a fine Microplane, grate the garlic into the food processor bowl and pulse to combine the ingredients. With the machine running, begin adding the oil through the lid of the food

For the Bagna Cauda Croutons

4 tablespoons (½ stick) unsalted butter

½ cup extra-virgin olive oil

10 Cetara anchovy fillets in oil (or another quality, oil-packed variety; or 5 whole salt-packed anchovies, rinsed and backbones removed)

4 large garlic cloves, peeled

Half of a 1-pound loaf of rustic bread

For the Parsley

Canola oil (or olive oil) for deep-frying

1 cup fresh Italian parsley leaves

½ teaspoon kosher salt

For the Dressing

2 tablespoons fresh lime juice, plus more to taste

1 teaspoon red wine vinegar

½ teaspoon Tabasco sauce

½ teaspoon Worcestershire sauce

½ cup extra-virgin olive oil

½ cup canola oil (or another neutral-flavored oil)

1 extra-large egg yolk, at room temperature

2 teaspoons kosher salt, plus more to taste

10 anchovy fillets (preferably salt-packed; rinsed and backbones removed if salt-packed)

4 large garlic cloves, peeled

1 teaspoon fresh coarsely ground black pepper

1½ cups finely grated Parmesan

processor, blending continuously, until the oil and egg are emulsified and creamy looking; you will have added about ¼ cup of the oil. Turn off the machine, take off the lid, scrape down the sides of the bowl with a rubber spatula, and add one-third of the lime juice–vinegar mixture. Return the lid and pulse to combine. Add the remaining oil in a slow, steady drizzle, adding the remaining lime juice–vinegar mixture when the dressing gets very thick. Turn off the machine and transfer the dressing to a medium bowl, scraping down the sides of the food processor bowl. Add the pepper and Parmesan and stir to combine. Add more lime juice or salt to taste.

To prepare the salad, cut off and discard the root end of the escarole. Remove the dark green outer leaves until only the tender, light yellow leaves remain. (Reserve the outer leaves to make Braised Greens, page 297.) Tear the remaining leaves from the core and put them in a large wide-mouth bowl.

Trim the cauliflower and cut it into quarters, keeping the core intact. Adjust the blade of a mandoline to slice ⅛ inch thick. Slice 2 slices of cauliflower and check that the slices are just thick enough that they don't fall apart. If they are thick, like slabs, adjust the mandoline to slice thinner. If they are so thin that they crumble into pieces, adjust the blade to slice thicker. Continue slicing the cauliflower, stopping just before your fingers get dangerously close to the blade; snack on the end piece.

Squeeze the juice of the lemon half and sprinkle the salt over the escarole, and toss to coat the escarole with the lemon juice and salt. Drizzle 1 cup of the dressing over the escarole and massage with your hands to coat the escarole with the dressing. Add the cauliflower and the residual cauliflower crumbles and toss again, gently tossing to coat the vegetables and adding more dressing if needed to coat them thoroughly; take care not to break up the cauliflower.

To serve, building the salad in two layers and choosing the largest leaves of escarole first, arrange half of the escarole leaves and cauliflower slices to cover the surface of a large platter or wide-mouth bowl. Scatter half of the croutons over the lettuce and drape half of the anchovies in the nooks and crannies of the salad. Build a second layer using the remaining escarole, cauliflower, croutons, and anchovies. Use a fine Microplane to zest the bright orange outer layer of the orange and grate a thin blanket of Parmesan over the salad. Scatter the fried parsley and grind a generous amount of pepper over the top.

For the Salad

1 head escarole (preferably "blanched" escarole)

¼ large head cauliflower (about ½ pound)

½ lemon

½ teaspoon kosher salt

6 Cetara anchovy fillets in oil (or another quality oil-packed variety; or 3 whole salt-packed anchovies; rinsed and backbones removed)

1 orange

A chunk of Parmesan for grating

Fresh coarsely ground black pepper

Making Aioli by Hand

When I make aioli, which is the French word for garlic mayonnaise, at home, I always do it by hand. (I use the word "aioli," but the following applies to any type of mayonnaise and also Caesar salad dressing, which is essentially a doctored up mayonnaise.) That said, I've found, from doing cooking demonstrations, that many home cooks are overwhelmed by the idea of making aioli by hand, so in these recipes, I provide the less intimidating, foolproof, mini–food processor method. Whether you're making aioli (or any of its cousins) by hand or with a machine, the challenge is to form an emulsion, which is what happens when you combine two ingredients that normally don't mix—oil and water (or other thin liquids), for instance. If you were to look at an emulsion under a microscope, rather than the oil and other liquids being separate, the molecules are all mixed together. The way to form an emulsion is to add an ingredient that mixes with both oil and water—in the case of aioli, an egg yolk. You then add the oil to the egg yolk very slowly until the mixture is white and creamy—emulsified. When making aioli by hand, you add the oil *excruciatingly slowly,* drop by drop, whisking constantly while you add it. Once you've formed an emulsion, you can begin adding the oil a bit more quickly, in a slow, steady stream. As you add the oil, the aioli will become very thick; at this point, you have to thin it out or it will break (separate) as a result if its own weight. When making aioli, the liquids used to thin it are often the ingredients you're seasoning the aioli with, such as lemon juice or vinegar, but water also does the trick. (If you make aioli or Caesar salad dressing by hand, you will need to add water in addition to the thin liquids called for in the recipes.) Follow these step-by-step instructions and you will have success every time.

- First thing have all your ingredients at room temperature, which means putting your egg out on the counter to warm up a bit before you start.

- Next, pick a small bowl to make the aioli in. I prefer a deep bowl (the shape of the bowl of a stand mixer, but much smaller), so the ingredients don't spread out too much. If you have a bowl with a rubber bottom, even better, as you will need to keep the bowl steady when you start whisking. If you don't have a rubber-bottomed bowl, you need to do something to keep the bowl steady; you're going to be whisking vigorously with one hand while drizzling with the other, and the bowl is going to tend to flop all over the place. To keep the bowl steady, wet a clean kitchen towel, wring out the excess water, and then twist it into a rope. Wrap the towel around the base of the bowl you're making your aioli in to keep it in place. Another method for steadying the bowl is to set the bowl over a saucepan filled with water to weigh it down.

- If you are working with more than one kind of oil, mix the oils together into one vessel. I use a measuring cup with a spout, which makes it easy to drizzle the oil.

- Mix all of your thin ingredients, such as vinegar, lemon juice, or lime juice together. In the case of Caesar salad dressing, this also includes Worcestershire sauce and Tabasco sauce.

- Crack the egg yolk into the mixing bowl and discard the white. Add the salt and mustard and garlic to the bowl with the yolk. Garlic and mustard, like egg yolk, are natural emulsifiers and starting with this mixture will make it easier to form an emulsion.

- Begin adding the oil, drop by drop, vigorously whisking as you add it. You really cannot do this too slowly. After you've added about one-third of the oil, you will see that an emulsion has formed because the mixture will look white, satiny, and homogenous (like one substance), not separate or "broken." At this point, you can begin to drizzle the oil in a slow, steady stream.

- When you begin adding the oil a bit faster, it will become so thick that it is almost impossible to whisk. At this point, drizzle in some of the thin liquids, whisk them in, and then resume adding the oil. Continue adding the oil and the thin liquids (or additional water) whenever the emulsion gets too thick.

- Taste the aioli and add more salt or lemon juice as desired.

Misticanza: Shaved Vegetable Salad
with Radicchio and Sherry Dijon Vinaigrette

Serves 4

Misticanza means "mixture" or "mixed salad," in Italian, and that's what this is: a light tossed salad of shaved crunchy vegetables dressed in a tangy vinaigrette. Just what you want to accompany a rich, meaty dinner.

You will need a large platter or large wide-mouth bowl to serve this salad.

To make the vinaigrette, combine the shallot, vinegar, mustard, kosher salt, and a few turns of pepper in a small bowl. Gradually add the extra-virgin olive oil, whisking constantly.

To make the salad, adjust the blade of a mandoline to slice ⅛ inch thick. Holding a beet by the stem, slice 2 slices on the mandoline and check their thickness; you want the slices just thick enough that they don't fall apart. If they are thick, like slabs, adjust the mandoline to slice thinner. If they are so thin that they tear or don't maintain their shape, adjust the blade to slice thicker. Continue slicing the beets, stopping just before your fingers get dangerously close to the blade and discarding the end you are holding. Put the beet slices into a large bowl.

Slice the radishes and turnips in the same way, checking the thickness of the slices and adjusting the mandoline as needed, and adding them to the bowl with the beets. Drizzle the vegetables with 2 tablespoons of the vinaigrette and toss, massaging with your hands to coat the vegetables with the vinaigrette.

Trim and discard the root ends of the radicchio and cut the heads in half through the cores. Remove and discard the outer leaves. Pull the remaining leaves from the core and drop them into the bowl with the shaved vegetables; discard the cores. Squeeze the juice from the half lemon and crush about ½ teaspoon flaky sea salt between your fingertips over the salad; toss gently to coat the radicchio. Drizzle the remaining vinaigrette over the salad and toss, massaging the vinaigrette into the leaves with your hands.

For the Vinaigrette

1 medium shallot, peeled and finely chopped

2 tablespoons sherry vinegar

1 teaspoon Dijon mustard

¼ teaspoon kosher salt

Fresh coarsely ground black pepper

¼ cup extra-virgin olive oil

For the Salad

2 small beets (any color), scrubbed

3 large radishes (such as Easter egg, watermelon, or large breakfast radishes), scrubbed

2 small turnips (preferably Tokyo turnips, not baby turnips), scrubbed

12 to 14 ounces radicchio (about 2 medium heads)

½ lemon

Flaky sea salt

3 tablespoons fresh dill (tufts pulled from the stems)

To serve, building the salad in three layers and choosing the largest leaves of radicchio first, arrange one-third of the radicchio leaves on a large platter or wide-mouth bowl with the "cups" of the lettuce facing up, in concentric circles like the petals of a flower. Grab a small handful of the shaved vegetables from the bowl, and put them in the cups formed by the radicchio, and scatter one-third of the dill over the salad. Continue, building two more layers the same as the first, using the medium leaves for the second layer and reserving the smallest leaves for the top layer, and making each layer smaller than the one before it. Crush a big pinch of flaky sea salt between your fingers and scatter it and the remaining dill over the salad.

Heirloom Tomato Panzanella
with Olive Bread Croutons and Feta Yogurt

Serves 4

This salad (see photo, page ii) is a marriage between Italian panzanella, which is traditionally made with tomatoes, cucumbers, and stale bread, and the Greek salad with feta and olives that I started making at Campanile back in the 1980s. Where panzanella is traditionally made with untoasted chunks of bread that get wet and soggy when they absorb the liquid in the tomatoes, I toast the bread to make croutons, which stay crunchy even when dressed. And rather than mix the feta into the salad and muddy the beautiful tomatoes, I mix it in with yogurt and put that underneath the tomatoes; I also lay thin slices of feta on top of the finished salad. It's a new way of presenting familiar flavors. It is a summer salad; I can't stress enough how important it is to start with delicious, in-season heirloom tomatoes, preferably from a farmers' market. Choose different varieties of tomatoes—that mix of colors, shapes, sizes, and flavors of the different tomatoes makes this salad beautiful; each variety also has a subtly unique flavor. Buy a 6-ounce or larger chunk of water-packed feta; Bulgarian has great flavor without being too salty.

You will need an extra-large platter to serve this salad.

To make the croutons, adjust the oven rack to the center position and preheat the oven to 350°F.

Pull the inside of the bread out of the crust into 1- to 1½-inch chunks and put the chunks on a large baking sheet. (Reserve the crusts to snack on or discard them.) Add the olives, drizzle with the extra-virgin olive oil, sprinkle with the salt, and toss to distribute the olives and salt and coat the bread and olives with the oil. Spread the bread chunks and olives out on the baking sheet and bake for 10 to 12 minutes, until the bread chunks are golden brown and crispy, stirring them and rotating the baking sheet from front to back halfway through that time for even browning. Remove the croutons from the oven and set aside to cool to room temperature.

For the Olive Bread Croutons

Half of a 1-pound loaf of olive bread (or rustic bread)

1 cup pitted olives, such as Picholine, Taggiasche, Niçoise, or Kalamata

½ cup extra-virgin olive oil

1 teaspoon kosher salt

To make the feta yogurt, cut the cucumber in half lengthwise and then slice it into ⅛-inch half-moons. Place the pieces in a large bowl, sprinkle with ¼ teaspoon of the salt, and toss to coat them with the salt. Add the yogurt, lemon juice, and the remaining ½ teaspoon salt and stir to combine; do not stir more than necessary because the yogurt will become thin and runny. Crumble ½ cup from the chunk of feta into the bowl in ½-inch chunks and gently stir to combine. Set the remaining chunk aside to thinly slice as a garnish.

To prepare the salad, cut the heirloom tomatoes in half through the stems. Cut each half in half again, or into thirds or quarters depending on their size, and put them in a large bowl. Remove and discard the stems from the cherry tomatoes, cut them in half through the stems, and add them to the bowl with the heirloom tomatoes. Drizzle the finishing-quality olive oil and vinegar and sprinkle the salt over the tomatoes. Stir vigorously with a large spoon to emulsify the natural dressing made by the oil and the juice from the tomatoes.

Peel the onion and cut it in half again, root to tip. Separate the layers of the onion, stack two or three layers on top of one another, and slice them lengthwise 1/16 inch thick. Add them to the bowl with the tomatoes and toss to combine.

To serve, spoon the feta yogurt onto an extra-large platter and use the back of the spoon to spread it toward the edges in organic, uneven swirls. Add the croutons to the bowl with the tomatoes and toss to coat them with the juices from the tomatoes. Pile the tomatoes and croutons on top of the yogurt. Using a large sharp knife, cut 6 to 8 very thin slices from the block of feta. Lay the sheets of feta on top of the tomatoes and sprinkle the oregano over the salad.

For the Yogurt

1 Persian cucumber
(about 6 inches)

¾ teaspoon kosher salt,
plus more to taste

1 cup Straus Family Creamery
Organic Greek Yogurt
(or another plain, whole-milk,
not overly thick yogurt)

2 tablespoons fresh lemon juice,
plus more to taste

2 ounces from a chunk of
water-packed feta
(preferably Bulgarian feta)

For the Salad

2 pounds mixed heirloom
tomatoes

1 pint small cherry tomatoes
(preferably Sun Gold)

¾ cup finishing-quality
extra-virgin olive oil

2 tablespoons red wine vinegar

1 teaspoon kosher salt

½ red onion (halved root to tip)

A chunk of water-packed feta
(preferably Bulgarian feta)

2 teaspoons dried oregano
(preferably Sicilian oregano
on the branch)

Butter Lettuce and Herb Salad
with Lemon Dijon Vinaigrette

Serves 4

A combination of tender butter lettuce, soft herbs, and zingy vinaigrette, this simple, refreshing salad seems to make its way into every book I write, and a version of it is also on the menu of every restaurant I own. It complements any dish and satisfies the request "Do you have a simple green salad?" This recipe calls for the combination of herbs that I like best, but I also understand that for the home cook, using a selection of six herbs can be challenging, so feel free to use more of one and less of another to make up the difference. I like the butter lettuces I see at farmers' markets, but you can also find nice butter lettuce with the roots still attached sold in plastic clamshells in just about any grocery store; one of the nice things about this lettuce is that because it's not grown in dirt, you don't need to wash it.

You will need a large platter or large wide-mouth bowl to serve the salad.

To make the vinaigrette, combine the lemon juice, vinegar, shallots, mustard, kosher salt, and a few turns of pepper in a small bowl. Add the extra-virgin olive oil, whisking constantly.

To make the salad, put half of the chervil, dill, celery leaves, tarragon, and parsley in a medium bowl. Put the remaining half of the herbs on a cutting board and finely chop them. Add the chopped herbs to the bowl with the whole herbs. Cut the chives into 1-inch bâtons and add them to the bowl. Toss to combine.

Remove and discard the roots from the heads of lettuce if they are still attached. Remove and discard the outermost bruised leaves of the lettuce. Tear the remaining leaves from the cores and put them in a large wide-mouth bowl. Discard the cores. Sprinkle half the herbs over the lettuce. Squeeze the juice of the lemon half and sprinkle the kosher salt over the lettuce, and toss to coat the lettuce with the lemon juice and salt. Drizzle the vinaigrette over the salad and toss, gently massaging the leaves with your hands to coat them with the vinaigrette.

For the Vinaigrette

¼ cup plus 2 tablespoons fresh lemon juice

3 tablespoons champagne vinegar

3 tablespoons peeled and minced shallots

1 tablespoon Dijon mustard

1½ teaspoons kosher salt

Fresh coarsely ground black pepper

¼ cup plus 2 tablespoons extra-virgin olive oil

For the Salad

½ cup loosely packed fresh chervil leaves

½ cup loosely packed fresh dill (tufts pulled from the stems)

To serve, building the salad in three layers and choosing the largest lettuce leaves first, arrange about one-third of the lettuce leaves with the "cups" of the lettuce facing upward, in concentric circles—like the petals of a flower—on a large platter or in a wide-mouth bowl; make sure some of the dressed herbs come along with the lettuce leaves. Sprinkle one-third of the reserved, undressed herbs into the cups formed by the lettuce. Continue, building two more layers the same as the first, using the medium leaves for the second layer and the smallest leaves for the top layer, and making each layer smaller than the one before it. Crush about 1 teaspoon flaky sea salt between your fingertips and grind a few turns of pepper over the salad.

½ cup loosely packed fresh hearts of celery leaves (look for the palest leaves, which are located closer to the core)

¼ cup loosely packed fresh tarragon leaves

2 tablespoons finely chopped fresh Italian parsley leaves

½ cup loosely packed fresh chives

2 heads butter lettuce

½ lemon

¾ teaspoon kosher salt

Flaky sea salt

Fresh coarsely ground black pepper

Indian-Spiced Chicken Salad with Mixed Lettuces, Walnuts, and Preserved Lemon Vinaigrette

Serves 4

When I am in San Francisco, I always try to make time to eat at Boulettes Larder, a one-of-a-kind food shop/restaurant in the Ferry Plaza Farmers Market. I have never eaten there and not been inspired. When I ordered their Indian chicken salad, I loved it so much I basically tried to replicate it as closely as possible, right down to the mix of escarole and Little Gem lettuces that are the base of the salad.

When shopping for escarole, look for "blanched escarole" at farmers' markets and specialty food stores. Blanched escarole is light green, almost white, in color, and sweeter and crunchier than traditional escarole. It is grown the same way white endive and white asparagus are grown, by shielding the young plants from direct sunlight, so they don't go through photosynthesis, which is what gives all plants their green color. If you can't find blanched escarole, buy conventional escarole and remove the dark, floppy outer leaves as described in the recipe.

You will need a large platter or large wide-mouth bowl to serve this salad.

To prepare the chicken salad, adjust the oven rack to the center position and preheat the oven to 325°F.

Spread the walnuts on a baking sheet and toast them in the oven for 10 to 12 minutes, until they're toasted and fragrant, shaking the baking sheet and rotating it from front to back halfway through that time so the nuts brown evenly. Remove the walnuts from the oven and set aside until they are cool enough to touch. Finely chop the walnuts.

Increase the oven temperature to 350°F.

While the nuts are toasting, to make the vinaigrette, combine the shallots, lemon juice, vinegar, salt, and a few turns of black pepper in a small bowl. Gradually add the extra-virgin olive oil, whisking constantly.

Season the chicken breast on both sides with the salt. Sprinkle 1 tablespoon of the garam masala on the chicken breast, rubbing it to coat both →

For the Chicken Salad

¼ cup shelled walnuts, halves or pieces

1 boneless, skinless chicken breast (about ¾ pound)

¾ teaspoon kosher salt

2 tablespoons Garam Masala (page 21; or store-bought)

4 Preserved Lemon halves (page 23; or store-bought)

¼ teaspoon red pepper flakes

1 teaspoon finishing-quality extra-virgin olive oil

sides evenly. Lay the chicken on a baking sheet and roast it in the oven for about 25 minutes, rotating the baking sheet from front to back halfway through that time so the chicken browns evenly, until the juices run clear when the chicken is pierced with a sharp knife. Remove the baking sheet from the oven and set aside for the chicken to cool to room temperature. Shred the chicken into the longest shreds possible into a medium bowl.

Rinse the preserved lemons to remove the sugar and salt and drain well. Use a paring knife to remove the pulp, pith, and seeds and discard, so you are left with only the bright yellow peel. Finely chop the peel and add 1 tablespoon to the bowl with the chicken. Add half of the walnuts, the remaining 1 tablespoon of the garam masala, and the red pepper flakes. Drizzle with the finishing-quality olive oil and toss to distribute the ingredients and coat them with the oil. Taste and add more salt if desired.

To prepare the green salad, cut off and discard the root end of the escarole. Remove the dark green outer leaves until only the tender, light yellow leaves remain. (Reserve the outer leaves to make Braised Greens, page 297.) Tear the remaining leaves from the core and put them into a large wide-mouth bowl.

Remove and discard any unappealing outer leaves from the head of the Little Gem lettuce. Tear the remaining leaves from the core and drop the leaves into the bowl with the escarole, discarding the core. Squeeze the lemon half over the lettuces, sprinkle with the salt, and toss to coat the lettuces. Drizzle ¼ cup of the vinaigrette over the salad and toss to coat, gently massaging the leaves with your hands to coat them with the vinaigrette. Add the remaining chopped preserved lemon peel and half of the cilantro and toss gently to distribute them.

To serve, building the salad in three layers and choosing the largest leaves first, arrange one-third of the leaves to cover the surface of a large platter or wide-mouth bowl. Scatter one-third of the chicken-walnut mixture over the lettuces, leaving the edges of the lettuce layer visible. Scatter one-third of the remaining chopped walnuts, one-third of the chopped preserved lemon, and one-third of the cilantro from the bowl the salad was tossed in over the salad. Continue, building two more layers the same as the first one, using the medium leaves for the second layer and the smallest leaves for the top layer, and making each layer smaller than the one before. Sprinkle the reserved undressed cilantro over the salad.

For the Vinaigrette

¼ cup peeled and minced shallots

¼ cup fresh lemon juice

1 tablespoon champagne vinegar

1 teaspoon kosher salt

Fresh coarsely ground black pepper

½ cup extra-virgin olive oil

For the Green Salad

1 head escarole (preferably "blanched" escarole)

1 head Little Gem lettuce

½ lemon

½ teaspoon kosher salt

¼ cup micro cilantro (or finely chopped fresh cilantro leaves)

Roasted Beets with Chicories, Yogurt, and Lemon Zest

Serves 4

Traveling is one of my favorite (and most surefire) ways to get inspiration. A recent trip to Israel inspired many dishes, including this one. Until then, I had always rubbed the skins off of roasted beets. Then, at North Abraxass, my favorite restaurant in Tel Aviv, I was served a plate of roasted beets with the skins intact. The beets had been roasted until they were charred black on the outside, and they were sliced into disks, so you could see the bright-colored flesh outlined by the crinkled papery skin. It was so pretty! It reminded me of that type of sushi called *maki* that has papery nori wrapped around the perimeter. The beets covered the entire plate in a single layer and were topped with a dollop of rich, creamy yogurt. So delicious! Even though you can find beets in the supermarket year-round, it doesn't mean that they're good year-round. My favorite time for medium beets is summer and late fall, and, of course, my favorite place to get them is at farmers' markets.

Castelfranco is a chicory with pretty, very light green leaves mottled with pink spots. The leaves have a ruffle-like quality. The way I serve them here, layered on top of one another, reminds me of the pretty layers of a petticoat.

You will need a large platter to serve this salad.

To prepare the beets, adjust the oven rack to the center position and preheat the oven to 400°F.

Trim the tops off of the beets, leaving the tails intact. (Use the tops for making Braised Greens, page 297.) Scrub the beets and put them on a baking sheet. Drizzle with the olive oil, sprinkle with the kosher salt, and toss to coat the beets with the oil and salt.

Roast the beets in the oven until the skins are charred and wrinkled and the beets are tender when pierced with a sharp knife, about 45 minutes, rotating the baking sheet from front to back so they cook evenly. Remove the beets from the oven and set aside to cool to room temperature.

Meanwhile, to make the vinaigrette, combine the shallot, vinegar, mustard, kosher salt, and a few turns of pepper in a small bowl. Gradually add the extra-virgin olive oil, whisking constantly. →

For the Beets

2 pounds medium beets
(red, yellow, or orange)

¼ cup olive oil

1 tablespoon kosher salt

For the Vinaigrette

1 medium shallot, peeled and
finely chopped

2 tablespoons sherry vinegar

1 teaspoon Dijon mustard

¼ teaspoon kosher salt

Fresh coarsely ground black
pepper

¼ cup extra-virgin olive oil

Cut off the stem ends of the beets; snack on or discard them. Slice the beets ½ inch thick, leaving the thin, crunchy tails attached to the last slice. (If the tails are thick and soggy, cut off and discard them.)

Lay the beet slices to cover the surface of a large platter, putting the slices with the tails around the edges of the platter so they stick out from the platter decoratively. Drizzle about 2 tablespoons finishing-quality olive oil over the beets and gently pat the oil onto the beets with your fingers so the beets glisten. Crush about 1 teaspoon flaky sea salt with your fingertips over the beets.

To prepare the salad, remove and discard any unappealing outer leaves from the head of Castelfranco. Remove the remaining leaves from the cores and drop them into a large wide-mouth bowl, taking care to keep the leaves whole if possible; discard the cores. Squeeze the lemon half over the Castelfranco, sprinkle with the kosher salt, and toss to coat the leaves with the lemon and salt. Drizzle the vinaigrette over the salad and toss with your hands, massaging the dressing to coat each leaf.

To serve, arrange the largest leaves of Castelfranco to begin to build four large "nests" on top of the beets. Continue building the nests, nestling the medium leaves and then the smallest leaves inside the large leaves. Use a soupspoon to dollop the yogurt into the "cups," dividing it evenly. Use a fine Microplane to zest the bright yellow outer layer of half of the lemon over each nest, dividing it evenly, and reserve the lemon to juice another time.

For the Salad

1 head Castelfranco (or another chicory, such as radicchio)

½ lemon

¼ teaspoon kosher salt

For Serving

Finishing-quality extra-virgin olive oil

Flaky sea salt

2 cups Straus Family Creamery Organic Greek Yogurt (or another plain, whole-milk, not overly thick yogurt)

1 lemon

BLTA Salad with Aioli and Herb Bread Crumbs

Serves 4

This salad is made up of all the same components as a BLTA (bacon, lettuce, tomato, and avocado) sandwich, right down to the bread (in this case, in the form of bread crumbs) and the aioli (aka garlic mayonnaise) that it is dressed with. It is a summer salad; make it when tomatoes are sweet and flavorful.

Look for watercress from a farmers' market, which is spicier and more flavorful than upland cress, which you often find in supermarkets; upland cress is also more fragile and wilts too easily.

This recipe calls for you to make the aioli in a mini food processor. To make it by hand, see Making Aioli by Hand (page 104).

You will need a large platter or large wide-mouth bowl to serve this salad.

To make the bread crumbs, adjust the oven rack to the center position and preheat the oven to 350°F.

Pull the inside of the bread out of the crust into 1- to 1½-inch chunks and put the chunks on a large baking sheet. (Reserve the crusts to snack on or discard them.) Drizzle the bread with the olive oil, sprinkle with the kosher salt, and toss to coat the bread chunks with the oil and salt. Spread the bread chunks out on the baking sheet and bake for 10 to 12 minutes, until the bread chunks are golden brown and crispy, stirring them and rotating the baking sheet from front to back halfway through that time for even browning. Remove the croutons from the oven and set them aside to cool. Transfer the croutons to a food processor fitted with a metal blade and pulse until they are fine bread crumbs. Transfer the bread crumbs to a medium bowl. Add the chives, tarragon, and parsley and stir to combine. Return the bread crumbs to the baking sheet and return the sheet to the oven for 2 to 3 minutes, until the herbs are brown. Remove the bread crumbs from the oven and set them aside to cool to room temperature. (You will use ½ cup of the bread crumbs for this salad; store the remaining bread crumbs in a covered container at room temperature for as long as 1 week.)

For the Herb Bread Crumbs

Half of a 1-pound loaf of rustic bread

½ cup olive oil

1 teaspoon kosher salt

2 tablespoons finely chopped fresh chives

2 tablespoons finely chopped fresh tarragon leaves

2 tablespoons finely chopped fresh Italian parsley leaves

For the Aioli

2 teaspoons champagne vinegar

2 teaspoons fresh lemon juice, plus more to taste

¾ cup canola oil (or another neutral-flavored oil)

¼ cup extra-virgin olive oil

To make the aioli, combine the vinegar and lemon juice in a small measuring cup or bowl. Combine the canola oil and extra-virgin olive oil in a measuring cup with a spout.

Put the egg yolk and kosher salt in the bowl of a mini food processor. Using a fine Microplane, grate the garlic into the food processor bowl and pulse to combine the ingredients. With the machine running, begin adding the oils through the lid of the food processor, blending continuously, until the oils and egg are emulsified and creamy looking; you will have added about ¼ cup of the oils. Turn off the machine, take off the lid, scrape down the sides of the bowl with a rubber spatula, and add one-third of the lemon juice–vinegar mixture. Return the lid and pulse to combine. Add the remaining oils in a slow, steady drizzle, adding the remaining lemon juice–vinegar mixture when the aioli gets very thick. Turn off the machine and transfer the aioli to a small bowl, scraping down the sides of the food processor bowl. Add more lemon juice or kosher salt to taste.

To prepare the salad, place the bacon on a baking sheet and cook it in the oven for 16 to 20 minutes, until it is cooked but not crisp, rotating the baking sheet from front to back halfway through that time so the bacon cooks evenly. Meanwhile, create a bed of paper towels. Remove the bacon from the oven and transfer it to the paper towels to drain. Finely chop the bacon.

Cut the avocados in half lengthwise and twist each half in opposite directions to separate them. Plunge the edge of a large knife into the pit and twist the knife to release the pit from each avocado; discard the pits. With the avocados still in their skins, slice each avocado half lengthwise into 4 equal slices, making sure not to cut through the skins. Crush about 1 tablespoon flaky sea salt between your fingertips over the avocado halves.

Cut the heirloom tomatoes in half through the stems and cut them in half again into quarters. Put the quartered tomatoes in a medium bowl. Remove the stems from the cherry tomatoes and cut them in half through the stem ends. Add them to the bowl with the heirlooms. Drizzle the tomatoes with the finishing-quality olive oil, sprinkle with the kosher salt, and squeeze the lemon half into the bowl. Stir vigorously with a large spoon to emulsify the natural dressing made by the oil and the juices from the tomatoes. →

1 extra-large egg yolk, at room temperature

1 teaspoon kosher salt, plus more to taste

1 large garlic clove, peeled

For the Salad

8 ounces applewood-smoked slab bacon, cut into ½-inch cubes (or thick-sliced applewood-smoked bacon)

2 ripe but firm avocados (preferably Pinkerton, Fuerte, or Hass)

Flaky sea salt

4 medium heirloom tomatoes (about 5 ounces each)

1 cup small cherry tomatoes (preferably Sun Gold), stems removed

¼ cup finishing-quality extra-virgin olive oil

1½ tablespoons kosher salt

1 lemon, halved

8 cups watercress (about 2 bunches)

Trim and discard the stems from the watercress, leaving about 2 inches of the stems intact.

To serve, spoon the aioli into the center of a large platter or large wide-mouth bowl and use the back of the spoon to spread toward the edges in organic, uneven swirls.

Building the salad in two layers, lay half of the tomatoes over the aioli. Use a large spoon to scoop the avocado slices out of the skins and nestle the slices from one avocado in random directions in the crevices between the tomatoes. Sprinkle half of the bacon over the tomatoes and avocado slices and sprinkle ¼ cup of the bread crumbs over the bacon. Reserve a small handful of watercress and arrange the remaining watercress over the tomatoes and avocado, leaving the edges of the tomato and avocado layer visible. Build a second layer, laying the remaining tomatoes and avocado slices on top of the watercress, leaving the edges of the watercress visible. Sprinkle the remaining bacon and the remaining bread crumbs over the tomatoes and avocados and pile the reserved watercress in the center on top of the salad.

Grains and Seeds Salad with Escarole, Avocado, Bacon, Egg, and Horseradish Dressing

Serves 4

I conceived this salad during the height of the recent grain renaissance, although, having come of age as a cook during the 1970s, I have been cooking with grains for decades. I fry the grains before adding them to this delicious mess of a salad, so they're crispy and crunchy, but still light and tender.

If you want to use fewer varieties of grains and seeds, just make sure the total adds up to one-half cup. Alternatively, you may want to fry more of each of these grains and keep them around to sprinkle over salads, eggs, vegetables, or yogurt in the days ahead. (Think of them as whole-grain bread crumbs!) You need to plan ahead to make this salad if you're going to make it with farro, which has to be cooked and dried overnight before you fry it in order to crisp. If you have leftover farro from another dish (though there is not one in this book), that would be the perfect excuse to make this salad.

When shopping for escarole, look for "blanched escarole" at farmers' markets and specialty food stores. Blanched escarole is light green, almost white, in color, and sweeter and crunchier than traditional escarole. It is grown the same way white endive and white asparagus are grown, by shielding the young plants from direct sunlight, so they don't go through photosynthesis, which is what gives all plants their green color. If you can't find blanched escarole, buy conventional escarole and remove the dark, floppy outer leaves as described in the recipe. The eggs for this salad are cooked to what I call "wet but set." They are not cooked as long as I would to grate eggs, but they are not so runny that you can't slice them.

You will need a large wide-mouth bowl to serve this salad.

To cook the farro, bring 4 cups water to a boil in a small saucepan over high heat and stir in the kosher salt. Add the farro and cook for about 14 minutes, until it is tender. Drain the farro using a mesh strainer and transfer to a small baking sheet. Drizzle with the olive oil and spread the farro out over the surface of the baking sheet. Refrigerate, uncovered, overnight to dry out the farro. →

For the Farro

1 scant tablespoon kosher salt

¼ cup farro

1 tablespoon olive oil

To cook the eggs, bring a large saucepan of water to a boil over high heat and add the kosher salt. (The salt does not penetrate the egg shells and season the eggs; it helps the whites to solidify quickly if there is a crack in an egg.) Carefully lower the eggs into the water and reduce the heat so the water is gently simmering. Cook the eggs for 5 minutes. While the eggs are cooking, prepare an ice bath in a small bowl. Turn off the heat and transfer the eggs to the ice bath to chill. Peel them under a gentle stream of running water.

Meanwhile, to make the dressing, combine the onion, vinegar, horseradish, and kosher salt in a medium bowl. Stir to combine and set aside for 5 to 10 minutes to allow the onion to marinate. Stir in the aioli and mustard. Add the extra-virgin olive oil in a thin, steady stream, whisking constantly.

To toast the seeds and fry the grains, adjust the oven rack to the center position and preheat the oven to 350°F.

Spread the sunflower seeds on a baking sheet, drizzle with 1 tablespoon of the extra-virgin olive oil, sprinkle with ½ teaspoon of the kosher salt, and toss to coat. Toast the seeds in the oven for 5 to 6 minutes, until they are toasted and fragrant, stirring the seeds halfway through that time so the seeds brown evenly. Remove the seeds from the oven and transfer them to a medium bowl. Leave the oven on for cooking the bacon.

Meanwhile, put the pumpkin seeds in a small skillet, drizzle with 1 tablespoon of the extra-virgin olive oil, sprinkle with ½ teaspoon of the kosher salt, and toss to coat. Toast the seeds over medium heat for 3 to 5 minutes, until they are toasted and start to pop in the pan, stirring often so they don't burn. Transfer the pumpkin seeds to the bowl with the sunflower seeds.

Put the flaxseeds in the skillet and toast them (without oil) over medium heat for about 2 minutes, shaking the pan so they cook evenly, until the seeds start to pop. Transfer the flaxseeds to the bowl with the other seeds.

To fry the grains, pour enough canola oil into a small deep saucepan to fill it 1½ to 2 inches deep. Fasten a deep-fry thermometer, if you have one, to the side of the pan, and heat the oil over medium-high heat until the thermometer registers 400°F or a pinch of salt sizzles when dropped into the oil. While the oil is heating, remove the farro from →

For the Eggs

1 tablespoon kosher salt

3 extra-large eggs

For the Dressing

½ large yellow Spanish onion, peeled and grated on the medium holes of a box grater

3 tablespoons champagne vinegar

3 tablespoons prepared horseradish (preferably Atomic Extra Hot Horseradish Sauce)

1 teaspoon kosher salt

1 tablespoon Aioli (page 104; or store-bought mayonnaise)

1 tablespoon Dijon mustard

¼ cup plus 1 tablespoon extra-virgin olive oil

For the Seeds and Grains

¼ cup raw hulled sunflower seeds

2 tablespoons extra-virgin olive oil

1 tablespoon kosher salt

¼ cup raw hulled pumpkin seeds

¼ cup flaxseeds

3 cups canola oil (or another neutral-flavored oil), or as needed

¼ cup wild rice

¼ cup quinoa

the refrigerator. Line a baking sheet with paper towels and have a small mesh strainer handy.

Add the farro to the oil, taking care as the oil may splatter when you add the grains, and fry for about 6 minutes, until the bubbles subside and the grains are browned. Use the strainer to lift the farro out of the oil. Shake the strainer to drain the excess oil and spread the grains out on the prepared baking sheet. Sprinkle with ½ teaspoon of the kosher salt.

Turn off the heat, add the wild rice to the oil, and fry until the grains are puffed and crispy, about 10 seconds. Lift the wild rice out of the oil with the strainer, shake the strainer to drain the excess oil and then add the wild rice to the baking sheet with the farro. Sprinkle with ½ teaspoon of the kosher salt.

Add the quinoa to the oil and fry for 10 seconds, until the grains pop. Lift the quinoa out of the oil with the strainer, shake the strainer to drain the excess oil, and add the quinoa to the baking sheet with the other grains. Sprinkle with ½ teaspoon of the kosher salt. Add the wild rice, quinoa, and farro to the bowl with the toasted seeds. Sprinkle with the remaining ½ teaspoon kosher salt and toss to combine.

To make the salad, place the bacon on a baking sheet and cook it in the oven for 16 to 20 minutes, until it is cooked but not crisp, rotating the baking sheet from front to back halfway through that time so the bacon cooks evenly. Meanwhile, create a bed of paper towels. Remove the bacon from the oven and transfer it to the paper towels to drain. Cut the bacon on an extreme bias into ⅛-inch threads.

Cut off and discard the root ends of the escarole. Remove the dark green outer leaves until only the tender, light yellow leaves remain. (Reserve the outer leaves to make Braised Greens, page 297.) Tear the remaining leaves from the core and put them in a large wide-mouth bowl.

Cut the avocado in half lengthwise and twist each half in opposite directions to separate them. Plunge the edge of a large knife into the pit and twist the knife to release the pit from the avocado; discard the pit. With the avocado still in its skin, slice each avocado in half lengthwise into 4 equal slices, making sure not to cut through the skins. Crush about 1 teaspoon flaky sea salt between your fingertips over the avocado halves.

For the Salad

3 ounces thick-sliced applewood-smoked bacon

2 heads escarole (preferably "blanched" escarole)

1 ripe but firm avocado (preferably Pinkerton, Fuerte, or Hass)

Flaky sea salt

½ lemon

½ teaspoon kosher salt

Squeeze the lemon half over the escarole, sprinkle with the kosher salt, and toss to coat the escarole with the lemon and salt. Drizzle half of the dressing over the escarole and toss with your hands, massaging the dressing to coat each leaf.

To serve, cut the eggs in half lengthwise. Building the salad in three layers and choosing the largest leaves first, arrange one-third of the escarole to cover the bottom of a large wide-mouth bowl. Use a large spoon to scoop the avocado slices out of the skin and lay one-third of the avocado slices in different directions over the escarole. Scatter one-third of the bacon threads and one-third of the grains and seeds over and around the salad. Continue, building two more layers the same as the first, using the medium leaves for the second layer and the smallest leaves for the top layer, and making each layer smaller than the one before. Nestle the halved eggs into the top layer of the salad and crush a pinch of flaky sea salt between your fingertips over each egg. Drizzle the remaining dressing over the entire salad.

Burrata and Stone Fruit Salad
with Mizuna and Sweet Peppers

Serves 4

I'm not one to put fruit in my salad (and that goes for dried cranberries too), but in this recipe, the fruit *is* the salad. It is a dish to make only during the height of summer, when sweet, juicy stone fruit, a category that refers to fruits with "stones" or pits in them, such as peaches, nectarines, plums, and apricots, can be found at farmers' markets. The salad is all about contrasts: the sweet, soft fruit with the crunchy peppers, a slightly spicy, garlicky vinaigrette, and a good amount of minerally flaky sea salt. The "lettuce" for this salad is mizuna, a delicate Asian green, with soft, mild, spiky-shaped leaves. Burrata is a rich, luxurious fresh cheese in the mozzarella family, from Puglia, the boot heel of Italy, consisting of a thin mozzarella "sack," filled with *straciatella* (shredded mozzarella) and *panna* (Italian heavy cream).

You will need a large platter to serve this salad.

To make the vinaigrette, combine the parsley, lemon juice, garlic, red pepper flakes, mustard, and kosher salt in a small bowl. Gradually add the extra-virgin olive oil, whisking constantly.

To make the salad, cut the nectarines in half and remove and discard the pits. Lay each half flat side down, cut them into ¼-inch-thick slices, and put them into a large bowl.

Place one plum on a cutting board and cut four slabs off the pit. Repeat with the remaining plums. Add the plum slabs to the bowl with the peaches and discard the pits.

Remove and discard the stems from the peppers. Cut each pepper in half lengthwise and remove and discard the seeds. Slice the peppers ⅛ inch thick lengthwise and add them to the bowl with the fruit. Squeeze one lemon half over the fruit and peppers, sprinkle with ½ teaspoon of the kosher salt, and toss to coat the ingredients with the lemon and salt. Drizzle with half of the vinaigrette and toss gently to coat the fruit and peppers with the vinaigrette.

For the Vinaigrette

¼ cup finely chopped fresh Italian parsley leaves

3 tablespoons fresh lemon juice

2 large garlic cloves, peeled and minced

½ teaspoon red pepper flakes

½ teaspoon Dijon mustard

½ teaspoon kosher salt

¼ cup extra-virgin olive oil

For the Salad

2 ripe but firm nectarines (about 5 ounces each)

3 ripe but firm plums (such as Santa Rosa or Elephant Heart, about 3 ounces each)

Spoon half of the burrata in 1-inch clumps over the surface of a large platter. Crush about 1½ teaspoons flaky sea salt between your fingertips over the burrata. Mound the stone fruit and peppers on top of the burrata, leaving the edges of the burrata layer visible.

Put the mizuna and mint in the bowl the fruit and peppers were tossed in. Squeeze the remaining lemon half and sprinkle the remaining ½ teaspoon kosher salt over the mizuna and mint and toss to coat the greens with the lemon and salt. Drizzle the remaining vinaigrette over the greens and toss gently to coat them with the vinaigrette.

Pile three-quarters of the mizuna and mint on top of the fruit, leaving the edges of the fruit layer visible. Spoon the remaining burrata in 1-inch pieces evenly over the mizuna and crush about 1½ teaspoons flaky sea salt between your fingertips over the burrata. Pile the remaining mizuna in the center of the burrata, leaving the edges of the burrata visible.

4 baby sweet peppers (any variety, such as baby bell peppers, Tinkerbell peppers, or another sweet variety)

1 lemon, halved

1 teaspoon kosher salt

8 ounces burrata

Flaky sea salt

8 cups mizuna (or a wild arugula)

12 to 15 fresh mint leaves, each torn into 3 or 4 pieces

BEEF AND VEAL   133

Bistecca Fiorentina   134

Carne Cruda, Osteria Style   136

Carne Cruda, "Tartufo Povero"   139

Grilled Porcini-Rubbed Short Ribs
with Salsa Verde and Scallions   141

Standing Rib Roast, APL Style   143

Coffee-Rubbed Grilled Tri-Tip   146

Beef Cheek and Bone Marrow Pie   149

Braised Brisket with Salsa Verde
and Horseradish Crème Fraîche   156

Pepper Steak "Dal Rae"   161

Milk-Braised Veal Breast with Hazelnuts   163

Porcini-Rubbed Double-Bone Veal Chops with
Roasted Onions and Brown Butter Jus   166

PORK   168

Grilled Tomahawk Pork Chop
with Fennel Pollen   169

Pork Tenderloin, Segreto Style,
with Lemon-Anchovy Salsa Rustica   172

Grilled Pork-and-Veal Meatballs with
Fresh Ricotta and Braised Greens   175

Pork al Latte with Fennel Pollen
and Crispy Sage   177

Parmesan Soufflé with Ragù Bolognese   180

Pork Tonnato with Crispy Capers   183

Pork Shoulder Blade Chops
with Chipotle and Apple Cider Syrup   187

LAMB   189

Braised Lamb Necks with Castelvetrano
Olives and Preserved Lemon   191

Roasted Lamb Rack with Dried Persian Lime
Tahini and Grilled Broccolini and Scallions   193

Moorish Lamb Shoulder Chops
with Mint Yogurt   196

Armenian-Style Lamb Ribs with Jajik   198

Grilled Lamb Sausage Coils
with Onion and Peppers   201

Moroccan-Braised Lamb Shanks with
Pistachio Gremolata and Celeriac Purée   204

DUCK, RABBIT, AND CHICKEN   207

Chicken Stock   159

Lacquered Duck with Honey-Balsamic Glaze
and Crispy Black Rice   208

Pancetta-Wrapped Rabbit with Braised
Greens   212

Pollo alla Diavola on Toast   216

Carne

Meat is the centerpiece of the Chi Spacca menu, the showstoppers to build your meal around. While a few of these recipes call for luxurious cuts that are simply grilled, even more utilize lesser-known, often less expensive meats, including "butcher's cuts," which historically the butcher, unable to sell them (either because there were too few of them on the animal to market or because they weren't in demand), took home for the family. Prepared correctly, these underutilized pieces are as tender and flavorful as their better-known counterparts.

Ryan's Meat Tutorial

The most important factor when buying meat of any kind—whether it's beef, pork, lamb, chicken, whatever—is to buy it from a reliable source, meaning a butcher shop or a grocery store with a good butcher counter. As a chef, I do a lot of research to find out where the meat I am buying comes from, what breed it is, how it was raised, and, finally, how it tastes. A good butcher does the same research, and by shopping with him or her, you are benefiting from their legwork and expertise. See Sources (page 357) for where to buy meat, poultry, and game that meet the standards I describe below.

Beef

First let's talk about breed. The majority of beef we use at Chi Spacca comes from Angus cattle, a breed that is known for its well-marbled beef with a large cap of fat. Marbling refers to the intramuscular fat that creates the white striations in a piece of raw meat. The fat in meat translates to flavor and also juiciness. The Angus beef we use is grass-raised, grain-finished, which means it is raised on grass for 80 percent of its life and finished on a diet of ground corncobs. This results in beef that is well marbled with great flavor.

A second breed that has become popular in recent years for its beef is Holstein. Traditionally a "milking cow" and not used for meat, it is much leaner than other breeds, but nevertheless has beautiful marbling and an intense, beefy flavor. For our Bistecca Fiorentina (page 134), which is our premier steak, we offer a choice of Angus and Holstein, which we sell as "Flannery" beef, named after Brian Flannery, the distributor who gets the Holsteins for us. Flannery sources only the best Holstein cows, and as a result, the beef is even more flavorful (and also more expensive) than the Angus we sell.

Another option and a major buzzword when it comes to beef is Wagyu, the American version of Kobe beef that is known for being tender, fatty, and flavorful. Where Kobe is prohibitively expensive, Wagyu is much more affordable, and it is becoming readily available. Wagyu is highly marbled, which makes it a good choice for preparations where the meat is cooked for a short time, such as grilled rare or medium-rare steaks. The downside of Wagyu is that it has *so* much marbling that you don't want to eat very much of it. If you were to feel like splurging on Wagyu, either the Carne Cruda, Osteria Style (page 136) or Carne Cruda, "Tartufo Povero" (page 139) would be the perfect place for it.

DRY-AGED BEEF

Dry aging is a process used to add flavor and tenderness to meat. The process of dry aging involves storing meat in a well-aerated temperature-controlled room to allow the meat to dry out. The layer of mold that grows on the outside of the meat tenderizes the meat and also gives it a funky, almost mushroomy flavor. In the aging process the steak loses moisture, so the flavor becomes more concentrated. (Because the meat essentially shrinks, it also becomes more expensive the longer it ages.) Dry-aged meat is best used in preparations where the meat is grilled or seared and served rare or medium-rare. Although Italians don't typically use dry-aged meat, our Bistecca Fiorentina (page 134) is the perfect way to show-case the effects of dry aging. At Chi Spacca, we age our beef for thirty and forty days—which is enough time to concentrate the flavor, but not so long that the meat starts to taste *too* funky—but some steak houses age their steaks for as long as one hundred days. Dry aging has become very popular over the last ten years, and today, most butcher shops dry age, as do many specialty grocery stores. Many mail-order sources (see Sources, page 357) carry dry-aged beef.

There are two grades to consider when buying beef: prime and choice. The grades, which are regulated by the USDA, signify the amount of marbling in the beef: the more marbling, the higher the grade. It's important to choose prime meats for grilling, searing, or roasting. But if you're braising the meat, such as for the Braised Brisket (page 156), the extra marbling that prime beef guarantees is not going to make a significant difference in the finished product.

Veal

Strict regulations around veal ensure that all of the veal on the market is humanely raised. And, in fact, veal is a natural by-product of the dairy industry; in order for cows to produce milk, they must give birth at least once a year, and the male offspring are raised and sold as veal. When shopping for veal, look for "nature veal," which is milk-fed, or grain-fed veal, also called red veal. We use grain-fed veal, which has a meatier color and flavor, but either will work in these recipes. →

Pork

Do you remember the "other white meat" campaign where they tried to convince people that pork wasn't fattening? Well, thanks to that campaign, the vast majority of pork in this country has been raised to have so little fat in it that no matter how you cook it, it turns out dry and lacking in flavor. To ensure that your pork is fatty, juicy, and flavorful, the way pork should be, look for heritage breeds that have not had the fat bred out of them. The one you will see most often is Berkshire (also called Kurobuta). Other heritage breeds on the market are Duroc, Tamworth, Mangalitsa, and Red Wattle. All of them are great. It is especially important to look for heritage breeds when you are cooking pork loin and tenderloin. These cuts can tend to be dry, but not so with the heritage breeds. In buying the better breed, you have improved your finished dish before you even start cooking.

Lamb

If you're someone who shies away from lamb because of its gamy flavor, look for domestic lamb from small producers, such as that labeled Colorado lamb or Sonoma lamb. Raised on a diet of grains and legumes, domestic lamb has a sweeter, milder flavor than lamb imported from Australia and New Zealand. Australian and New Zealand lamb is comparable in size and can be used in place of domestic in these recipes; it is also easier to find and considerably less expensive.

Beef and Veal

Bistecca Fiorentina

Serves 2 to 4

Chi Spacca is designed like a big open home kitchen; when our customers walk in, they see everything happening right in front them, and very often, they see a bistecca Fiorentina (or several) standing upright on the grill. Bistecca Fiorentina (see photo page 133), the iconic steak of Tuscany, is a very thick porterhouse steak, with a New York steak on one side of the bone and a fillet, or tenderloin, on the other. What makes the Fiorentina unique is how large and thick it is. According to the unwritten rules of the Tuscan kitchen, a bistecca Fiorentina must be at least 2 inches thick and weigh a minimum of 1 kilo (35 ounces, or 2¼ pounds). (We sell it by the kilo for a minimum of two people; ours are often as big as 1½ kilos, or 50 ounces, or just over 3 pounds.) The thick cut enables us to cook the steak just the way we want it. We sear it, so it has a beautiful, caramelized crust, and then we cook it so that it is an even rare all the way through, rather than being well-done and gray toward the edges, graduating to rare in the very center. The way we achieve the even rare center is by grilling the steak over a hot fire and then letting it stand on the bone over indirect heat for a long time.

Ask your butcher for a porterhouse steak (preferably dry-aged), cut 2½ to 3 inches thick and weighing 2½ to 3 pounds.

You will need an extra-large platter to serve this steak.

To prepare the steak, remove it from the refrigerator and place it on a baking sheet or in a baking dish. Set aside for 30 minutes to 1 hour to come to room temperature.

Prepare a wood, charcoal, or gas grill for direct and indirect heat. (For detailed instructions, see Ryan's Chi Spacca Grilling Class, page 27.)

Very coarsely grind the peppercorns with a mortar or spice grinder. Pour 1 tablespoon of the olive oil over the steak and massage with your hands to coat the meat with the oil. Sprinkle the kosher salt evenly on all sides of the steak. Pour the remaining olive oil over the steak and massage to coat. (We apply oil before and after the salt on this steak to ensure the salt adheres to the meat during the long cooking time.) Sprinkle the pepper evenly on all sides of the steak and press it in with your hands to adhere.

For the Steak

1 (2½- to 3-inch-thick) porterhouse steak (preferably dry-aged; about 3 pounds)

¼ cup black peppercorns

2 tablespoons olive oil

2 tablespoons kosher salt

Place the steak on the grill over direct heat for 5 to 6 minutes, until both sides are deeply caramelized with a thin crust. Move the steak to the indirect heat side of the grill, standing the steak on the bone with the larger New York section of the meat facing the hot fire and the smaller tenderloin facing away from the fire. Cook the steak standing up for 14 to 20 minutes, until an instant-read thermometer registers 100°F when inserted deep into the side of the steak.

Transfer the steak to a cutting board to rest for 5 to 10 minutes.

To serve, place your knife along one side the bone that runs down the center of the steak and run the knife down the side of the bone to cut off the loin (New York steak). Cut down the other side of the bone to remove the tenderloin. Place the bone standing upright at the end of a large platter or cutting board. Slice the loin and tenderloin 1 inch thick. Slide your knife under the slices and then transfer the slices to the platter or cutting board, fanning the slices out so they look like they slid off the bone and onto the platter. Slide your knife under the tenderloin and fan the slices out next to the loin slices, as if they slid down the other side of the bone. Drizzle the finishing-quality olive oil and crush the flaky sea salt between your fingers over the steak and the bone. (We season the bone along with the meat because we expect people to pick it up and eat it. I don't know about you, but the bone is the first thing I reach for.)

For Serving

¼ cup plus 2 tablespoons finishing-quality extra-virgin olive oil

Flaky sea salt

Carne Cruda, Osteria Style

Serves 4

Carne cruda translates as "raw meat" and is Italy's version of steak tartare. Where the French enrich their raw steak with egg yolks, the Italians do it with their own fat of choice: fruity olive oil. We make our carne cruda with hanger steak, a flavorful cut that hangs down the center of the animal. Hanger steak's downfall is that it can be tough, but that doesn't matter with carne cruda, where the meat is chopped. We spoon the tartare over two large thin slices of toasted bread that, laid side by side, form a circle. Then we sprinkle fried, thinly sliced garlic and capers on top, which are very delicate, crunchy, and flavorful.

Ask your butcher for 1½ pounds of hanger steak with the silver skin and fat removed. If hanger is not available, ask for beef shoulder clod (also called Denver steak), or another lean, non-sinewy cut.

You will need two medium round plates or a long cutting board to serve the carne cruda.

To make the toast, adjust the oven rack to the center position and preheat the oven to 350°F.

Place the bread in the freezer until it is firm but not frozen, about 30 minutes. Remove the bread from the freezer and use a large serrated knife to cut 4 slices from the center of the loaf. Reserve the rest of the loaf to enjoy in whatever way you like.

Place the slices of bread on a large baking sheet and brush them lightly with olive oil and toast them in the oven until they are golden brown and slightly crunchy. Remove the toast from the oven and rub with the garlic clove.

To fry the garlic and capers, adjust the blade of a mandoline to slice ⅛ inch thick. Slice the garlic lengthwise, stopping just before your fingers get dangerously close to the blade; reserve the garlic ends to chop for another use. Put the garlic slices in a small saucepan. Add 3 cups cold water and bring the water to a boil over high heat. Create a bed of paper towels and have a mesh strainer handy. When the water just starts to boil,

For the Toast

1 (1-pound) round loaf of rustic bread

Olive oil

1 large garlic clove, peeled

For the Fried Garlic and Capers

¾ cup large garlic cloves (about 30), peeled

2 cups olive oil, or as needed

1 teaspoon kosher salt

½ cup capers (preferably salt-packed), soaked for 15 minutes if salt-packed, rinsed and drained turn off the heat and strain the garlic over the sink. Return the garlic to the saucepan. Add 3 cups cold water and repeat, boiling and draining the garlic two more times. Transfer the garlic slices to the paper towels to drain thoroughly. Create a bed of paper towels and have a mesh strainer handy. Fill a small saucepan 1½ to 2 inches deep with olive oil. Add the garlic and heat the oil and garlic together over medium-high heat, stirring often, until the garlic is light golden, 6 to 7 minutes. Use the strainer to remove the garlic slices from the oil and transfer them to the paper towels to drain. Season the garlic slices with the kosher salt and set aside to cool to room temperature.

Fasten a deep-fry thermometer, if you have one, to the side of the saucepan with the oil you fried the garlic in and heat the oil over medium-high heat until the thermometer registers 350°F or a pinch of salt sizzles when dropped into the oil. While the oil is heating, create another bed of paper towels. Turn off the heat, add the capers, and fry them for 30 seconds, until the buds open up. Use the mesh strainer or a slotted spoon to lift the capers out of the oil and transfer them to the paper towels to drain. Let the oil cool and strain it into a container; cover and reserve the oil to cook with another time.

To prepare the carne cruda, very coarsely grind the peppercorns using a mortar, spice grinder, or an antique coffee grinder.

Cut the beef into ¼-inch cubes and put them in a large bowl. Add the (unfried) capers and oregano. Crush the flaky sea salt between your fingertips into the bowl and add the pepper. Use a fine Microplane to zest the bright yellow outer layer of half of the lemon over the meat. (Reserve the lemon to juice at another time.) Drizzle the finishing-quality olive oil into the bowl and fold the ingredients together.

To serve, lay 2 toasts on each of the round plates or lay all 4 on a long cutting board, facing the straight edges of the bread (the bottoms, when the bread was baked) toward each other so 2 of the slices together form a circle. Spoon one-fourth of the carne cruda onto each slice of bread, using the back of the spoon to spread it out in an even layer, leaving the edges of the bread visible. Sprinkle the whole oregano leaves and fried capers over the meat. Use the Microplane to zest the bright yellow outer layer of the remaining lemon and scatter the garlic slices over the meat. (Reserve the lemon to juice at another time.)

For the Carne Cruda

1 tablespoon black peppercorns

1½ pounds hanger steak, trimmed of silver skin and fat

2 tablespoons capers (preferably salt-packed), soaked for 15 minutes if salt-packed, rinsed and drained, finely chopped

2 tablespoons finely chopped fresh oregano leaves

2 teaspoons flaky sea salt

1 lemon

2 tablespoons finishing-quality extra-virgin olive oil

For Serving

2 tablespoons fresh whole oregano leaves

1 lemon

Carne Cruda, "Tartufo Povero"

Serves 4

Tartufo povero means, essentially, "poor man's truffle." We gave this dish that name because the carne cruda is served with a blanket of white button mushrooms shaved the way you would shave truffles generously over a pasta, letting them rain over the top, concealing what is beneath. Look for fresh, pretty button mushrooms that are tight, with the cap intact, not open with the gills showing.

Ask your butcher for 1½ pounds of hanger steak and specify that the silver skin and fat be removed. If hanger is not available, ask for beef shoulder clod (also called Denver steak), or another lean, non-sinewy cut.

You will need a large platter to serve the carne cruda.

To prepare the carne cruda, very coarsely grind the peppercorns using a mortar, spice grinder, or an antique coffee grinder.

Cut the beef into ¼-inch cubes and put them in a large bowl. Crush the flaky sea salt between your fingertips over the meat and add the pepper. Drizzle the finishing-quality olive oil into the bowl and fold the ingredients together.

Spoon the meat onto a small platter and use the back of the spoon to gently spread it in uneven waves toward the edges of the platter without smashing it.

Clean the outsides of the mushrooms with a damp towel and trim and discard the very ends of the stems; don't trim too much as you want to maintain the shape of the stemmed mushrooms. Adjust the blade of a mandoline or truffle slicer to slice as thinly as possible. Slice the mushrooms to fall like a blanket over the carne, stopping just before your fingers get dangerously close to the blade; snack on the remaining parts of the mushrooms or reserve them to make stock.

To serve, squeeze the juice of the lemon half over the mushrooms, drizzle with about 2 tablespoons finishing-quality olive oil, and crush about 1 teaspoon flaky sea salt between your fingertips over them.

For the Carne Cruda and "Tartufi"

2 tablespoons black peppercorns

1½ pounds hanger steak, trimmed of silver skin and fat

2 tablespoons flaky sea salt

2 tablespoons finishing-quality extra-virgin olive oil

2 large button mushrooms

For Serving

½ lemon

Finishing-quality extra-virgin olive oil

Flaky sea salt

Grilled Porcini-Rubbed Short Ribs
with Salsa Verde and Scallions

Serves 4

When you think of short ribs, you probably imagine braised, fall-off-the-bone tender meat in a rich, winey sauce. Well, think again! These are "Korean-cut" short ribs, which refers to ribs that are cut very thin, marinated to tenderize them, and then grilled. It's really remarkable how cutting and marinating allow you to take a cut of meat that normally takes hours to cook and lets you cook it in minutes. The secret is the marinade, which we learned from Jenee Kim, who owns Parks BBQ, a legendary restaurant in Koreatown in Los Angeles. It so happens that Jenee's daughter is Liz Hong, the executive chef at Osteria Mozza, and Jenee was nice enough to share it with us. The ribs are cut so thin there is something kind of dainty about them. They invite you to pick them up and gnaw the meat off the bones—my favorite way to eat meat. You marinate the short ribs for at least two hours, but no longer than four; the marinade is such an effective tenderizer that any longer than four hours and the meat will break down too much and get an unpleasant texture.

Ask your butcher for 12 (½- to ¾-inch-thick) flanken-style short ribs, aka Korean-style short ribs, and ask him or her to remove the silver skin.

You will need an extra-large platter to serve the ribs.

To marinate the ribs, cut the onion into quarters, root to tip. Separate the layers of the onion, stack two or three layers at a time on top of one another, and slice ¼ inch thick lengthwise. Put the onions in a large baking dish or divide them between two large resealable plastic bags. Using a sharp knife, score the meat of each short rib on both sides in a ¼-inch diamond, crosshatch pattern, making sure not to cut all the way through the meat; scoring the meat helps the marinade to penetrate. Put the ribs in the baking dish or bags with the onion.

Combine the balsamic vinegar, olive oil, honey, and kiwi in the jar of a blender and blend until puréed. Pour the marinade into the dish or bags, dividing it evenly. Massage the marinade into the meat with your hands. Cover the dish with plastic wrap or close the bags and put the ribs in the refrigerator for at least 2 hours and no more than 4 to marinate. →

For the Ribs

1 red onion, peeled

12 (½- to ¾-inch-thick) flanken-style short ribs, trimmed of silver skin

1 cup balsamic vinegar

1 cup olive oil

¼ cup honey

1 kiwi, peeled and roughly chopped (or 1 ripe pear, core and stem removed and roughly chopped)

1 recipe Porcini Rub (page 22)

3 large scallions

While the short ribs are marinating, to make the salsa verde combine the oregano, mint, capers, lemon juice, kosher salt, and red pepper flakes in a medium bowl. Use a fine Microplane to grate the garlic into the bowl and stir to combine. Gradually add the finishing-quality olive oil, stirring constantly.

Remove the short ribs from the refrigerator and uncover. Remove the ribs from the marinade and discard the marinade and onion. Scrape off the excess marinade with your hands and lay the ribs in a single layer on a large baking sheet or cutting board. Pat both sides of the ribs dry with paper towels. Sprinkle the porcini rub on both sides of the ribs and massage to thoroughly coat the ribs. Use the meat to mop up any rub that falls onto the baking sheet. Set aside for about 30 minutes to let the seasonings penetrate the ribs and for the ribs to come to room temperature.

Prepare a hot fire in a wood-burning or charcoal grill or preheat a gas grill for high heat. (For detailed instructions, see Ryan's Chi Spacca Grilling Class, page 27.)

While the grill is heating, trim any wilted greens from the scallions. Starting at the green ends and moving toward the white ends, slice the scallions ⅛ inch thick on an extreme bias. Put the scallion slices in a small bowl; discard the root ends.

Place the short ribs on the grill, leaving about 1 inch between each rib (if the ribs are too close to each other, they will steam from the water released during the cooking, rather than sear and caramelize). Grill the short ribs until they have black grill marks on both sides, 3 to 4 minutes per side. Remove the ribs from the grill and place them on a large dry baking sheet.

To serve, stir the salsa verde to recombine the ingredients and spoon it over the ribs, using the back of the spoon to dress the ribs with the salsa. Transfer the ribs to a large platter, crisscrossing them and fanning the crisscrosses to cover the platter. Drizzle about 2 teaspoons finishing-quality olive oil and crush about ½ teaspoon flaky sea salt with your fingertips over the scallions. Mix the scallions with your fingers to dress them and drop them in clumps on the ribs.

For the Salsa Verde

¼ cup finely chopped fresh oregano leaves

1 tablespoon finely chopped fresh mint leaves

1 tablespoon capers (preferably salt-packed), soaked for 15 minutes if salt-packed, rinsed, drained, and finely chopped

2 teaspoons fresh lemon juice, plus more to taste

2 teaspoons kosher salt, plus more to taste

½ teaspoon red pepper flakes

2 large garlic cloves, peeled

¼ cup finishing-quality extra-virgin olive oil

For Serving

Finishing-quality extra-virgin olive oil

Flaky sea salt

Standing Rib Roast, APL Style

Serves 7 to 12

This brilliant treatment of a standing rib roast came about as the result of a happy accident, when, researching something unrelated, I came across a video of the late food writer Josh Ozersky making a rib roast with Adam Perry Lang, a chef known for the delicious things he does with barbecue and meat in general. The video showed Adam scoring the top, fat layer, creating nooks and crannies that get golden brown and crispy in the oven—nothing *so* unusual. But then he did something I'd never seen or considered. He took a big knife and carved off the entire fat layer—all those charred bits that I love to snack on. He put all that good stuff on a cutting board, cut it up, and mixed it with fresh parsley and garlic, and made a sort of salsa out of it. It looked so good. And what a great idea! Meat with meat sauce.

A standing rib roast is a roast consisting of the same meat as rib-eye steaks. It gets its name from the fact that it is roasted standing upright, on the rib bone. Even when the roast is boneless, like this one, it still goes by the same name. It is often referred to as a "prime rib," a reference to the grade of meat, even when the rib roast might be made with a lower grade of meat, such as choice. We use exclusively prime for our prime rib roast.

Ask your butcher for an 8-pound boneless standing beef rib roast, preferably prime.

You will need a long cutting board or an extra-large platter to serve the rib roast.

To cook the rib roast, place it in a large baking dish or on a baking sheet and season it all over with the kosher salt. Cover the dish with plastic wrap and refrigerate overnight or for at least 6 hours.

Remove the rib roast from the refrigerator and set aside for 30 minutes to 1 hour to come to room temperature.

Put the peppercorns in a mortar or spice grinder and very coarsely grind them.

Adjust the oven rack to the center position and preheat the oven to 375°F.

Transfer the rib roast, fat side up, to a cutting board. Make 5 long cuts about 1 inch deep into the fat cap of the roast, running the knife along the length of the meat. Rotate the roast 45 degrees and make 5 or 6 cuts of the same depth running the width of the meat, creating a →

For the Roast

1 (8-pound) boneless standing beef rib roast (preferably prime)

2 tablespoons plus 2 teaspoons kosher salt

2 tablespoons black peppercorns

For the Topping

4 large garlic cloves, peeled

1 cup fresh Italian parsley leaves

1 lemon

1 teaspoon kosher salt

¼ cup finishing-quality extra-virgin olive oil

diamond pattern. Sprinkle the pepper evenly over the surface of the roast. Use the meat to mop up any fallen pepper and press it into the meat with your hands to adhere. Put a roasting rack, if you have one, in a roasting pan and put the prime rib, fat side up, on the rack (or in the pan). Roast the meat for about 1 hour, until the top is deeply caramelized and crispy in places. Remove the pan from the oven and transfer the meat to a large cutting board.

Reduce the oven temperature to 325°F.

With your knife parallel to the roast, insert it where the fat layer meets the meat to carve off the layer of squares created by scoring. Place the chunks in a bowl and set aside.

Return the roast to the roasting pan and return it to the oven to cook until an instant-read thermometer inserted into the deepest part of the meat reads 125°F, 50 to 75 minutes. Remove the roasting pan from the oven and let the meat rest in the pan for 20 to 30 minutes; resting meat allows the juices to disperse evenly throughout the meat, which is especially important with a large roast such as this. Leave the oven on.

To prepare the topping, while the meat is cooking, put the garlic and parsley together in a mound on a cutting board. Use a vegetable peeler to peel the bright yellow outer layer of zest from the lemon onto the mound and sprinkle with the kosher salt. Finely chop the parsley, garlic, and lemon zest together.

Just before serving, spread the trimmings on a baking sheet and put them in the oven for 2 to 3 minutes to warm them slightly, until the fat is glistening. Remove the baking sheet from the oven, transfer the trimmings to a cutting board, and chop them into ½-inch pieces. Put the trimmings into a medium bowl and add the chopped garlic, parsley, and lemon zest. Cut the lemon you zested in half, squeeze the juice into the bowl, and stir to combine. Gradually add the finishing-quality olive oil, stirring constantly.

To serve, transfer the rib roast to a cutting board and cut it into 1-inch-thick slices. Slide the knife under the slices and transfer them to a long cutting board or an extra-large platter, fanning them out to cover the board or platter. Spoon the chopped meat mixture over the meat slices and crush about 1 teaspoon flaky sea salt between your fingertips over the meat.

Coffee-Rubbed Grilled Tri-Tip

Serves 4

Tri-tip, a classic cut from Santa Maria, north of Santa Barbara, was one of the items in my mom's small cooking repertoire. She prepared it in the oven, and I remember its always being a bit dry and chewy. Ryan also grew up eating tri-tip that his dad cooked on the grill, and he swore it was never chewy. When Ryan and I had the opportunity to cook for a barbecue-themed event, we decided, together, that it was time to revisit this California classic. I put Ryan to the challenge of showing me that tri-tip could be a tender cut. For once, he proved me wrong! The key, it turns out, is cooking the meat properly (in other words: not overcooking it), and, as is the case with so many tough cuts, slicing it against the grain. We wouldn't even consider serving this without Chris Feldmeier's Rancho Beans (page 302). Beans are a typical component of traditional Santa Maria barbecue, and Chris Feldmeier, a dear friend and former Mozza chef, makes the best version I've ever tasted.

Chipotle chiles are dried, smoked jalapeño chiles; they have a wonderful, deeply smoky flavor. If you can't find chipotle chile powder, use smoked paprika (sweet or hot) or another quality chile powder.

Ask your butcher for a (4- to 5-pound) beef tri-tip with the fat cap trimmed to about ½ inch thick.

You will need an extra-large platter to serve the tri-tip.

To make the rub, put the peppercorns, coriander seeds, cumin seeds, fennel seeds, and mustard seeds in a mortar or spice grinder and very coarsely grind them. If you're using a spice grinder, transfer the spices to a small bowl. Add the ground coffee beans, kosher salt, brown sugar, paprika, chipotle chile powder, garlic powder, and onion powder and stir to combine.

To prepare the tri-tip, place it on a large baking sheet or in a baking dish. Pour the olive oil over the meat and massage with your hands to coat the meat with the oil. Reserve 1 tablespoon of the rub, sprinkle the remaining rub on the meat, and use your hands to press the rub into the meat. Set aside for 30 minutes to 1 hour to let the seasonings penetrate the meat and to come to room temperature.

For the Rub

1 heaping tablespoon black peppercorns

1 heaping tablespoon coriander seeds

1 heaping tablespoon cumin seeds

1 heaping teaspoon fennel seeds

1 heaping teaspoon yellow mustard seeds

½ cup ground coffee beans

½ cup kosher salt

Prepare a wood, charcoal, or gas grill for direct and indirect heat. (For detailed instructions, see Ryan's Chi Spacca Grilling Class, page 27.)

While the grill is heating, to make the basting liquid put the cider vinegar, lemon juice, tomato paste, and the reserved spice rub in a small saucepan and whisk to combine the ingredients. Bring the mixture to a boil over high heat. Reduce the heat and cook for 1 to 2 minutes, stirring, until the tomato paste is combined with the vinegar. Turn off the heat.

Lay the tri-tip on the direct-heat side of the grill and cook for 4 to 5 minutes, until the meat is deeply caramelized and almost black. (The coffee in the rub will cause the meat to look burned. Don't be afraid; the deeply caramelized exterior is what makes this special.) Turn the meat and cook for 4 to 5 minutes, until the second side is deeply caramelized and almost black. Move the meat to the side of the grill where there are no coals and cook over indirect heat for 10 minutes. Begin basting the meat and continue cooking, basting often, for another 5 to 10 minutes, until an instant-read thermometer reads 120°F when inserted deep into the thickest part of the meat. Remove the meat from the grill and place it on a cutting board to rest for about 20 minutes. This resting time allows the juices to distribute in the meat, as with any large cut of meat, but in this case, it also allows the glaze to cool slightly and adhere to the steak.

Cut the tri-tip into ½-inch-thick slices against the grain. (To see the grain, press down lightly on the meat and look closely; you will see the fibers of meat running in one direction. That is the grain. By slicing the meat against the grain, you are cutting through those fibers, which makes the meat more tender.)

To serve, slide your knife under the slices of meat. Transfer the slices to an extra-large platter and fan them out to cover the surface of the platter. Lightly brush the remaining basting liquid on the meat and crush flaky sea salt between your fingertips over it.

½ cup light or dark brown sugar

2 tablespoons sweet smoked paprika

1 tablespoon ground chipotle chile (or sweet or hot smoked paprika or another chile powder)

1 tablespoon garlic powder

1 tablespoon onion powder

For the Meat

1 (4- to 5-pound) beef tri-tip, fat cap trimmed to about ½ inch thick

2 tablespoons olive oil

For the Basting Liquid

1½ cups apple cider vinegar

1 tablespoon fresh lemon juice

1 tablespoon double-concentrated tomato paste

For Serving

Flaky sea salt

Beef Cheek and Bone Marrow Pie

Makes 2 (6-inch) pies; serves 4

Okay, here it is: The recipe you've been waiting for. This pie, with a rich filling of beef cheeks braised in red wine encased in a flaky, buttery crust and baked with a marrow bone sticking out of the center, is by far the most talked-about, photographed, and Instagrammed item we have at the restaurant. It's a head turner. I had eaten all sorts of meat pies before, but I had never had one with a bone in it until a few years ago when I was working in the kitchen during a food festival in Melbourne, Australia, and one of the participants, knowing it was something I would appreciate, brought me this meat pie from the nearby Middle Park Hotel. I remember looking at the pie, seeing that bone, and thinking: "That is *insane*! And brilliant." This is my version of that pie. Besides acting as a smokestack for the pie, the marrow inside the bone melts back into the pie as it bakes, which further enriches the filling.

You may want to make this pie over three days: Make the stock and season the meat on the first day. Braise the meat and make the dough on the second day. And assemble, bake, and enjoy the pie on the third day. This recipe calls for homemade chicken stock, which doesn't contain any sodium. If the stock you are using does contain sodium, cut the salt in this recipe by half.

Ask your butcher for two 3-inch cylindrical-cut marrow bones and 2 pounds beef cheeks, cut into 1-inch cubes.

You will need two (6-inch-wide, 1½-inch-deep) pie pans to make this.

You will need two 10-inch plates to serve these pies.

To make the stock, heat the olive oil in a large saucepan over medium-high heat for 2 to 3 minutes, until the oil slides easily and is smoking around the edges of the pan. Add the onion, carrot, celery, and garlic and sauté for 8 to 10 minutes, until the vegetables are deeply caramelized, stirring often so they don't burn. Move the vegetables to one side of the pan. Add the tomato paste to the space created and cook for about 2 minutes to caramelize the tomato paste, stirring constantly so it doesn't burn. Add the red wine and cook for 2 to 3 minutes, until it has almost all evaporated, scraping to release any bits stuck to the bottom of the pan. Add the chicken, thyme, bay leaves, parsley, and 3 quarts (12 cups) water. Increase the heat to high and bring the liquid to a boil. Reduce the heat to low to maintain a gentle simmer and cook the →

For the Stock

2 tablespoons olive oil

1 large yellow Spanish onion, peeled and roughly chopped

1 large carrot, roughly chopped

1 celery stalk, roughly chopped

5 large garlic cloves, peeled and thinly sliced lengthwise

1 tablespoon double-concentrated tomato paste

2 cups dry red wine

stock for 45 minutes, skimming off any foam that rises to the top. Turn off the heat and let the stock cool slightly. Put a mesh strainer over a large pot or bowl and strain the stock, pressing on the solids to extract as much liquid as possible. Discard the solids. Measure out 2 quarts (8 cups) of the stock to use for the filling and reserve remaining stock, if there is any, for another use. (If you are shy of 8 cups, add enough water to make up the difference.) If you are making the stock in advance, let it come to room temperature and refrigerate, covered, for up to 3 days.

To prepare the meat and marrow bones, place the beef cheeks in a baking dish and season them on all sides with the kosher salt and pepper. Cover the dish and refrigerate overnight or for at least 6 hours.

Adjust the oven rack to the center position and preheat the oven to 350°F.

Crush a pinch of flaky sea salt between your fingertips to fall on the circle of fat at the center of each side of each bone. Lay the bones on a baking sheet and roast the bones for 8 to 10 minutes, until they begin to look soft and a bit of fat begins to drain onto the baking sheet; the bones will still look raw and not brown. Remove the bones from the oven and set aside to cool to room temperature. Cover the bones and refrigerate until you're ready to use them.

To make the filling, wipe the mushrooms with a damp towel to clean them. Trim and discard the bottoms of the stems and cut the mushrooms into quarters.

Remove the beef cheeks from the refrigerator and uncover them. Heat 2 tablespoons of the olive oil in a large skillet over medium-high heat for 2 to 3 minutes, until the oil slides easily and is smoking around the edges of the pan. Add the beef cheeks and sear until they are deeply caramelized on all sides, 12 to 15 minutes, turning the pieces individually to cook them on all sides. Remove the beef cheeks from the skillet and return them to the baking dish. Add the remaining 2 tablespoons olive oil to the skillet. Add the mushrooms, cippolini onions, garlic, and thyme, and cook over medium-high heat for 10 to 12 minutes, until the vegetables are deeply caramelized, stirring occasionally so they don't burn. Turn off the heat, remove the vegetables from the skillet, and set them aside.

In the skillet you cooked the vegetables in, melt the butter over medium heat. Add the flour and cook until the mixture begins to bubble, about 3 minutes, whisking constantly. Gradually add 1 cup of the stock, whisk-

4 pounds chicken feet,
chicken wings,
or a combination

5 fresh thyme sprigs

3 bay leaves (preferably fresh)

½ bunch fresh Italian parsley

For the Meat

2 pounds beef cheeks,
cut into 1-inch cubes

2 teaspoons kosher salt

½ teaspoon fresh coarsely
ground black pepper

Flaky sea salt

2 (3-inch) cylindrical-cut beef
marrow bones

For the Filling

8 large button mushrooms,
caps intact

¼ cup olive oil

6 large cippolini onions,
peeled and quartered through
the core

4 large garlic cloves, peeled
and thinly sliced lengthwise

2 tablespoons fresh thyme
leaves

2 tablespoons unsalted butter

2 tablespoons unbleached
all-purpose flour

For the Dough

¼ cup heavy cream

¼ cup plus 2 tablespoons cold
water

4 cups unbleached all-purpose
flour, plus more for dusting

1 tablespoon plus 1 teaspoon
kosher salt

ing until no lumps remain. Gradually add the remaining stock, whisking constantly. Increase the heat to high and bring the stock to a boil. Return the meat to the skillet and return the liquid to a boil. Reduce the heat to medium-low to maintain a gentle simmer and cook for about 2 hours, until fork-tender. To test for doneness, insert a fork into the meat and turn it slightly; if the meat pulls apart with very little effort, it's done. Add the vegetables and cook them for about 10 minutes to meld the flavors. Add more kosher salt to taste. Turn off the heat and set aside to room temperature; transfer the filling to a covered container and refrigerate to chill.

To make the dough, whisk the cream and water together in a small bowl.

Combine the flour and kosher salt in the bowl of a stand mixer. Fit the mixer with the paddle attachment and mix on low speed to distribute the salt. Add the butter and mix on low speed until the flour and butter come together into pea-size clumps. Add the cream and water and mix on low speed until the dough comes together.

Lightly dust a large flat work surface with flour and transfer the dough to the floured surface. Gather the dough together into a ball and cut it into 4 equal pieces. Pat each piece into two 2-inch-thick disks. Wrap each disk separately in plastic wrap and place them in the refrigerator to chill until the dough is firm, about 2 hours.

To roll out the dough and line the pie pans, line a baking sheet with parchment paper and lightly dust the parchment with flour.

Lightly dust a large work surface with flour. Remove one disk of dough from the refrigerator, unwrap it, and place it on the floured surface. Cut the dough into large chunks and pound each chunk with a rolling pin to soften the dough. Bring the chunks together into a ball and gently knead until the dough is malleable. Dust the dough and rolling pin lightly with flour and roll the dough into a ⅛-inch-thick (at least 10-inch) circle, dusting the dough, rolling pin, and work surface with flour as needed. Place the dough round on the prepared baking sheet and lightly dust it with flour. Repeat with the remaining 3 pieces of dough, adding them to the baking sheet after they're rolled out, and dusting with flour between each dough round. Place the dough in the refrigerator to chill until it is firm. →

1 pound (4 sticks) unsalted butter, cut into 1-inch cubes and frozen for at least 1 hour, plus more for buttering the pans

2 extra-large eggs

Flaky sea salt

To Serve
Garlic Mashed Potatoes (page 299)

Butter the bottom and sides of two 6-inch pie pans.

Remove one dough round from the refrigerator and place it over one of the prepared pans, centering it so that the dough overhangs evenly around the pan. Working your way around the pan, lift the edge of the dough with one hand and let it drop down into the pan; at the same time, with your other hand, dip the flat side of the knuckle of your index finger in flour and use it to gently press the dough against the edges and into the creases of the pan to create straight, not sloping sides. (Don't stretch the dough to fit into the pan or it will shrink when it is baked.) Repeat: remove a second dough round from the refrigerator and line the second pie pan in the same way. Using kitchen shears, trim the dough so there is ¾ inch overhanging all around each pie pan; discard the scraps. Place the piecrusts in the refrigerator to chill.

Remove the piecrusts, dough rounds, and filling from the refrigerator. Stand one marrow bone with the smaller end facing up in the center of each piecrust.

Spoon half of the filling into each piecrust around the marrow bone and use your hands or a spoon to press down on the filling and smooth out the top.

Whisk the eggs in a small bowl with 1 teaspoon water to make an egg wash. Brush the exposed rim of dough with the egg wash and reserve the remaining egg wash to brush the tops of the pies.

Using a 2-inch-round cookie cutter, cut a hole in the center of each dough round; discard the pieces of dough that you cut out.

Lay the rounds on top of each pie, fitting the marrow bone through the hole in the dough.

Press the top and bottom sheets of dough together around the edges against the pie filling.

Trim the dough so the top and bottom sheets of dough are overhanging the edge of the pan by ¾ inch; discard the scraps. →

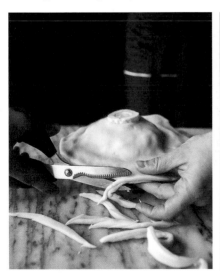 

Lightly dust your fingers with flour and roll the edges of the dough tightly underneath themselves to create a smooth rolled lip around the edges.

To crimp the pies, press the thumb or forefinger of your dominant hand on the lip of the dough, pointing outward, and pinch around it with the thumb and forefinger of your nondominant hand to create a scallop shape.

Continue, "leapfrogging" your fingers around the perimeter of the pies to create a scalloped edge. Brush half of the egg wash over the pies.

Place the pies in the refrigerator to chill until the dough is firm, about 2 hours.

Adjust the oven rack to the center position and preheat the oven to 350°F.

Remove the pies from the refrigerator and brush them with the remaining egg wash. Crush about 1 teaspoon flaky sea salt between your fingertips and scatter over the pies.

Place the pies on a baking sheet to catch any juices that may bubble over and bake for 35 minutes, until the crusts are golden brown and the filling is bubbling out of the tops, rotating the baking sheet from front to back halfway through that time so the pies brown evenly. Remove the baking sheet from the oven.

While the pies are baking, make the Garlic Mashed Potatoes (page 299).

To serve, slide an offset spatula or small knife around the inside perimeter of each pie pan to release any stuck bits. Place a plate facedown on one pie and with one hand on the pie and one on the plate, quickly flip it to invert the pie onto the plate. With your hand on top of the pie, quickly invert the pie again onto a 10-inch plate. Do the same with the second pie, inverting it onto a second 10-inch plate. (If you're not confident in your inverting skills, you can put the pies, in their pans, directly onto the plates.) Serve the pies with the mashed potatoes in a large bowl on the side.

Braised Brisket with Salsa Verde and Horseradish Crème Fraîche

Serves 6

My mother loved to experiment with "exotic" recipes from international cookbooks, but nothing gave her more pleasure than cooking a brisket; my dad, my sister, and I loved eating it as much as she liked making it. No matter where you are from, there is something about brisket—tender, juicy meat served in a rich, gravy-like sauce—that just tastes like home.

This brisket recipe is pretty traditional. To give it the contrasting flavors and textures that take a dish over the top, I serve this with an herbaceous salsa verde, which really livens it up, and cool, spicy horseradish crème fraîche, which is the MVP of this recipe. The "secret" to the crème fraîche is the horseradish itself, which is a bottled product that you can buy at many conventional supermarkets, butcher shops, and even (of all places) Smart & Final. I discovered Atomic through my friend the chef Suzanne Tracht, who serves a horseradish crème fraîche on which this recipe is based with her pot roast and the house-made potato chips she offers at the bar at her steak house, Jar. For years, every time I dined there, I was blown away by how strong the burn was from the horseradish. We share the same produce purveyor, so I asked him, "What kind of horseradish do you sell to Suzanne?" And he said, "Atomic." I figured this was the name of a rare heirloom variety of the world's best horseradish root, and then he came out of the truck holding a jar and handed it to me: "Atomic Extra Hot Horseradish Sauce."

This recipe calls for homemade chicken stock, which doesn't contain any sodium. If the stock you are using does contain sodium, cut the salt in this recipe by half.

You will need an extra-large platter to serve the brisket.

To season the brisket, place it in a baking dish. Combine the fennel seeds, mustard seeds, and coriander seeds in a mortar or spice grinder and very coarsely grind them. If you're using a spice grinder, transfer the spices to a small bowl. Add the kosher salt, paprika, brown sugar, red pepper flakes, and ground ginger to the mortar or bowl and stir to combine. Sprinkle the rub evenly over the brisket and use the meat to mop up any rub that falls into the baking dish. Press the rub into the meat with your hands to adhere. Cover the dish with plastic wrap and refrigerate overnight or for at least 6 hours.

For Seasoning the Brisket

1 (6-pound) beef brisket, trimmed of excess fat

1 tablespoon fennel seeds

1 tablespoon mustard seeds

1 tablespoon coriander seeds

2 tablespoons kosher salt

2 tablespoons sweet smoked paprika

Remove the brisket from the refrigerator and set it aside for 30 minutes to 1 hour to come to room temperature.

Adjust the oven rack to the center position and preheat the oven to 300°F.

To cook the brisket, heat the olive oil in a large Dutch oven over medium-high heat for 2 to 3 minutes, until the oil slides easily and is smoking around the edges of the pan. Place the brisket, fat side down, in the pan, reduce the heat to medium, and sear for 12 to 15 minutes, until it is deeply caramelized on both sides. Remove the brisket from the pan and return it to the baking dish. Turn off the heat and discard all but a thin layer of fat in the pan. (Brisket is very fatty so you will most likely have an excess of fat left over.) Add the onion, carrot, and garlic to the pan you cooked the brisket in and sauté over medium-high heat for 8 to 10 minutes, until the vegetables are deeply caramelized, stirring often so they don't burn. Move the vegetables to one side of the pan. Add the tomato paste to the space created and cook for about 2 minutes to caramelize the tomato paste, stirring constantly so it doesn't burn. Add the red wine and cook for 2 to 3 minutes, until it has almost all evaporated, scraping to release any bits stuck to the bottom of the pan. Return the brisket to the pan. Add the beer, pouring it around the brisket, not over it, so you don't rinse off the seared exterior. Pour the chicken stock around the brisket, adding as much as needed to come to the top of the brisket but not submerge it. Add the rosemary and bay leaves and bring the liquid to a boil over high heat. Turn off the heat and put the lid on.

Put the brisket in the oven to braise for 3 to 4 hours, until fork-tender. To test for doneness, remove the lid from the Dutch oven, insert a fork into the brisket, and turn it slightly; if the meat pulls apart with very little effort, it's done. Remove the brisket from the oven, uncover, and allow the brisket to rest in the liquid for 20 to 30 minutes.

While the brisket is braising, to make the salsa verde, combine the oregano, mint, capers, lemon juice, kosher salt, and red pepper flakes in a medium bowl. Use a fine Microplane to grate the garlic into the bowl and stir to combine. Gradually add the finishing-quality olive oil, stirring constantly. Before serving, transfer the salsa verde to a small pretty bowl. →

1 tablespoon light or dark brown sugar

1 teaspoon red pepper flakes

1 teaspoon ground ginger

For Cooking the Brisket

2 tablespoons olive oil

1 large yellow Spanish onion, peeled and quartered, root to tip

1 carrot, cut into 1-inch pieces

2 heads garlic, peeled and sliced in half through the middle

1 tablespoon double-concentrated tomato paste

3 cups dry red wine

3 cups beer (preferably lager, or another medium-bodied beer)

2 cups Chicken Stock (page 159; or sodium-free or low-sodium store-bought)

2 fresh rosemary sprigs

2 bay leaves (preferably fresh)

For the Salsa Verde

¼ cup finely chopped fresh oregano leaves

1 tablespoon finely chopped fresh mint leaves

1 tablespoon capers (preferably salt-packed), soaked for 15 minutes if salt-packed, rinsed, drained, and finely chopped

2 teaspoons fresh lemon juice, plus more to taste

2 teaspoons kosher salt, plus more to taste

½ teaspoon red pepper flakes

2 large garlic cloves, peeled

¼ cup finishing-quality extra-virgin olive oil

To make the horseradish crème fraîche, put the crème fraîche, prepared horseradish, and freshly grated horseradish in a small bowl and stir to combine. Add the kosher salt, black pepper, lemon juice, Tabasco, and Worcestershire sauce and stir to combine. Add more lemon juice or kosher salt to taste. Before serving, transfer the horseradish crème fraîche to a small pretty bowl.

To serve, remove the brisket from the liquid and place it, fat side down, on a cutting board. Place a mesh strainer over a large saucepan and strain the braising liquid into the saucepan, pressing on the solids to extract as much liquid as possible; discard the solids. Warm the liquid over medium-high heat. Cut the brisket into ½-inch-thick slices against the grain. (To see the grain, press down lightly on the meat and look closely; you will see the fibers of meat running in one direction. That is the grain. By slicing the meat against the grain, you are cutting through those fibers, which makes the meat more tender.) Slide the knife under the slices and place them on an extra-large platter, fanning them out to cover the platter. Spoon 1 cup of the warm braising liquid over them and crush the flaky sea salt between your fingertips over the meat. (Reserve the remaining braising liquid to make soup another time.) Serve with the bowls of horseradish crème fraîche and salsa verde on the side.

For the Horseradish Crème Fraîche

2 cups crème fraîche (preferably Bellwether Farms sheep's milk crème fraîche)

¼ cup plus 1 tablespoon drained and packed Atomic Extra Hot Horseradish Sauce

2 tablespoons fresh grated horseradish (from a 2- to 2½-inch piece, peeled and grated on a coarse Microplane)

2 teaspoons kosher salt, plus more to taste

1 teaspoon fresh coarsely ground black pepper

1 teaspoon fresh lemon juice, plus more to taste

1 teaspoon Tabasco sauce

1 teaspoon Worcestershire sauce

To Serve

Flaky sea salt

Chicken Stock

Makes about 2 quarts (8 cups)

We make this chicken stock with feet and wings. Both are high in collagen, which makes the stock gelatinous and in turn gives the sauces made with it body and sheen. Chicken wings are available anywhere chicken is sold. You can find chicken feet in any butcher shop and many specialty food stores.

Put the chicken, onion, carrot, celery, and peppercorns in a tall stockpot. Add 4 quarts (16 cups) water or enough to cover by 1 inch and bring the water to a boil over high heat. Reduce the heat to low to maintain a gentle simmer and simmer for 2 hours, skimming off any foam that rises to the top. Turn off the heat and let the stock cool slightly.

Put a mesh strainer over a large pot or bowl and strain the stock, pressing on the solids to extract as much liquid as possible. Discard the solids. Use the stock, or let it cool to room temperature, transfer to a covered container, and refrigerate for as long as 3 days; or freeze for as long as 3 months.

5 pounds chicken feet, chicken wings, or a combination

1 large yellow Spanish onion, peeled and roughly chopped

1 large carrot, roughly chopped

1 celery stalk, roughly chopped

1 tablespoon black peppercorns

Pepper Steak "Dal Rae"

Serves 4

If a party of two comes in to Chi Spacca and they want steak, the Bistecca Fiorentina (page 134) may be too big, so I wanted to put a smaller steak on the menu. I didn't want to just offer a New York steak and simply grill it. I wanted to do something special, so I reached far back into my memory and recalled how much I loved the pepper steak that I used to eat at Dal Rae Restaurant in Pico Rivera, in southeastern L.A. County, where I've been going since the early 1980s. A pepper-crusted steak with a bacon-scallion "salad" piled on top, it's a very dramatic presentation and it couldn't be more delicious. You can cook these steaks on an outdoor grill or inside, in a cast-iron skillet or grill pan. If you have a two-burner rectangular griddle, you can cook all of the steaks at one time.

Ask your butcher for boneless New York steaks, dry-aged, if you like.

To season the steaks, put the peppercorns in a mortar or spice grinder and very coarsely grind them.

Place the steaks in a large baking dish or on a cutting board. Pour the olive oil over them and with your hands massage to coat the steaks all over with the oil. Sprinkle the salt and half of the pepper evenly over the steaks. Use the meat to mop up the fallen salt and pepper and press the salt and pepper into the meat with your hands to adhere. Set the steaks aside for at least 30 minutes to come to room temperature.

To make the bacon topping, adjust the oven rack to the center position and preheat the oven to 350°F.

Place the bacon on a baking sheet and cook it in the oven for 16 to 20 minutes, until it is cooked but not crisp, rotating the baking sheet from front to back halfway through that time so the bacon cooks evenly. Meanwhile, create a bed of paper towels. Remove the bacon from the oven and transfer it to the paper towels to drain. Chop the bacon into ¼-inch pieces and put them in a medium bowl.

Trim and discard the hairy root ends from the scallions and slice the scallions (both the white and green parts) into ¼-inch-thick rings. →

To Season the Steaks

½ cup black peppercorns

4 (1-inch-thick) New York steaks (about 12 ounces each)

¼ cup olive oil

2 teaspoons kosher salt

For the Bacon Topping

2 ounces applewood-smoked slab bacon, cut into ½-inch cubes (or thick-sliced applewood-smoked bacon)

4 bunches large scallions

4 tablespoons (½ stick) unsalted butter

3 large garlic cloves, peeled and finely chopped

2 tablespoons finely chopped fresh Italian parsley leaves

1 teaspoon kosher salt

¼ cup olive oil

Melt the butter in a large saucepan over medium-high heat. Add the scallions and garlic and cook for 10 minutes, stirring frequently, until the scallions are soft. Add the cooked bacon, the parsley, salt, and the remaining cracked pepper. Add the oil, stir to combine, and cook for 2 to 3 minutes, until the bacon is warmed through. Turn off the heat.

If you are grilling the steaks, prepare a hot fire in a wood-burning or charcoal grill or preheat a gas grill for high heat. (For detailed instructions, see Ryan's Chi Spacca Grilling Class, page 27.)

If you are cooking the steaks in a skillet or a grill pan, heat 2 tablespoons of the olive oil in a large cast-iron skillet over high heat for 2 to 3 minutes, until the oil slides easily and is smoking around the edges of the pan. If you're using a two-burner griddle, heat all of the oil. (You won't need the oil if you are cooking the steaks on the grill or in a grill pan.)

Add the steaks to the grill, skillet, or grill pan; if you are using a skillet, add only 2 of the steaks. Sear for 3 to 4 minutes, until the steaks are deeply caramelized and a crust has formed on the surface. Turn the steaks and cook the second sides for 2 to 3 minutes, until an instant-read thermometer reads 115°F when inserted into the deepest part of the steaks for medium-rare. Remove the steaks from the pan and place them on a large platter. If you're using a skillet, wipe the pan clean with paper towels and add the remaining 2 tablespoons olive oil to the pan. Heat it for 30 seconds to 1 minute, until it just begins to smoke. Add the remaining 2 steaks and cook them as you did the first two. When they are done, place the steaks on the platter with the first two steaks.

To serve, spoon the bacon topping onto the steaks, dividing it evenly, and sprinkle with the chives.

To Cook and Serve the Steaks

½ cup olive oil (only if you are cooking the steaks in a skillet or grill pan)

2 tablespoons finely chopped fresh chives

Milk-Braised Veal Breast with Hazelnuts

Serves 4 to 6

Veal breast is a cut that refers to the veal belly, which is fatty and flavorful. Where veal is normally expensive, the breast is very reasonably priced. The first chef I ever worked for, Bobby Miller, at 464 Magnolia, in Marin County, used to make veal breast that he stuffed with sausage and sewed closed. I had never seen such a large slab of meat before that, and I was so impressed! For veal lovers, the breast is like a best-kept secret. Now I guess the secret's out.

For the hazelnuts in this recipe, we use ones from Trufflebert Farm in Oregon, which are big and flavorful and, in my opinion, the best hazelnuts in the world. This recipe calls for homemade chicken stock, which doesn't contain any sodium. If the stock you are using does contain sodium, cut the salt in this recipe by half. The finished veal is seasoned with fennel pollen, a fragrant powder harvested from wild fennel in the hillsides of Tuscany and Umbria. You can find it at specialty food markets and online sources (see Sources, page 357).

Ask your butcher to debone, roll, and tie the veal breast; the trickiest part of this recipe, which appears in the first step, will be done for you.

You will need an extra-large platter to serve the veal breast.

To prepare the veal breast, place it on a large baking sheet, sprinkle 1 tablespoon plus 1 teaspoon of the salt and the pepper evenly over both sides. If your butcher did not roll and tie the breast for you, cut 8 (20-inch) lengths of butcher's twine. Roll the breast tightly lengthwise into a log shape and tie it at 1-inch intervals with the twine. Cover the baking sheet with plastic wrap and refrigerate overnight or for at least 6 hours.

Remove the veal breast from the refrigerator and let it rest for 30 minutes to 1 hour to come to room temperature.

Adjust the oven rack to the center position and preheat the oven to 325°F.

Spread the hazelnuts on a large baking sheet and toast them in the oven until they are fragrant and toasted, 12 to 15 minutes, gently shaking the baking sheet and rotating it from front to back halfway through that time so the nuts brown evenly. Remove the baking sheet from the oven →

For Seasoning the Veal

1 boneless veal breast (about 4 pounds), deboned, rolled, and tied

1 tablespoon plus 2 teaspoons kosher salt

2 teaspoons fresh coarsely ground black pepper

2 cups hazelnuts

¼ cup plus 1 tablespoon olive oil

1 large yellow Spanish onion, peeled and roughly chopped

6 large garlic cloves, peeled and roughly chopped

4 cups whole milk

and set it aside until the nuts are cool enough to touch. Gather the hazelnuts into a clean dish towel and rub them together inside the towel to remove the skins. Discard the skins. Transfer the nuts to a cutting board and crush them with the back of a pan or coarsely chop them so that each nut breaks into a few pieces. Transfer the nuts to a small bowl.

Reduce the oven temperature to 300°F.

Heat ¼ cup of the olive oil in an extra-large Dutch oven over medium-high heat for 2 to 3 minutes, until the oil slides easily and is smoking around the edges of the pan. Place the veal breast in the Dutch oven and sear it for 10 to 12 minutes, until it is deeply caramelized on both sides. Remove the veal from the pan and return it to the baking sheet. Add the onion and garlic to the Dutch oven, sprinkle with the remaining 1 teaspoon salt, and cook them over medium heat for 6 to 8 minutes, until the onion is soft and light golden, stirring often so the onion or garlic doesn't brown. Return the veal breast to the Dutch oven. Add the milk, pouring it around not over the veal so you don't rinse off the seared exterior. Pour the chicken stock around the veal, adding as much as needed to come to the top of the veal but not submerge it. Add the rosemary and 1 cup of the hazelnuts. Increase the heat to high and bring the liquid to a boil. Turn off the heat and put the lid on the Dutch oven.

Put the veal in the oven to braise for 2½ to 3 hours, until fork-tender. To test for doneness, remove the lid from the Dutch oven, insert a fork into the veal, and turn it slightly; if the meat pulls apart with very little effort, it's done. Remove the veal from the oven, uncover, and allow the veal breast to rest in the liquid for 20 to 30 minutes.

While the veal is braising, to fry the sage, pour enough oil into a small saucepan to fill it 1½ to 2 inches deep. Fasten a deep-fry thermometer, if you have one, to the side of the pan, and heat the oil over medium-high heat until the thermometer registers 350°F or a pinch of salt sizzles when dropped into the oil. While the oil is heating, create a bed of paper towels and have a slotted spoon or mesh strainer handy. Turn off the heat, add the sage leaves, and fry for about 30 seconds, until the leaves are crispy but not brown. Use the slotted spoon or strainer to lift the sage leaves out of the pan and transfer them to the paper towels to drain. Sprinkle with the salt. Let the oil cool and strain it into a container; cover and reserve the oil to cook with another time.

2 cups Chicken Stock (page 159; or sodium-free or low-sodium store-bought), or as needed

2 fresh rosemary sprigs

For the Sage

2 cups olive oil, or as needed

½ cup fresh sage leaves

½ teaspoon kosher salt

For Serving

Finishing-quality extra-virgin olive oil

1 tablespoon fennel pollen

Remove the veal breast from the braising liquid and place it on a cutting board. Put a mesh strainer over a medium saucepan and strain the braising ingredients, pressing on the solids to extract as much liquid as possible. Discard the solids. Bring the liquid to a boil over high heat. Reduce the heat to medium-low and simmer for 10 to 15 minutes, until the liquid is thick enough to coat the back of a spoon.

To serve, snip off and discard the butcher's twine and slice the veal breast into 1-inch-thick disks. Transfer the veal slices to an extra-large platter, arranging them in a ring formation if you are using a round or oval platter, or in a line down the length of a rectangular platter, overlapping the slices slightly. Spoon the sauce over the slices and use the back of a spoon to dress the slices with the sauce, leaving the edges of the meat visible. Drizzle about ¼ cup finishing-quality olive oil over the veal and sprinkle the veal with the fennel pollen. Scatter the remaining hazelnuts and the fried sage leaves over and around the veal.

Porcini-Rubbed Double-Bone Veal Chops
with Roasted Onions and Brown Butter Jus

Serves 4

A double-bone veal chop is a tender, juicy, luxurious cut of meat. In this preparation, we coat the meat in porcini rub, which gives it an umami flavor, and then cook it in brown butter on a bed of sweet onions. It's such a simple dish, and so good.

Ask your butcher for four double-bone, Frenched veal loin chops. A "Frenched" bone refers to a bone with the meat cut off of it, leaving you with a thick loin with two long, dramatic, rib bones attached.

You will need an extra-large platter to serve the chops.

To prepare the veal chops, adjust the oven rack to the center position and preheat the oven to 300°F.

Place the chops on a baking sheet or cutting board and sprinkle 1 tablespoon of the porcini rub over each chop. Use the meat to mop up the fallen rub and massage with your hands to thoroughly coat the chops with the rub. Set aside for 30 minutes to 1 hour to let the seasonings penetrate the veal and for the veal to come to room temperature.

Keeping the rings of onion intact as much as possible, lay them and the garlic cloves in the bottom of a large roasting pan. Sprinkle with the remaining porcini rub and lay the veal chops on top, leaving space between each chop so they cook evenly. Place a piece of butter on each chop.

Roast the veal in the oven for 15 minutes. Remove the pan from the oven, flip the chops, and return them to the oven to roast for 15 minutes. Remove the veal chops from the oven. Use a large spoon to spoon the melted butter and juices out of the roasting pan into a small saucepan. Return the chops to the oven to cook for about 10 minutes, until an instant-read thermometer inserted deep into the chop registers 115°F. Remove the veal from the oven.

4 (1-inch-thick) bone-in double-bone veal loin chops (about 1 pound each)

1 recipe Porcini Rub (page 22)

2 large red onions, peeled and sliced into ¼-inch-thick rings

16 large garlic cloves, peeled

8 tablespoons (1 stick) unsalted butter, cut into 4 equal pieces

Flaky sea salt

Meanwhile, heat the juices and butter from the pan over medium heat to brown the butter, swirling the pan occasionally so the butter cooks evenly. Cook until the foam that develops has subsided and the butter is coffee colored and has a toasted aroma, about 10 minutes. Turn off the heat and scrape the bottom to release the solids.

To serve, remove the veal chops from the pan. Arrange the onions and garlic on a large platter and nestle the veal chops on top. Spoon the brown butter jus over the chops and crush about 1 teaspoon flaky sea salt between your fingertips over them.

Pork

Grilled Tomahawk Pork Chop
with Fennel Pollen

Serves 4

Every restaurant needs at least one dish that people are willing to drive across town for, and this enormous, Flintstone-esque cut of pork, along with the Beef Cheek and Bone Marrow Pie (page 149), is that item at Chi Spacca. New customers come in just to try it, and our regular customers come in with it on their minds. It's a thick, double-cut pork loin (the cut you most often see in the form of pork chops), perfectly cooked to medium-rare, attached to two very long rib bones. Normally when you see a tomahawk, whether at a butcher shop or in a restaurant, that belly meat has been stripped from the bone; the long bone is just there for looks, but these rib bones still have the belly meat attached. After cooking the chop, we put the ribs back on the grill to crisp up the fatty belly. We slice the belly and then serve the bones on the side. I love to see customers gnawing every last bit of meat off the bone, which is the first thing I do when I get a bone. (You don't need me to tell you that that's the best part!) The finished pork is seasoned with fennel pollen, a fragrant powder harvested from wild fennel that grows on the hillsides of Tuscany and Umbria. You can find it at specialty food markets and online sources. (See Sources, page 357.)

We brine this chop before grilling it. *Brining* refers to infusing meat with a solution usually consisting of water and either salt or a combination of salt and sugar. You can brine meat by soaking it in the solution or by injecting the solution into the meat. (We do the latter.) Brining tenderizes the meat, makes it juicier, and also seasons it on the inside. It is especially important with thick cuts of meat where the seasoning on the outside will have no effect whatsoever on the inside, and pork, in particular, which can tend to be dry. To brine this chop, you will need a flavor injector, an inexpensive gadget that is available wherever cooking supplies are sold.

Ask your butcher for a double-bone pork loin chop with the rib and belly attached (about 42 ounces). If you can't find a butcher who will cut a tomahawk for you, use two thick-cut pork porterhouse chops (or other thick-cut, bone-in pork chops) instead.

You will need an extra-large platter to serve the chop on. →

To prepare the pork, place it on a large baking sheet. Combine the kosher salt, sugar, and ¼ cup water in a small bowl to make a brine and whisk to dissolve the salt and sugar. Fill the flavor syringe with the brine. Inject half of the brine into the belly of the pork and half into the center of the loin and pat the pork dry with paper towels. Pour the olive oil over the pork and with your hands massage to coat all parts of the chop. Sprinkle the fennel rub evenly over the pork. Use the meat to mop up any fallen rub and press the rub into the meat with your hands to adhere. Set aside for 30 minutes to 1 hour to let the seasonings penetrate the pork and for the pork to come to room temperature.

Prepare a wood, charcoal, or gas grill for direct and indirect heat. (For detailed instructions, see Ryan's Chi Spacca Grilling Class, page 27.)

Place the chop on the direct heat and grill until it is deeply caramelized with black grill marks on both sides, 5 to 8 minutes per side. Move the chop to the indirect-heat side of the grill and set it on its edge with the fatty, rounded side facing down; point the rib toward the indirect heat and the loin toward the direct heat. Cook the chop on its side for 30 to 40 minutes, until an instant-read thermometer inserted deep into the center of the loin reads 120°F. (If you are cooking another cut of pork chop, cook the chops over the direct heat for the same amount of time. Transfer them and rest them on the bone—if they are porterhouse—or on their side, to the indirect heat and cook until the thermometer reaches 120°F; begin checking the temperature after 15 minutes to avoid overcooking the chops.)

Transfer the pork chop to a cutting board to rest for about 10 minutes.

Turn the chop on its back with the fat side facing up. Put your knife where the loin begins (about 4 inches from the top of the loin) and cut through to the bone. Turn the knife and cut along the bone to separate it from the loin. Set it aside.

Cut between the two rib bones to separate them. Return the ribs, cut sides down, to the direct heat and grill for 3 to 4 minutes, until the belly meat is golden brown and crispy. Transfer the rib bones to the cutting board.

For the Pork

1 double-bone pork loin chop, bone-in, belly attached (about 42 ounces; or 2 thick-cut pork porterhouse or other bone-in pork chops)

1½ teaspoons kosher salt

1½ teaspoons sugar

2 tablespoons olive oil

1 recipe Fennel Rub (page 20)

For Serving

¼ cup plus 2 tablespoons finishing-quality extra-virgin olive oil

Flaky sea salt

1 tablespoon fennel pollen

To serve, slice the loin ½ inch thick. Slide the knife under the meat to keep the slices intact and transfer them to an extra-large platter, fanning them out to cover the platter.

With your knife parallel to the rib bone, cut between the belly and the bone to slice the belly off of each bone. Slice the belly ½ inch thick. One at a time, slide the knife under the sliced belly and transfer the slices to the platter, fanning them out. Rest the rib bones against the sliced loin like a pair of crossed legs. Drizzle the finishing-quality olive oil and crush about 1 teaspoon flaky sea salt between your fingertips over the loin and ribs. Sprinkle with the fennel pollen. Encourage your guests to pick up the ribs and eat with their hands. Since there are only two bones, presumably for four people, you may have to pass the rib bones around and share, although if I were at the table, I may not give mine up.

Pork Tenderloin, Segreto Style,
with Lemon-Anchovy Salsa Rustica

Serves 4

Segreto, which means "secret" in Italian, is what is known as a *butcher's cut,* a term that refers to cuts that butchers save for themselves, historically because nobody wants them, or because there are so few on an animal that it would be pointless to try to sell them, so the butcher takes them home. Segreto, a small, tender and flavorful "roast" hidden inside the tough pork shoulder, is the latter. We kept the name (because who doesn't love "secret pork"), but adapted this recipe to pork tenderloin, which is easy to find.

Ask your butcher for two pork tenderloins (about 1½ pounds each). But before you do that, you might try asking for pork "segreto." He or she will probably say they don't have it, but it will start a conversation between you and your butcher, which is a good thing. Specify Kurobuta (or another heritage breed) pork. Seeking out heritage pork is especially beneficial with pork tenderloin (and loin), which has little fat and can tend to be dry. Pork from heritage breeds has more marbling and is moister and more flavorful.

You will need a large platter to serve the pork.

To prepare the pork, place the tenderloins on a large baking sheet.

Put the peppercorns in a mortar or spice grinder and very coarsely grind them.

Combine the rosemary, garlic, and ¼ cup of the olive oil in the jar of a blender and purée to make a rub.

Drizzle the remaining 2 tablespoons olive oil over the tenderloins and massage with your hands to coat the meat with the oil. Sprinkle the salt and pepper evenly over the tenderloins, dividing them evenly, and press them into the meat with your hands to adhere. Divide the rub between the 2 tenderloins and massage to coat the meat with the seasonings. Set aside for 30 minutes to 1 hour to let the seasonings penetrate the pork and for the pork to come to room temperature.

To make the salsa, cut off and discard the top and bottom of the lemon at the point where you can see the flesh. Place the lemon upright on a cutting

For the Pork

2 (1½-pound) pork tenderloins

1 tablespoon black peppercorns

¼ cup fresh rosemary

4 large garlic cloves, peeled and roughly chopped

¼ cup plus 2 tablespoons olive oil

2 tablespoons kosher salt

For the Lemon-Anchovy Salsa Rustica

1 lemon

4 Cetara anchovy fillets (or another quality, oil-packed anchovy), finely chopped

board and cut down the side at the point where the pith meets the flesh, following the natural curve of the fruit to remove the pith along with the peel. Discard the pith and peels. Turn the lemon on its side and cut along one of the membranes toward the center of the fruit. Working your way around the lemons, cut along both sides of each membrane to release all the segments from the core. Chop the segments into ½-inch pieces and put them in a medium bowl. Squeeze the core of the lemon over the bowl to extract as much juice as you can. Add the anchovies, shallot, capers, and parsley and use a fork to mash and stir the ingredients together. Gradually add the finishing-quality olive oil, stirring constantly.

Prepare a wood, charcoal, or gas grill for direct and indirect heat. (For detailed instructions, see Ryan's Chi Spacca Grilling Class, page 27.)

Place the tenderloins over the direct heat and grill for 8 to 10 minutes, until they are deeply caramelized on both sides. Move the tenderloins to the indirect-heat side of the grill and cook for about 15 minutes, rotating the loins 180 degrees every 5 minutes so they cook evenly, until an instant-read thermometer inserted deep into the side of the tenderloins reads 130°F.

Place a rack on the baking sheet the pork was resting on previously. Transfer the tenderloins to the rack to rest for 5 minutes; resting the tenderloins on a rack allows the heat to escape and prevents the tenderloins from overcooking.

To serve, transfer the tenderloins to a cutting board and slice them ½ inch thick. Slide your knife under the slices and transfer them to a large platter, fanning the slices out down the length of the platter. Spoon the salsa rustica over the pork and use the back of the spoon to dress the slices, leaving the edges of the slices visible.

1 small shallot, peeled and minced

2 tablespoons capers (preferably salt-packed), soaked for 15 minutes if salt-packed, rinsed, drained, and finely chopped

2 tablespoons roughly chopped fresh Italian parsley leaves

½ cup finishing-quality extra-virgin olive oil

Grilled Pork-and-Veal Meatballs
with Fresh Ricotta and Braised Greens

Serves 6

Ryan and I developed this meatball recipe for a collaborative dinner that we did with Franco Pepe, a great Italian chef and legendary pizza maker from Calabria, near Naples. He had created an all-pizza menu, and we wanted to serve a few dishes to go with it. We add N'duja (page 58), Calabrian spiced ground pork fat, to the meatballs and serve them with braised greens, on a bed of soft, fluffy ricotta. Look for quality fresh sheep's or cow's milk ricotta, such as Bellwether Farms Sheep Milk Basket Ricotta or Di Stefano Premium Ricotta Cheese from a cheese shop or specialty food store.

You will need a large platter to serve the meatballs.

To prepare the meatballs, toast the fennel seeds in a small skillet over medium heat for 1 to 2 minutes, until they are fragrant and toasted, shaking the pan so they don't burn. Transfer the seeds to a mortar or spice grinder and very coarsely grind them.

Combine the pork, veal, fennel seeds, n'duja, onion, parsley, oregano, sage, and rosemary in a large bowl. Using a fine Microplane, grate the garlic into the bowl. Add the salt and mix with your hands to combine the ingredients without smashing the meat. Add the ricotta, pecorino, and eggs and mix them in with your hands.

Shape the meat into 3-ounce (½-cup) meatballs, gently pressing the meat between your palms to shape the balls without crushing them. Place the balls on a large baking sheet as they are formed. Cover the baking sheet with plastic wrap and refrigerate the meatballs for at least 2 hours to chill. (Refrigerating them helps the meatballs retain their shape when they're cooked.)

While the meatballs are chilling, make the Braised Greens (page 297).

To grill the meatballs, prepare a hot fire in a wood-burning or charcoal grill or preheat a gas grill for high heat. (For detailed instructions, see Ryan's Chi Spacca Grilling Class, page 27.) →

1 teaspoon fennel seeds

1 pound ground pork

1 pound ground veal

½ pound N'duja
(page 58; or store-bought)

1 large yellow Spanish onion,
peeled and finely chopped

¼ cup finely chopped fresh
parsley leaves

¼ cup finely chopped fresh
oregano leaves

¼ cup finely chopped fresh
sage leaves

¼ cup finely chopped fresh
rosemary leaves

5 large garlic cloves, peeled

1 teaspoon kosher salt

½ cup fresh ricotta
(preferably sheep's milk)

¼ cup finely grated pecorino
Romano

Place the meatballs on the grill and grill them for 5 minutes, until the undersides are deeply caramelized with dark grill marks. Gently slide a metal spatula under the meatballs to release them from the grill and cook them on the other side until they are deeply caramelized.

To serve, while the meatballs are on the grill, spoon the ricotta onto a large platter and use the spoon to spread the ricotta toward the edges in organic, uneven swirls. Lay the greens on the ricotta, leaving the edges of the ricotta visible. Remove the meatballs from the grill, nestle them on top of the greens, and sprinkle the parsley over them.

2 extra-large eggs, lightly beaten

For Serving

Braised Greens (page 297)

1½ cups fresh ricotta (preferably sheep's milk)

1 tablespoon finely chopped fresh Italian parsley leaves

Pork al Latte with Fennel Pollen and Crispy Sage

Serves 4 to 6

Pork braised in milk is a classic Italian preparation and results in juicy, flavorful meat. There is lemon in the braising liquid, and the combination of the milk with the acid causes the milk to form curds. Ryan likes to say it looks like a failed culinary school assignment, but I think the pillowy curds look pretty in a very rustic way. This recipe calls for a pork loin, a large cut of meat that becomes tender when braised; this is not to be confused with the smaller, thinner tenderloin, which should be grilled or seared, rather than slow cooked.

We brine this roast before grilling it. *Brining* refers to infusing meat with a solution usually consisting of water and either salt or a combination of salt and sugar. You can brine meat by soaking it in the solution or by injecting the solution into the meat. (We do the latter.) Brining tenderizes the meat, makes it juicier, and also seasons it on the inside. It is especially important with thick cuts of meat where the seasoning on the outside will have no effect whatsoever on the inside, and pork in particular, which can tend to be dry. To brine this roast, you will need a flavor injector, an inexpensive gadget that is available wherever cooking supplies are sold. The finished pork is seasoned with fennel pollen, a fragrant powder harvested from wild fennel in the hillsides of Tuscany and Umbria. You can find it at specialty food markets and online sources. (See Sources, page 357.)

Ask your butcher for a (4-pound) bone-in pork loin roast with a nice fat cap. Pork loin does not have much marbling of fat in it, so the fat cap is essential.

You will need an extra-large platter to serve the pork on.

To prepare the pork, place it in a large baking dish or on a baking sheet. Combine the salt, sugar, and ¼ cup water in a small bowl to make a brine and whisk to dissolve the salt and sugar. Fill the flavor syringe with the brine. Entering through the side of the roast, inject half of the brine deep into the center of the roast. Remove the syringe and inject the remaining brine deep into the roast through the other side. Pat the roast dry with paper towels. Reserve 2 teaspoons of the fennel rub and sprinkle the remaining rub evenly over the pork. Use the meat to mop up any fallen rub and press the rub into the meat with your hands to adhere. Set →

For the Pork

1 center-cut pork loin
(about 4 pounds)

1½ teaspoons kosher salt

1½ teaspoons sugar

1 recipe Fennel Rub (page 20)

2 lemons

1½ cups whole milk,
plus more as needed

aside for 30 minutes to 1 hour to let the seasonings penetrate the pork and for the pork to come to room temperature.

Adjust the oven rack to the center position and preheat the oven to 325°F.

Cut off and discard the top and bottom of the lemons at the point where you can see the flesh. One at a time, place the lemons upright on a cutting board and cut down the sides at the point where the pith meets the flesh, following the natural curve of the fruit to remove the pith along with the peel. Discard the pith and peels. Turn the lemons on their sides and cut along one of the membranes toward the center of the fruit. Working your way around the lemons, cut along both sides of each membrane to release all the segments from the cores.

Combine the lemon segments, milk, shallots, bay leaves, and the reserved 2 teaspoons fennel rub in a large Dutch oven and stir to combine. Place the pork in the Dutch oven and add more milk if needed to come halfway up the sides of the pork. Warm the milk over medium-high heat until it begins to bubble around the edges, about 5 minutes. Turn off the heat.

Roast the pork in the oven for 45 minutes to 1 hour, until an instant-read temperature registers 125°F when inserted deep into the side of the pork. Remove the pork from the oven and set aside for 10 to 20 minutes to allow the pork to rest and for the milk to form curds as it cools.

While the pork is braising, to fry the sage, pour enough oil into a small saucepan to fill it 1½ to 2 inches deep. Fasten a deep-fry thermometer, if you have one, to the side of the pan and heat the oil over medium-high heat until the thermometer registers 350°F or a pinch of salt sizzles when dropped into the oil. While the oil is heating, create a bed of paper towels and have a slotted spoon or mesh strainer handy. Turn off the heat, add the sage leaves, and fry for about 30 seconds, until the leaves are crispy but not brown. Use the slotted spoon or strainer to lift the sage leaves out of the pan and transfer them to the paper towels to drain. Sprinkle with the salt. Let the oil cool and strain it into a container; cover and reserve the oil to cook with another time.

2 medium shallots, peeled and sliced ¼ inch thick lengthwise

2 bay leaves (preferably fresh)

For the Sage

2 cups olive oil, or as needed

½ cup fresh sage leaves

½ teaspoon kosher salt

For Serving

1 tablespoon fennel pollen

Remove the pork loin from the Dutch oven and place it on a cutting board with the bones facing up.

Using a slotted spoon, gently scoop the curds out of the pan, letting the liquid drain for a few seconds before gently dropping the curds onto an extra-large platter. When you have harvested all of the curds, slice the pork. With your knife parallel to and resting alongside the rib bones, slide your knife down the bones to release the loin, leaving as little meat on the bones as possible. Slice the loin ½ inch thick. Slide your knife under the slices and lay them fanned out over the curds so the curds are peeking out around the slices. Cut between the rib bones and pile them on the platter for people to gnaw on. Drizzle the liquid left in the pan over and around the pork slices and bones to moisten them. Sprinkle the fennel pollen and scatter the sage leaves over the pork.

Parmesan Soufflé with Ragù Bolognese

Serves 4

This recipe dates back to the early days at Chi Spacca, when it was a cooking school and event space. We were playing with the idea of turning the space into a restaurant, and we started by hosting family-style dinners one night a week. Each week, we celebrated a different ingredient, which we featured in every dish. For our pork-themed dinner, Matt Molina and Chad Colby, Chi Spacca's founding chefs, were looking for creative ways to incorporate pork into the menu without having it all be steaks and chops. Matt came up with this presentation of Parmesan soufflé with Bolognese spooned over it. Ragù served over polenta is nothing unusual, but this is an inventive, playful extension of that idea. A soufflé isn't difficult to make, but you want to time it right so you can serve it straight from the oven, because it will collapse over time. I suggest you make the ragù a day or two in advance. It starts with a long-cooked soffritto, the combination of onion, carrots, and celery that is the bedrock of Italian slow cooking, so from beginning to end, the ragù takes about five hours to cook.

This recipe calls for homemade chicken stock, which doesn't contain any sodium. If the stock you are using does contain sodium, cut the salt in this recipe by half.

You will need a 12- × 7-inch oval ceramic baking dish (or another baking dish with a 12-cup capacity) to make and serve the soufflé, and a medium serving bowl to serve the ragù Bolognese.

To make the ragù Bolognese, heat 1½ cups of the olive oil in a large sauté pan over medium-high heat for 2 to 3 minutes, until the oil slides easily and is smoking around the edges of the pan. Add the onions, carrots, and celery, reduce the heat to medium, and cook for 30 minutes, stirring often, until the vegetables are tender and translucent. Reduce the heat to low and cook for 2 to 3 hours, stirring often, until the vegetables are dark brown and have almost completely broken down into a paste. Transfer the soffritto (vegetables) to a bowl. Add the remaining 2 tablespoons olive oil and heat it until it slides easily and is smoking around the edges of the pan. Add the pancetta and garlic, reduce the heat to medium, and cook for 5 minutes, stirring often, until the fat from the pancetta has rendered (melted) and the garlic is golden brown. Return

For the Ragù Bolognese

1½ cups plus 2 tablespoons olive oil

3 large yellow Spanish onions (about 1 pound), peeled and finely chopped

2 large carrots, finely chopped

5 celery stalks, finely chopped

¼ pound pancetta, cut into ½-inch pieces

1 head garlic (about 10 cloves), peeled and finely chopped

the soffritto to the pan and cook for 2 to 3 minutes, stirring occasionally, to cook the vegetables in the pancetta fat. Move the vegetables and pancetta to one side of the pan. Add the tomato paste to the space created and cook for about 2 minutes to caramelize the tomato paste, stirring constantly so it doesn't burn.

Add the ground veal and pork, sprinkle the salt, black pepper, and nutmeg over it, and stir to distribute the seasonings. Cook over medium heat for 10 to 15 minutes, until the juices from the meat have cooked off, leaving the pan almost dry. Add the white wine and cook for about 10 minutes, until it is almost all evaporated. Add about one-third of the chicken stock, reduce the heat to low, and cook the ragù for about 2 hours, adding the remaining chicken stock in thirds, until the last of the chicken stock has cooked off. Stir in the milk and cook for another 30 minutes, until the ragù has a thick, saucy consistency. Turn off the heat. If you are making the ragù to serve another day, let it cool to room temperature, then transfer it to a covered container and refrigerate until you're ready to serve it.

To make the soufflé, adjust the oven rack to the center position and preheat the oven to 425°F.

Butter the bottom and sides of a 12-inch (or another 12-cup-capacity) baking dish.

Separate 3 of the eggs, dropping the whites into the bowl of a stand mixer and the yolks into a separate large bowl. Separate the remaining 5 eggs, adding the whites to the mixer bowl with the other whites and reserving the remaining 5 yolks to use another time. (You will use all 8 egg whites, but only 3 egg yolks.)

Add the Parmesan to the bowl with the egg yolks and whisk to combine.

Combine the butter, onion, árbol chile, and bay leaves in a medium saucepan and cook over medium heat until the onion is tender and translucent, about 10 minutes, stirring often to prevent the onion from browning. Add the flour and cook until the mixture begins to bubble, about 3 minutes, whisking constantly. Gradually add the milk and cream, whisking constantly. Increase the heat to high and bring the sauce to a boil, stirring constantly with the whisk. Reduce the heat to low and cook for 3 to 4 minutes, stirring constantly, until the sauce is thick enough to coat the back of a spoon. Turn off the heat, place a mesh strainer over →

¼ cup double-concentrated tomato paste

1 pound ground veal

1 pound ground pork

1 teaspoon kosher salt

½ teaspoon fresh coarsely ground black pepper

¼ teaspoon freshly grated nutmeg (grated with a fine Microplane or a nutmeg grater from a whole nutmeg)

1 cup dry white wine

3 cups Chicken Stock (page 159, or sodium-free or low-sodium store-bought), plus more as needed

1 cup whole milk

For the Soufflé

4 tablespoons (½ stick) unsalted butter, plus more for buttering the baking dish

8 extra-large eggs

¾ cup finely grated Parmesan

½ large yellow Spanish onion, peeled and cut into ½-inch dice

1 árbol chile

2 bay leaves (preferably fresh)

¼ cup all-purpose flour

1½ cups whole milk

1½ cups heavy cream

1 teaspoon kosher salt

⅛ teaspoon cayenne pepper

⅛ teaspoon freshly grated nutmeg (grated with a fine Microplane or a nutmeg grater from a whole nutmeg)

¼ teaspoon fresh coarsely ground black pepper

a medium bowl, and strain the sauce into the bowl. Add the salt, cayenne, nutmeg, and black papper, and stir to combine. Gradually add ½ cup of the warm cream sauce to the bowl with the egg yolks and cheese, stirring constantly with the whisk to prevent the hot liquid from cooking the eggs. Add another cup or ladleful of the cream sauce, stirring constantly. Gradually add the contents of the bowl back to the saucepan with the remaining sauce, stirring as you add it.

Put the mixer bowl with the egg whites on the stand and fit the mixer with the whisk attachment. Beat the egg whites on high speed for 2 to 3 minutes, until they reach stiff peaks. (When you lift the whisk out of the bowl and turn it upside down, stiff peaks will stand up, not droop over.) Remove the bowl from the stand. Add one-quarter of the egg whites to the saucepan with the sauce and use a rubber spatula to stir it in with the eggs until they are completely combined. Add the remaining egg whites, folding them to combine.

Pour the soufflé batter into the baking dish and smooth out the top. Place the baking dish in a roasting pan and add enough water to reach halfway up the sides of the dish and place the pan in the oven. Bake the soufflé for 20 to 25 minutes, until it has tripled in size and the top is a deep golden brown. Remove the roasting pan from the oven and carefully remove the baking dish.

To serve, while the soufflé is baking, warm the Bolognese in a saucepan (or the pan you cooked it in) over medium heat, stirring occasionally, adding chicken stock or water as needed to give it a thick but spoonable consistency. Transfer the Bolognese ragù to a medium serving bowl and serve with a large spoon. Serve the soufflé with a second large spoon for people to serve themselves, scooping large mounds of soufflé onto their plate, and topping it with a generous helping of Bolognese. Using a fine Microplane, grate a generous layer of Parmesan over the Bolognese.

For Serving

A chunk of Parmesan for grating

Pork Tonnato with Crispy Capers

Serves 4

Veal tonnato is an unlikely dish of cold, sliced, roasted veal topped with a sauce that is, essentially, a loose aioli with tuna mixed in. It is a classic dish from Piedmonte, in northern Italy. Although the plating sometimes varies, until recently, the dish never strayed from veal. The first time I ever saw tonnato made with pork was at Jonathan Waxman's iconic New York restaurant Barbuto. I thought, "Wow! That's unusual." But it also made sense, because pork, like veal, has a mild flavor and buttery texture. If you were to close your eyes and take a bite of each one, I'm not sure you could even tell the difference. We poach our own tuna, which is very easy to do, but you could also make this with quality, oil-packed bottled or canned tuna.

Ask your butcher for Kurobuta (or another heritage breed) pork. Seeking out heritage pork is especially beneficial with pork loin (and tenderloin), which has little fat and can tend to be dry. Pork from heritage breeds has more marbling and is moister and more flavorful.

This recipe calls for you to make the tomato sauce in a mini food processor. To make it by hand, see Making Aioli by Hand (page 104).

You will need a large platter to serve the pork tonnato.

To prepare the pork, adjust the oven rack to the center position and preheat the oven to 450°F.

Place the pork in a baking dish or on a baking sheet. Reserve 1 tablespoon of the fennel rub and sprinkle the remaining rub evenly over the pork. Use the meat to mop up any rub that falls onto the dish or baking sheet and let the pork rest at room temperature for at least 30 minutes and up to 1 hour.

Put the pork in the oven to roast for 10 minutes. Reduce the oven temperature to 250°F and roast the pork for 20 to 30 minutes, until an instant-read thermometer reads 125°F when inserted deep into the center of the loin. Remove the pork from the oven and set aside to come to room temperature. Wrap the pork tightly in plastic wrap and refrigerate for at least 2 hours to chill.

Preheat the oven to 350°F. →

For the Pork

1 (1½-pound) boneless pork loin

1 recipe Fennel Rub (page 20)

For the Poached Tuna

8 ounces (2-inch-thick) albacore tuna

1½ teaspoons kosher salt

1 teaspoon fresh coarsely ground black pepper

2 tablespoons champagne vinegar (or white wine vinegar)

1 bay leaf (preferably fresh)

1 large garlic clove, peeled and sliced ⅛ inch thick lengthwise

1 árbol chile

Place the tuna in a saucepan just large enough to hold it. Sprinkle the kosher salt and pepper evenly over both sides of the tuna and set aside for 30 minutes to come to room temperature.

Add the vinegar, bay leaf, garlic, árbol chile, and rosemary to the saucepan with the tuna. Use a vegetable peeler to peel the bright yellow outer layer of zest from the lemon and add the zest to the baking dish. Slice the lemons into ¼-inch rounds. Remove the seeds and add the lemons to the baking dish. Add enough olive oil to cover the tuna.

Put the tuna in the oven to poach, uncovered, for 25 to 35 minutes, until a thermometer inserted into the deepest part of the tuna reaches 120°F. Remove the baking dish from the oven and set aside to allow the tuna and oil to cool to room temperature.

Set a mesh strainer over a medium bowl. Remove the tuna from the baking dish and place it in a medium bowl. Strain the oil into the bowl. Discard the contents of the strainer. Reserve 1 cup of the oil to make the tonnato sauce. Reserve the rest of the oil for another use where the flavor of fish is welcome.

To fry the capers, pour enough olive oil into a small saucepan to fill it 1½ to 2 inches deep. Fasten a deep-fry thermometer, if you have one, to the side of the pan, and heat the oil over medium-high heat until the thermometer registers 350°F or a pinch of salt sizzles when dropped into the oil. While the oil is heating, create a bed of paper towels and have a small mesh strainer or slotted spoon handy. Turn off the heat, add the capers, and fry them for 30 seconds, until the buds open up. Use the strainer to lift the capers out of the oil and transfer them to the paper towels to drain. Let the oil cool and strain it into a container; cover and reserve the oil to cook with another time.

To make the tonnato sauce, combine the egg yolk and kosher salt in the bowl of a mini food processor fitted with a metal blade. Finely chop the anchovies with a large knife, use the flat side of the knife to smash them into a paste, and add the paste to the bowl of the mini food processor. Using a fine Microplane, grate the garlic into the food processor bowl and pulse to combine the ingredients. With the machine running, begin adding the extra-virgin olive oil through the lid of the food processor, blending continuously, until the oil and egg are emulsified and creamy looking; you will have added about ¼ cup of the oil. Turn off the machine, take off

1 fresh rosemary sprig

1 lemon

1¼ cups olive oil, or as needed

For the Capers

2 cups olive oil, or as needed

2 tablespoons capers (preferably salt-packed), soaked for 15 minutes if salt-packed, rinsed and drained

For the Tonnato Sauce

1 extra-large egg yolk, at room temperature

½ teaspoon kosher salt, plus more to taste

4 anchovy fillets (preferably salt-packed; rinsed and backbones removed if salt-packed)

1 large garlic clove, peeled

1 cup extra-virgin olive oil (if you poached your own tuna, use the oil you poached the tuna in)

2 tablespoons fresh lemon juice, plus more to taste

1 tablespoon capers (preferably salt-packed), soaked for 15 minutes if salt-packed, rinsed and drained

½ teaspoon fresh coarsely ground black pepper

For Serving

1 cup arugula (preferably wild arugula)

Finishing-quality extra-virgin olive oil

Flaky sea salt

the lid, scrape down the sides of the bowl with a rubber spatula, and add one-third of the lemon juice. Return the lid and pulse to combine. Add the remaining ¾ cup oil in a slow, steady drizzle, adding the remaining lemon juice when the aioli gets very thick. Turn off the machine, remove the lid, and add half of the tuna. Purée the tuna with the aioli and transfer it to a medium bowl, scraping down the sides of the food processor bowl. Stir in the capers and pepper. Add more kosher salt or lemon juice to taste. Flake the remaining tuna into the bowl in roughly ½-inch pieces and stir gently to combine.

To serve, remove the pork from the refrigerator, unwrap it, and place it on a cutting board. Slice the pork loin as thinly as possible.

Spoon 1 cup of the tonnato sauce onto a large platter and use the back of the spoon to spread it toward the edges of the platter in organic, uneven swirls. Slide your knife under the slices and transfer them to the platter, fanning them out over the tonnato sauce. Spoon the remaining tonnato sauce over the pork slices and use the back of the spoon to dress the slices with the sauce, leaving the edges of the slices visible. Scatter the arugula leaves unevenly over the pork slices. Drizzle about 2 tablespoons finishing-quality olive oil over the pork and arugula, making sure the undressed edges of the slices get oiled. Crush about 1 teaspoon flaky sea salt between your fingertips and scatter the fried capers over the pork and arugula.

Pork Shoulder Blade Chops with Chipotle and Apple Cider Syrup

Serves 4

Many of the cuts of pork that we offer at Chi Spacca are the result of our wanting to use the entire animal. This recipe is borne of that goal. The shoulder blade chop, which comes, obviously, from the shoulder, fulfills the expectations of a typical pork chop, which comes from the loin. Putting a cut like this on the menu introduces our customers not just to a cut they might not already know, but to the idea that there is a whole world of animal cuts out there, many of which they may not have tried. If you want to use the more widely known pork loin chops for this recipe, they will work, too.

If we were playing a game of what-goes-with-what, and you said, "Pork," I'd say, "Apples." The apple flavor is incorporated here in the form of an apple cider syrup that we glaze these chops with, something that also satisfies my love of acidic foods. We use Carr's Ciderhouse Cider Syrup, an artisanal product from the Berkshires that my friend the food writer Ruth Reichl introduced me to when I was at her house in Hudson, New York. I liked it so much that she sent me home with a bottle. If you don't want to seek out that product, we have provided a recipe for making a glaze using standard apple cider vinegar. Chipotle chiles are dried, smoked jalapeño chiles; they have a wonderful, deeply smoky flavor. If you can't find chipotle chile powder, use sweet smoked paprika or another quality chile powder.

Ask your butcher for 2 (¾-inch-thick) pork shoulder blade chops, about 1 pound each.

You will need a large platter to serve the chops.

To make the syrup, combine the apple cider vinegar, apple cider, and balsamic vinegar in a medium saucepan and bring to a simmer over medium-high heat. Reduce the heat to low to maintain a gentle simmer and cook for 30 to 40 minutes, until the liquid has reduced to a syrupy consistency.

To prepare the pork, first make the rub: grind the coriander seeds in a spice grinder and transfer them to a small bowl. Add the chipotle chile powder, salt, and brown sugar and stir to combine. →

For the Syrup
(if you are not buying Carr's Ciderhouse Cider Syrup)

1 cup apple cider vinegar

1 cup apple cider

2 tablespoons balsamic vinegar

Put the chops in a baking dish or on a large plate. Sprinkle the rub evenly over the meat and use the meat to mop up any rub that falls onto the dish or plate. Set aside for 30 minutes to 1 hour to let the seasonings penetrate the pork and for the pork to come to room temperature.

Prepare a hot fire in a charcoal grill. Move all of the coals to one side of the grill so you have both direct and indirect heat. If you have a gas grill, preheat one side for high heat and leave one side of the grill with no heat on; if it is an option, close the lid on the side with no heat.

While the grill is heating, place the onions in a large sauté pan. Add the cider vinegar and bring it to a boil over high heat. Reduce the heat to medium-high and gently boil the vinegar and onions for 5 to 10 minutes, stirring often, until the onions are tender and the vinegar coats them like a glaze. Turn off the heat.

Place the pork chops on the grill over the direct heat and grill for about 4 minutes, until the undersides are golden brown with dark grill marks. Move the pork chops to the side of the grill where there is no flame and cook over the indirect heat, uncovered, for about 10 minutes, until the meat is firm to the touch. Remove the pork chops from the grill and place them on a large serving platter.

To serve, drizzle the apple cider syrup over the pork chops and lay the onions on and around the pork chops, leaving the meat in the center of the platter visible.

For the Pork

1 tablespoon ground coriander seeds

1 tablespoon chipotle chile powder (or smoked sweet paprika or another chile powder)

1 tablespoon kosher salt

1 tablespoon light brown sugar

2 (¾-inch-thick) pork shoulder blade chops (about 1 pound each)

For the Onions

2 large yellow Spanish onions, peeled and sliced into ½-inch rings

2 cups apple cider vinegar

Braised Lamb Necks with Castelvetrano Olives and Preserved Lemon

Serves 4 to 6

Necks are an underused and very affordable cut of lamb. They are a bit like oxtails: they're all bone, with bits of fatty, gelatinous meat tucked into the nooks and crannies that you have to dig to get to. Just the way I like to eat! There are many North African flavors in Sicilian cooking, and the flavor combination in this braising liquid—including anchovies, orange, green olives, and preserved lemons—reflects both North Africa and Sicily. Castelvetrano olives are large, green, fresh (unbrined) olives with a meaty texture. They're cooked with the lamb so they absorb the braising liquid in this dish and are just delicious.

This recipe calls for homemade chicken stock, which doesn't contain any sodium. If the stock you are using does contain sodium, cut the salt in this recipe by half.

Ask your butcher for 4 lamb necks, halved through the middle to form two semicircles.

To prepare the lamb necks, put them in a large baking dish and sprinkle the salt evenly over them. Cover the dish tightly with plastic wrap and refrigerate overnight or for at least 6 hours.

Adjust the oven rack to the center position and preheat the oven to 325°F.

Remove the lamb necks from the refrigerator and uncover them.

Cut off and discard the root and tip ends of the onion. Peel the onion and cut it into quarters, root to tip.

Heat the olive oil in an extra-large Dutch oven over medium-high heat for 2 to 3 minutes, until the oil slides easily and is smoking around the edges of the pan. Lay the lamb necks in the Dutch oven in a single layer and sear them until they are deeply caramelized on both sides, about 5 minutes per side. Turn off the heat, remove the lamb necks from the Dutch oven, and return them to the baking dish. Add the onion and garlic to the Dutch oven and sauté them over medium-high heat until they are deeply caramelized, 6 to 8 minutes, stirring occasionally so they don't burn. Add the white wine and cook for 2 to 3 minutes, until it has almost all evaporated, scraping to release any bits stuck to the bottom of the $\rightarrow$

For the Lamb

4 whole lamb necks
(1 to 1½ pounds each), halved

1 tablespoon kosher salt

1 red onion

¼ cup olive oil

10 large garlic cloves,
peeled and thinly sliced
lengthwise

1 cup dry white wine

2 quarts Chicken Stock
(page 159; or sodium-free
or low-sodium store-bought),
or as needed

1 cup Castelvetrano olives

2 oranges, cut into quarters,
seeds removed and discarded

8 anchovy fillets (preferably salt-
packed; rinsed and backbones
removed if salt-packed)

pan. Add the chicken stock, pouring it around the necks, not over them, so you don't rinse off the seared exterior; add as much stock as needed to come just to the edge of the necks but not submerge them. Scatter the olives over the lamb necks. Cut a doubled piece of cheesecloth 2 inches larger than the pan and place it on top of the liquid. Add the oranges, anchovies, and rosemary sprigs and gently press on the cheesecloth to make sure the ingredients on top of it are submerged. Bring the liquid to a boil over high heat. Turn off the heat and put the lid on the Dutch oven.

Braise the lamb necks in the oven for 2½ to 3 hours, until fork-tender. To test for doneness, remove the lid from the Dutch oven, insert a fork into the meaty part of the neck, and turn it slightly; if the meat pulls apart with very little effort, the necks are done. Remove the lamb necks from the oven and remove the lid of the Dutch oven. Increase the heat to 500°F and wait 10 minutes for the oven to heat up. Lift off the cheesecloth and discard it and the ingredients that were on it.

Meanwhile, rinse the preserved lemon to remove the sugar and salt and drain well. Use a paring knife to remove the pulp, pith, and seeds, and discard, so you are left with only the bright yellow peel of the lemon. Finely chop the peel.

Add half of the chopped preserved lemon peel to the Dutch oven with the lamb and olives and return the lamb to the oven, uncovered, for 10 to 15 minutes, until the exposed parts of the lamb necks are charred and crispy. Remove the lamb necks from the oven and let them rest in the braising liquid for 5 to 10 minutes.

To serve, sprinkle the remaining chopped preserved lemon and drizzle about 2 tablespoons finishing-quality olive oil over the lamb necks. Sprinkle with the chopped parsley and tear the mint leaves into 3 or 4 pieces each so they drop onto the lamb.

4 fresh rosemary sprigs

2 Preserved Lemon halves (page 23; or store-bought)

For Serving

Finishing-quality extra-virgin olive oil

¼ cup finely chopped fresh Italian parsley leaves

½ cup whole fresh mint leaves

Roasted Lamb Rack with
Dried Persian Lime Tahini and
Grilled Broccolini and Scallions

Serves 4

Debbie Michail is a talented cook who worked at Osteria Mozza for a few years. She has since gone on to do whole-animal-themed pop-ups around Los Angeles. I attended several of these dinners and was so enthralled with the way she wove Persian, Turkish, and Israeli influences together that I asked her to create a lamb dish for us. She came up with this lamb rack, which is marinated in a paste made with tahini and dried lime. Dried limes are as hard and brittle as ping-pong balls; who would think you could cook with them! They are so out of my wheelhouse; they have an unusual, acidic flavor, and I am grateful to Debbie for showing us how to use them. We serve this with Grilled Broccolini and Scallions (page 310), and I think you'll be happy if you do the same.

We use Soom, a small-batch brand of tahini made in Philadelphia. If you can't find Soom, seek out another brand of tahini from a Middle Eastern market.

To season and sear the lamb, place the lamb rack in a baking dish. Sprinkle the kosher salt evenly over the rack and set aside for 30 minutes to 1 hour to come to room temperature.

To make the marinade, if you are using whole dried limes, cut them in half and pick out and discard the seeds. Working in batches, finely grind the limes in a spice grinder and transfer them to a measuring cup. You will need ¼ cup ground lime.

Toast the coriander seeds in a small skillet over medium heat for 1 to 2 minutes, until they are fragrant and toasted, shaking the pan often so they don't burn. Finely grind the seeds in the spice grinder and add them to the measuring cup with the dried lime.

Put the tahini in the bowl of a food processor fitted with a metal blade. Use a fine Microplane to grate the garlic into the food processor and pulse just to combine. Add the ground lime and coriander, the smoked →

For the Lamb

1 (8-bone) rack of lamb
(about 2 pounds)

2 teaspoons kosher salt

¼ cup olive oil

1 tablespoon fresh coarsely
ground black pepper

For the Marinade

10 dried Persian limes,
or as needed (or ¼ cup ground
Persian lime)

1 tablespoon coriander seeds

1½ cups tahini (preferably Soom)

6 large garlic cloves, peeled

paprika, kosher salt, and black pepper, and blend for 20 to 30 seconds, until all the spices have mixed in evenly. While the machine is still running, slowly add the olive oil in a thin stream to emulsify it with the tahini.

To cook the lamb, heat the olive oil in a large cast-iron skillet over medium-high heat for 2 to 3 minutes, until the oil slides easily and is smoking around the edges of the pan. Place the lamb rack, fat side down, in the pan and sear for 3 to 4 minutes, until it is deeply caramelized. Turn the rack to sear each of the meaty ends (not the bone side) until they are deeply caramelized. Remove the lamb from the skillet and return it to the baking dish. Set the lamb aside to cool to room temperature, about 20 minutes.

Reserve ½ cup of the marinade and slather the remaining marinade on the lamb, massaging with your hands to coat the lamb with the marinade. Cover the baking dish with plastic wrap and marinate the lamb at room temperature for 1 hour.

Adjust the oven rack to the center position and preheat the oven to 350°F.

Uncover the baking dish and sprinkle the pepper evenly over all sides of the lamb. Use the meat to mop up any fallen pepper and press it into the meat with your hands to adhere.

Place the lamb rack, bone side down, on a baking sheet, and roast it in the oven for 35 minutes, until an instant-read thermometer reads 135°F when inserted deep into the loin through the side of the rack. Remove the baking sheet from the oven and let the lamb rack rest for 5 to 7 minutes before cutting into it.

While the lamb is roasting, make the grilled broccolini and scallions.

To serve, spoon the reserved ½ cup marinade onto a large platter and use the back of the spoon to spread it toward the edges in organic, uneven swirls. Lay the grilled broccolini and scallions on the platter, leaving the edges of the marinade visible.

Transfer the lamb to a cutting board and cut between each rib to cut the rack into individual chops. Fan the lamb chops out on the greens with 2 crossed over each other like pairs of legs. Drizzle about 2 tablespoons finishing-quality olive oil and crush about 1 teaspoon flaky sea salt between your fingertips over the meat. Sprinkle the za'atar and tear the mint leaves into 3 or 4 pieces each to fall over the meat.

2 tablespoons sweet smoked paprika

1 teaspoon kosher salt

1 tablespoon fresh coarsely black pepper

¼ cup olive oil

For Serving

Grilled Broccolini and Scallions (page 310)

Finishing-quality extra-virgin olive oil

Flaky sea salt

2 tablespoons Za'atar (page 25; or store-bought)

10 fresh mint leaves

Moorish Lamb Shoulder Chops
with Mint Yogurt

Serves 4

Theoretically, every menu I create is a collection of things I want to eat. But when it comes down to it and I have to order something at one of my restaurants for myself, I tend to order the same thing over and over again. At Chi Spacca, these marinated, grilled shoulder chops are that thing. Shoulder chops are a lesser-known, economical cut of lamb. The shoulder of any animal tends to be tough, and is generally reserved for long cooking. If you were to just throw one of these on the grill, it would be inedibly tough. But the yogurt in the marinade tenderizes the meat. It's never going to have the buttery, melt-in-your mouth quality of the more luxurious (and considerably more expensive) lamb loin chop, and it's not meant to. Instead, it has a chewy, steak-like quality, which I like. For the same reason that it tenderizes the shoulder, you don't want to leave meat in this marinade for more than 30 minutes or the yogurt will turn it into a mealy texture.

Ask your butcher for 4 (¾-inch-thick) lamb shoulder chops (6 to 8 ounces each).

You will need an extra-large platter to serve the chops.

To marinate the lamb chops, put them in a large baking dish or two large resealable plastic bags.

Toast the fennel seeds, peppercorns, and cardamom pods in a small skillet over medium heat for 1 to 2 minutes, until they are fragrant and toasted, shaking the pan often so the spices don't burn. Transfer the spices to a mortar or spice grinder and finely grind them. Put the yogurt in a medium bowl. Add the cilantro, mint, paprika, and the ground spices. Use a fine Microplane to grate the garlic into the bowl and stir to thoroughly combine. Pour the marinade over the lamb chops and massage with your hands to coat the chops with the marinade. Cover the baking dish or close the bags and set the chops aside to marinate for 30 minutes; any longer and the marinade will turn the meat mealy.

While the lamb chops are marinating, to make the yogurt sauce, put the yogurt, extra-virgin olive oil, lemon juice, and kosher salt in a medium bowl. Using a fine Microplane, grate the garlic into the bowl and stir to

For the Lamb Chops

4 (¾-inch-thick) lamb shoulder chops (6 to 8 ounces each)

1 teaspoon fennel seeds

1 teaspoon black peppercorns

1 teaspoon cardamom pods

1 cup Straus Family Creamery Organic Greek Yogurt (or another plain, whole milk, not overly thick yogurt)

2 tablespoons finely chopped fresh cilantro leaves

2 tablespoons finely chopped fresh mint leaves

¾ teaspoon sweet smoked paprika

3 large garlic cloves, peeled

combine. Stir in the mint. Before serving, transfer the yogurt sauce to a small pretty bowl.

To grill the lamb and lemons, cut the lemons in half through the middle and trim and discard ½ inch from each end, so the lemon halves have two flat surfaces. Brush both cut ends of the lemon halves with olive oil and set them aside.

Put the peppercorns in a mortar or spice grinder and very coarsely grind them.

Prepare a hot fire in a charcoal grill. (Alternatively, to cook the chops indoors, preheat a cast-iron grill pan or skillet over high heat. The cooking method and times will be the same as for grilling.)

Remove the chops from the marinade, scrape off the excess marinade with your hands, and lay the chops in a single layer on a baking sheet. Sprinkle the chops with 1 tablespoon plus 1 teaspoon of the kosher salt and sprinkle the pepper evenly over both sides. Use the meat to mop up the fallen pepper and press it into the meat with your hands to adhere. Drizzle with the olive oil and massage to coat the chops with the oil.

Grill the chops over direct heat for about 6 minutes, until they are charred on both sides. Remove the chops from the grill.

Place the lemon halves, center sides down, on the grill or in the grill pan with the chops and grill for about 2 minutes, until they are deeply caramelized. Turn and cook the smaller sides of the lemon halves for about 30 seconds just to warm them. Remove them from the grill.

To serve, lay the chops slightly overlapping one another on an extra-large platter with the bones all facing the same direction and arrange the lemon halves with the center sides facing up, around them. Drizzle the chops with about 2 tablespoons finishing-quality olive oil and crush about ½ teaspoon flaky sea salt between your fingertips over them. Drop tangles of the cilantro over and around the chops and serve with the bowl of yogurt sauce on the side.

For the Yogurt Sauce

2 cups Straus Family Creamery Organic Greek Yogurt (or another plain, whole-milk, not overly thick yogurt)

¼ cup extra-virgin olive oil

2 tablespoons fresh lemon juice, plus more to taste

1 teaspoon kosher salt, plus more to taste

3 large garlic cloves, peeled

½ cup finely chopped fresh mint leaves

For Grilling the Lamb and Lemons

2 lemons

2 tablespoons olive oil, plus more for the lemons

1 teaspoon black peppercorns

1 tablespoon plus 1 teaspoon kosher salt

For Serving

Finishing-quality extra-virgin olive oil

Flaky sea salt

8 long fresh cilantro sprigs

Armenian-Style Lamb Ribs with Jajik

Serves 4

Lamb ribs are as tender as they are flavorful, and yet when was the last time you were served lamb ribs? This Armenian-inspired preparation is in honor of our friend Michael Krikorian, who refers to any Armenian he meets (and even if he doesn't meet them) as his "cousin." I had thought of the ribs as Turkish, because of the blend of spices we season them with, but then Michael told Ryan, "If you call these Armenian-style, the one hundred thousand Armenians living in Los Angeles will love you for it. If you call them Turkish, the five Turks in L.A. won't care." I don't know whether that's true, but, in fact, when we served them at an event at the Hotel Bel-Air, we got more than one comment from "cousins" of Michael's saying how happy they were. We serve the ribs with jajik, a yogurt sauce with grated cucumber and other delicious things in it; it's a classic Armenian condiment and the perfect, cooling accompaniment to these heavily spiced ribs. I love yogurt sauces, so it's right up my alley. This one is a bit unusual: in addition to the cucumber, it also contains ginger and lemon zest. I have one Armenian in Los Angeles to thank for that.

Ask your butcher for 4 racks of Denver lamb ribs (also called spareribs; about 1 pound each). You will need an extra-large platter to serve the ribs.

To prepare the lamb ribs, sprinkle the kosher salt evenly over both sides of the ribs. Place the ribs on a baking sheet, cover with plastic wrap, and refrigerate overnight or for at least 6 hours.

Combine the fennel seeds, cumin seeds, caraway seeds, and coriander seeds in a mortar or spice grinder and very coarsely grind them. If you're using a spice grinder, transfer the spices to a small bowl. Add the paprika, ginger, turmeric, and red pepper flakes to the mortar or bowl and stir to combine.

When you're ready to cook the ribs, adjust the oven rack so one is in the top third and one is in the bottom third and preheat the oven to 275°F.

Remove the lamb ribs from the refrigerator. Unwrap the lamb ribs and move 2 of the ribs to a second baking sheet. Set the lamb aside for 30 minutes to 1 hour to come to room temperature. Pour the olive oil over them, and massage with your hands to coat the ribs with the oil.

For the Lamb

1 tablespoon plus 1 teaspoon kosher salt

4 (8-bone) lamb rib racks (about 1 pound each)

2 tablespoons fennel seeds

2 tablespoons cumin seeds

2 teaspoons caraway seeds

2 tablespoons coriander seeds

2 tablespoons sweet smoked paprika

2 teaspoons ginger

1 teaspoon ground turmeric

1 teaspoon red pepper flakes

2 tablespoons olive oil

Roast the lamb ribs in the oven for 3 to 3½ hours, until the outside is crusty and the ribs tear apart easily, rotating them from front to back and from one rack to another halfway through that time so the ribs cook evenly. Remove the ribs from the oven. Transfer them to a cutting board and cut them into two-bone pieces.

While the lamb is roasting, to make the jajik, put the yogurt in a medium bowl. Grate the cucumber on the largest holes of a box grater until you have ½ cup; reserve the remaining cucumber for another use. Add the grated cucumber to the bowl with the yogurt. Use a fine Microplane to grate the garlic, ginger, and the bright yellow outer layer of lemon zest into the bowl. Cut the lemon in half, juice it, and add 2 tablespoons of the juice to the bowl. Remove and discard the stem from the Fresno chile, cut it in half, and remove and discard the seeds. Mince the chile and add it to the bowl. Add the dill and kosher salt and stir to combine. Add more lemon juice or kosher salt to taste. Transfer to a small pretty bowl before serving.

To serve, lay the ribs on an extra-large platter, stacking them against one another like fallen logs. Crush about 2 teaspoons flaky sea salt with your fingertips over the ribs and serve with the jajik in a bowl on the side.

For the Jajik

2 cups Straus Family Creamery Organic Greek Yogurt (or another plain, whole-milk, not overly thick yogurt)

1 Persian cucumber (about 3 inches)

2 large garlic cloves, peeled

1-inch piece of fresh ginger, peeled

1 lemon

1 Fresno chile

1 tablespoon finely chopped fresh dill

1 teaspoon kosher salt, plus more to taste

For Serving

Flaky sea salt

Grilled Lamb Sausage Coils
with Onion and Peppers

Makes 4 (2-foot) links

Long before I had a butchery-centric restaurant, a selection of sausage, purchased from my local butcher, Huntington Meats, grilled in my outdoor fireplace, has been one of my favorite things to serve when I have a dinner party. Every butcher has their own recipe for sausages; after opening Chi Spacca, it was my turn to develop my own. I started with lamb because it has so much flavor, and I like the spicy seasonings that are often associated with lamb sausages. I formed the sausages into thin coils, which make for such a pretty presentation, and pile grilled shishito peppers and onions on top. It's my interpretation of the old-school Italian American favorite: sausage and peppers. The "secret ingredient" in this dish is the Calabrian chile peppers, often sold as Calabrian chile paste or Calabrian chile "Bomba." The chopped peppers make a delicious condiment on their own, but for this recipe, we use them as a base for a salsa, which we use to dress the lamb as well as the salad.

If you don't want to make your own sausage, substitute 24 ounces lamb Merguez sausage (coils, if you can find them).

You will need a meat grinder or meat grinding attachment to a stand mixer as well as a ½-inch sausage stuffing tube to make this. You will also need 4 (at least 8-inch) wooden skewers and a large cast-iron skillet.

Ask your butcher for beef trimmings (preferably dry-aged), consisting of 80 percent fat and 20 percent meat. Also ask for sheep's casing. Most butchers sell these in 8-ounce packages; you need a fraction of that but you can freeze the remaining casings for another time.

You will need an extra-large platter or large cutting board to serve the sausages.

To make the sausage, put the lamb shoulder and beef trimmings in a large container or medium bowl. Add the paprika, salt, black pepper, oregano, and cayenne. Use a fine Microplane to grate the garlic cloves into the container or bowl and toss to coat the meat with the seasonings. Cover and refrigerate the meat for 24 hours and up to 2 days to marinate.

When you are ready to grind the meat, remove it from the refrigerator and transfer it to the freezer along with the meat grinding attachment, including the smallest die, the blade, and the stuffing tube, and chill →

For the Sausage

1½ pounds lamb shoulder, cut into 1-inch cubes

8 ounces beef trimmings (preferably dry-aged; including meat and fat)

2 tablespoons hot smoked paprika

1 tablespoon kosher salt

for 10 to 15 minutes. (You don't want to freeze the meat; you just want to chill it so it firms up, which makes it easier to grind.)

Remove the meat grinding attachment and the meat from the freezer and fit the mixer with the grinding attachment. Place a bowl under the mixer attachment. Add the ice water to the meat mixture and pass the meat through the grinder into the bowl. Pass half of the ground meat through the grinder a second time. Cover the bowl with plastic wrap and refrigerate it for 30 minutes to 1 hour to chill and firm the meat before stuffing it into a casing.

Fit the sausage stuffing attachment with a ½-inch plastic stuffing tube and fit the attachment onto the mixer. Put a baking sheet or large bowl below the stuffing tube to catch your sausage as it is stuffed. Carefully slide the sheep's casing onto the stuffing tube, gathering as much casing as you can onto the tube. Leave about 3 inches of casing to hang off the tube and tie that in a knot. Begin cranking the sausage into the casing, guiding the casing with your hands to help stuff it evenly. When all the sausage has been stuffed, slide the casing off the tube. (When you're stuffing sausage, there will always be some meat left in the stuffer. Pat this into small patties and fry it up for breakfast.)

Transfer the sausage to a cutting board and cut it into four equal lengths; each will be about 2 feet long. Form each length of sausage into a coil and run a skewer through the coil to hold it in place. Place the sausage coils in a single layer on a large baking sheet. Refrigerate, uncovered, overnight to allow the casing to dry out and firm up slightly; this prevents the casing from falling apart when cooked.

Meanwhile, to make the Calabrian chile salsa, put the chopped cherry peppers in a medium bowl. Add the vinegar, lemon juice, cilantro, parsley, mint, and salt. Using a fine Microplane, grate the garlic into the bowl and stir to combine. Gradually add the extra-virgin olive oil, stirring constantly. Add more lemon juice or salt to taste.

To cook the onion and peppers, prepare a hot fire in a charcoal grill (see Ryan's Chi Spacca Grilling Class, page 27). Move all of the coals to one side of the grill so you have both direct and indirect heat. If you have a gas grill, preheat one side for high heat and leave one side of the grill with no heat on; if it is an option, close the lid on the side with no heat.

1 tablespoon fresh coarsely ground black pepper

1 tablespoon dried oregano (preferably Sicilian oregano on the branch)

½ teaspoon cayenne pepper

2 large garlic cloves, peeled

2 tablespoons ice water

10 feet sheep's sausage casings

For the Calabrian Chile Salsa

1 tablespoon finely chopped oil-packed Calabrian cherry peppers

2 tablespoons red wine vinegar

2 tablespoons fresh lemon juice, plus more to taste

2 tablespoons finely chopped fresh cilantro leaves

2 tablespoons finely chopped fresh Italian parsley leaves

1 tablespoon finely chopped fresh mint leaves

½ teaspoon kosher salt, plus more to taste

1 large garlic clove, peeled

¾ cup extra-virgin olive oil

For the Onion and Peppers

1 large yellow Spanish onion, peeled and sliced into ½-inch rings

¼ cup olive oil

1 teaspoon kosher salt

2 cups shishito peppers (about ¼ pound; or padrón, Jimmy Nardello, or any variety of small mild pepper)

Put the onion slices in a large cast-iron skillet. Add 2 tablespoons of the olive oil and ½ teaspoon of the salt and toss to coat the slices with the oil and salt. Place the skillet on the hot side of the grill (or over high heat) and sauté for 10 to 12 minutes, until they are light golden brown and tender, stirring often so they don't burn. Remove the skillet from the heat.

Put the shishito peppers in a medium bowl. Drizzle with the remaining 2 tablespoons olive oil and ½ teaspoon salt and toss to coat.

Remove the sausage coils from the refrigerator. Spoon 1 tablespoon of the Calabrian chile salsa onto each coil and massage with your hands to coat. Place the sausages on the grill on the direct-heat side of the grill and sear them for about 5 minutes on each side, until the coils are red with very dark grill marks. Move the sausages to the indirect-heat side of the grill and cover the grill, if possible. Cook the sausage coils over indirect heat for 5 minutes; finishing the sausage over indirect heat ensures the insides are cooked fully and evenly. Remove the sausages from the grill.

While the sausage coils are cooking, put the shishito peppers on the direct-heat side of the grill and cook them for about 5 minutes, until they are soft and charred in places. Transfer the peppers to the skillet with the onion slices and toss to combine them.

To serve, remove and discard the skewers from the sausage coils and arrange the coils on an extra-large platter or cutting board, overlapping one another haphazardly and leaving space on the cutting board for the salad that will be piled there. Reserve ¼ cup of the remaining salsa and spoon the rest of the salsa over the sausages, dividing it evenly. Pile the onions and peppers over and around the sausage coils, letting the meat peek through the vegetables.

Put the arugula, cilantro, and mint in a medium bowl. Drizzle with the reserved ¼ cup Calabrian chile salsa and the lemon juice and toss to dress the greens. Mound the salad on the side of the sausage coils.

For Serving

4 cups arugula leaves (preferably wild arugula)

1 cup fresh whole cilantro leaves

½ cup whole fresh mint leaves

Juice of ½ lemon

Moroccan-Braised Lamb Shanks
with Pistachio Gremolata
and Celeriac Purée

Serves 4

Oftentimes when we feel the urge to add a new dish to the menu at Chi Spacca, we start by seeing if there are any holes in our selections. That's how this Moroccan-inspired lamb dish was born. I threw out the question: What are we missing? And Ryan and Francis Chua, our gifted line cook at the time, answered in unison: lamb shank! It would be difficult to find someone more beautiful to watch on the line than Francis; he worked with such grace. Whether he was cutting, stirring, or plating, his movements were orchestrated like a dance. *Shank* refers to the shinbone of the animal. The meat is normally very tough but, when braised, becomes so tender it falls off the bone in juicy shreds. What comes to the table when someone orders this, is a big bone with a chunk of delicious meat on it, covered in a rich braising sauce. This recipe calls for four shanks, which is a pretty hefty portion. Ryan and Francis looked to North Africa for inspiration, seasoning the shanks with ras el hanout, a spice blend from that part of the world. For the braise, they circled back to Italy and use Lambrusco, Italian sparkling red wine.

This is one of the few meat dishes at Chi Spacca that is served with a side dish—in this case, a celeriac purée. The celery flavor is the perfect complement to the intense spices that the lamb is seasoned with, enough that the boys thought it was a must with this dish.

Both black and white unhulled toasted sesame seeds are sold as "roasted sesame seeds" in shaker canisters in the Japanese section of supermarkets. If you can't find them, use the more widely available hulled white sesame seeds and toast them along with the other seeds in this recipe. This recipe calls for homemade chicken stock, which doesn't contain any sodium. If the stock you are using does contain sodium, cut the salt in this recipe by half. A citrus zester is a one-trick tool used to peel long, threadlike strips from citrus. The strips are really pretty made this way, but if you don't want to invest in one just for this, you can get more or less the same results by peeling citrus with a vegetable peeler and then cutting it into long thin strips.

Ask your butcher for 4 (¾-pound) bone-in lamb shanks.

You will need an extra-large platter to serve the lamb shanks.

To prepare the lamb, place the shanks in a baking dish and sprinkle the kosher salt evenly over them. Cover the dish with plastic wrap and refrigerate the lamb overnight or for at least 6 hours.

Meanwhile, to make the gremolata, adjust the oven rack to the center position and preheat the oven to 325°F.

Spread the pistachios on a baking sheet and toast them in the oven for about 6 minutes, until they're fragrant and toasted, shaking the baking sheet and rotating it from front to back halfway through that time so the nuts brown evenly. Remove the baking sheet from the oven and set aside to cool slightly. Finely chop the pistachios and transfer them to a medium bowl.

Toast the cumin seeds and caraway seeds in a small skillet over medium heat for 1 to 2 minutes, until they are fragrant and toasted, shaking the pan so they don't burn. Transfer the seeds to a mortar or spice grinder. Add the flaky sea salt, sesame seeds, and ras el hanout and very coarsely grind the ingredients. Add the mixture to the bowl with the pistachios.

If you have a citrus zester, use it to zest half of the bright yellow outer layer of the lemon into long threads. If you do not have a citrus zester, use a vegetable peeler to peel the bright yellow outer layer of lemon zest in wide strips, and thinly slice the strips into long threads. (Reserve the lemon to juice at another time.) Add the zest, along with the cilantro and mint, to the bowl with the nuts and seeds and stir to combine.

To braise the lamb shanks, remove the shanks from the refrigerator and unwrap them. Heat the olive oil in an extra-large Dutch oven over medium-high heat for 2 to 3 minutes, until the oil slides easily and is smoking around the edges of the pan. Add the lamb shanks in a single layer and sear them until they are deeply caramelized on both sides, about 5 minutes per side. Turn off the heat, remove the lamb shanks from the Dutch oven, and return them to the baking dish. Add the shallots, garlic, and ginger to the Dutch oven and cook them over medium heat for about 6 minutes, until the shallots are soft and light golden, stirring often so the vegetables don't brown. Move the vegetables to one side of the pan. Add the tomato paste to the space created and cook for 2 to 3 minutes to caramelize the tomato paste, stirring constantly so it doesn't burn. Add the Lambrusco and cook for 2 to 3 minutes until almost all the wine has evaporated, scraping to release any bits stuck to the bottom of the pan. Add the chicken →

For the Lamb

4 bone-in lamb shanks
(about 12 ounces each)

2 tablespoons kosher salt

For the Pistachio Gremolata

1½ cups shelled pistachios

1 tablespoon cumin seeds

1 teaspoon caraway seeds

1 teaspoon flaky sea salt

1 teaspoon unhulled toasted sesame seeds (preferably black sesame seeds)

1 teaspoon Ras el Hanout
(page 24; or store-bought)

1 lemon

1 tablespoon finely chopped fresh cilantro leaves

1 teaspoon finely chopped fresh mint leaves

For Braising the Lamb

¼ cup plus 2 tablespoons olive oil

4 large shallots, peeled and sliced ½ inch thick lengthwise

10 large garlic cloves, peeled and halved lengthwise

¼ pound fresh ginger, peeled and sliced into ½-inch rings

2 tablespoons double-concentrated tomato paste

2 cups Lambrusco
(or dry red wine)

2 quarts (8 cups) Chicken Stock (page 159; or sodium-free or low-sodium store-bought), plus more as needed

¼ cup Ras el Hanout
(page 24; or store-bought)

2 tablespoons wildflower honey (or another mild-flavored honey)

stock, ras el hanout, and honey and bring the liquid to a boil over high heat. Turn off the heat and let the liquid cool slightly. (You will be blending the ingredients in the next step; if you blend the ingredients while they're hot, they will expand from the heat and blow the lid off the blender when you turn it on.) Working in batches, transfer the stock and vegetables to a blender and purée until smooth. Pour the purée into a bowl or another pan and continue until you've puréed all of the ingredients.

Return the lamb shanks to the Dutch oven. Add as much of the puréed liquid as needed to come three-fourths of the way up the side of the lamb, pouring it around the shanks, not over them, so you don't rinse off the seared surface of the meat. If you don't have enough liquid, add chicken stock. If you have excess liquid, use it in another braise or in soup, or discard it. Put the lid on the Dutch oven.

Braise the lamb shanks in the preheated oven for 2½ to 3 hours, until fork-tender. To test for doneness, remove the lid from the Dutch oven, insert a fork into a shank, and turn it slightly; if the meat pulls apart with very little effort, it's done. Remove the lamb shanks from the oven, uncover, and allow the shanks to rest in the liquid for 20 to 30 minutes.

While the lamb is braising, make the celeriac purée.

Remove the lamb shanks from the braising liquid and transfer them to an extra-large platter with the bones standing upright. Place the Dutch oven on the stove and bring the braising liquid to a boil over high heat. Reduce the heat to medium-low and simmer for 10 to 15 minutes, until the sauce is thick enough to coat the back of a spoon.

To serve, pour ½ cup of the sauce over each lamb shank and drizzle each shank with about 1 tablespoon finishing-quality olive oil. Sprinkle the pistachio gremolata over the shanks, dividing it evenly, and drop the cilantro in a few tangles around them. Serve the remaining sauce in a small bowl on the side and the celeriac purée on the side in a large bowl.

For Serving

Celeriac Purée (page 315)

Finishing-quality extra-virgin olive oil

½ cup fresh cilantro sprigs

Duck, Rabbit, and Chicken

Lacquered Duck with Honey-Balsamic Glaze and Crispy Black Rice

Serves 4

You have Francis Chua, one of our former line cooks, to thank for this beautiful, lacquered duck. Francis worked for us in Singapore, where he came to appreciate and love eating Peking duck, and he wanted to do something resembling that at Chi Spacca. The first renditions he brought me were too Asian for Spacca, and too sweet for my taste. We worked together until we landed on a roasted duck that had the best qualities of Peking duck—that crisp, lacquered skin and moist, flavorful meat—but with a flavor profile more befitting Chi Spacca. Keep in mind when you're planning to cook this recipe that this is not fast food. The duck marinates for at least two days, and then needs to dry out in the refrigerator for at least one day and up to a week—the longer the better.

We serve this duck with crispy black rice, which people often call by the brand name Forbidden Rice. A whole grain, it has a nutty, wholesome depth of flavor and an exotic, shiny black appearance. We cook the rice in duck fat until it's crispy and close to burned on the bottom. In the tradition of so many great rice dishes—the *socarrat* (crispy bottom layer) that is the benchmark of good paella and the crispy-bottomed Middle Eastern rice dish tahdig—the crispy-chewy stuck-to-the-bottom grains are the best part. The rice dish contains Chinese sausage, a slender, hard, spicy sausage with a unique flavor redolent of five-spice powder; find it at Asian food stores, or use hard, dry-cured Italian salami instead.

This recipe calls for homemade chicken stock, which doesn't contain any sodium. If the stock you are using does contain sodium, cut the salt in this recipe by half. We dry the orange peel for the spice blend in the oven. You can always skip this step and use packaged dried orange peel, available at Middle Eastern markets, instead. Sambal oelek is an Asian chile and garlic paste. It is readily available in the Asian section of grocery stores.

Ask your butcher to split the duck in half down the middle; seek out Peking duck that is meaty, flavorful, and the ideal size for this recipe. Buy duck fat from a butcher or the meat section of a specialty food store.

You will need a large cast-iron skillet to cook and serve the rice and an extra-large platter to serve the duck.

To make the marinade, put the pear in the bowl of a food processor fitted with a metal blade. Trim and discard the root end of the scallion, cut the scallion into 1-inch pieces, and add the pieces to the food processor. Add the ginger, garlic, kosher salt, brown sugar, five-spice powder, and red pepper flakes. Use a fine Microplane to zest the bright orange outer layer of the orange into the food processor bowl. Pulse the machine until the ingredients are chopped but not puréed. Transfer the ingredients to a medium bowl. Juice the orange and add the orange juice and hoisin sauce to the marinade; stir to combine.

Place the duck halves in a large bowl or baking dish. Pour 1 cup of the marinade over them and massage with your hands to coat each duck half. Cover with plastic wrap and place the duck in the refrigerator to marinate for at least 24 hours and up to 48 hours. Transfer the remaining marinade to a covered container and refrigerate until you're ready to cook the duck.

Remove the reserved marinade from the refrigerator and pour it into a large soup pot. Add 6 quarts water and bring to a simmer over high heat. Reduce the heat to low to keep the liquid warm. Place a cooling rack on a baking sheet and set it near the soup pot. Have a small saucepan handy to use as a ladle (or have a large ladle handy). Remove the duck from the refrigerator and remove and discard the plastic wrap. Pick up one duck half with a pair of tongs and hold it over the saucepan. Ladle the hot liquid, taking care not to splash yourself, over the duck to baste it, letting the liquid drop back into the pot. Baste the duck with the hot liquid about twenty times, until the skin tightens and darkens to a light brown color. Move the duck to the cooling rack to drain. Baste the second duck half and add it to the cooling rack with the first half. Place the pan with the duck in the refrigerator and allow the duck to sit, uncovered, for at least 3 days and up to 1 week. (The longer the duck rests in the refrigerator, the more the skin will dry out and the crispier it will get when roasted.)

To make the spice blend, peel the bright orange outer layer of orange zest with a vegetable peeler and put the peels on a baking sheet. Adjust the oven rack to the center position and put the baking sheet in the oven. Preheat the oven, with the orange peels inside, to 300°F. Cook the peels for 30 to 40 minutes, until they are dried out and slightly crunchy. Remove the orange peels from the oven and set them aside to cool slightly. Transfer to a mortar or spice grinder and finely grind them. If you're using a spice grinder, transfer the orange peels to a small bowl. →

For the Marinade

1 ripe pear, core and stem removed and roughly chopped

1 large scallion

1 (1-ounce) piece of fresh ginger, peeled and roughly chopped

2 large garlic cloves, peeled

2 tablespoons kosher salt

1 teaspoon dark or light brown sugar

1 teaspoon five-spice powder

½ teaspoon red pepper flakes

1 orange

¾ cup bottled hoisin sauce

1 (5- to 6-pound) whole duck (preferably Peking duck), halved

For the Spice Blend

1 orange (or 1 teaspoon dried orange peel)

1½ tablespoons coriander seeds

1½ tablespoons fennel seeds

2 cardamom pods

1 teaspoon Szechuan peppercorns

For the Rice

3 large scallions

¼ cup duck fat

¼ pound Chinese sausage (or dry-cured Italian salami), cut into ½-inch cubes

2 cups black rice (preferably Lotus Foods Forbidden Rice)

½ cup sherry vinegar

2 cups Chicken Stock (page 159; or sodium-free or low-sodium store-bought)

2 teaspoons sambal oelek

½ teaspoon kosher salt

Increase the oven temperature to 350°F.

Toast the coriander seeds, fennel seeds, cardamom pods, and Szechuan peppercorns in a small skillet over medium heat for 1 to 2 minutes, until they are fragrant and toasted, shaking the skillet often so the spices don't burn. Add the spices to the mortar or spice grinder and very coarsely grind them. Transfer the spices to the bowl with the orange peel and stir to combine.

Remove the duck halves from the refrigerator and set them aside for 30 minutes to 1 hour to come to room temperature. Remove the ducks from the rack. Wash and dry the rack and baking sheet and return the rack to the baking sheet.

Wrap each duck half separately in aluminum foil, making sure they are completely covered, and return them, skin side up, to the rack. Roast the duck in the oven for 18 to 20 minutes, until an instant-read thermometer registers 100°F when inserted deep into the breast. Remove the duck from the oven and set aside for 2 or 3 minutes until the foil is cool enough to touch. Remove and discard the foil and place the duck halves, skin side up, on the rack, making sure there is ample space between them.

While the duck is roasting, to make the rice, trim and discard any wilted greens from the scallions. Starting at the green ends and moving toward the white ends, slice the scallions ⅛ inch thick on an extreme bias, keeping the green and white parts separate. Put the green scallion slices in a small bowl and set the white slices aside; discard the root ends.

Heat 2 tablespoons of the duck fat in a large cast-iron skillet over medium-high heat to melt it. Add the Chinese sausage and cook for 3 to 4 minutes, stirring occasionally, until it is golden brown and slightly crispy. Add the rice, stir to coat it with the fat, and toast it, stirring occasionally, for 3 to 4 minutes, until it starts to stick to the pan. Add the sherry vinegar and cook until the liquid has evaporated, about 1 minute. Add the chicken stock, increase the heat to high, and bring it to a boil. Reduce the heat to low, cover the pan with a lid, and cook for 45 minutes, stirring occasionally, until the liquid is absorbed. Turn off the heat and let the rice rest, covered, for 10 minutes, to continue cooking. Uncover the skillet and transfer the rice to a large bowl. Add the white scallion slices, the sambal oelek, and the kosher salt, and gently fold them in.

Wipe out the skillet. Add the remaining 2 tablespoons duck fat and heat it over medium-high heat until it slides easily and is smoking around

For the Glaze

1 cup balsamic vinegar

2 bay leaves (preferably fresh)

½ cup honey (such as wildflower or another mild-flavored honey)

For the Charred Scallions

4 large scallions

1 tablespoon olive oil

½ teaspoon kosher salt

For Serving

½ teaspoon flaky sea salt

the edges of the pan. Return the rice to the pan and cook it for 10 to 15 minutes to crisp the rice, scraping the bottom of the pan occasionally to crisp all of the rice. Turn off the heat and return the lid to the skillet to keep the rice warm.

To make the glaze, while the rice is cooking, put the balsamic vinegar and bay leaves in a small saucepan and bring it to a boil over high heat. Reduce the heat to medium and simmer until the liquid is reduced to a syrupy consistency, about 20 minutes. Add the honey in a slow stream, whisking constantly. Increase the heat to high and return the glaze to a boil. Turn off the heat. Brush the glaze on the duck halves, coating the skin completely; don't brush the bottom of the duck where there is no skin. Immediately sprinkle the spice blend evenly over the duck. Return the duck halves to the oven to cook for 10 minutes, until the instant-read thermometer registers 120°F. Remove the duck halves from the oven.

Increase the oven temperature to 450°F.

To char the scallions, trim and discard the root ends and put the scallions on a baking sheet. Drizzle with the olive oil, sprinkle with the kosher salt, and massage with your hands to coat the scallions. Spread the scallions out in a single layer and roast them in the oven for 6 to 8 minutes, until they are wilted and charred in places. (You don't have to wait for the oven to warm up to 450° for the scallions as you did for the duck because they are not as sensitive to temperature as the duck.) Remove the scallions from the oven.

Return the duck to the oven for 3 to 5 minutes, until the skin is dark brown and crispy. Remove the duck from the oven.

To serve, transfer the duck to a cutting board. Cut the leg and thigh away from each breast in one piece. Cut the leg and thigh at the joint into two pieces. With your knife parallel to the counter, slice between the breast bone and the breast meat to remove the breast from the bone in one piece. Discard the breast bone or add it to your next batch of Chicken Stock (page 159). Slice the duck breasts 1 inch thick. Slide your knife under the slices and transfer them to an extra-large platter, fanning them out slightly. Pile the legs around the breast slices. Crush the flaky sea salt between your fingertips over the duck slices and drape the charred scallions over the top. Scatter the reserved green scallion slices over the rice and serve the rice in the skillet it was cooked in.

Pancetta-Wrapped Rabbit
with Braised Greens

Serves 4

You'll find *coniglio,* or "rabbit," on the menu of just about any restaurant in Umbria and Tuscany, where I spend my summers. I order it often—it is always roasted with rosemary and served with simple, delicious roasted potatoes—and I am never disappointed. I wanted to re-create that experience at Chi Spacca, but when Ryan and I tried, it never tasted as good as it did in Italy. So we changed the cooking method entirely. We wrap the rabbit in pancetta, braise it, and then sprinkle fried rosemary over the top. I still think of Italy every time I see (or eat) it.

This recipe calls for homemade chicken stock, which doesn't contain any sodium. If the stock you are using does contain sodium, cut the salt in this recipe by half.

Ask your butcher for a whole (5-pound) rabbit, legs separated from the carcass and loin separate.

You will need an extra-large platter to serve the rabbit and greens.

To prepare the rabbit, place it in a large baking dish and sprinkle the salt evenly over all sides of the rabbit. Cover with plastic wrap and refrigerate for at least 2 hours and as long as 1 day.

Remove the rabbit from the refrigerator and remove and discard the plastic wrap. Remove the rabbit from the baking dish, rinse it under cold water to remove the salt, rinse and dry the baking dish, and return the rabbit to the dish. Pour the milk into the dish, adding enough to submerge the rabbit. Re-cover the dish with plastic and refrigerate overnight or for at least 6 hours.

Remove the rabbit from the refrigerator and remove and discard the plastic wrap. Remove the rabbit from the milk, discard the milk, and pat the rabbit dry. Clean and dry the baking dish and return the rabbit legs to the dish.

For the Rabbit

1 whole rabbit (about 5 pounds), legs separated from the carcass, loin separate

1 tablespoon kosher salt

4 cups whole milk, plus more as needed

10 (⅛-inch-thick) pancetta slices

15 fresh sage leaves

10 large garlic cloves, peeled

½ cup olive oil

1 large yellow Spanish onion, peeled and sliced into ¼-inch slices

Cut a 12-inch piece of plastic wrap (from a standard, 12-inch-wide roll) and lay it on a clean work surface. Uncoil the pancetta slices and lay them, slightly overlapping, to cover the square of plastic wrap. Lay the rabbit loin, skin side down, on the pancetta with the long side of the loin parallel to the counter's edge, and lay the sage leaves on the loin, distributing them evenly. Lift the edge of the plastic wrap closest to the counter's edge over the loin to wrap the pancetta around the loin. Roll the rabbit away from you to form a tight roll, pulling the plastic wrap out from under the rabbit as you roll; discard the plastic. Cut 8 (10-inch) lengths of butcher's twine and tie the loin at 1-inch intervals. Place the rabbit loin in the baking dish with the legs, cover with plastic wrap, and refrigerate for at least 1 hour to chill.

Adjust the oven rack to the center position and preheat the oven to 325°F.

Adjust the blade of a mandoline to slice ⅛ inch thick. Slice the garlic lengthwise, stopping just before your fingers get dangerously close to the blade; reserve the garlic ends to chop for another use.

Remove the rabbit from the refrigerator and remove and discard the plastic wrap. Heat ¼ cup of the olive oil in a large Dutch oven over medium-high heat for 2 to 3 minutes, until the oil slides easily and is smoking around the edges of the pan. Add the rabbit legs to the Dutch oven in a single layer and sear for 6 to 8 minutes, until both sides are golden brown. Remove the legs and return them to the baking dish. Add the remaining ¼ cup olive oil and heat it over medium-high heat until the oil slides easily and is smoking around the edges of the pan. Place the rabbit loin in the pan and sear it for 12 to 15 minutes, until it is deeply caramelized all over, turning the loin so it browns evenly. Transfer the loin to the baking dish with the legs.

Add the onion and garlic to the Dutch oven you cooked the rabbit in and sauté over medium-high heat for 6 to 8 minutes, until they are soft and deeply caramelized, stirring to prevent them from burning. Move the vegetables to one side of the pan. Add the tomato paste to the space created and cook for about 2 minutes to caramelize the tomato paste, stirring constantly so it doesn't burn. Add the white wine and cook for 2 to 3 minutes, until it has almost all evaporated, scraping to release any bits stuck to the bottom of the pan. Add the rosemary sprigs and →

1 tablespoon double-concentrated tomato paste

1 cup dry white wine

2 fresh rosemary sprigs

2 oranges, cut into quarters through the core

6 cups Chicken Stock (page 159; or sodium-free or low-sodium store-bought)

For the Fried Rosemary

2 cups olive oil (or canola oil), or as needed

½ cup fresh rosemary leaves

½ teaspoon kosher salt

For Serving

Braised Greens (page 297)

Finishing-quality extra-virgin olive oil

oranges. Turn off the heat and add all of the rabbit pieces in a single layer. Add the chicken stock, pouring it around, not over, the rabbit so you don't wash off the seared exterior, adding as much as needed to come just to the top of the rabbit without submerging it. Bring the liquid to a boil over high heat and turn off the heat. Put the lid on the Dutch oven and put the pan in the oven to braise the rabbit for 30 to 40 minutes, until an instant-read thermometer inserted deep into the center of the loin registers 145°F to 155°F.

While the rabbit is braising, to fry the rosemary, pour enough olive oil into a small saucepan to fill it 1½ to 2 inches deep. Fasten a deep-fry thermometer, if you have one, to the side of the pan and heat the oil over medium-high heat until the thermometer registers 350°F or a pinch of salt sizzles when dropped into the oil. While the oil is heating, create a bed of paper towels and have a slotted spoon or mesh strainer handy. Turn off the heat, add the rosemary leaves, and fry for about 30 seconds, until the leaves are crispy but not brown. Use the slotted spoon or strainer to lift the rosemary leaves out of the pot and transfer them to the paper towels to drain. Sprinkle with the salt. Let the oil cool and strain it into a container; cover and reserve the oil to cook with another time.

While the rabbit is in the oven, make the braised greens.

Remove the rabbit from the oven and remove the lid from the Dutch oven. Transfer the loin to a baking dish large enough to hold all the rabbit pieces in a single layer. Return the lid to the Dutch oven and return it to the oven to cook the legs for 10 to 20 minutes, until fork-tender. To test for doneness, remove the lid from the Dutch oven, insert a fork into a rabbit leg, and turn it slightly; if the meat pulls apart with very little effort, it's done. Remove the rabbit legs from the oven, uncover, and transfer the legs to the baking dish with the loin.

Increase the oven temperature to 375°F and wait about 10 minutes for the oven to heat up.

Place a mesh strainer over a large saucepan and strain the braising liquid into the saucepan, pressing on the solids to extract as much liquid as possible. Bring the liquid to a boil over high heat. Reduce the heat to medium to maintain a steady simmer and cook the liquid for 10 to 15 minutes, until it is thick enough to coat the back of a spoon.

While the sauce is reducing, place the baking dish with the rabbit legs and loin in the oven to roast until the pancetta is crisp, 5 to 7 minutes. Remove the baking dish from the oven. Place the loin on a cutting board and snip off and discard the ties.

To serve, lay the braised greens in a bed on an extra-large platter. Slice the rabbit loin 1 inch thick. Slide your knife under the loin to pick up the slices and lay them on the bed of greens, fanning them out down the center of the platter. Place the legs around the loin and spoon the sauce over the legs and loin. Drizzle about 2 tablespoons finishing-quality olive oil over the rabbit and scatter the fried rosemary over the top.

Pollo alla Diavola on Toast

Serves 4

I have so many things to say about this chicken dish, starting with the fact that it's really not about the chicken. It's about the toast that the chicken is roasted and served on. The chicken, which is coated in spicy seasonings, is roasted on thick slices of bread, so the juices, fat, and spices drip down into the toast, which gets saturated with flavor but stays crunchy around the edges. The chicken is good, but the bread you just can't stop eating! In the kitchen, we refer to this dish as "chicken French toast." We tell customers: Just discard the chicken and eat the toast. We're kidding, of course. Sort of.

This recipe calls for homemade chicken stock, which doesn't contain any sodium. If the stock you are using does contain sodium, cut the salt in this recipe by half.

Ask your butcher for one whole (3- to 4-pound) chicken, halved.

You will need four dinner plates to serve the chicken and toast.

To prepare the chicken, adjust the oven racks so one is in the top third and the other is in the bottom third and preheat the oven to 375°F.

Place the chicken in a large baking dish or on a baking sheet. Stir the paprika, salt, black pepper, and cayenne together in a small bowl. Reserve 1 tablespoon of the seasonings and sprinkle the rest evenly over the chicken. Set aside for 30 minutes to 1 hour to come to room temperature.

Lay the onion slices in a single layer in a large baking dish. Add enough chicken stock to come halfway up the sides of the onions and sprinkle with the reserved seasonings. Place the onions on the top rack of the oven and roast for 35 minutes, until they are soft and translucent. Remove the onions from the oven.

While the onions are roasting, pour ¼ cup of the olive oil into a large roasting pan and lay the bread slices in the pan. Place one chicken half, skin side up, on each slice of bread. Put the chicken and bread on the bottom rack of the oven and roast it for 45 minutes, until an instant-read thermometer registers 155°F when inserted deep into the thigh.

For the Chicken, Toast, and Onions

1 whole (3½- to 4-pound) chicken, halved

2 tablespoons sweet smoked paprika

1 tablespoon kosher salt

1 tablespoon fresh coarsely ground black pepper

½ teaspoon cayenne pepper

2 large yellow Spanish onions, peeled and sliced through the middle (not root to tip) into ¾- to 1-inch-thick rounds

1½ cups Chicken Stock (page 159; or sodium-free or low-sodium store-bought), or as needed

Remove the chicken and bread from the oven and transfer the chicken to a cutting board.

Heat the remaining 2 tablespoons olive oil in a large skillet over medium-high heat for 2 to 3 minutes, until the oil slides easily and is smoking around the edges of the pan. Carefully slide a metal spatula under the bread to release it from the roasting pan, taking care not to let the crunchy bits of bread stick to the pan, and put the bread, bottom side down, into the skillet. Toast the bread for about 4 minutes, until it is deeply caramelized and crunchy. Transfer the bread to a cutting board, cut each slice in half, and put each half on a dinner plate.

Cut the lemon in half through the middle. Trim and discard ½ inch from each end so each half has two flat surfaces. Brush both cut ends of the lemon halves with olive oil and set aside.

Remove the onions from the baking dish and place them in a small bowl. Pour the juice from the baking dish you cooked the onions in into the roasting pan in which you cooked the chicken and bread and place it on the stove. Cook the sauce over high heat, scraping up any bits stuck to the bottom of the pan, until it is thick and syrupy, about 5 minutes. Turn off the heat.

To serve, cut the thigh and leg off each chicken breast half and cut each chicken breast in half. Put one chicken breast half and a thigh and leg on each toast. Nestle the onions next to the toast, dividing them evenly. Spoon enough pan sauce over each serving of chicken so it's glistening, drizzle each serving with about ½ tablespoon finishing-quality olive oil, and sprinkle with the parsley, dividing it evenly. Serve the remaining pan sauce on the side. Place the lemon halves with the larger cut sides facing up on the platter.

¼ cup plus 2 tablespoons olive oil

2 (1½-inch-thick) slices from the center of a 1-pound loaf of rustic bread

For Serving

1 lemon

Olive oil for the lemon

Finishing-quality extra-virgin olive oil

2 tablespoons finely chopped fresh Italian parsley leaves

Roasted Amberjack Collars with Labneh, Zhug, and Radish Salad   221

Branzino alla Piastra with Wilted Soft Herbs   225

Fried Calamari alla Piccata   227

Baked Mussels and Clams with N'duja and Aioli, and Toast for Dipping   230

Fish Stock   232

Roasted Salmon Steaks with Remoulade Butter   233

Fideus a la Catalana with Sweet Sherry and Garlic Aioli   236

Lobster Potpie   239

Skate Wing with Braised Leeks, Brown Butter, and Capers   243

Roasted Yellowtail with Spring or Summer Vegetables   246

Spring: Snap Peas with Chive Vinaigrette   246

Summer: Charred Beans with Mustard Vinaigrette   247

Mischiato Potente: Mixed Pasta and Seafood Stew   249

Fried Whole Branzino with Pickled Peppers and Charred Scallions   253

Salt-Baked Fish with Green Olive and Charred Lemon Salmoriglio   257

Pesce

It's easy for seafood to get lost or forgotten at a meat-centric restaurant, but not so at Chi Spacca. Our seafood offerings embody what we think an Italian butcher would do if she or he were to suddenly change careers and become a fishmonger. Whether it's thick salmon steaks with the meaty quality of a New York strip, amberjack collars to pick from like oxtails, skate wing served on the "bone," or a butterflied branzino that lies flat on a plate with its face looking up at the diner, this is fish as seen through the lens of a butcher.

Roasted Amberjack Collars with Labneh, Zhug, and Radish Salad

Serves 4

We butcher whole fish at Chi Spacca, so we had collars left over, which Ryan was grilling and serving, along with tortillas and salsa to make tacos, for staff meal. Fish collars are cut from behind the head of the fish, and are a fatty, flavorful cut, which you most often see grilled at Japanese restaurants. I love any meat that I can pick off the bone with my fingers, and fish collars definitely fit that bill. When I walked by and saw what the staff was eating, I said, "Wow, I love these! Let's put them on the menu!" So the staff's loss was the customers' gain, because we no longer serve the collars for staff meal, but now we have this delicious fish, served on a bed of labneh and zhug, a Middle Eastern herb sauce, and topped with a refreshing radish salad on the menu instead.

You can find amberjack (also called kanpachi) in good fish markets. If you can't find it, use yellowtail (also called hamachi), an equally mild-flavored, buttery-textured fish instead. Labneh is a fresh cheese traditional to Middle Eastern cuisine made by straining plain, whole milk yogurt through cheesecloth to drain out the whey. It takes three days to make. For a shortcut, substitute 2 cups quality labneh, from a Middle Eastern grocery store. Chipotle chiles are dried, smoked jalapeño chiles; they have a wonderful, deeply smoky flavor. If you can't find chipotle chile powder, use sweet smoked paprika or another quality chile powder.

You will need a large platter to serve the collars.

To make the labneh, put the yogurt in a medium bowl. Using a fine Microplane, zest the bright yellow outer layer of the lemon into the bowl. Cut the lemon in half and juice it; add 3 tablespoons of the lemon juice to the bowl. Add the kosher salt and stir to combine. Line a second bowl with a double layer of cheesecloth; make sure to cut a large enough piece of cheesecloth so it flops over the top of the bowl. Pour the yogurt mixture over the cheesecloth and gather the edges of the cheesecloth at the middle to form a loose bundle; you don't want the bundle so tight that the yogurt squishes out of the cheesecloth. Tie the bundle closed at the top with kitchen twine. Slide the handle of a long wooden spoon through the cheesecloth, piercing the cloth just under the knot so →

For the Labneh

4 cups Straus Family Creamery Organic Greek Yogurt (or another plain, whole-milk, not overly thick yogurt)

1 lemon

¾ teaspoon kosher salt

For the Rub

1 tablespoon coriander seeds

2 tablespoons kosher salt

the handle goes all the way through and the bundle hangs from it and looks like a "hobo stick." Drop the bundle down into a tall container, such as a stockpot, so the spoon handle rests across the top of the container and the bundle hangs down into the container with at least 2 inches of clearance at the bottom. If the yogurt bundle is touching the bottom of the container, use a taller container. Refrigerate for 3 days to drain the whey from the yogurt. Remove the yogurt from the refrigerator and remove and discard the cheesecloth. Transfer the labneh to a bowl, and discard the whey. Refrigerate, covered, until you're ready to use it.

To make the rub to season the amberjack, on the second day that your labneh is hanging, put the collars in a single layer in a large baking dish or on a baking sheet. Finely grind the coriander seeds in a mortar or spice grinder and put them in a small bowl. Add the salt, brown sugar, and chile powder, and stir to combine. Sprinkle the seasonings evenly over the collars, massaging them with your hands to coat the collars completely. Cover with plastic wrap and refrigerate the collars overnight or for at least 6 hours.

To make the zhug, toast the cumin seeds, coriander seeds, and cardamom pod in a small skillet over medium heat for 1 to 2 minutes, until they are fragrant and toasted, shaking the pan often so they don't burn. Transfer the spices to a mortar or spice grinder and very coarsely grind them. If you are using a spice grinder, transfer the spices to a small bowl.

Remove and discard the stems from the Fresno and jalapeño chiles. Cut the chiles in half and remove and discard the seeds. Finely chop the chiles and add them to the mortar or bowl. Use a fine Microplane to grate the garlic into the mortar or bowl. Add the kosher salt and stir to combine; if you are using a mortar, use the pestle to grind the chiles slightly. Add the cilantro, parsley, and mint leaves and stir or grind to combine. Add the lemon juice and stir to combine. Drizzle in the finishing-quality olive oil, stirring constantly. Add more lemon juice or kosher salt to taste.

To make the radish salad, adjust the blade of a mandoline to slice ⅛ inch thick. Cut the radishes lengthwise into slices ⅛ inch thick, stopping just before your fingers get dangerously close to the blade and discarding or snacking on the first slice and the part that you are holding so you're left with only thin slices. Place the radishes in a small bowl. Add

1 tablespoon light brown sugar

1 tablespoon ground chipotle chile powder (or sweet smoked paprika or another chile powder)

For the Collars

4 amberjack collars (or yellowtail collars; about 8 ounces each)

¼ cup olive oil, plus more for the lemons

2 lemons

For the Zhug

1 tablespoon cumin seeds

1 tablespoon coriander seeds

1 cardamom pod

2 Fresno chiles

1 jalapeño chile

1 large garlic clove, peeled

2 teaspoons kosher salt, plus more to taste

¼ cup finely chopped fresh cilantro leaves

¼ cup finely chopped fresh Italian parsley leaves

1 tablespoon finely chopped fresh mint leaves

¼ cup fresh lemon juice, plus more to taste

½ cup finishing-quality extra-virgin olive oil

the dill tufts and tear the mint leaves into 3 or 4 pieces to drop into the bowl. Wrap the bowl in plastic wrap and refrigerate the salad until you're ready to dress and serve it. To cook the collars, adjust the oven racks so none is near the oven floor; you'll be putting a baking sheet directly on the oven floor. If you are using an electric oven or another oven where you can't put anything on the floor, place the rack as close to the floor as possible and put a pizza steel or stone, if you have one, on it. Preheat the oven to 400°F.

Remove the collars from the refrigerator and remove and discard the plastic wrap. Drizzle 1 tablespoon of the olive oil onto each collar and massage with your hands to coat, making sure to get the oil into all the nooks and crannies of the collars. Arrange the collars, skin side up, on the baking sheet.

Put the baking sheet on the oven floor and roast the collars for 20 minutes. Remove the baking sheet from the oven and turn the broiler on. Wait 5 minutes for the broiler to heat up, then place the collars under the broiler until the skin is crispy and deep golden brown, about 3 minutes. Remove the baking sheet from the broiler.

While the collars are roasting, cut the 2 lemons in half through the middle and trim and discard ½ inch from each end, so the lemon halves have two flat surfaces. Brush both cut ends of the lemon halves with olive oil. Heat a large skillet over medium-high heat. Place the lemon halves, center sides down, in the skillet and cook for about 2 minutes, until they are deeply caramelized. Turn and cook the smaller sides of the lemon halves for about 30 seconds just to warm them. Turn off the heat.

Squeeze the juice of the lemon half and sprinkle the kosher salt over the radishes and herbs and toss to coat them with the lemon juice and salt. Drizzle with the finishing-quality olive oil and toss to combine.

To serve, spoon the labneh into the center of a large platter. Use the back of the spoon to spread it to the edges of the platter in organic, uneven swirls, creating a shallow reservoir. Spoon the zhug into the reservoir and use the back of the spoon to spread it to the edges. Place the collars on the reservoir of labneh and zhug. Nestle the lemon halves, center sides up, around the fish and pile the radish salad into the center of each collar, dividing it evenly. Crush the flaky sea salt between your fingertips and sprinkle the parsley over the fish.

For the Radish Salad

2 bunches French breakfast radishes (or another small radish variety)

1 cup fresh dill tufts (pulled from the stems)

1 cup fresh mint leaves

½ lemon

1 teaspoon kosher salt

1 tablespoon finishing-quality extra-virgin olive oil

For Serving

Flaky sea salt

2 tablespoons finely chopped fresh Italian parsley leaves

Branzino alla Piastra
with Wilted Soft Herbs

Serves 4

One of my favorite things to order as a customer at Chi Spacca is this whole branzino. The fish is butterflied and lies flat, covering the entire plate. Served on a bed of wilted fresh herbs, it's the epitome of simplicity. The hot fish steams the herbs and brings out their aromas. Hayley Porter, the lead line cook at Chi Spacca, calls the herbs "the unsung hero" of this dish. They're almost totally hidden under the fish, but they are what takes this dish over the top.

Ideally, you will cook both branzinos at the same time, so if you're looking for an excuse to buy a two-burner cast-iron griddle, this is it. If you have two large skillets (preferably cast-iron), you can also cook them simultaneously in two different skillets. That said, this recipe calls for you to cook the fish one at a time, and to keep the first fish warm in the oven while you cook the second one.

Ask your fishmonger for 2 whole (1-pound) branzinos (or rockfish, cod, or snapper), heads attached, gutted, scaled, pin bones and spine removed, and butterflied.

You will need two large platters to serve the branzinos.

To prepare the herbs, combine the chervil, chives, tarragon, celery leaves, dill, and mint in a medium bowl and set aside.

To cook the fish, adjust the oven rack to the center position and preheat the oven to 250°F. (If you are cooking both fish at the same time, either in two skillets or a two-burner cast-iron griddle, skip this step.)

Cut the lemon in half through the middle. Trim and discard ½ inch from each end so each half has two flat surfaces. Brush both cut ends of the lemon halves with olive oil and set aside.

Pat the fish dry and place them, skin side down, on a large baking sheet or cutting board. Drizzle 1 tablespoon of the olive oil on each fish and massage with your hands to coat the fish with the oil. Sprinkle the kosher salt and a few turns of pepper evenly over both sides of the fish.

Have a baking sheet and a pot lid that fits inside the skillet you are cooking the fish in handy; you will use the lid to press down on the fish. →

For the Herbs

½ cup fresh chervil leaves

10 fresh chives, cut into 1-inch bâtons

¼ cup fresh tarragon leaves

½ cup fresh celery leaves (look for the palest leaves, which are located closer to the core)

½ cup fresh dill sprigs

10 fresh mint leaves

½ cup finishing-quality extra-virgin olive oil

½ teaspoon flaky sea salt

Heat 2 tablespoons of the remaining olive oil in a large skillet (preferably cast-iron) over medium-high heat for 2 to 3 minutes, until the oil slides easily and is smoking around the edges of the pan. Reduce the heat to medium and lay the fish, skin side down, in the pan. Place the lid on the fish and gently press for about 10 seconds to make sure the surface of the fish is touching the pan, which will ensure the skin crisps. Remove the pressure; if the fish begins to curl at the edges, re-apply the pressure for another 10 seconds and check again. Cook the fish over medium heat for 12 to 15 minutes, until the skin is golden brown and crispy. Slide a spatula under the fish to release the skin from the pan, taking care not to rip the skin, and lift the fish out of the pan. (The skin will release easily when it is ready to be turned. If it is sticking, cook the fish for another minute or two.) Flip the fish and cook the second side for 1 minute just to warm it through and coat the second side with the oil. Transfer the fish to the baking sheet and place it in the oven to stay warm. Wipe the skillet clean, add the remaining oil, and heat the oil until it slides easily and is smoking around the edges of the pan. Add the second fish and cook it as you did the first one. (If you are using a two-burner griddle or two large skillets, cook both fish at the same time.)

While the second fish is cooking, drizzle the finishing-quality olive oil and crush the flaky sea salt between your fingertips over the herbs. Gently toss to distribute the herbs and dress them with the oil and salt. Lay the herbs equally to cover the surface of the two platters, dividing them evenly. Place the lemon halves, with the center sides down, in the skillet with the fish, finding space for them around the fish, and cook for about 2 minutes, until they are deeply caramelized. Turn and cook the smaller sides for about 30 seconds just to warm them.

To serve, remove the fish from the skillet or baking sheet and lay one fish, skin side up, on each platter on top of the herbs. Crush about ½ teaspoon flaky sea salt between your fingertips over each fish.

Place one lemon half with the center side facing up on each platter of herbs.

For the Fish

1 lemon

¼ cup plus 2 tablespoons olive oil, plus more for the lemon

2 whole branzinos (about 1 pound each), heads attached, gutted, scaled, pin bones and spine removed, and butterflied

2 teaspoons kosher salt

Fresh coarsely ground black pepper

For Serving

Flaky sea salt

Fried Calamari alla Piccata

Serves 4

We borrowed this unusual calamari preparation from one of our sister restaurants, Del Posto, in New York. It's not your typical breaded and fried calamari, served with marinara dipping sauce. Although it is battered and fried, it's then tossed in "piccata sauce," which is white wine, lemon, and capers. The calamari are crunchy with a delicious, light glaze on the outside, like an Italian version of Chinese food. When you're serving these, make sure to have your table set, guests seated, and wine poured before you put the calamari in the oil to fry. Take them out, toss them in the sauce, and serve them as quickly as possible. The key is to enjoy them while the calamari are still slightly crunchy.

Use Koda Farms Blue Star Mochiko rice flour to make this. It results in the ideal batter consistency and a crispy, crunchy exterior. It is available at specialty food stores and online sources. This recipe calls for homemade chicken stock, which doesn't contain any sodium. If the stock you are using does contain sodium, cut the salt in this recipe by half.

You will need a large platter to serve the calamari.

To fry the calamari, pour enough oil into a large saucepan to fill it 3 to 4 inches deep. Fasten a deep-fry thermometer, if you have one, to the side of the pan and heat the oil over medium-high heat until the thermometer registers 350°F or a pinch of salt sizzles when dropped into the oil. Line a large plate or baking sheet with paper towels and have a slotted spoon handy. Have a large platter ready.

While the oil is heating, to make the piccata sauce, adjust the blade of a mandoline to slice ⅛ inch thick. Slice the garlic lengthwise, stopping just before your fingers get dangerously close to the blade; reserve the remaining garlic to chop for another use.

Heat the olive oil in a medium saucepan over medium heat for 1 minute to warm it slightly. Add the garlic and cook until it is fragrant, 3 to 4 minutes, stirring constantly so it doesn't burn. Add the sugar and cook for 2 to 3 minutes, until the garlic is light golden. Add the white wine and red pepper flakes and cook for about 5 minutes, until almost all the wine →

For the Calamari

2 quarts (8 cups) canola oil
(or another neutral-flavored oil),
or as needed

1 cup Koda Farms Blue Star
Mochiko rice flour

½ cup club soda, plus more
as needed

1 pound calamari tubes
and tentacles

1 teaspoon kosher salt

For the Piccata Sauce

3 large garlic cloves, peeled

1 tablespoon olive oil

½ teaspoon sugar

½ cup dry white wine

has evaporated. Add the chicken stock and capers and simmer for about 10 minutes, until the liquid is reduced to a syrupy consistency, thick enough to coat the back of a spoon. Reduce the heat to low. Add the butter a few cubes at a time, whisking as you add it, until the butter has disappeared into the sauce, and waiting until the butter has melted before adding more. If the butter is melting immediately, before you have the chance to whisk it in, remove the pan from the heat and wait a minute or two for the sauce to cool down before adding more butter. When you have whisked in all the butter, turn off the heat and whisk in the lemon juice and salt, adding more lemon juice and salt to taste. Leave the sauce on or near the stove to stay warm while you fry the calamari.

Put the rice flour in a medium bowl. Add the club soda and whisk to combine. Gradually add more club soda, whisking constantly, until the mixture is the consistency of thin pancake batter. Add the calamari to the bowl with the batter and mix until the calamari are completely coated with batter.

Working in three or more batches, lift the calamari pieces out of the batter one by one, allow the batter to drip into the bowl for a few seconds, and place them in the hot oil, adding only as many as will fit in a single layer in the oil. (If you add too many calamari to the oil at once, the oil temperature will drop, resulting in oily, soggy batter.) Fry the calamari for 3 to 4 minutes, until the batter looks cooked and crispy, turning the calamari so they fry evenly. Remove the calamari from the oil and spread them out in a single layer on the paper towels to drain. Season with one quarter of the salt while the calamari are hot, so the salt sticks to the batter. Fry the remaining calamari in two or three additional batches, adding it to the paper towels in a single layer and salting the fried calamari immediately after removing them from the oil.

To serve, put half of the fried calamari in a large bowl, drizzle with half of the piccata sauce, and gently fold the calamari with the sauce to coat them. Transfer the calamari to the large platter and repeat, tossing the remaining calamari with the remaining sauce and adding them to the platter. Squeeze the lemon half over the calamari and sprinkle with the parsley.

½ teaspoon red pepper flakes

1½ cups Chicken Stock (page 159; or sodium-free or low-sodium store-bought)

2 tablespoons capers (preferably salt-packed), soaked for 15 minutes if salt-packed, rinsed and drained

8 tablespoons (1 stick) cold unsalted butter, cut into 1-inch cubes

1 tablespoon fresh lemon juice, plus more to taste

½ teaspoon kosher salt, plus more to taste

To Serve

½ lemon

1 tablespoon finely chopped fresh Italian parsley leaves

Baked Mussels and Clams with N'duja and Aioli, and Toast for Dipping

Serves 4

N'duja is a spiced pork fat and meat mixture from the southern Italian region of Calabria. Mussels with n'duja is a classic combination, similar to the Spanish dish of mussels with chorizo. I love mussels with aioli, or garlic mayonnaise; we drizzle some over the top and serve the rest on the side.

   This recipe calls for you to make the aioli in a mini food processor. To make it by hand, see Making Aioli by Hand (page 104).

   You will need a 14-inch oval ceramic baking dish (or another 16-cup-capacity baking dish) to make and serve this.

To make the aioli, combine the vinegar and lemon juice in a small measuring cup or bowl. Combine the canola oil and extra-virgin olive oil in a measuring cup with a spout.

Put the egg yolk and kosher salt in the bowl of a mini food processor. Using a fine Microplane, grate the garlic into the food processor bowl and pulse to combine the ingredients. With the machine running, begin adding the oils through the lid of the food processor, blending continuously, until the oils and egg are emulsified and creamy looking; you will have added about ¼ cup of the oils. Turn off the machine, take off the lid, scrape down the sides of the bowl with a rubber spatula, and add one-third of the lemon juice–vinegar mixture. Return the lid and pulse to combine. Add the remaining oils in a slow, steady drizzle, adding the remaining lemon juice–vinegar mixture when the aioli gets very thick. Turn off the machine and transfer the aioli to a small bowl, scraping down the sides of the food processor bowl. Add more lemon juice or kosher salt to taste.

Adjust the oven rack to the center position and preheat the oven to 350°F.

To make the toasts, lay the bread on a baking sheet and brush the tops with olive oil. Toast the bread in the oven for about 12 minutes, until it is golden brown but not crunchy. Remove the toast from the oven and transfer it to a cutting board.

For the Aioli

2 teaspoons champagne vinegar

2 teaspoons fresh lemon juice, plus more to taste

¾ cup canola oil (or another neutral-flavored oil)

¼ cup extra-virgin olive oil

1 extra-large egg yolk, at room temperature

1 teaspoon kosher salt, plus more to taste

1 large garlic clove, peeled

For the Toasts

4 (1-inch-thick) slices from the center of a 1-pound loaf of rustic bread

Olive oil

1 large garlic clove, peeled

Finishing-quality extra-virgin olive oil

Flaky sea salt

Rub one side of the bread vigorously with the garlic clove, rubbing hard enough that bits of the garlic end up on the toast. Drizzle about 1 teaspoon finishing-quality olive oil and crush a big pinch of flaky sea salt between your fingertips onto each piece of toast. Cut each toast in half on an extreme bias.

To prepare the mussels, clams, and n'duja, scrub the mussels and clams under cold running water to clean them thoroughly, and pull off and discard the beards from the mussels, if they are still attached. Put the mussels and clams into a 14-inch (or similar capacity) baking dish.

Warm the n'duja in a large skillet over medium heat for about 2 minutes, until it melts. Add the shallots and garlic and cook for about 5 minutes, stirring occasionally, until they are soft and fragrant, stirring often so they don't brown. Add the white wine and cook for 2 to 3 minutes, until it has almost all evaporated, scraping to release any bits stuck to the bottom. Turn off the heat and add the fish stock. Pour this mixture over the mussels and clams.

Bake the mussels and clams in the oven for 20 to 25 minutes, until all (or the vast majority) of the mussels and clams have opened. Remove the baking dish from the oven. If a few of the shellfish have refused to open, remove and discard them.

To serve, squeeze the lemon half and drizzle all of the aioli over the mussels and clams. Pile the bread on a small plate to serve alongside the mussels and clams.

For the Mussels, Clams, and N'duja

2 pounds black mussels

2 pounds Manila clams (or littleneck clams or another small clam variety)

2 cups N'duja (page 58; or store-bought)

2 medium shallots, peeled and minced

10 large garlic cloves, peeled and minced

2 cups dry white wine

3 cups Fish Stock (page 232; or store-bought)

To Serve

½ lemon

Fish Stock

Makes about 4 cups

We use this rich seafood stock for the Baked Mussels and Clams with N'duja and Aioli, and Toast for Dipping (page 230) and the Mischiato Potente (page 249). In both cases, it makes about 1 cup more than you will need in the recipe. Add kosher salt to taste, and enjoy it on its own.

To make the stock, heat the oil in a large stockpot over medium-high heat for 1 minute just to warm it slightly. Add the onions, carrot, celery, and garlic and cook for 5 to 6 minutes, until the vegetables are soft, stirring occasionally so the vegetables don't brown. Move the vegetables to one side of the pan. Add the tomato paste to the space created and cook for about 2 minutes to caramelize the tomato paste, stirring constantly so it doesn't burn. Add the fish bones and white wine and cook for 2 to 3 minutes, until almost all the wine has evaporated, scraping to release any bits stuck to the bottom of the pot. Add the tomatoes, lemon, oregano, tarragon, rosemary, and 2 quarts water, or enough to cover the fish bones by 1 inch. Increase the heat to high and bring the water to a boil. Reduce the heat to low to maintain a gentle simmer and simmer the stock for 1 hour 20 minutes, skimming off any foam that rises to the top. Turn off the heat and let the stock cool slightly. Put a mesh strainer over a large pot or bowl and strain the stock, pressing on the solids to extract as much liquid as possible. Discard the solids.

2 tablespoons olive oil

1 large yellow onion, peeled and roughly chopped

1 large carrot, roughly chopped

1 celery stalk, roughly chopped

10 large garlic cloves, peeled

2 tablespoons double-concentrated tomato paste

2 pounds fish bones (preferably with heads on)

1 cup dry white wine

2 large tomatoes, chopped (or 2 cups canned tomatoes, strained)

1 lemon, cut into quarters

5 fresh oregano sprigs

3 fresh tarragon sprigs

3 fresh rosemary sprigs

Roasted Salmon Steaks
with Remoulade Butter

Serves 4

A lot of times in expanding the menu, Ryan and I will have a conversation about old-school dishes that we miss. In one such conversation, we got to talking about the presentation of a salmon steak, as opposed to the more modern fillet. When I started my cooking journey, back in the mid-1970s, salmon steak was the only cut you saw, and that's how I learned to cook salmon, whereas now you almost always see salmon fillets. Like the name suggests, the iconic, horseshoe-shaped cut seems like a steak. In this recipe, the salmon is seared in a hot pan to give it a beautiful caramelized exterior, and then it is roasted in the oven and served topped with an herby compound butter.

This recipe calls for you to cook two salmon steaks at a time in a large skillet (preferably cast-iron). To cook all four steaks at one time, use a two-burner cast-iron griddle.

Ask your fishmonger for 4 (1-inch-thick) salmon steaks (10 to 12 ounces each), preferably cut from the center.

You will need a large platter to serve the salmon.

To make the herb butter, put the butter, parsley, dill, chives, tarragon, capers, shallot, lemon juice, and salt in the bowl of a stand mixer. Finely chop the anchovies with a large knife and use the flat side of the knife to smash them into a paste. Add the paste to the bowl with the other ingredients. Using a fine Microplane, grate the garlic into the bowl. Fit the mixer with the paddle attachment and mix on medium speed until the herbs and other flavorings are combined with the butter, stopping to scrape down the sides of the mixer as needed. Transfer the butter to a small bowl and set it aside.

To cook the salmon, adjust the oven racks so none is near the oven floor; you'll be putting a baking sheet directly on the oven floor. If you are using an electric oven or another oven where you can't put anything on the floor, place a rack as close to the floor as possible and put a pizza steel or stone, if you have one, on it. Preheat the oven to 350°F. →

For the Herb Butter

½ pound (2 sticks) unsalted butter, softened at room temperature

¼ cup finely chopped fresh Italian parsley leaves

2 tablespoons finely chopped fresh dill

2 tablespoons finely chopped fresh chives

1 tablespoon finely chopped fresh tarragon leaves

2 tablespoons capers (preferably salt-packed), soaked for 15 minutes if salt-packed, rinsed and drained

Pat the salmon steaks dry and place them in a large baking dish or on a plate. Wrap a length of kitchen twine around the perimeter of each salmon steak and tie the ends closed. (Tying the salmon steaks helps maintain their shape.) Cut off and discard the excess twine. Drizzle with 2 tablespoons of the olive oil and massage with your hands to coat the fish with the oil. Sprinkle the salt and a few turns of pepper evenly over both sides of the fish.

Heat 1 tablespoon of the olive oil in a large cast-iron skillet (or another heavy skillet) over medium-high heat for 2 to 3 minutes, until the oil slides easily and is smoking around the edges of the pan. Add 2 of the salmon steaks and sear for 5 to 6 minutes, until they are deeply caramelized on both sides. Remove the salmon steaks from the pan and place them on a baking sheet. Wipe the pan clean, add the remaining 1 tablespoon oil, and heat the oil until it is almost smoking. Add the remaining 2 salmon steaks and cook them as you did the first steaks. Add them to the baking sheet, in a single layer, with the other cooked salmon. (If you are using a two-burner griddle, heat all of the oil and cook all 4 steaks at the same time.)

Put the baking sheet on the oven floor or the lowest rack and roast the salmon for 5 minutes. Remove the baking dish from the oven, flip the steaks, and return them to the oven to roast for 2 minutes. Remove the baking sheet from the oven.

To serve, transfer the salmon steaks to a large platter. Working quickly so the butter doesn't melt, dollop a big spoonful of herb butter onto each steak and use the back of the spoon to spread it out in one quick motion. Squeeze the lemon juice over the steaks.

1 medium shallot, peeled and finely chopped

2 tablespoons fresh lemon juice

1 teaspoon kosher salt

4 anchovy fillets (preferably salt-packed; rinsed and backbones removed if salt-packed)

1 large garlic clove, peeled

For the Salmon

4 (1-inch-thick) salmon steaks (10 to 12 ounces each)

¼ cup olive oil

2 tablespoons kosher salt

Fresh coarsely ground black pepper

To Serve

½ lemon

Fideus a la Catalana with Sweet Sherry and Garlic Aioli

Serves 4

Both Ryan and I are huge fans of Spanish food, so it was only natural that we invited Anthony Sasso, the executive chef from one of our sister restaurants, Casa Mono, in New York City, to do a collaborative dinner at Chi Spacca. The entire menu was delicious, but this fideus, a traditional Spanish dish made of broken angel hair pasta, baked into a sort of casserole, was, for me, the standout. Anthony makes an aioli to go with this recipe, using garlic caramelized with Pedro Ximénez aged sweet sherry. The flavor is very unusual. It really makes this dish. We use carabineros prawns from Spain for this, which are a beautiful orange-red hue; they remind me of baby lobsters. Any quality, large prawns, such as spot prawns or blue prawns, will work. The pasta that sticks to the bottom of the dish is the best part, so make sure to scrape it up and enjoy it.

This recipe calls for you to make the aioli in a mini food processor. To make it by hand, see Making Aioli by Hand (page 104).

The aioli for this dish calls for 30 cloves of garlic. (No, it is not a typo.) The garlic is poached in sweet sherry until it is very soft and mild flavored. When puréed into the aioli, it adds delicious flavor and is not at all overwhelming.

You will need a 12-inch stovetop-to-oven cooking vessel, such as a handle-free sauté pan, a cast-iron skillet, or a stovetop-proof clay *casuela* to make and serve the fideus.

To make the aioli, combine the garlic and sherry in a small saucepan and bring to a simmer over medium heat. Reduce the heat to low to maintain a steady simmer and cook the garlic for 15 to 20 minutes, until the cloves are very soft and the sherry has reduced and thickened to a syrupy consistency. Turn off the heat and set aside to cool to room temperature.

Transfer the garlic and sherry to the bowl of a mini food processor fitted with a metal blade. Add the egg yolk and blend until the garlic is puréed. With the machine running, begin adding the olive oil through the lid of the food processor, blending continuously, until the oil and egg are emulsified and creamy looking; you will have added about ¼ cup of the oil. Turn off the machine, take off the lid, scrape down the sides of the bowl with a rubber spatula, and add one-third of the lemon juice. Return the

For the Aioli

¾ cup large garlic cloves, peeled (about 30 cloves)

1½ cups Pedro Ximénez sherry (or another dry sherry)

1 extra-large egg yolk, at room temperature

1 cup olive oil

¼ cup fresh lemon juice, plus more to taste

¼ teaspoon kosher salt, plus more to taste

lid and pulse to combine. Add the remaining oil in a slow, steady drizzle, adding the remaining lemon juice when the aioli gets very thick. Turn off the machine and transfer the aioli to a small bowl, scraping down the sides of the food processor bowl. Stir to combine. Add salt or more lemon juice to taste. Cover and refrigerate the aioli until you're ready to use it.

To prepare the fideus, adjust the oven rack to the center position and preheat the oven to 350°F.

Spread the pasta in an even layer on a large baking sheet and toast it in the oven for 7 to 10 minutes, until golden brown, shaking the pan once or twice during that time so the pasta browns evenly. Remove the baking sheet from the oven and set aside until the pasta is cool enough to touch. Break the pasta into 1½-inch pieces.

Scrub the mussels and clams under cold water to clean them, and pull off and discard the beards from the mussels, if they are still attached.

Heat a 12-inch handle-free sauté pan, a cast-iron skillet, or a stovetop-proof clay *casuela* over medium heat. Add the guanciale and cook until the fat begins to melt, about 8 minutes. Add the chorizo, garlic, and shallots, and cook for 6 to 8 minutes, until the garlic and shallots begin to brown, but not crisp. Add the pasta and cook, stirring occasionally, until the pasta has softened slightly. Add the white wine and cook for 2 to 3 minutes, until it has almost all evaporated, scraping to release any bits stuck to the bottom. Add the chicken stock and the salt. Increase the heat to high and bring the liquid to a boil. Reduce the heat to medium to maintain a steady simmer, and cook for 6 to 7 minutes, until so much of the liquid has cooked off that the pasta is beginning to stick to the bottom of the pan. Add the mussels and clams and stir to distribute the shellfish evenly.

Bake the fideus in the oven, uncovered, for 8 to 10 minutes, until all of the liquid has been cooked off. Remove from the oven and lay the prawns facing different directions on top of the pasta. Drizzle the prawns with the finishing-quality olive oil and return the fideus to the oven for 8 to 12 minutes, until the pasta on top is golden brown and crisp, and the prawns are red and cooked through. Remove the fideus from the oven and squeeze the half lemon over the top.

To serve, generously dollop half of the aioli in one big spoonful on the dish. Sprinkle with the chopped parsley. Serve the remaining aioli in a small bowl on the side.

For the Fideus

½ pound angel hair pasta

½ pound black mussels

½ pound Manila clams (or littleneck clams, or another small clam variety)

½ pound (½-inch-thick) guanciale (or pancetta) slices, cut into ½-inch pieces

¼ pound Spanish (hard) chorizo (or another spicy salami), skin removed, cut into ½-inch pieces

4 large garlic cloves, peeled and thinly sliced lengthwise

2 medium shallots, peeled and minced

1 cup dry white wine

3 cups Chicken Stock (page 159; or sodium-free or low-sodium store-bought)

1 teaspoon kosher salt

8 prawns (heads intact; about 1 pound)

2 tablespoons finishing-quality extra-virgin olive oil

½ lemon

To Serve

½ cup finely chopped fresh parsley leaves

Lobster Potpie

Serves 4

As a chef, one of the "perks" of being honored at charity functions is that you get to impose on all your friends to cook at the event. At a recent No Kid Hungry by Share Our Strength dinner in Los Angeles, Michael Cimarusti, the chef at Providence in Los Angeles, was one of my victims. I assigned him the main course; Michael's specialty is seafood, and for that dinner, which was served family style, he served a lobster potpie. And what a pie! Lucky for us, Michael shared his recipe for this book.

After blanching the lobsters, you need to shock them in ice water to stop them from cooking. If you don't want to buy a bag of ice, use whatever you have in your freezer.

You may want to make this pie over three days: Cook the lobsters and make the stock the first day. Make the dough and filling on the second day. And assemble, bake, and enjoy the pie on the third day.

You will need a 12-inch shallow oval copper pan to make and serve the potpie.

To cook the lobsters, combine 2 gallons water and 2 tablespoons of the salt in a large stockpot and bring the water to a boil over high heat. Create an ice bath in a separate large stockpot or a large bowl. Add the remaining 1 tablespoon salt and stir to dissolve the salt.

Place the lobsters in the boiling water and cook for 2 to 3 minutes, until they are bright red. Remove the lobsters from the boiling water and place them in the ice water. Add more ice and water if needed to submerge the lobsters and keep them in the water until they are completely cooled, about 5 minutes. Lift the lobsters out of the ice water, letting the water drip off, and place them on a baking sheet to drain for about 5 minutes, pouring off any water that accumulates on the baking sheet.

With a kitchen towel in each hand, hold the body of one lobster in one hand and twist off the claws with the other. Set the claws aside. Repeat with the second lobster. Keep the kitchen towels in your hands and place one hand on the tail and one on the head; twist forcibly in opposite directions until the tail is separated from the head. Set the tail aside with the claws and put the head in a large bowl. Repeat with the second lobster. →

For Cooking the Lobsters

3 tablespoons kosher salt

2 whole lobsters
(about 1 pound each)

For the Stock

2 tablespoons canola oil
(or another neutral-flavored oil)

1 small yellow onion, peeled
and roughly chopped

10 large garlic cloves, peeled

1 large carrot, roughly chopped

1 celery stalk, roughly chopped

1 tablespoon double-
concentrated tomato paste

1 teaspoon fresh coarsely
ground black pepper

½ cup brandy

Crack the claws with a mallet (or the back of a pan) and break them in half at the knuckles. Remove the meat from the claws and knuckles and place it in a separate bowl. Place the shells in the bowl with the heads. Crack the tail shells and remove the meat. Slice the tail meat into 1-inch chunks and add them to the bowl with the claw and knuckle meat. Place the tail shells in the bowl with the claw shells and heads. Cover the bowl of meat with plastic wrap and place it in the refrigerator.

To make the stock, heat the canola oil in a large stockpot over medium-high heat until the oil slides easily in the pan and is almost smoking. Add the lobster heads and shells and cook for 3 to 4 minutes, turning to cook on all sides, until the lobster shells are deep red. Reduce the heat to medium and add the onion, garlic, carrot, and celery. Cook the vegetables with the shells for 6 to 8 minutes, until the vegetables begin to brown slightly, stirring occasionally to prevent them from burning. Move the vegetables and shells to one side of the pan, add the tomato paste to the space created, and cook for about 2 minutes to caramelize the tomato paste, stirring constantly so it doesn't burn. Add the pepper and brandy, taking care when adding the brandy because it may flare up. Cook for 1 to 2 minutes to burn off the alcohol. Add the white wine and cook for 2 to 3 minutes, until it has almost all evaporated, scraping to release any bits stuck to the bottom. Add the tomato, bay leaf, thyme, and 3 quarts (12 cups) water. Increase the heat to high and bring the liquid to a boil. Reduce the heat to low to maintain a gentle simmer and cook the stock for 45 minutes, skimming off any foam that rises to the top. Turn off the heat and let the stock cool slightly. Put a mesh strainer over a large pot or bowl and strain the stock, pressing on the solids to extract as much liquid as possible. Discard the solids. Measure out 5 cups of the stock and reserve any remaining stock for another use. (This recipe will make about a cup more than you need for the potpie.) If you are making the stock in advance, let it come to room temperature, transfer it to a covered container, and refrigerate it for up to 3 days.

To make the dough, combine the flour, sugar, and salt in the bowl of a stand mixer. Fit the mixer with the paddle attachment and mix on low speed to distribute the sugar and salt. Add the butter and mix on low until the ingredients come together into pea-size clumps. Add the water and mix on low until the dough comes together.

Lightly dust a large flat work surface with flour and transfer the dough to the floured surface. Gather the dough together into a ball and cut it into

½ cup dry white wine

1 medium tomato, roughly chopped

1 bay leaf (preferably fresh)

3 fresh thyme sprigs

For the Dough

3¼ cups unbleached all-purpose flour, plus more for dusting

1½ tablespoons sugar

1½ teaspoons kosher salt

1¼ cups (2½ sticks) unsalted butter, cut into small pieces and frozen for at least 10 minutes

½ cup cold water

For the Filling

1 medium leek

8 large white button mushrooms, caps intact

½ pound (2 sticks) unsalted butter

2 medium carrots, peeled and cut into ¼-inch half-moons

7 large cippolini onions, peeled and quartered through the core

2 teaspoons kosher salt, plus more to taste

¾ cup unbleached all-purpose flour

½ cup heavy cream

¼ cup brandy

3 tablespoons finely chopped fresh chives

3 tablespoons finely chopped fresh chervil leaves

3 tablespoons finely chopped fresh tarragon leaves

2 pieces, one that consists of two-thirds of the dough and one that consists of one-third. Pat each hunk of dough into a 2-inch-thick block. Wrap each block separately in plastic wrap and place both in the refrigerator to chill until the dough is firm, about 2 hours.

Lightly dust a large flat work surface with flour and line two large baking sheets with parchment paper. Remove the larger block of dough from the refrigerator, unwrap it, and place it on the floured surface. Cut the dough into large chunks and pound each chunk with a rolling pin to soften the dough. Bring the chunks together into a ball and gently knead until the dough is malleable. Pat the dough into a 2-inch-thick disk. Dust the dough and rolling pin lightly with flour and roll the dough into a 3/16-inch-thick oval, dusting the dough, rolling pin, and work surface as needed. Loosely roll the dough around the rolling pin and transfer it to one of the prepared baking sheets. Place the dough in the refrigerator to chill until it is firm, about 1 hour.

Remove the second block of dough from the refrigerator and unwrap it. Cut the dough into large chunks and pound each chunk with a rolling pin to soften. Bring the chunks together into a ball and gently knead until the dough is malleable. Pat the dough into a 2-inch-thick rectangle. Dust the dough and rolling pin lightly with flour and roll into a 3/16-inch-thick rectangle, dusting the dough, rolling pin, and work surface as needed. Loosely roll the dough around the rolling pin and transfer it to the second baking sheet. Cut lobster claw shapes out of the dough with a sharp knife. Remove and discard the trimmings and place the baking sheet in the refrigerator to chill the dough until it is firm, about 1 hour.

To make the filling, remove and discard the outer layer of the leek and trim and discard the hairy end. Cut the leek in half lengthwise. Lay the leek halves, cut sides down, and slice them into ½-inch half-moons. Put the half-moons in a bowl, fill the bowl with water, and swish them around with your hands to release any dirt. Drain in a colander.

Wipe the mushrooms with a damp towel to clean them. Trim and discard the bottoms of the stems and cut the mushrooms into quarters.

Melt 4 tablespoons of the butter in a large sauté pan over medium heat. Add the carrots and cook them for 5 to 7 minutes, stirring occasionally, until they start to brown. Add the mushrooms, cippolini onions, 1 cup of the lobster stock, and 1 teaspoon of the salt and cook for 7 to 10 minutes, stirring periodically, until the vegetables are tender and the →

3 tablespoons finely chopped fresh celery leaves (look for the palest leaves, which are located closer to the core)

For Assembling the Pie

1 extra-large egg

stock has thickened and coats the vegetables. Add the leek half-moons and cook for 1 minute to soften them slightly. Turn off the heat.

Melt the remaining 12 tablespoons butter in a large saucepan over medium heat. Add the flour and cook until the mixture begins to bubble, about 3 minutes, whisking constantly. Gradually add 1 cup of the remaining stock, whisking until no lumps remain. Gradually add the remaining 3 cups stock, whisking constantly. Increase the heat to high and bring the stock to a boil. Turn off the heat. Add the cream and brandy and stir to combine. Set aside to come to room temperature.

Remove the bowl of lobster meat from the refrigerator and add the meat to the saucepan with the cream sauce. Add the cooked vegetables, the chives, chervil, tarragon, celery leaves, and the remaining 1 teaspoon salt to the saucepan and stir to combine. Add more salt to taste. Transfer to a covered container and refrigerate to chill.

While the filling is chilling, adjust the oven rack to the center position and preheat the oven to 425°F.

To assemble the pie, whisk the egg in a small bowl with 1 teaspoon water to make an egg wash. Brush the top edges of a 12-inch copper pan with the egg wash. Remove the filling from the refrigerator, spoon the filling onto the copper pan, and use the spoon to smooth out the top. Remove the baking sheet with the oval of dough from the refrigerator and drape it, centering it, over the pan. Turn the parchment paper over and set the baking sheet aside. Trim any dough that is hanging so low that it is touching the baking sheet; discard the trimmings. (Normally I trim piecrust shorter and more neatly, but in this case, I leave the excess so that after the potpie is baked, you can break off the crust and use it to dip into the pie filling.) Use your fingers to press the edges of dough onto the edges of the pan and brush the crust with egg wash. Remove the baking sheet with the dough claws from the refrigerator and arrange the claws on the pie. Press down on the claws to adhere and brush them with the remaining egg wash.

Place the potpie on the reserved parchment-lined baking sheet and bake in the oven for 10 minutes. Rotate the baking sheet from front to back. Reduce the oven temperature to 350°F and bake for about 25 minutes, until the crust is golden brown. Remove the pie from the oven.

Skate Wing with Braised Leeks, Brown Butter, and Capers

Serves 4

Skate, a thin, flat, mild-tasting fish shaped like a wing, is one of those "lost" foods that you don't see often. We cook and serve it on the cartilage wing, which keeps the fish moist and makes for a dramatic presentation that is also very fitting for Chi Spacca. To eat it, you have to scrape the fish off the wing and you basically shred it in the process. If you were to try to carve nice fillets of fish off of the wing, like you would a whole branzino or rock cod, you would be setting yourself up for failure. Instead, put the fish on a large platter and let your guests dig in with their forks.

This recipe calls for you to cook the fish one at a time in a large skillet, and to keep the first fish warm in the oven while you cook the second one. To cook both skate wings at the same time, use a two-burner cast-iron griddle or two large skillets (preferably cast-iron) simultaneously. The recipe for leeks makes more than you will need for this, but leeks cook best when they fit snugly in the baking dish. The method for cooking leeks is designed to work with the 9- × 13-inch Pyrex pan that I think everyone owns. Enjoy the leftover leeks as a side dish, drizzled with finishing-quality extra-virgin olive oil and sprinkled with flaky sea salt.

You will need Koda Farms Blue Star Mochiko rice flour to make this. It results in the ideal batter consistency and a crispy, crunchy exterior. It is available at specialty food stores and online sources.

Ask your fishmonger for 2 skate wings (about 1 pound each), on the cartilage, cleaned and skinned.

You will need an extra-large platter to serve the skate.

To braise the leeks, adjust the oven rack to the center position and preheat the oven to 350°F.

Remove and discard the outer layer of each leek and trim and discard the hairy ends, cutting as little as necessary so the layers stay intact. Put the leeks in a bowl, fill the bowl with water, and swish them around with your hands to release any dirt. Drain the leeks in a colander.

Place the leeks in a shallow baking dish just large enough to hold them in a single layer. Drizzle the olive oil and sprinkle the salt over them and →

For the Leeks

6 medium leeks
(about 1 pound)

¼ cup olive oil

1 teaspoon kosher salt

1½ cups Chicken Stock
(page 159; or store-bought
sodium-free or low-sodium),
or as needed

massage with your hands to coat the leeks with the oil and salt. Arrange the leeks, cut sides up, in the dish. Pour the chicken stock to come three-fourths of the way up the sides of the leeks. Lay the lemon slices, thyme, and butter on top of the leeks, and cover the baking dish with aluminum foil.

Place the dish in the oven to braise the leeks for 45 minutes. Remove the baking dish from the oven.

Increase the oven temperature to 400°F.

Remove and discard the foil, and remove and discard the lemon and thyme. Return the leeks to the oven to cook for 1 hour to 1 hour 15 minutes, until the liquid has cooked down to a syrupy consistency and the leeks are golden brown and glazed looking. Remove the leeks from the oven.

While the leeks are cooking, to make the sauce, use a fine Microplane to zest the bright yellow outer layer of the lemon into a small bowl.

Cut off and discard the top and bottom of the lemon at the point where you can see the flesh. Place the lemon upright on a cutting board and cut down the side at the point where the pith meets the flesh, following the natural curve of the fruit to remove the pith. Discard the pith. Turn the lemon on its side and cut along one of the membranes toward the center of the fruit. Working your way around the lemon, cut along both sides of each membrane to release all the segments from the core. Add the segments to the bowl with the zest.

Melt the butter in a small saucepan over medium heat to begin to make brown butter. Cook the butter for about 10 minutes, swirling the pan occasionally so the butter browns evenly, until the foam has subsided and the butter is coffee colored with a toasted aroma. Turn off the heat. Add the garlic and let it cook in the warm butter for about 2 minutes, until it is soft and fragrant, stirring so it doesn't brown. Add the lemon zest and segments, the capers, parsley, and salt, and stir to combine. Add more salt to taste. Leave the sauce in a warm place on or near the stove while you cook the skate.

To cook the skate, adjust the oven rack to the center position and preheat the oven to 250°F. (If you are cooking both fish at the same time, either in two skillets or on a two-burner cast-iron griddle, skip this step.)

½ lemon, sliced into ¼-inch rounds, end discarded

10 fresh thyme sprigs

½ pound (2 sticks) unsalted butter, cubed

For the Sauce

1 lemon

½ pound (2 sticks) unsalted butter

3 large garlic cloves, peeled and minced

3 tablespoons capers (preferably salt-packed), soaked for 15 minutes if salt-packed, rinsed and drained

¼ cup finely chopped fresh Italian parsley leaves

½ teaspoon kosher salt, plus more to taste

For the Skate

1 cup Koda Farms Blue Star Mochiko rice flour

2 skate wings (about 1 pound each), cleaned and skinned

2 teaspoons kosher salt

1 cup olive oil

For Serving

¼ cup finely chopped fresh parsley leaves

Put the rice flour in a baking dish large enough to hold a skate wing. Put the skate wings on a baking sheet. Pat them dry and sprinkle both sides with the salt. One at a time, dredge the skate wings in the rice flour, turning them three or four times to coat them evenly. Shake off the excess flour and return them to the baking sheet.

Have a second baking sheet and a pot lid that fits inside the skillet you are cooking the fish in handy; you will use this to press down on the fish.

Heat ¼ cup of the olive oil in a large skillet over medium-high heat for 2 to 3 minutes, until the oil slides easily and is smoking around the edges of the pan. Place one of the skate wings in the pan and press on it with the lid for 10 seconds to make sure the surface of the fish is touching the pan, which will ensure that the fish is brown and crisp all over. Remove the pressure; if the fish begins to curl at the edges, re-apply the pressure for another 10 seconds or so. Cook the fish for 6 to 8 minutes, until the underside is golden brown and crispy. Slide a spatula under the fish to release the skin from the pan, taking care not to rip the fish, and lift the fish out of the pan. Add ¼ cup of the olive oil to the pan and let it heat for about 30 seconds. Flip the fish and cook the other side for 2 minutes, until it is golden brown and crispy. Turn off the heat, remove the fish from the pan, and transfer it to the baking sheet. Place it in the oven to stay warm while you cook the second skate wing.

Wipe the pan clean, add ¼ cup of the olive oil, and let it heat for about 30 seconds, until it is almost smoking and slides easily in the pan. Add the second skate wing and fry it as you did the first wing, adding the remaining ¼ cup oil to the pan when you flip the fish. (If you are using a two-burner griddle, cook both fish at the same time, using all of the oil at once and skip the step of keeping them warm in the oven.)

To serve, if the sauce has cooled, warm it over low heat. Lay the leeks, cut sides up, on an extra-large platter. Spoon the brown butter sauce over the leeks and use the back of the spoon to dress each leek with the sauce. Lay the skate wings on top of the leeks and sprinkle the parsley over the wings.

Roasted Yellowtail with Spring
or Summer Vegetables

Serves 4

This roasted fish, served with snap peas or string beans, is a super-simple recipe, and the payoff is equally great. Ben Giron, a sous-chef at the Pizzeria, created it for a Friday *piatto,* or daily special. After tasting it, Ryan immediately stole it for the purposes of this book. There are two different versions of this recipe, one made with raw sugar snap peas, for spring, when those are in season, and the other with charred green beans, to make during the summer. The green beans are roasted in a cast-iron skillet that is preheated in the oven while the oven is preheating; this is our way of replicating the radiant surface heat we get from our wood-burning ovens. By adding the vegetables to an already-hot skillet, you are able to caramelize without overcooking them. If you are making the summer version, you will need a large cast-iron skillet to roast the beans.

You will need a large platter to serve the fish and vegetables.

For the spring, sugar snap pea option, combine the shallots, vinegar, salt, and red pepper flakes in a small bowl. Gradually add the extra-virgin olive oil, whisking constantly. Stir in the chives. Slice the sugar snap peas 1 inch thick on such an extreme bias that you are almost slicing lengthwise and put them in a medium bowl. Drizzle 1 cup of the chive vinaigrette over the sugar snap peas and toss to coat the peas.

For the green bean option, adjust the oven racks so none is near the oven floor; you'll be putting a baking sheet directly on the oven floor. If you are using an electric oven or another oven where you can't put anything on the floor, place an oven rack as close to the floor as possible and put a pizza steel or stone, if you have one, on it. Place a large cast-iron skillet on the floor or the lowest rack or stone. Preheat the oven and skillet to 500°F.

To make the vinaigrette, rinse the preserved lemon to remove the sugar and salt and drain well. Use a paring knife to remove the pulp, pith, and seeds, so you are left with only the bright yellow peel; finely chop.

Combine the whole-grain mustard, Dijon mustard, lemon juice, and salt in a small bowl. Gradually add the extra-virgin olive oil, whisking constantly. Add the chopped lemon peel and stir to combine.

**Spring: Snap Peas
with Chive Vinaigrette**

**3 tablespoons peeled and
minced shallots**

**3 tablespoons champagne
vinegar**

½ teaspoon kosher salt

½ teaspoon red pepper flakes

**¼ cup plus 2 tablespoons
extra-virgin olive oil**

**3 tablespoons finely chopped
fresh chives**

**1 pound sugar snap peas,
strings removed and discarded**

Put the beans and shallots in a large bowl. Drizzle the olive oil over them, sprinkle with the salt, and toss to coat the vegetables with the oil and salt. Open the oven and transfer the vegetables to the cast-iron skillet, spreading them out to cover the surface. Roast them on the oven floor or lowest rack until they're tender and blistered in places but not soggy, 10 to 12 minutes, shaking the baking sheet and rotating it from front to back halfway through that time so the vegetables cook evenly. Remove the baking sheet from the oven.

Reduce the oven temperature to 400°F.

Transfer the beans and shallots to a medium bowl. Drizzle 1 cup of the vinaigrette and sprinkle the chopped mint over the vegetables and toss to coat the vegetables and distribute the mint.

To prepare the fish, pat the fillets dry and place them in a baking dish or on a baking sheet. Drizzle with 2 tablespoons of the olive oil and massage with your hands to coat the fish with the oil. Sprinkle the salt and a few turns of black pepper evenly over both sides of the fish.

Heat the remaining 2 tablespoons olive oil in a large sauté pan over medium-high heat for 2 to 3 minutes, until the oil slides easily and is smoking around the edges of the pan. Lay the fish fillets in a single layer in the pan and sear for 1 to 2 minutes, until the undersides are golden brown. Flip the fish fillets. Place the sauté pan on the oven floor or lowest rack and bake for 5 to 6 minutes, until the fish is cooked through. To check for doneness, insert a toothpick into the center of a fillet, hold it there for 3 to 4 seconds, and then remove it and press it between your fingertips. The temperature of the toothpick will tell you what the temperature is inside the fish. If it feels cold, cook the fish for another minute and test it again. If it is warm, remove the sauté pan from the oven. Squeeze the juice of the lemon evenly over the fish.

While the fish is cooking, to prepare the salad, place the mizuna in a large bowl. Just before serving, drizzle with the extra-virgin olive oil and lemon juice, sprinkle with the salt, and toss to coat.

To serve, pile the sugar snap peas or green beans and shallots on a large platter. Nestle the fish fillets side by side on top of the vegetables. Spoon the remaining vinaigrette over the fish and use the back of the spoon to dress the fish, leaving the edges of each fillet visible. Top each fillet with a tangle of salad.

Summer: Charred Beans with Mustard Vinaigrette

For the Vinaigrette

2 Preserved Lemon halves (page 23; or store-bought)

2 tablespoons whole-grain mustard

1 tablespoon Dijon mustard

2 tablespoons fresh lemon juice

½ teaspoon kosher salt

2 tablespoons extra-virgin olive oil

For the Green Beans

1 pound mixed fresh string beans (such as green beans, yellow string beans, and Romano beans), stems removed and discarded, tails intact

2 large shallots, peeled and sliced ½ inch thick lengthwise

¼ cup olive oil

½ teaspoon kosher salt

2 tablespoons chopped fresh mint leaves

For the Fish

4 skinless yellowtail fillets (about 6 ounces each)

¼ cup olive oil

1 tablespoon kosher salt

Fresh coarsely ground black pepper

Juice of 1 lemon

For the Salad

4 cups mizuna (or wild arugula)

1 teaspoon extra-virgin olive oil

1 teaspoon fresh lemon juice

½ teaspoon kosher salt

Mischiato Potente:
Mixed Pasta and Seafood Stew

Serves 4

We often host wine dinners at Chi Spacca, building a menu around a winemaker or a region. It's a great opportunity to stretch ourselves and to expand our menu. When we were hosting a wine dinner for Franco Pepe, the legendary pizza maker and chef extraordinaire from Campagna, I remembered a soup that Faith Willinger, a dear friend and an authority on Italian cuisine, had told me about called *mischiato potente.* The south of Italy is known for its *cucina povera,* or "poverty cooking" (which, in my opinion happens to be some of the best food in all of Italy), and this soup is made from scraps of uncooked, dried pasta. Back in the day, pasta was sold in bags as high as my waist. At the bottoms of the bags would be broken pieces of pasta, which the shopkeepers would sell, all mixed together. The various shapes require different cooking times, so when they're cooked together, some are al dente while others are soft. I just loved that in a country where people normally obsess about cooking pasta properly, for this, they just let it go! For Chi Spacca, we turned the soup into a rich fish stew. Today, one of the premier pasta makers in Campagna, Pastificio dei Campi, packages those mixed shapes and sells them as "mischiato potente." I like how it's gone full circle—that the product is no longer a by-product, nor is it *povera.*

Colatura di alici is a by-product of curing anchovies in salt; the fish cure for about a year and in the process, they release liquid, which is colatura. It has an intense, briny flavor that adds depth to this stew. You can find it in Italian and specialty food markets, and from online sources. If it's not the season for great tomatoes, use quality, imported jarred or canned small tomatoes. Look for the words *datterini* or *Corbari* (both are varieties of tomatoes), or *pomodorini* (which refers to cherry tomatoes in general); drain the tomatoes before using them.

Ask your fishmonger for one (2-pound) sea bass (or striped bass, black bass, or branzino), filleted, skin on (each fillet will weigh about 6 ounces each). Ask him or her to reserve the head and bones for you to make the fish stock; you will need a total of 2 pounds of bones for the stock.

You will need a 12-inch stovetop-to-oven cooking vessel, such as a handle-free sauté pan, a cast-iron skillet, or a clay *casuela* to make and serve this stew. →

To make the salad, trim the tops off the fennel at the point where the bulb starts to sprout into separate stalks. (Trimming the fennel this way shows off its pretty shape when sliced.) Trim the very bottom of the root end, making sure to leave enough of the core so that the bulb stays intact. Remove any brown or unappealing outer layers. Chop the fennel trimmings and set them aside to use in the stock. Adjust a mandoline to slice ⅛ inch thick. Cut the fennel in half lengthwise. Lay the fennel, cut sides down, on the mandoline. Slice 2 slices and check their thickness; you want the slices just thick enough that they don't fall apart. If they are thick, like slabs, adjust the mandoline to slice thinner. If they are so thin that they tear or don't hold their shape, adjust the blade to slice thicker. Continue slicing the fennel, stopping when your fingers get dangerously close to the blade; snack on the end piece or reserve it for stock. Place the fennel slices in a medium bowl, cover them with a damp paper towel, and set aside until you're ready to serve the mischiato.

To prepare the mischiato, adjust the oven rack to the center position and preheat the oven to 375°F.

Pat the sea bass dry and place them in a baking dish or on a plate. Drizzle 1 tablespoon of the olive oil onto each fish and massage with your hands to coat. Sprinkle the salt and a few turns of pepper evenly over both sides of the fish.

Heat the remaining ¼ cup olive oil in a large sauté pan over medium-high heat for 2 to 3 minutes, until the oil slides easily and is smoking around the edges of the pan. Have a pot lid that fits inside the pan you are cooking the fish in handy; you will use this to press down on the fish. Reduce the heat to medium and place the fish fillets, skin side down, in the pan. Place the lid on one fish and gently press for about 10 seconds to make sure the surface is touching the pan, which will ensure the skin crisps. Remove the pressure; if the fish begins to curl at the edges, re-apply the pressure for another 10 seconds and check again. Repeat with the second fish. Reduce the heat to medium and cook the fish for 10 to 12 minutes, until the skin is crispy. Turn off the heat.

While the fish is cooking, pour the fish stock into a 12-inch stovetop-to-oven cooking vessel and bring the stock to a boil over high heat. (Reserve the remaining stock for another use.) Add the pasta and cook for 4 minutes to soften it slightly. Add the tomatoes. Squeeze the juice of

For the Fennel Salad

1 large fennel bulb
(preferably with the tops;
about 1 pound, or 12 ounces
for the bulb)

½ lemon

½ teaspoon kosher salt

1 tablespoon finishing-quality
extra-virgin olive oil

1 tablespoon finely chopped
fresh Italian parsley leaves

For the Mischiato

2 sea bass fillets
(or striped bass, black bass,
or branzino; about 6 ounces
each), skin on

¼ cup plus 2 tablespoons
olive oil

1 teaspoon kosher salt

Fresh coarsely ground black
pepper

3 cups Fish Stock (page 232)

¼ pound mixed pastas
(such as penne, trofie,
orecchiette, fusilli, and
spaghetti; if you use longer
shapes, like spaghetti, break
them into 2- to 3-inch pieces;
or a packaged mix of
pasta shapes)

1 cup small red cherry tomatoes
(or jarred Italian cherry
tomatoes, drained of liquid)

½ lemon

1 tablespoon colatura di alici

2 tablespoons finely chopped
fresh Italian parsley leaves

2 tablespoons finishing-quality
extra-virgin olive oil

the lemon half and drizzle the colatura into the broth and stir to combine. Remove the fish from the sauté pan, taking care not to tear off the skin and place it, skin side up, in the pan with the stock.

Bake the mischiato, uncovered, for 8 to 10 minutes, until the largest pasta shapes are al dente. Remove the mischiato from the oven.

To finish the salad: Uncover the fennel slices and squeeze the juice of the lemon half and sprinkle the salt over them. Toss to coat the fennel with the lemon and salt. Drizzle the finishing-quality olive oil and sprinkle the parsley over the fennel and toss again to combine.

To serve, drop the fennel salad in tangles on top of the fish, dividing it evenly. Sprinkle the parsley over the mischiato and drizzle with the finishing-quality olive oil.

Fried Whole Branzino
with Pickled Cherry Peppers
and Charred Scallions

Serves 4

There are always a handful of cooks at the restaurants who love to come up with additions to our menus. Jess Ziman is one of those cooks, and she introduced this fish to our repertoire. She skewers it so it holds a C shape, fries the fish whole, and then sets the fish upright on the plate, as if it were swimming. It looks like the sort of presentation you would see in an Asian restaurant. It's really a stunner. It is served with pickled peppers, which are sweet, spicy, and acidic—just what you want with fried food. You need to start making the peppers two to three days in advance so they have time to pickle, so plan ahead—or cheat and substitute 1 heaping cup store-bought pickled cherry peppers.

Ask your fishmonger for 2 whole bone-in branzinos (or rockfish, rock cod, snapper, or trout; 1 to 1½ pounds each).

You will need 2 (8-inch) wooden skewers to make this. You will need a large platter to serve the branzino.

To pickle the peppers, combine the vinegar, sugar, kosher salt, mustard seeds, fennel seeds, peppercorns, bay leaf, and 2 cups water in a medium saucepan and bring the liquid to a boil over high heat, stirring occasionally to dissolve the sugar and salt. Reduce the heat to medium-low and simmer for 10 minutes to infuse the liquid with the seasonings. Turn off the heat.

Put the cherry peppers in a large container with a lid and add enough of the pickling liquid to fill the container; discard the remaining liquid. Set aside for the peppers and pickling liquid to cool to room temperature. Cover and refrigerate the peppers for at least 2 days and up to 1 month. (To store leftover pickles even longer, strain the peppers from the pickling liquid, return them to the container you pickled them in, and add enough extra-virgin olive oil to cover. Place the peppers in the refrigerator for as long as several months.) →

For the Pickled Peppers

2 cups champagne vinegar
(or white wine vinegar)

2 teaspoons sugar

1 teaspoon kosher salt

½ teaspoon mustard seeds

½ teaspoon fennel seeds

½ teaspoon pink peppercorns

1 bay leaf (preferably fresh)

½ pound cherry peppers
(or Fresno chiles, or another
small mild pepper)

2 cups extra-virgin olive oil,
or as needed (if you are storing
the pickles)

To prepare the scallions and peppers, adjust the oven racks so none is near the oven floor; you'll be putting a baking sheet directly on the oven floor. If you are using an electric oven or another oven where you can't put anything on the floor, place an oven rack as close to the floor as possible and put a pizza steel or stone, if you have one, on it. Preheat the oven to 500°F.

Trim and discard the root ends from the scallions and put the scallions on a baking sheet. Drizzle with the olive oil, sprinkle with ½ teaspoon of the kosher salt, and massage with your hands to coat the scallions. Spread the scallions in a single layer and place the baking sheet on the oven floor or lowest rack and cook until they are charred in places, about 6 minutes. Remove the baking sheet from the oven and set aside until the scallions are cool enough to handle.

Toast the coriander seeds in a small sauté pan over medium heat for 1 to 2 minutes, until they are golden brown and fragrant, shaking the pan so they don't burn. Transfer the seeds to a mortar or spice grinder and very coarsely grind them. Transfer the seeds to a medium bowl.

Remove and discard the stems from the cherry peppers. Cut the peppers in half and remove and discard the seeds. Slice the peppers ¼ inch thick and add them to the bowl with the coriander. Chop the scallions into 1-inch pieces. Add them to the bowl. Add the cherry pepper pickling liquid, finishing-quality olive oil, and the remaining ½ teaspoon of kosher salt and stir to combine. Set aside until you're ready to serve the fish.

To prepare the fish, trim and discard the root ends from the scallions and cut the scallions into 1-inch pieces. Pat the branzino dry and place them on a cutting board. Score the skins of both fish in a ½-inch diagonal crosshatch pattern, taking care not to cut all the way through the skin to the flesh of the fish. Stuff the belly cavities with the scallions. Lay the fish on their sides and bend them into a slight C shape. Run an 8-inch wooden skewer through one side of the head to the other and then through the tail, so the skewer holds the fish in the C. Season the fish evenly with the kosher salt.

Pour the canola oil into a large saucepan. Fasten a deep-fry thermometer, if you have one, to the side of the pan and heat the oil over medium-high heat until the thermometer registers 350°F or a pinch of salt sizzles when dropped into the oil. Line a large plate or baking sheet with paper towels. Have a slotted spoon handy.

For the Scallions and Peppers

1 bunch large scallions

1 tablespoon olive oil

1 teaspoon kosher salt

1 teaspoon coriander seeds

2 tablespoons pickling liquid from the cherry peppers (see above)

1 tablespoon finishing-quality extra-virgin olive oil

For the Fish

4 large scallions

2 whole branzino (or rockfish, rock cod, snapper, or trout; about 1 pound each)

2 teaspoons kosher salt

3 quarts (12 cups) canola oil (or another neutral-flavored oil), plus more as needed

Flaky sea salt

Carefully slide one fish into the oil and cook it for 5 minutes, until it is crispy all over; use the slotted spoon to turn the fish halfway through so the fish cooks evenly. Remove the fish from the pan and place it on the paper towels to drain. Immediately crush about 1 teaspoon flaky sea salt over the fish; the salt will attach to the fish better if applied while the oil is hot. Repeat, frying the second fish in the same way, placing it on the paper towels to drain, and salting it.

To serve, carefully remove the skewer from both fish, and place the fish upright on a large platter so they are standing up as if they are swimming. Pile the charred scallions and peppers next to the fish.

Salt-Baked Fish with Green Olive and Charred Lemon Salmoriglio

Serves 4

A few years ago, some of the chefs from our restaurants were invited on a sponsored trip to Italy. Joe Tagorda, the sous-chef at Chi Spacca, was among them. As hard as it is for us to get by without Joe—he's the rock in the Spacca kitchen—we let him go to Italy. In exchange for the time off, I gave all of the cooks an assignment: they had to come home with a dish that inspired them. Joe came back excited about a whole fish, baked in a thick salt crust, that he had in Naples.

Salt-baked fish is one of the iconic foods of Italy. The salt crust is deceptively easy to do: just mix egg whites with salt to make a grainy paste, pack it around the fish, then stick the fish in the oven and forget about it. It's such an effective way to cook fish. The mixture, when baked, forms a crust, which acts like an oven around the fish, so it stays really moist. We add spices to the salt mixture and aromatic herbs and lemon, to infuse the fish with flavor. This is served with a salsa made with charred lemons and Castelvetrano olives. It's just the kind of thing I love to eat—simple, but with bold flavors. It made it worth it to lose Joe for a week.

We make it easy on the home cook by starting with a deboned side of fish (half of a whole fish). We serve this with a bundle of fresh herbs. As pretty as they are, they're not just for decoration—they're for flavor. The idea is that each person picks up the bundle and tears the herbs over their portion.

A citrus zester is a one-trick tool used to peel long, threadlike strips from citrus. The strips are really pretty made this way, but if you don't want to invest in one just for this, you can get more or less the same results by peeling citrus with a vegetable peeler and then cutting it into long thin strips.

Ask your fishmonger for a 3- to 4-pound side of fish, boned, gutted, and scaled. You can use any flaky fish of this size (including rockfish, rock cod, snapper, branzino, salmon, or striped bass).

You will need a large platter to serve the fish. →

To make the salmoriglio, adjust the oven racks so one is in the center position and none is near the oven floor; you'll be putting a baking sheet directly on the oven floor. If you are using an electric oven or another type of oven where you cannot put anything on the floor, place the rack as close to the floor as possible and put a pizza steel or stone on it, if you have one. Preheat the oven to 300°F. Line a large baking sheet with parchment paper.

Slice one of the lemons into ¼-inch rounds using a mandoline or a sharp knife. Remove and discard the seeds from each slice, throw away the 2 end pieces from each lemon, and put the lemon slices in a medium bowl. Drizzle the lemon slices with 1 tablespoon of the extra-virgin olive oil, sprinkle with the sugar and salt, and toss to coat the lemon slices. Lay the lemon slices in a single layer on a baking sheet and put the baking sheet on the oven floor or the lowest rack to roast the lemons for 10 to 12 minutes, until the rind is crispy and the insides are still soft, shaking the baking sheet and rotating it from front to back halfway through that time so the lemons cook evenly. Remove the baking sheet from the oven. Immediately turn each lemon slice so the charred side is facing up; if you don't do this just after the lemons come out of the oven, the lemons will stick to the baking sheet. Set the charred lemons aside until they are cool enough to touch.

To prepare the fish, increase the oven temperature to 350°F.

Put the salt, peppercorns, coriander seeds, and cumin seeds in a large bowl. If you have a citrus zester, use it to zest half of the bright yellow outer layer of the whole lemon into long threads. If you do not have a citrus zester, use a vegetable peeler to peel the bright yellow outer layer of lemon zest in wide strips, and thinly slice the strips into long threads. Add the zest to the bowl. (Reserve the lemon to juice to make the salmoriglio.) Add the egg whites and stir to combine, adding more as needed to achieve the consistency of wet beach sand.

Lay the lemon rounds side by side on a large baking sheet to form a bed for the fish. Lay one-third of the dill, oregano, and mint sprigs and one-third of the chives on the lemon rounds and lay the fish on top of the lemons and herbs. Lay half of the remaining dill, oregano, mint, and chives on top of the fish. Use your hands to pack the salt on the fish, leaving the tail and the very end of the head side exposed. Patch up any holes in the crust with your hands to create an airtight surface. Bake the fish

For the Green Olive and Charred Lemon Salmoriglio

3 lemons (preferably Meyer lemons)

½ cup plus 1 tablespoon extra-virgin olive oil

2 teaspoons sugar

1 teaspoon kosher salt

1 cup Castelvetrano olives, pitted and coarsely chopped

¼ cup finely chopped fresh Italian parsley leaves

¼ cup finely chopped fresh oregano leaves

½ teaspoon red pepper flakes

For the Fish

4 cups kosher salt

2 tablespoons pink peppercorns

2 tablespoons coriander seeds

2 tablespoons cumin seeds

2 lemons, 1 left whole and 1 sliced into ¼-inch-thick rounds, ends discarded

6 extra-large egg whites, plus more as needed

1 bunch (or 2 clamshells) fresh dill sprigs

1 bunch (or 2 clamshells) fresh oregano sprigs

1 bunch (or 2 clamshells) fresh mint sprigs

½ bunch (or 1 clamshell) fresh chives

1 (4-pound) side of fish (use rockfish, rock cod, snapper, branzino, salmon, or striped bass; half of an 8-pound fish)

½ bunch (or 1 clamshell) fresh cilantro sprigs

in the oven until the crust is light golden brown, about 30 minutes. Remove the pan from the oven and let the fish rest for 5 minutes.

While the fish is cooking, to finish the salmoriglio, cut off and discard the top and bottom of the remaining 2 lemons at the point where you can see the flesh. Place the lemons upright on a cutting board and cut down the side to remove the peel at the point where the pith meets the flesh, following the natural curve of the fruit. Discard the peels. Turn the lemons on their sides and cut along one of the membranes toward the center of the fruit. Continue, working your way around the lemons, cutting along both sides of each membrane to release all the segments from the cores. Put the segments in a medium bowl. Squeeze the core of the lemons over the bowl to extract as much juice as you can. Add the olives, parsley, oregano, and red pepper flakes to the bowl and mash the ingredients together with a fork. Gradually add the remaining ½ cup extra-virgin olive oil, whisking constantly. Roughly chop the charred lemon slices and discard any bits that were charred too much. Using the flat side of your knife, scoop the lemons off the cutting board, including all of the flesh stuck to the board, and transfer to a medium bowl, discarding the blackened bits. Stir the lemon into the relish.

To finish the fish, bundle the cilantro sprigs along with the remaining dill, oregano, and mint sprigs like a bouquet of flowers. Tie the bundle with 1 or 2 of the remaining chives.

Tap on the fish crust with the side of a large spoon to crack it. (Do this assertively to avoid the crust shattering into small pieces that could potentially crumble into your food. It's the same concept as cracking an egg.) Remove and discard the crust and the herbs on top of the fish. Grab the skin of the fish with the tines of a fork and gently pull it off of the fish, slowly twisting the fork as you pull to keep the skin from breaking. Discard the skin. With a metal spatula, cut off the head end of the fish. Cut the remaining fish into 4 equal portions. Discard the collar and tail.

To serve, transfer the fish, along with the lemon slices and herbs they were cooked on, to a large platter. Spoon about 1 tablespoon of the salmoriglio over each portion of fish and use the back of a spoon to dress the fish with the sauce, leaving the edges without any sauce. Serve with the remaining salmoriglio on the side and the herb bundle for each person to pick from and sprinkle over their fish for flavor.

Whole Roasted Cauliflower with Green Garlic Crème Fraîche
and Sunflower Seed Crumble   262

Whole Roasted Sweet Potatoes with Orange–Brown Butter Glaze and Mascarpone   265

Whole Roasted Eggplant with Chickpea Purée and Zhug   267

Roasted Cabbage with Bagna Cauda Yogurt and Crunchy Grains   271

Roasted Cabbage with Toasted Caraway Vinaigrette   274

Whole Roasted Fennel with Salsa Verde and Gremolata Bread Crumbs   276

Roasted Cauliflower Wedges with Crushed Lemon Bagna Cauda   278

Roasted Parsnips with Chestnut Honey, Garlic, and Thyme   281

Whole Roasted Carrots with Cracked Coriander and Cumin and Dill Yogurt   283

Asparagus al Cartoccio with Butter, Mint, and Parmesan   285

Charred Sugar Snap Peas with Yogurt, Guanciale, and Lemon Zest   287

Roasted Honeynut Squash with Pistachio-Hazelnut Dukkah   291

Dario's Baked Potatoes with Whipped Lardo   293

Roasted Ricotta-Stuffed Squash Blossoms with Tomato Vinaigrette   295

Braised Greens   297

Creamed Summer Corn   298

Garlic Mashed Potatoes   299

Lardo Asador Potatoes   301

Chris Feldmeier's Rancho Beans   302

Yorkshire Pudding with Aged Beef Trimmings   304

Plate of Citrus with Olio Nuovo and Fresh Mint   306

Creamed Spinach   308

Grilled Broccolini and Scallions   310

Dario's Tuscan White Beans   312

Classic Vichy Carrots   314

Celeriac Purée   315

Contorni

Contrary as it might seem, with an ever-changing, always growing selection of seasonal side dishes, Chi Spacca is a vegetable lover's dream. We like to present vegetables in ways that show off their natural shapes and beauty: giant whole roasted carrots, halved winter squash, baby sweet potatoes, whole heads of baby cabbage, cauliflower wedges, caramelized fennel bulbs, and seared sugar snap peas. Cooked in a hot oven to achieve Chi Spacca's hallmark caramelization and layered with contrasting flavors, textures, temperatures, and even colors, these could easily take center stage alongside our assertive meat and fish dishes.

Whole Roasted Cauliflower with Green Garlic Crème Fraîche and Sunflower Seed Crumble

Serves 4

When I went to Israel with my friend Steven Rothfeld, it seemed that every contemporary chef was serving a whole roasted head of cauliflower. The trick to getting that beautiful brown color, for me, anyway, was in massaging a healthy amount of olive oil into the nooks and crannies between the florets. The amount of oil may seem extreme, but the resulting cauliflower is as beautiful as it is delicious.

We serve our cauliflower with green garlic crème fraîche on the side, which is like a fancy version of the classic potato chip dip made with French onion soup mix. Green garlic looks similar to a scallion and has a fresh, grassy, garlicky flavor. If you can't find green garlic, go ahead and use scallions in its place—still tasty, just a different flavor. Seek out Bellwether Farms sheep's milk crème fraîche, which is rich, creamy, and flavorful (although you can also use sour cream).

You will need a 10-inch round platter or plate to serve the cauliflower.

To prepare the cauliflower, fill a large pot with enough water to submerge the cauliflower, adding 1 scant tablespoon kosher salt per quart of water. Bring the water to a boil over high heat.

Cut off and discard the stem of the cauliflower, making sure to cut it straight so the cauliflower can rest on the remaining stem later when you serve it, and cutting as little as possible so the cauliflower will stay intact. Remove and discard the large leaves from the cauliflower, leaving the tender ones that envelop it intact. Add the cauliflower to the water and cook it for 6 to 8 minutes, until the core is tender when poked with a sharp knife, pushing the cauliflower down as it boils to keep it submerged.

While the cauliflower is cooking, adjust the oven rack to the center position and preheat the oven to 450°F.

Prepare an ice bath in a deep medium bowl. Drain the cauliflower in a colander and put it in the ice bath for about 5 minutes to cool completely.

For the Cauliflower

Kosher salt

1 large head cauliflower (about 2 pounds)

½ cup extra-virgin olive oil, plus more as needed

Return the cauliflower to the colander, stem side up, to drain for at least 10 minutes.

Put the cauliflower on a baking sheet. Pour the extra-virgin olive oil over the cauliflower and use your hands to massage the oil into its nooks and crannies, separating the florets to create crevices for the oil to flow into; add more oil as you are massaging until the entire head and the crevices are generously coated. Set the cauliflower on the stem so it is upright. Roast the cauliflower in the oven for 15 to 20 minutes, until deep brown, rotating the head from front to back halfway through that time so it browns evenly. Remove the cauliflower from the oven.

To make the sunflower seed crumble, combine the olive oil and sunflower seeds in a small sauté pan. Smash 3 of the garlic cloves with the side of a knife and add them to the sauté pan. Cook over medium heat for 3 to 4 minutes, until the garlic is light golden brown and the seeds are toasted, stirring so the garlic and seeds brown evenly. Turn off the heat and set aside for about 5 minutes to cool slightly. Transfer the contents of the pan to a mortar or the bowl of a mini food processor. Using a fine Microplane, grate the remaining 2 garlic cloves into the mortar. Use the Microplane to grate the bright yellow outer layer of the lemon into the mortar or food processor bowl. (Reserve the lemon to juice for the green garlic crème fraîche.) Crack the sunflower seeds and garlic with the pestle or pulse the food processor until they are a crumbly texture. If you're using a food processor, transfer the mixture to a small bowl. Add the oregano, thyme, and flaky sea salt and stir to combine.

To prepare the green garlic crème fraîche, put the crème fraîche in a small bowl. Trim the root ends of the green garlic stalks and remove and discard any limp or unappealing outer greens; discard the trimmings. Finely chop the stalks and add them to the bowl with the crème fraîche. (If using scallions, chop them finely and add them to the crème fraiche, then use a fine Microplane to grate the peeled garlic cloves into the bowl.) Add the lemon juice and kosher salt and stir to combine. Add more lemon juice and salt to taste. Before serving, transfer the crème fraîche to a small, pretty wide-mouth bowl.

To serve, put the cauliflower on a round platter. Crush about ½ teaspoon flaky sea salt between your fingertips over the cauliflower and sprinkle the sunflower seed crumble evenly over it. Serve with a long knife to cut into it and the green garlic crème fraîche on the side to dip into.

For the Sunflower Seed Crumble

¼ cup olive oil

¼ cup raw hulled sunflower seeds

5 large garlic cloves, peeled

1 lemon

2 tablespoons finely chopped fresh oregano leaves

1 teaspoon finely chopped fresh thyme leaves

½ teaspoon flaky sea salt

For the Green Garlic Crème Fraîche

1 cup crème fraîche (preferably Bellwether Farms; or sour cream)

2 stalks green garlic (or 4 large scallions plus 2 large garlic cloves, peeled)

1 tablespoon fresh lemon juice, plus more to taste

½ teaspoon kosher salt, plus more to taste

For Serving

Flaky sea salt

Whole Roasted Sweet Potatoes
with Orange–Brown Butter Glaze
and Mascarpone

Serves 4

One fall, the Chi Spacca team and I took a field trip to Chino Family Farm in San Diego County, a two-hour drive from Los Angeles. Chino's is a very special place; everything they grow—green beans, strawberries, figs, winter squash, summer squash, even celery—is as beautiful as it is delicious. On this trip, it was winter, and they had a large array of sweet potatoes: purple-skinned with white flesh, red with orange flesh, and yellow-skinned with purple flesh. When I find something that precious, I want to find a way to use it. I scooped up the sweet potatoes and said to Ryan, "Let's do a side dish of super-simple sweet potatoes!" We came up with this preparation, where the potatoes are baked whole, coated in an orange–brown butter glaze, and nestled on a bed of creamy mascarpone. They're rich and decadent, but not sweet, like candied yams. We use Di Stefano mascarpone, which has a spreadable, buttery consistency that I like. If the mascarpone you get is stiffer than that, whisk in enough heavy cream until it is spreadable.

A citrus zester is a one-trick tool used to peel long, threadlike strips from citrus. The strips are really pretty made this way, but if you don't want to invest in one just for this, you can get more or less the same results by peeling citrus with a vegetable peeler and then cutting it into long thin strips.

You will need a large platter to serve the sweet potatoes.

If you have a citrus zester, use it to zest the bright orange outer layer of the orange. If you do not have a citrus zester, peel the bright orange outer layer of zest in wide strips using a vegetable peeler and then very thinly slice it into long threads. Set the zest aside for garnish.

Cut the oranges in half and juice them. Measure out 1 cup.

Adjust the oven rack to the center position and preheat the oven to 350°F.

Put the sweet potatoes on a baking sheet. Drizzle them with the olive oil, sprinkle with the salt, and use your hands to coat the sweet potatoes with the oil and salt. →

For the Sweet Potatoes

3 oranges

8 baby sweet potatoes
(2 to 3 ounces each;
or 4 small sweet potatoes,
about 2 pounds)

2 tablespoons olive oil

1 tablespoon kosher salt

8 tablespoons (1 stick)
unsalted butter

Roast the sweet potatoes in the oven until the skin feels crisp and papery and the sweet potato is soft when you gently squeeze it, 15 to 20 minutes for baby sweet potatoes, 30 to 40 minutes for larger sweet potatoes.

While the sweet potatoes are cooking, put the orange juice in a small saucepan and bring it to a boil over high heat. Reduce the heat to low to maintain a steady simmer and cook for about 15 minutes, until the juice has reduced to a syrupy consistency. Turn off the heat and pour the juice into the jar of a blender.

Put the butter in the saucepan you cooked the orange juice in and melt it over medium heat to begin to make brown butter. Cook the butter for about 10 minutes, swirling the pan occasionally so the butter browns evenly, until the foam has subsided and the butter is coffee colored with a toasted aroma. Turn off the heat and scrape the bottom to release the solids. Set aside to cool slightly.

Turn on the blender and add the butter in a slow, steady stream through the feed hole. Transfer the orange butter to a bowl.

Remove the sweet potatoes from the oven and drizzle each potato generously with the orange butter. Return the sweet potatoes to the oven for 3 minutes to bake on the glaze. Remove the sweet potatoes from the oven.

To serve, spoon the mascarpone into the center of a large platter and use the back of the spoon to spread it out toward the edges in organic, uneven swirls. Gently nestle the sweet potatoes on the mascarpone, piling them on top of one another if you are using baby potatoes. Drizzle the orange butter from the baking sheet over the sweet potatoes. Sprinkle the chives over the sweet potatoes, use a fine Microplane to grate a generous amount of Parmesan, and scatter the orange zest over the top.

For Serving

½ cup mascarpone (preferably Di Stefano), at room temperature

¼ cup finely chopped fresh chives

A chunk of Parmesan for grating

Whole Roasted Eggplant
with Chickpea Purée and Zhug

Serves 4

The same trip to Israel where I discovered whole roasted cauliflower, I also discovered whole roasted eggplant that was sauced with hummus and garnished with a super-tasty sauce of chopped herbs and chiles, which I learned was called zhug. There are several components to this recipe, and it's those components that provide the layers of flavors and textures that make these eggplants memorable. Trust me; they're worth it. Spoon leftover zhug onto grilled lamb, fish, or vegetables. Plan ahead before you make this, because the chickpeas need to soak for at least eight hours before you cook them.

We use Soom, a small-batch brand of tahini made in Philadelphia. If you can't find Soom, seek out another brand of tahini from a Middle Eastern market.

You will need a large oval platter to serve the eggplants.

To prepare the chickpeas, put them in a large bowl, cover with water, and soak overnight or for at least 8 hours. Drain the chickpeas, transfer them to a large pot, and add enough water to cover them by 1½ to 2 inches. Stir in the extra-virgin olive oil and salt. Add the onion, carrot, celery, garlic, sage, bay leaves, árbol chiles, and rosemary and bring to a boil over high heat. Reduce the heat to medium-low to maintain a gentle simmer and simmer the chickpeas for about 2 hours, until they are tender and creamy, not chalky or al dente but also not falling apart, stirring occasionally and adding more water as needed to keep the chickpeas covered at all times. Skim off and discard any foam that rises to the top while the beans are cooking. To test for doneness, press one chickpea between your fingers; if it is creamy and silky, it's done. Turn off the heat.

Set a large mesh strainer over a large bowl and strain the chickpeas. Transfer the liquid to a container and reserve it to use in place of stock to make soup another day. Remove the onion, carrot, and celery. (Rather than discarding them, I like to season them with olive oil and salt and snack on them.) Transfer the chickpeas to the bowl you strained →

For Cooking the Chickpeas

1 pound dried chickpeas (about 2 cups)

½ cup extra-virgin olive oil

¼ cup kosher salt

1 small yellow onion, peeled and halved root to tip

1 carrot, halved horizontally

1 celery stalk, halved horizontally

1 head of garlic, unpeeled and halved through the middle

5 fresh sage leaves

2 bay leaves (preferably fresh)

2 árbol chiles

1 fresh rosemary sprig

them over. Remove the garlic and squeeze the cloves out of the skins into the bowl with the chickpeas; discard the skins. Remove and discard the herbs and árbol chiles.

To make the chickpea purée, place the tahini in the bowl of a food processor. Use a fine Microplane to grate 3 of the garlic cloves into the food processor bowl. Add ¼ cup of the lemon juice and 2 teaspoons of the salt and purée. Slowly pour in the water through the feed tube of the food processor while it is running and blend until the tahini is smooth, adding more water if necessary for a spreadable consistency. (When you add water to tahini, it actually thickens and seizes. But as you add more water and blend it in, the tahini will thin out. Keep adding water gradually until you reach the desired consistency.) Turn off the food processor. Taste the purée and grate the remaining 2 cloves of garlic. Add the remaining 2 tablespoons lemon juice, if desired. Add more salt to taste.

Reserve 1 cup of the chickpeas and set them aside in a small bowl. Return the strainer to the large bowl and set it aside.

Put the remaining chickpeas in the food processor with the tahini mixture and purée them with the tahini. With the machine running, gradually add the extra-virgin olive oil through the feed tube and purée until smooth, about 2 minutes. Pass the purée through the strainer into the bowl using a rubber spatula to push it through.

To make the zhug, toast the cumin seeds, coriander seeds, and cardamom pod in a small skillet over medium heat for 1 to 2 minutes, until they are fragrant and toasted, shaking the pan often so they don't burn. Transfer the spices to a mortar or spice grinder and very coarsely grind them. If you are using a spice grinder, transfer the spices to a small bowl.

Remove and discard the stems from the Fresno and jalapeño chiles. Cut the chiles in half and remove and discard the seeds. Finely chop the chiles and add them to the mortar or bowl. Use a fine Microplane to grate the garlic into the mortar or bowl. Add the salt and stir to combine; if you are using a mortar, use the pestle to grind the chiles slightly. Add the cilantro, parsley, and mint and stir or grind to combine. Add the lemon juice and stir to combine. Drizzle in the finishing-quality olive oil, stirring constantly. Add more lemon juice or salt to taste.

For the Chickpea Purée

½ cup tahini (preferably Soom)

5 large garlic cloves (depending on taste), peeled

¼ cup plus 2 tablespoons fresh lemon juice

2 teaspoons kosher salt, plus more to taste

¼ cup ice-cold water, plus more as needed

¾ cup extra-virgin olive oil

For the Zhug

1 tablespoon cumin seeds

1 tablespoon coriander seeds

1 cardamom pod

2 Fresno chiles

1 jalapeño chile

1 large garlic clove, peeled

2 teaspoons kosher salt, plus more to taste

¼ cup finely chopped fresh cilantro leaves

¼ cup finely chopped fresh Italian parsley leaves

1 tablespoon finely chopped fresh mint leaves

¼ cup fresh lemon juice, plus more to taste

½ cup finishing-quality extra-virgin olive oil

For the Eggplants

4 medium eggplants (about 1 pound each)

2 tablespoons olive oil

1 tablespoon kosher salt

To cook the eggplants, adjust the oven rack to the center position and preheat the oven to 425°F.

Cut a shallow slit down the length of each eggplant to allow air to escape. Place the eggplants on a baking sheet. Drizzle the olive oil on the eggplants, sprinkle the salt, and massage with your hands to coat the eggplants with the oil and salt. Put the eggplants, cut sides up, on the baking sheet.

Roast the eggplants in the oven for 50 minutes to 1 hour, turning the baking sheet halfway through that time so they cook evenly, until the skin is wrinkled and the eggplants are soft and mushy. Remove the eggplants from the oven and set aside.

To serve, transfer the eggplants, open sides up, to a large oval platter. Gently open the eggplants at the slits to expose the insides and to create a well in each.

Spoon ½ cup of the chickpea purée into the opening of each eggplant. Use the back of the spoon to create a small crater in the purée and spoon the zhug into each crater, dividing it evenly. Scatter the reserved 1 cup chickpeas over the eggplants. Sprinkle the za'atar and tear each mint leaf into 2 or 3 pieces to fall over the eggplants.

For Serving
2 tablespoons Za'atar
(page 25; or store-bought)
12 fresh mint leaves

Roasted Cabbage with Bagna Cauda Yogurt and Crunchy Grains

Serves 4

My cooks often come to me with dishes they're working on to see if it's something I like enough to work on together and eventually possibly put on the menu. Rarely does anybody come to me with a dish that is perfect the first time around, but that's what happened with this dish, which comes to us courtesy of our Pizzeria sous-chef Ben Giron. I never would have thought to mix bagna cauda with yogurt, but Ben did, and it's *really* delicious. He sprinkles fried wild rice and sorghum over the cabbage, so you have all the textures and temperatures—hot, cold, creamy, and crunchy—that I love together in a dish. Sorghum, when popped or fried, looks like miniature popcorn. It's so adorable! The heart and soul of this dish is the cabbage with bagna cauda yogurt. If you don't want to deep-fry the grains, don't let that deter you from making this; just skip them. This recipe also calls for fried celery leaves as a garnish; this is if you happen to have a head of celery. I wouldn't want you to go out and buy one just for this.

Ben makes this using cone-shaped cabbage, a green cabbage traditionally used to make sauerkraut in Germany, or whole baby savoy cabbages. These are nearly impossible to find, so the recipe calls for cabbage halves or wedges instead. If you're lucky enough to get your hands on the softball-size cabbages, just note that instead of turning to brown each cut side, you will roll them around on the baking sheet to brown them all over. Depending on the size of the cone cabbage you will halve or quarter it.

You will need a large platter to serve the cabbages.

To make the bagna cauda yogurt, combine the butter and extra-virgin olive oil in a small saucepan. Finely chop the anchovies with a large knife and use the flat side of the knife to smash them into a paste; add the paste to the saucepan. Using a fine Microplane, grate the garlic into the saucepan and heat the bagna cauda over low heat for 5 minutes, stirring occasionally, to melt the butter and meld the flavors. Turn off the heat. Use the Microplane to zest the bright yellow outer layer of the lemon into the saucepan and let the bagna cauda cool to room temperature. Cut the lemon in half and squeeze 1 tablespoon lemon juice into the bagna cauda; reserve the remaining lemon to juice another time. →

For the Bagna Cauda Yogurt

2 tablespoons unsalted butter

¼ cup extra-virgin olive oil

5 anchovy fillets (preferably salt-packed; rinsed and backbones removed if salt-packed)

2 large garlic cloves, peeled

1 lemon

Put the yogurt in a medium bowl, add the bagna cauda, and whisk to combine. Place a mesh strainer over a small bowl and strain the yogurt into the bowl, using a rubber spatula or spoon to push it through.

To fry the grains, pour enough canola oil into a deep small saucepan to fill it 1½ to 2 inches deep. Fasten a deep-fry thermometer, if you have one, to the side of the pan and heat the oil over medium-high heat until the thermometer registers 400°F or a pinch of salt sizzles when dropped into the oil. Line a baking sheet or large plate with paper towels and have a small mesh strainer handy.

Turn off the heat, add the wild rice to the oil, and fry until the grains are puffed and crispy, about 10 seconds. Lift the wild rice out of the oil with the strainer, shake the strainer to drain the excess oil, and spread the grains out on the paper towels to drain. Sprinkle with ½ teaspoon of the salt.

Add the sorghum to the oil and fry for about 10 seconds, until the majority of the grains have popped open like popcorn; not all of the grains will pop. Lift the popped sorghum out of the oil with the strainer, leaving any unpopped grains in the oil, and shake the strainer to drain the excess oil. Add the sorghum to the paper towels with the wild rice and sprinkle with the remaining ½ teaspoon salt.

If you are garnishing with the celery leaves, add the celery leaves to the oil, stepping back when you add them because the moisture in the celery will cause the oil to splatter. Cook the leaves for 5 seconds. Use the strainer to lift the celery out of the oil and spread them out on paper towels to drain.

To prepare the cabbage, adjust the oven rack to the center position and preheat the oven to 400°F.

Trim the root ends of the cabbages, trimming as little as possible so the heads stay intact. Cut each head in half through the root end. If you are using conventional-size cabbages, cut each half into 3 wedges. Put the cabbage halves or wedges on a large baking sheet. Pour the olive oil over the cabbages and with your hands massage to coat them with the oil, rubbing it into the nooks and crannies between the layers. Sprinkle the salt and a few turns of pepper over the cabbages and toss to coat them with the seasonings. Arrange the halves or wedges, cut sides down, on the baking sheet.

1 cup Straus Family Creamery Organic Greek Yogurt
(or another plain, whole-milk, not overly thick yogurt)

For the Grains and Celery Leaf Garnish

3 cups canola oil
(or another neutral-flavored oil), or as needed

2 tablespoons wild rice

1 teaspoon kosher salt

1 tablespoon sorghum grains

10 to 12 fresh celery leaves
(optional; look for the palest leaves, which are located closer to the core)

For the Cabbage

3 pounds baby cone cabbage, baby savoy cabbage, or savoy cabbage

½ cup olive oil

1 tablespoon kosher salt

Fresh coarsely ground black pepper

1 lemon, halved

Roast the cabbages in the oven for about 20 minutes (8 to 10 minutes for baby cabbages), until the undersides are deep brown and caramelized. Turn the cabbage wedges onto the second cut sides and roast for another 10 minutes, until the second sides are caramelized and the cores of the cabbages are tender when pierced with a sharp knife. Remove the baking sheet from the oven and squeeze the lemon halves over the cabbages while the cabbages are on the baking sheet.

To serve, spoon the bagna cauda yogurt onto the bottom of a large platter and use the back of the spoon to spread it toward the edges in organic, uneven swirls. Pile the cabbages side by side on top of the yogurt. Use the back of the spoon to spread the remaining yogurt over the cabbages and sprinkle 1 cup of the fried rice and sorghum over them; reserve the remaining fried grains for another use. Scatter the fried celery leaves, if you are using them, over the top.

Roasted Cabbage with
Toasted Caraway Vinaigrette

Serves 4

I often talk about underused, underappreciated vegetables, and how happy I am when I see one resurrected. For a while it was celery. Before that, kale. As I write this, the vegetable having its "15 minutes" is cabbage. It may be old news by the time you're reading this, but right now, cabbage—*cooked* cabbage—is all the rage. Caramelized, like we prepare it, it is sweet, tender, and so flavorful. I have to admit, as much as I have always loved raw cabbage in various renditions of coleslaw, it wasn't until the current cabbage renaissance that I really embraced it cooked.

We use baby savoy cabbages for this dish, and each person gets one whole cabbage. The likelihood of your finding baby cabbages is slim, so I give you instructions for starting with conventional heads of savoy cabbage. If you're lucky enough to get your hands on the softball-size cabbages, just note that instead of turning to brown each cut side, you will roll them around on the baking sheet to brown them all over. Another good option is cone cabbage, which is a cone-shaped green cabbage traditionally used to make sauerkraut. Depending on the size, you will halve or quarter the cone cabbage.

You will need a large platter to serve the cabbages.

To make the vinaigrette, toast the caraway seeds in a small sauté pan over medium heat for 1 to 2 minutes, until they are golden brown and fragrant, shaking the pan so they don't burn. Transfer the seeds to a mortar or spice grinder and very coarsely grind them. Transfer the seeds to a small bowl. Add the lemon juice, vinegar, shallots, mustard, kosher salt, and pepper to the bowl with the caraway seeds. Gradually add the extra-virgin olive oil, whisking constantly.

To prepare the cabbages, adjust the oven rack to the center position and preheat the oven to 425°F.

Trim the root ends of the cabbages, trimming as little as possible so the heads stay intact. Cut each head in half through the root end. If you are using conventional-size cabbages, cut each half into 3 wedges. Put the

For the Caraway Vinaigrette

1 tablespoon caraway seeds

3 tablespoons fresh lemon juice

1 tablespoon champagne vinegar

3 tablespoons peeled and minced shallots

1 tablespoon Dijon mustard

1½ teaspoons kosher salt

Fresh coarsely ground black pepper

¼ cup extra-virgin olive oil

cabbage halves or wedges on a large baking sheet. Pour the olive oil over the cabbages and with your hands massage to coat them with the oil, rubbing it into the nooks and crannies between the layers. Sprinkle the kosher salt and a few turns of pepper over the cabbages and toss to coat them with the seasonings. Arrange the halves or wedges, cut sides down, on the baking sheet.

Roast the cabbages in the oven for about 20 minutes (8 to 10 minutes for baby cabbages), until the undersides are deep brown and caramelized. Turn the cabbage wedges onto the second cut sides and roast for another 10 minutes, until the second sides are caramelized and the cores of the cabbages are tender when pierced with a sharp knife. Remove the baking sheet from the oven. Transfer the cabbages to a large bowl and drizzle the vinaigrette over them. Gently toss to coat the wedges with the vinaigrette.

To serve, pile the cabbages on a large platter and crush about 1 teaspoon flaky sea salt between your fingertips over them.

For the Cabbages

3 pounds baby savoy cabbage, baby cone cabbage, or savoy cabbage

½ cup olive oil

2 teaspoons kosher salt

Fresh coarsely ground black pepper

For Serving

Flaky sea salt

Whole Roasted Fennel with Salsa Verde and Gremolata Bread Crumbs

Serves 4

Roasting turns fennel sweet and almost buttery, and it also mellows out the licorice flavor. If you think you don't like fennel, try this recipe and think again. It's a great accompaniment to any pork or fish dish. You could use any size fennel bulb to make this, but the timing of this recipe is based on 12-ounce (¾-pound) bulbs.

The recipe makes more bread crumbs than you will need for this recipe; store them at room temperature and use them in the week ahead on salads, pasta, or other roasted vegetables.

You will need a medium platter to serve the fennel.

To make the bread crumbs, adjust the oven rack to the center position and preheat the oven to 350°F.

Pull the inside of the bread out of the crust in 1- to 1½-inch chunks and put the chunks on a large baking sheet. (Reserve the crusts to snack on or discard them.) Drizzle with the olive oil, sprinkle with the kosher salt, and toss to coat the bread chunks. Spread the bread chunks out on the baking sheet and bake for 10 to 12 minutes, until the bread chunks are golden brown and crispy, stirring them and rotating the baking sheet from front to back halfway through that time for even browning. Remove the croutons from the oven and set aside to cool slightly. Transfer the croutons to a food processor fitted with a metal blade and pulse until they are fine bread crumbs. Transfer the bread crumbs to a medium bowl. Add the parsley and thyme and stir to combine. Use a fine Microplane to grate the bright yellow outer layer of zest from both lemons and about ¼ cup Parmesan into the bowl. Stir to combine. (Juice the lemons for the salsa verde.)

To make the salsa verde, combine the oregano, mint, capers, lemon juice, kosher salt, and red pepper flakes in a medium bowl. Use a fine Microplane to grate the garlic into the bowl and stir to combine. Gradually add the finishing-quality olive oil, stirring constantly.

For the Gremolata Bread Crumbs

Half of a 1-pound loaf of rustic bread

½ cup olive oil

1 teaspoon kosher salt

¼ cup finely chopped fresh Italian parsley leaves

1 tablespoon fresh thyme leaves

2 lemons

A chunk of Parmesan for grating

For the Salsa Verde

¼ cup finely chopped fresh oregano leaves

1 tablespoon finely chopped fresh mint leaves

1 tablespoon capers (preferably salt-packed), soaked for 15 minutes if salt-packed, rinsed, drained, and finely chopped

To prepare the fennel, adjust the oven rack to the center position and preheat the oven to 450°F.

Cut off the fronds from the fennel bulb, if they are still attached, at the point where the bulb starts to sprout into separate stalks and discard them. (Trimming the fennel this way shows off its pretty shape when sliced.) Trim the very bottom of the root end, making sure to leave enough of the core so that the bulb stays intact. Remove the brown or unappealing outer layers and reserve them for another use, such as to make stock, or discard. Cut the fennel bulbs in half lengthwise.

Place the fennel halves on a large baking sheet. Pour the olive oil over the fennel, sprinkle with the kosher salt, and toss to coat the fennel with the oil and salt, massaging the oil into the crevices. Arrange the fennel, cut sides down, on the baking sheet and roast them in the oven for 40 to 50 minutes, until the undersides are deeply caramelized and the fennel is tender when pierced with a sharp knife, rotating the baking sheet from front to back halfway through that time for even browning. Remove the fennel from the oven.

To serve, transfer the fennel halves, cut sides up, to a medium platter. Spoon the salsa verde over the top of each fennel half and use the back of the spoon to dress the fennel with the salsa. Crush about 1 teaspoon flaky sea salt between your fingertips and sprinkle the bread crumbs over the fennel.

2 teaspoons fresh lemon juice

2 teaspoons kosher salt

½ teaspoon red pepper flakes

2 large garlic cloves, peeled

¼ cup finishing-quality extra-virgin olive oil

For the Fennel

2 large fennel bulbs (about 12 ounces each)

½ cup olive oil

1 teaspoon kosher salt

For Serving

Flaky sea salt

Roasted Cauliflower Wedges with Crushed Lemon Bagna Cauda

Serves 4 to 6

These cauliflower wedges dressed with bagna cauda have been on the Chi Spacca menu since day one. We blanch the wedges and then roast them in a hot oven, so they're tender on the inside with a dark, caramelized exterior. They're really beautiful and delicious. *Bagna cauda* means "warm bath," in Italian, and is a traditional condiment made of butter, olive oil, anchovies, and garlic. We add crushed lemon segments to this version. It has an intense, bold flavor that makes the ideal accompaniment to the mild flavor of cauliflower.

A citrus zester is a one-trick tool used to peel long, threadlike strips from citrus. The strips are really pretty made this way, but if you don't want to invest in one just for this, you can get more or less the same results by peeling citrus with a vegetable peeler and then cutting it into long thin strips.

You will need a large platter to serve the cauliflower wedges.

To make the bagna cauda, combine the butter and extra-virgin olive oil in a small saucepan. Finely chop the anchovies with a large knife and use the flat side of the knife to smash them into a paste; add the paste to the saucepan. Using a fine Microplane, grate the garlic into the saucepan. Heat the bagna cauda over low heat for 5 minutes, stirring occasionally, to melt the butter and meld the flavors. Turn off the heat.

If you have a citrus zester, use it to zest the bright yellow outer layer of the lemon. If you do not have one, peel the bright yellow outer layer of lemon zest in wide strips using a vegetable peeler and then very thinly slice it into long threads. Set the zest aside for garnish.

Cut off and discard the top and bottom of the lemon at the point where you can see the flesh. Place the lemon upright on a cutting board and cut down the side at the point where the pith meets the flesh, following the natural curve of the fruit to remove the pith along with the peel. Discard the peels. Turn the lemon on its side and cut along one of the membranes toward the center of the fruit. Working your way around the lemon, cut along both sides of each membrane to release all the segments from the

For the Bagna Cauda

4 tablespoons (½ stick) unsalted butter

½ cup extra-virgin olive oil

10 anchovy fillets (preferably salt-packed; rinsed and backbones removed if salt-packed)

4 large garlic cloves, peeled

1 lemon

For the Cauliflower

2 teaspoons kosher salt, plus more for the boiling water

1 large head cauliflower (about 2 pounds)

¾ cup extra-virgin olive oil

1 tablespoon finely chopped fresh Italian parsley leaves

core. Add the segments to the bagna cauda and squeeze the core of the lemon over the saucepan to extract as much juice as you can. Crush the lemons into the bagna cauda.

To cook the cauliflower, fill a large pot with water and salt it to taste like the ocean, adding 1 scant tablespoon kosher salt per quart of water. Bring the water to a boil over high heat. Prepare an ice bath in a large bowl.

Cut off and discard the stem of the cauliflower, cutting as little as possible so the cauliflower will stay intact. Remove and discard the large leaves, leaving the tender ones that envelop the cauliflower intact. Cut the cauliflower in half and cut each half into 3 wedges.

Add the cauliflower wedges to the boiling water and cook for 2 to 3 minutes, until the core of one wedge is tender when poked with a knife. Drain the cauliflower in a colander and put it in the ice bath for about 2 minutes to cool completely. Return the cauliflower to the colander to drain for at least a few minutes. Pat the cauliflower dry with paper towels. (It's important that the cauliflower be completely dry, otherwise it will steam instead of roast when it goes into the oven in the next step.)

Adjust the oven rack to the center position and preheat the oven to 450°F.

Put the cauliflower wedges on a large baking sheet. Pour the extra-virgin olive oil over them and use your hands to massage the oil into the nooks and crannies. Sprinkle with the salt and massage it into the cauliflower. Arrange the wedges, cut sides down, on the baking sheet.

Roast the cauliflower wedges in the oven for 20 minutes, until the undersides are deeply caramelized. Turn the wedges onto the second cut sides and cook for another 20 minutes, until the cauliflower is tender when pierced with a sharp knife. Remove from the oven.

To serve, transfer the cauliflower to a large platter. Spoon the bagna cauda over the cauliflower wedges, dividing it evenly, and sprinkle the chopped parsley and lemon zest over them.

Roasted Parsnips with Chestnut Honey, Garlic, and Thyme

Serves 4

Parsnips, which look like white carrots but have a unique, distinct flavor, are one of the unsung heroes of the root vegetable world. They are at once very sweet, with a slight bitter, earthy taste. Roasting them with honey and whole garlic cloves turns this humble vegetable into a decadent side dish that is a real crowd-pleaser.

Chestnut honey has a distinct flavor and isn't as sweet as other varieties. You can find it at specialty food stores and cheese stores. If you can't find it, use buckwheat or avocado honey in its place. Look for long, slender parsnips that are sold like carrots often are, with the greens attached. You will probably have to go to a farmers' market to find them. If you are lucky enough to find baby parsnips, leave them whole.

You will need a large platter to serve the parsnips.

To cook the parsnips, adjust the oven rack to the center position and preheat the oven to 325°F.

Scrub the parsnips and, leaving the last ¾ inch of the stems attached, cut off and discard the greens, if they are attached. Cut the parsnips lengthwise into halves or quarters. (If you are using baby parsnips, leave them whole.)

Put the parsnips on a large baking sheet and add the garlic and thyme. Drizzle with the olive oil and sprinkle with the kosher salt and a few turns of pepper. Toss with your hands to coat the vegetables with the oil and seasonings and spread them out in a single layer on the baking sheet; if you've cut the parsnips, make sure they're cut sides down.

Roast the parsnips for 12 minutes to partially cook them, shaking the baking sheet once during that time so the parsnips cook evenly. Remove the baking sheet from the oven. Drizzle the honey over the parsnips and garlic and stir to coat the vegetables. Return the baking sheet to the oven and roast the vegetables for 5 to 7 minutes, until they are deep brown but not burned and are tender when pierced with a sharp →

For Cooking the Parsnips

1 pound parsnips (preferably long, slender parsnips with the greens attached, or baby parsnips)

2 garlic heads, cloves separated and peeled (about ½ cup)

8 fresh thyme sprigs

1 tablespoon olive oil

2 teaspoons kosher salt

Fresh coarsely ground black pepper

2 tablespoons chestnut honey (or buckwheat or avocado honey)

knife. Remove the baking sheet from the oven and gently roll the vegetables on the baking sheet to coat them with the honey, taking care not to smash them.

To serve, arrange the parsnips, garlic cloves, and thyme sprigs on a large platter. Crush about 1 teaspoon flaky sea salt between your fingertips over the vegetables and drizzle with about 2 tablespoons finishing-quality olive oil.

For Serving

Flaky sea salt

Finishing-quality extra-virgin olive oil

Whole Roasted Carrots with Cracked Coriander and Cumin and Dill Yogurt

Serves 4

I've roasted whole carrots for decades: baby carrots, Nantes carrots, rainbow carrots, but never the enormous carrots that you would ordinarily feed to horses. Where slender carrots, once roasted, shrivel away, with these, you get that caramelized exterior, but then the interior is creamy and meaty. The carrots should be 1 to 1½ inches in diameter. If you can't find carrots that large, use the biggest ones you can find, and keep an eye on them while they are roasting, because smaller carrots will take less time to cook.

You will need a large platter to serve the carrots.

To make the dill yogurt, combine the yogurt, dill, lemon juice, and kosher salt together in a medium bowl. Using a fine Microplane, grate the garlic into the bowl and stir to combine. Add more lemon juice and salt to taste.

To prepare the carrots, adjust the oven rack to the center position and preheat the oven to 450°F.

Put the coriander seeds and cumin seeds in a mortar or spice grinder and very coarsely grind them.

Put the carrots on a large baking sheet, drizzle with the olive oil, and sprinkle with the kosher salt and seeds. Toss with your hands to coat the carrots evenly with the oil, salt, and seeds. Spread the carrots out in a single layer.

Roast the carrots in the oven for 30 to 35 minutes, shaking the baking sheet and rotating it from front to back halfway through that time so they brown evenly. Remove the baking sheet from the oven.

To serve, spoon the yogurt into the center of a large platter and use the back of the spoon to spread it toward the edges in organic, uneven swirls. Lay the carrots on the yogurt. Crush about 1 teaspoon flaky sea salt between your fingertips and scatter it and the fresh dill tufts over the carrots.

For the Dill Yogurt

2 cups Straus Family Creamery Organic Greek Yogurt (or another plain, whole-milk, not overly thick yogurt)

½ cup finely chopped fresh dill

2 tablespoons fresh lemon juice, plus more to taste

1 teaspoon kosher salt, plus more to taste

2 large garlic cloves, peeled

For the Carrots

2 tablespoons coriander seeds

2 tablespoons cumin seeds

4 super-large carrots, (3 to 4 pounds), scrubbed

¼ cup olive oil

2 teaspoons kosher salt

For Serving

Flaky sea salt

¼ cup fresh dill (tufts pulled from the stems)

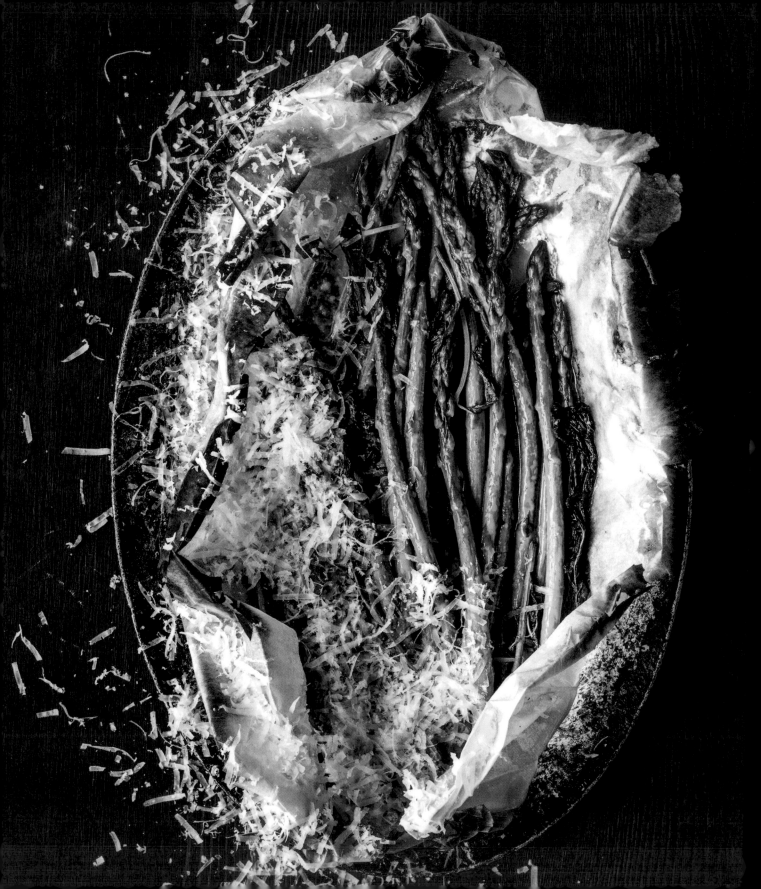

Asparagus al Cartoccio with Butter, Mint, and Parmesan

Serves 4

At one of my favorite restaurants in Tel Aviv, North Abraxass, I was served a dish of spinach stems *al cartoccio,* or spinach cooked in parchment. The paper packet came to the table unfolded, revealing the cooked green stems that were showered in Parmesan—so simple! It was obvious to me that the same cooking method would work on any long, slender vegetable. When I came home, I tried it with pencil asparagus. Cooking the slender asparagus spears in paper this way protects them from direct heat, so they retain their shape and color, rather than shriveling and drying up the way they do when roasted. They're basically steamed, but the paper packet gives the dish that "Wow!" factor. It's like a pretty present.

You will need a large platter to serve the asparagus packages.

Adjust the oven rack to the center position and preheat the oven to 450°F.

Lay a 13- × 18-inch sheet of parchment paper on a flat work surface with the long side parallel to the counter's edge and have another sheet handy. Lay half of the asparagus lengthwise in the center of the paper. Sprinkle the kosher salt and scatter half of the butter cubes over the spears and lay one mint sprig on top. Bring the top and bottom edges of the paper together and fold them over tightly to seal closed. Fold the sides inward like you were wrapping a present without tape and press down hard to seal them closed, so the asparagus are tightly wrapped in the paper. Repeat, wrapping the remaining asparagus, along with the butter, kosher salt, and mint, in the second sheet of parchment paper.

Place the asparagus packages on a large baking sheet and roast for about 10 minutes, until the paper is golden brown and the butter is bubbling out of the packages. Remove the baking sheet from the oven and let the packages cool for 1 minute on the baking sheet.

To serve, lay the packages on a large platter. Cut a slit lengthwise down the middle of each package, being careful of the steam that will arise. →

1 pound pencil asparagus

1 teaspoon kosher salt

2 tablespoons unsalted butter, cut into 1-inch cubes

2 fresh mint sprigs

Flaky sea salt

Fresh coarsely ground black pepper

A chunk of Parmesan for grating

Peel the sides of the parchment apart to expose the asparagus; remove and discard the mint sprigs.

Crush about ½ teaspoon flaky sea salt between your fingertips over the asparagus inside each package and grind a few turns of pepper into each package. Use a fine Microplane to grate a generous layer of Parmesan over one side of each package of asparagus, leaving one side free of cheese so you can see the asparagus.

Charred Sugar Snap Peas with Yogurt, Guanciale, and Lemon Zest

Serves 4

Most often, when I think of sugar snaps, my mind goes to serving them raw, thinly sliced and tossed in a spring salad along with other springtime ingredients, such as English peas, tiny radishes, and fresh herbs. When Ryan decided to char them, I was horrified at the thought, but he charred them just long enough so they were still crunchy with patches of green. I was won over. The sugar snap peas are roasted in a cast-iron skillet that is preheated while the oven is preheating; this is our way of replicating the intense heat we get from our wood-burning ovens. By adding the vegetables to an already-hot skillet, you are able to caramelize them without overcooking them.

You will need a large cast-iron skillet to make these.

You will need a large platter to serve the sugar snap peas.

To prepare the yogurt, combine the yogurt, lemon juice, shallot, olive oil, and salt in a small bowl and stir to combine.

To prepare the snap peas, arrange the oven racks so one is in the center and there is no rack near the oven floor; you'll be putting a baking sheet directly on the oven floor. If you are using an electric oven or another oven where you can't put anything on the floor, place one rack as close to the floor as possible and put a pizza steel or stone, if you have one, on it. Place a large cast-iron skillet on the floor or the lowest rack or stone. Preheat the oven and skillet to 500°F.

For the snap peas, place the guanciale on a baking sheet and cook it on the center rack of the oven until crispy, about 5 minutes. Line a plate with paper towels. Remove the baking sheet from the oven and transfer the guanciale to the plate to drain.

Put the snap peas in a large bowl, drizzle with the olive oil, sprinkle with the salt, and toss to coat the peas with the oil and salt. Open the oven and, using oven mitts, carefully pull out the hot skillet. Dump the sugar snap peas into the skillet and spread them out over the surface. →

For the Yogurt

½ cup Straus Family Creamery Organic Greek Yogurt (or another plain, whole-milk, not overly thick yogurt)

2 tablespoons fresh lemon juice

1 tablespoon peeled and minced shallot

1 tablespoon olive oil

½ teaspoon kosher salt

For the Snap Peas

¼ pound thinly sliced guanciale (or pancetta; sliced ¼ inch thick)

1 pound sugar snap peas, strings removed and discarded

2 tablespoons olive oil

1½ teaspoons kosher salt

1 lemon

Return the skillet to its original position, close the oven door, and cook until the snap peas are charred in places but still crisp, about 6 minutes, stirring them halfway through that time so they char evenly. Remove the skillet from the oven.

To serve, finely chop the guanciale. Spoon the yogurt into the middle of a large platter and use the back of the spoon to spread it toward the edges in organic, uneven swirls. Pile the snap peas on top of the yogurt and sprinkle the chopped guanciale on top. Using a fine Microplane, zest the bright yellow outer layer of the lemon over the snap peas. (Reserve the lemon to juice another time.)

Roasted Honeynut Squash with Pistachio-Hazelnut Dukkah

Serves 4

Honeynut squash is a variety of winter squash developed recently at the Cornell College of Agriculture and Life Sciences in collaboration with the chef Dan Barber. It is shaped like butternut squash, but smaller. It's a bit sweeter and more flavorful than butternut squash, but butternut squash, or any other flavorful winter squash, will work. The squash is cooked until the cut side is caramelized and just this side of burned, and then seasoned with an unusual mix of garam masala, an Indian spice blend, and dukkah, a blend of nuts, seeds, and spices traditional to Israeli and Egyptian cuisine. The word *dukkah* derives from Arabic for "to pound," and dukkah is ideally made using a mortar and pestle. It's like the dry "pesto" of Middle Eastern cuisine. It adds a lot of texture and flavor, and really turns the squash into a complete dish. I imagine that if vegetarians were to be served this as the centerpiece of their meal, they would feel totally satisfied.

Both black and white unhulled toasted sesame seeds are sold as "roasted sesame seeds" in shaker canisters in the Japanese section of supermarkets. If you can't find them, use the more widely available hulled white sesame seeds and toast them in a small skillet over medium heat for 1 to 2 minutes, until they're toasted and fragrant. We dry the orange peel for the dukkah in the oven. You can always skip this step and use packaged dried orange peel instead, available at Middle Eastern markets.

You will need a large platter to serve the squash.

To make the dukkah, peel the bright orange outer layer of orange zest with a vegetable peeler and put the peels on a baking sheet. Adjust the oven rack to the center position and put the baking sheet in the oven. Preheat the oven to 300°F, with the orange peels already inside. Cook the peels for 30 to 40 minutes, until they are dried out and slightly crunchy. Remove the orange peels from the oven and set them aside to cool slightly. Transfer to a mortar or spice grinder and finely grind them. If you're using a spice grinder, transfer the orange peels to a small bowl.

Increase the oven temperature to 325°F. →

For the Dukkah

1 orange (or 1 teaspoon dried orange peel)
¼ cup hazelnuts
¼ cup shelled pistachios
1 teaspoon coriander seeds
1 teaspoon black peppercorns
1 tablespoon unhulled roasted black or white sesame seeds (or hulled white sesame seeds, lightly toasted)
½ teaspoon kosher salt

Meanwhile, spread the hazelnuts out on a separate baking sheet and toast them in the oven until they are toasted and fragrant, shaking the baking sheet and rotating it from front to back halfway through that time so the nuts brown evenly. Remove them from the oven and set them aside to cool slightly. Gather the hazelnuts into a clean dish towel and rub them together inside the towel to remove the skins. Coarsely chop the hazelnuts and add them to the bowl with the orange peel.

Spread the pistachios on the baking sheet and toast them in the oven for about 6 minutes, until they're lightly browned and fragrant, shaking the baking sheet and rotating it from front to back halfway through that time so the nuts brown evenly. Remove the baking sheet from the oven and set aside to cool slightly. Coarsely chop the pistachios and add them to the bowl with the other dukkah ingredients.

While the nuts are toasting, put the coriander seeds and peppercorns in a small sauté pan and toast over medium heat for 1 to 2 minutes, until they are fragrant and toasted, shaking the pan so they don't burn. Transfer the seeds to the mortar or spice grinder and very coarsely grind them. Add them to the bowl with the dukkah. Add the sesame seeds and kosher salt and stir to combine.

To cook the squash, cut them (or it) in half lengthwise, scoop out and discard the seeds, and place the halves, cut sides up, on a large baking sheet. Drizzle with the olive oil, sprinkle with the kosher salt, and massage with your hands to coat all sides of the squash.

Lay the squash, cut sides down, on the baking sheet and roast in the oven for 45 minutes to 1 hour, until the undersides are deeply caramelized, the skin is golden brown and blistered, and the squash is tender when pierced with a sharp knife. Remove the baking sheet from the oven.

To serve, lay the squash, cut sides up, on a large platter. Sprinkle with the garam masala, dividing it evenly. Drizzle about 2 tablespoon finishing-quality olive oil and crush about 1 teaspoon flaky sea salt between your fingertips over the squash. Sprinkle ¼ cup of the dukkah over the squash, dividing it evenly. (Reserve the remaining dukkah to sprinkle over grilled vegetables or meats in the days ahead.)

For the Squash

2 honeynut squash
(or 1 medium to large butternut squash; 4 to 6 pounds)

¼ cup olive oil

2 teaspoons kosher salt

For Serving

1 tablespoon Garam Masala (page 21; or store-bought)

Finishing-quality extra-virgin olive oil

Flaky sea salt

Dario's Baked Potatoes
with Whipped Lardo

Serves 4

I love a good baked potato, and I always enjoy these when I go to my friend Dario Cecchini's steak house, Officina della Bistecca, in the Chianti region of Tuscany. Dario bakes and serves his potatoes wrapped in foil. In place of the typical butter and sour cream, he dollops a big spoonful of whipped lardo, or as he calls it, "Chianti butter," onto the baked potato, and then closes it back up again so it melts in the time it takes it to arrive at your table. It is an example of something so simple being so surprising and delicious.

You will need a medium platter to serve the baked potatoes.

Adjust the oven rack to the center position and preheat the oven to 350°F.

Scrub the potatoes and wrap them neatly in aluminum foil, keeping in mind that you will be unwrapping and rewrapping the potatoes in the same sheet of foil. Place the potatoes on a baking sheet and bake them in the oven for about 45 minutes, until they are tender when pierced with a sharp knife. Remove the potatoes from the oven and set aside until they're just cool enough to touch.

Unfold the foil to reveal the potato inside but leave the foil on. Cut a 1-inch-deep slit down the length of each potato. Squeeze the edges of each potato toward each other to push the inside up out of the skin. Spoon 2 tablespoons of the lardo into the opening of each potato. Close the potatoes with the lardo inside and fold the foil back around them.

To serve, transfer the potatoes, wrapped in foil, to a large platter.

4 medium russet potatoes

½ cup Whipped Lardo (page 59)

Roasted Ricotta-Stuffed Squash Blossoms with Tomato Vinaigrette

Serves 4 to 6

I had never seen beyond fried squash blossoms until a recent lunch in Tuscany, when a plate of squash blossoms came to the table *not* fried. The blossoms were stuffed with cheese, as usual, warmed ever so slightly, and served with a light tomato sauce. Since they weren't fried and there was no batter covering them, I could really see and appreciate the delicate flower. I brought this idea to Chi Spacca; we're always looking for lighter side dishes. We stuff the blossoms with creamy, flavorful Bellwether Farms sheep's milk ricotta, which is widely available in stores, and serve them on a light, acidic tomato vinaigrette. Look for squash blossoms that are very fresh and at least 2 inches in length; too-small or wilted blossoms can be very difficult to stuff. I prefer male blossoms, which are attached to the stem, rather than females, which are attached to the fruit. I think these look pretty with some of the stem attached.

If it's not the season for great tomatoes, use quality, imported jarred or canned small tomatoes. Look for the words *datterini* or *Corbari* (both are varieties of tomatoes), or *pomodorini* (which refers to cherry tomatoes in general); drain the tomatoes before using them.

You will need a large pastry bag with a ½-inch round tip, or a disposable pastry bag, to make these.

You will need a medium platter to serve the squash blossoms.

To make the vinaigrette, combine the cherry tomatoes and vinegar in the jar of a blender and purée. Put a mesh strainer over a medium bowl and strain the vinaigrette into the bowl. Gradually add the extra-virgin olive oil in a thin stream, whisking constantly to emulsify the vinaigrette; if the mixture looks visibly separated, continue whisking until it is emulsified. Add the salt and whisk to combine.

To prepare the squash blossoms, adjust the oven rack to the center position and preheat the oven to 350°F.

Trim the stems from the squash blossoms, leaving about 1 inch of the stems attached; if you can find only squash blossoms with the zucchini attached, break off the flower and reserve the zucchini to cook another time or to snack on. →

For the Vinaigrette

1 pint small cherry tomatoes (or 2 cups jarred or canned cherry tomatoes, drained)

3 tablespoons red wine vinegar

½ cup extra-virgin olive oil

1 teaspoon kosher salt

For the Squash Blossoms

12 large squash blossoms with stems attached (2 inches or longer, not including the stems)

Stir the ricotta, cream, salt, and pepper together in a small bowl.

Fit a large pastry bag with a ½-inch round tip or cut a ½-inch hole in the tip of a disposable pastry bag. Spoon the ricotta mixture into the bag and push it toward the tip. Twist the top of the bag until it puts enough pressure on the ricotta that it squeezes out of the bottom of the bag.

Place one squash blossom on your work surface and carefully open the petals with your fingers. Insert the piping bag into the opening and squeeze the bag gently to slowly release the ricotta mixture, until the blossom is stuffed about three-quarters full. (Each squash blossom will be stuffed with about 1 tablespoon of ricotta.) Gently twist the top of the blossom to seal the ricotta into the flower and place it on a baking sheet. Stuff the remaining blossoms with the remaining ricotta mixture, adding them to the baking sheet in a single layer.

Drizzle the olive oil over the blossoms and bake them for about 3 minutes. To check for doneness, squeeze the flower gently to see if the cheese is warm. The point of this is simply to warm the cheese, not cook the flowers. Remove the baking sheet from the oven.

While the blossoms are in the oven, warm the vinaigrette in a small saucepan over low heat for 3 to 4 minutes, being careful not to let it come to a simmer. Turn off the heat.

To serve, pour the vinaigrette to cover the surface of a medium platter. Transfer the squash blossoms to the platter and scatter the basil over them.

1 cup fresh ricotta
(preferably sheep's milk ricotta)

2 tablespoons heavy cream

½ teaspoon kosher salt

¼ teaspoon fresh coarsely ground black pepper

2 tablespoons olive oil

To Serve

12 fresh basil tufts
(delicate stems with young leaves attached; or 6 fresh basil leaves, torn into small pieces)

Braised Greens

Serves 4

We serve these unctuous braised greens with the Pancetta-Wrapped Rabbit (page 212) and Grilled Pork-and-Veal Meatballs with Fresh Ricotta (page 175). Slow-cooked with olive oil, onion, and garlic, this recipe is delicious made with any mix of dark, leafy greens. You could double the amount of one and skip another; or throw in the outer leaves of escarole, trimmed, to make a salad. This recipe calls for you to thinly slice the garlic on a mandoline because there is so much garlic and a mandoline works faster. If you prefer to use a knife, that's fine, too.

You will need a medium bowl to serve the greens.

Adjust the blade of a mandoline to slice ⅛ inch thick. Slice the garlic lengthwise, stopping just before your fingers get dangerously close to the blade; reserve the garlic ends to chop for another use. (Or thinly slice with a knife.) Cut off and discard the root and tip ends of the onion. Peel the onion and cut it into quarters, root to tip. Separate the layers of the onion, stack two or three layers on top of one another, and slice them ¹⁄₁₆ inch thick lengthwise. Pull the chard leaves from the ribs. Cut off and discard the very ends of the ribs and slice the ribs ¼ inch thick.

Cut the root from the escarole and remove the leaves from the core; discard the core. Pull the cavolo nero leaves from the stems and discard the stems. Tear the leaves into large pieces.

Heat the extra-virgin olive oil in a large skillet over medium-high heat. Add the chard ribs and cook for about 3 minutes, stirring occasionally, to begin to soften them. Add the onion, garlic, and 1 teaspoon of the salt and cook for about 10 minutes, stirring often, until the vegetables are tender and translucent. Add the chard leaves, escarole, cavolo nero, árbol chiles, and the remaining 1 teaspoon salt and stir to combine. Cover the pan, reduce the heat to medium-low, and cook the greens for 15 to 20 minutes, removing the lid and stirring often, until they are dark green and very soft, and the liquid released from them has cooked off. Turn off the heat. Transfer the greens to a medium bowl, unless you are using them for the rabbit or meatballs, in which case leave them in the skillet until you are ready to serve those dishes.

½ cup large garlic cloves, peeled

1 yellow Spanish onion

1 bunch Swiss chard (any color)

1 head escarole

1 bunch cavolo nero (Tuscan kale)

½ cup extra-virgin olive oil

2 teaspoons kosher salt, plus more to taste

2 árbol chiles

Creamed Summer Corn

Serves 4

This simple side dish of creamed corn is not to be confused with *cream* corn. There is no cream in it; the creaminess comes from the liquid extracted from the corn kernels. We started making this when Chi Spacca's original chef, Chad Colby, was making regular trips to Chino Family Farm in San Diego County. The Chino family is known for growing a lot of wonderful vegetables, but they're most famous for their corn. If you're going to make this recipe, you need to start with really delicious corn—taste it before you buy it. You can use yellow or white corn, but I prefer yellow. White corn can be too sugary for me, sweet but lacking in corn flavor.

On one of Chad's trips to Chino's, the Chino family gave him a gadget called Lee's Corn Cutter and Creamer, a simple, inexpensive, two-task tool made specifically for cutting corn off the cob and for "creaming," or grating, it. You can find them online or use a box grater to grate the kernels instead. The advantage of the corn creamer is that it shaves the corn smaller than a box grater does, and it's boat-shaped to accommodate the shape of an ear of corn, so you're surer to get all the corn off the cob, and with fewer turns.

You will need a medium bowl to serve the corn.

Using a corn creamer or the large holes on a box grater, grate the kernels off the corncobs into a large saucepan.

Place the saucepan over medium heat and cook the corn for 10 to 12 minutes, stirring often to prevent it from burning, until it releases liquid and the liquid is cooked off to resemble a thick pudding. Add the butter and cook, stirring often, to melt it. Remove the corn from the heat. Add the salt and several turns of pepper and stir to combine. Add more salt or pepper to taste.

To serve, transfer the corn to a medium bowl, drizzle the finishing-quality olive oil, and grind a few turns of pepper over the top.

6 ears of corn (preferably yellow corn), shucked

4 tablespoons (½ stick) unsalted butter, cut into 1-inch cubes

2 teaspoons kosher salt, plus more to taste

Fresh coarsely ground black pepper

1 tablespoon finishing-quality extra-virgin olive oil

Garlic Mashed Potatoes

Serves 4

The late, great chef Joël Robuchon gave us cooks permission to put as much cream and butter as we wanted into our mashed potatoes. At Chi Spacca, we do just that, so *merci,* Joël!

Our customers tell us ours are the best potatoes they've ever eaten. They don't want to know the amount of butter and cream it takes to make them that good! We use a food mill to purée the potatoes, and then pass them through a fine-mesh sieve to get a smooth, luxurious texture.

You will need a large bowl to serve the potatoes.

Set up a large pot with a steamer insert and fill the pot with a few inches of water. Bring the water to a boil over high heat. Add the potatoes and garlic to the steamer insert, cover the pot, and steam until the potatoes and garlic are tender when pierced with a sharp knife, 20 to 25 minutes.

Meanwhile, combine the cream, butter, and salt in a small saucepan and heat over low heat, stirring occasionally, until the butter has melted and the cream is gently simmering. Turn off the heat.

Set a food mill or ricer over a large bowl, spoon the potatoes and garlic into the mill or ricer, and mill or rice the potatoes and garlic into the bowl. Slowly add the hot cream mixture to the bowl, whisking to combine. Add more cream if needed for a loose consistency and add more salt to taste.

To serve, spoon the mashed potatoes into a large bowl.

2 pounds russet potatoes (3 to 4 medium), peeled and cut into 2-inch chunks

1 cup large garlic cloves (about 40 cloves), peeled

1½ cups heavy cream, plus more as needed

6 tablespoons unsalted butter, cut into 1-inch cubes

1 tablespoon kosher salt, plus more to taste

Lardo Asador Potatoes

Serves 4

These potatoes are thinly sliced, stacked on their sides, nestled together, and roasted until the outside edges are crispy and the insides are moist and tender. I borrowed the name, and the idea, from Anya Fernald, who has a recipe for her version of these, called Asador Potatoes, in her cookbook *Home Cooked.* The beautiful photograph of these sliced potatoes cooked in a cast-iron skillet caught my eye. She makes hers with butter, but at Chi Spacca we use lardo; we're always looking for ways to use up the pork fat we have from butchering whole hogs. It adds great flavor, but if you want to use melted butter instead, you can. It's important that you use potatoes that are larger around than the height of the skillet. That way, when sliced they stick up past the edge of the skillet and the edges of the potatoes get crispy and crackly.

You will need an 8- or 9-inch cast-iron skillet to make and serve these potatoes.

Adjust the oven rack to the center position and preheat the oven to 375°F.

Adjust the blade of a mandoline to slice ⅛ inch thick. Cut the first slice of potato to create a flat surface. Cut 2 more slices and check their thickness. If they are thick, like slabs, adjust the mandoline to slice thinner. If they are so thin that they tear or don't hold their shape, adjust the blade to slice thicker. Continue slicing the potato, stopping just before your fingers get dangerously close to the blade. Discard the first and last rounded slices and put the remaining slices in a medium bowl.

Put the lardo in a small skillet and melt it over medium-low heat. Pour the melted lardo or melted butter over the potatoes. Add the rosemary and salt and toss to coat the potatoes with them. Stack the potatoes and turn the stack so the edges of the slices are facing upright and lay the slices around the perimeter of the pan. Make a second circle of potatoes inside the first one to fill the pan.

Bake the potatoes in the oven for about 1 hour 20 minutes, until the top is deep golden brown and the interior of the potato slices is cooked all the way through.

Serve the potatoes straight from the oven in the pan they were cooked in.

2 pounds medium Yukon gold potatoes (about 12 potatoes)

3 ounces Whipped Lardo (page 59; about 3 tablespoons; or ¼ cup plus 2 tablespoons melted unsalted butter)

1 tablespoon finely chopped fresh rosemary leaves

1 tablespoon kosher salt

Chris Feldmeier's Rancho Beans

Serves 4 to 6

It's so hard with barbecue beans to get the right balance between sweet and spicy, and they're usually too sweet for my taste. My friend and one of my former chefs at Osteria Mozza, Chris Feldmeier, came up with the perfect version, enhanced by the smoky flavor of bacon. We stole it for Chi Spacca. They are a must-serve side if you're making Coffee-Rubbed Grilled Tri-Tip (page 146) because both are part of the traditional Santa Maria Barbecue, a feast that is a way of life in the central California town of Santa Maria. I like to serve these beans in the Dutch oven they're cooked in—it seems fitting for their "rancho" sensibility. Plan ahead to make these because the beans need to soak for at least 8 hours before you cook them.

This recipe calls for homemade chicken stock, which doesn't contain any sodium. If the stock you are using does contain sodium, cut the salt in this recipe by half.

Serve these in the pot they were made in, preferably a cast-iron or enameled Dutch oven.

Put the beans in a large bowl, cover them with water and soak overnight or for at least 8 hours. Drain the beans.

Cut off and discard the root and tip ends of the onion. Peel the onion and cut it into quarters, root to tip. Separate the layers of the onion, stack two or three layers on top of one another, and slice them ¼ inch thin lengthwise. Remove and discard the stem from the jalapeño. Cut it into quarters lengthwise and remove and discard the stems and seeds.

Heat the olive oil in a large Dutch oven or another large pot over medium-high heat for 2 to 3 minutes, until the oil slides easily and is smoking around the edges of the pan. Add the bacon, onion, and jalapeño, sprinkle with 1 teaspoon of the salt, and cook over medium-high heat for 12 to 15 minutes, stirring occasionally, until the onion and jalapeño are browned. Add the thyme, make space in the bottom of the pan, and add the garlic to the space. Cook, stirring occasionally, for about 4 minutes until the garlic cloves are golden brown all over. Create a space in the pan like you did for the garlic, add the tomato paste to the space, and cook for about 2 minutes to caramelize the tomato paste, stirring constantly so it

1 pound dried pinto beans (about 2 cups)

1 large yellow Spanish onion

1 small jalapeño chile

2 tablespoons olive oil

8 ounces slab bacon, bacon scraps, or thick-sliced bacon, cut into 2-inch pieces

1 tablespoon plus 1 teaspoon kosher salt, plus more to taste

10 fresh thyme sprigs

10 large garlic cloves, peeled

2 tablespoons double-concentrated tomato paste

2 quarts (8 cups) Chicken Stock (page 159; or sodium-free or low-sodium store-bought), or as needed

doesn't burn. Add the beans and enough chicken stock to cover them by 1½ to 2 inches. Stir in the remaining 1 tablespoon salt, increase the heat to high, and bring the stock to a boil. Reduce the heat to medium-low to maintain a gentle simmer. Simmer the beans for about 2 hours, until they are tender and creamy, not chalky or al dente but also not falling apart, stirring often and adding more stock to the pot as needed to keep the beans covered at all times. Skim off and discard any foam that rises to the top while the beans are cooking. To test the beans for doneness, press one bean between your fingers; if it is creamy and silky, it's done. Turn off the heat.

Serve the beans in the pot you cooked them in.

Yorkshire Pudding
with Aged Beef Trimmings

Makes 4 large Yorkshire puddings; serves 8

I love a challenge, so I welcomed the opportunity when I was asked by the organizers of a *Los Angeles Times* food event to re-create the classic sides from Lawry's, a legendary prime rib house in Los Angeles. Our executive pastry chef Dahlia Narvaez helped to create this next-level version of Yorkshire Pudding with Aged Beef Trimmings.

Yorkshire pudding is a custardy bread made of milk, eggs, and very little flour. Traditionally, the batter was poured into a pan and placed in the oven beneath a roast so the fat from the meat dripped down into the pudding. In more modern times, the pan is lined with beef drippings (or another fat) and the batter is poured over it. We use the melted trimmings from our aged steaks and dress up the batter with chopped fresh parsley and chives. Then we top the baked puddings with chopped roasted beef trimmings and fresh grated Parmesan. It's the perfect example of how we like to layer flavors at Chi Spacca. These are baked in cast-iron skillets and meant to be shared.

Ask your butcher for beef trimmings (preferably dry-aged), consisting of 80 percent fat and 20 percent meat.

The recipe makes enough for four Yorkshire puddings, each of which serves two. I didn't cut the recipe in half because it calls for an odd number of eggs. The batter will keep for up to two days, so bake them off as you desire; you could make two on one day and two on another.

You will need at least two (6½-inch) cast-iron skillets to make and serve the puddings.

To make the Yorkshire puddings, adjust the oven rack to the lowest position and preheat the oven to 400°F.

Spread the beef trimmings out in a single layer on a baking sheet and roast them in the oven for 12 to 15 minutes, until they are golden brown and crispy in places. Remove the trimmings from the oven and set aside until they are cool enough to touch. Chop the trimmings into ¼-inch cubes and put them in a small bowl. Pour the liquid fat from the baking sheet into a separate bowl.

For the Puddings

4 ounces beef trimmings (preferably dry-aged; including meat and fat; or melted lard)

¾ cup unbleached all-purpose flour

¾ teaspoon kosher salt

⅛ teaspoon baking powder

Reduce the oven temperature to 375°F. Place two skillets in the oven and preheat them for at least 10 minutes.

Combine the flour, salt, and baking powder in a medium bowl.

Crack the eggs into the bowl of a stand mixer. Fit the mixer with the whisk attachment and beat until the eggs have doubled in volume, about 5 minutes, stopping to scrape down the sides of the bowl at least once during that time. Turn off the mixer and add the dry ingredients. Beat on medium speed until no flour is visible. With the mixer running, slowly add the milk and beat until the batter is smooth, stopping to scrape down the sides of the bowl as needed. Turn off the mixer. Remove the bowl from the mixer stand and remove the whisk. Add the parsley and chives and fold them into the batter.

Carefully remove the skillets from the oven. Spoon 1 tablespoon of the liquid beef fat into each skillet and wait about 1 minute for the heat of the skillet to warm the fat. Tilt the pan so the fat spreads to the edges. Pour or ladle ½ cup of the batter into each of the skillets and use the back of the ladle to smooth out the tops.

Return the skillets to the oven and bake for 12 to 15 minutes, until the Yorkshire puddings are golden brown and have puffed up to about three times their original size. Remove the skillets from the oven and spoon 1 tablespoon of the chopped beef over each pudding. Use a fine Microplane to grate a generous amount of Parmesan to cover each pudding like a thin blanket of snow and grate a few turns of pepper over each.

Serve the Yorkshire puddings in the skillets you cooked them in and provide a big spoon for people to dig in. If you need the skillets to bake additional Yorkshire puddings, invert each pudding onto a plate and invert again so they are facing upright. Return the skillets to the oven to reheat as you did previously and repeat, baking the remaining batter and topping the second batch of puddings in the same way.

3 extra-large eggs

¾ cup whole milk

2 tablespoons finely chopped fresh Italian parsley leaves

2 tablespoons finely chopped fresh chives

For Serving

A chunk of Parmesan for grating

Fresh coarsely ground black pepper

Plate of Citrus with Olio Nuovo and Fresh Mint

Serves 4 to 6

I talk a lot about how important it is to use quality ingredients, but in this recipe, it's absolutely crucial, since (as the title suggests) it actually is simply a plate of citrus. There is nothing for the citrus to hide behind; it is dressed simply with *olio nuovo,* or "new olive oil," sea salt, a pinch of chile powder, and a few mint leaves. You can't just put an ordinary orange on a plate and expect it to be something special. The orange has to be special. You see citrus, especially lemons and oranges, in grocery stores around the country year-round, but citrus really has a season, and that season is winter. This recipe calls for very special varieties; look for them in farmers' markets. Keep a big bowlful on your counter and make your way through your centerpiece. The amounts called for are the ideal; if you can't find one variety, use more of another.

You will need a large platter to serve the citrus.

Peel the tangerines and set them aside.

Cut off and discard the tops and bottoms of the grapefruit, Cara Cara oranges, mandarin oranges, and blood oranges at the point where you can see the flesh. Working with one at a time, place the fruit upright on the cutting board and cut down the side to remove the peel at the point where the pith meets the flesh, following the natural curve of the fruit to remove the pith along with the peel. Discard the peels.

Turn a grapefruit on its side and cut along one of the membranes toward the center. Working your way around the grapefruit, cut along both sides of each membrane to release all the segments from the core. Discard the core of the grapefruit and set the segments aside. Repeat with the other grapefruit.

Cut the Cara Caras, mandarins, and blood oranges into ¼-inch-thick pinwheels. Remove and discard the seeds from the pinwheels.

4 Pixie tangerines (or Kishu mandarins), peeled

2 grapefruit (preferably Ruby Red or Oro Blanco)

2 Cara Cara oranges

2 mandarin oranges

2 blood oranges

¼ cup olio nuovo (or finishing-quality extra-virgin olive oil)

1 teaspoon Aleppo pepper (or another smoky chile powder, such as sweet smoked paprika)

Flaky sea salt

8 fresh mint leaves

To serve, arrange the pinwheels of Cara Caras, mandarins, and blood oranges, overlapping, to cover the surface of a large platter, evenly distributing the different varieties. Scatter the grapefruit segments over the pinwheels. Break the tangerines into segments and scatter them on the platter. Drizzle the olio nuovo, sprinkle the Aleppo pepper, and crush about 1 teaspoon flaky sea salt between your fingertips over the citrus. Tear the mint leaves to fall over all the citrus.

Creamed Spinach

Serves 4

I developed this classic steak-house side dish along with Herbie Yuen, the executive chef at the Pizzeria, as an ode to Lawry's, a legendary prime rib house in Los Angeles. It is the perfect green vegetable to serve with Standing Rib Roast, APL Style (page 143) and, of course, any steak.

Starting with prewashed spinach is always a welcome shortcut, especially if you buy it from a farmers' market. If you buy spinach by the bunch, pick the leaves from the stems, discard the stems, and wash the leaves a few times in a sink full of cold water, letting the dirt fall to the bottom of the sink. When no more dirt falls to the bottom, drain the spinach in a colander.

You will need a medium bowl to serve the spinach.

To make the béchamel sauce, cut off and discard the root and tip ends of the onion. Peel the onion and cut it into quarters, root to tip. Separate the layers of the onion, stack two or three layers on top of one another, and slice them 1⁄16 inch thick lengthwise. Combine the butter and onion in a medium saucepan and cook over medium-low heat until the onion is tender and translucent, about 10 minutes, stirring often to prevent the onion from browning. Add the flour and cook until the mixture begins to bubble, about 3 minutes, whisking constantly. Gradually add the cream, whisking constantly. Increase the heat to high and bring the sauce to a boil, stirring constantly with the whisk. Reduce the heat to low and cook for 3 to 4 minutes, stirring constantly, until the sauce is thick enough to coat the back of a spoon. Turn off the heat, place a mesh strainer over a medium bowl, and strain the sauce into the bowl. Add the salt and nutmeg and stir to combine.

To prepare the creamed spinach mixture, remove and discard the outer layer of the leek and trim and discard the hairy ends. Cut the leek into 3-inch segments and cut each segment in half lengthwise. Lay the leek segments cut sides flat and slice them 1⁄8 inch thick lengthwise. Put the leeks in a bowl, fill the bowl with water, and swish them around with your hands to release any dirt. Drain the leeks in a colander. Fill a large pot with water and salt it to taste like the ocean, adding 1 scant tablespoon

For the Béchamel Sauce

1 large yellow Spanish onion

4 tablespoons (1⁄2 stick) unsalted butter

2 tablespoons unbleached all-purpose flour

2 cups heavy cream

1 teaspoon kosher salt

1⁄8 teaspoon freshly grated nutmeg (grated with a fine Microplane or a nutmeg grater from a whole nutmeg)

For the Spinach

1 medium leek

1 teaspoon kosher salt, plus more for the boiling water and to taste

2 pounds spinach leaves

2 tablespoons unsalted butter

1 lemon

per quart of water. Bring the water to a boil over high heat. Prepare an ice bath in a large bowl. Have a large mesh strainer handy.

Add the spinach to the boiling water, pushing it down with a slotted spoon to submerge, and blanch it for about 1 minute, until it is bright green. Drain the spinach in a colander and plunge it into the ice water for about 2 minutes to stop it from cooking. Lift the spinach out of the ice bath with your hands and return it to the colander to drain for a few minutes. Lay a clean dish towel on your work surface and place the spinach on the dish towel. Gather the ends of the towel to create a bundle and wring out the spinach over the sink to extract as much water as possible. Transfer the spinach to a medium bowl.

Melt the butter in a large sauté pan over medium heat. Add the leeks and cook, stirring often, until they are tender and translucent, about 10 minutes. Add the spinach, béchamel, and salt and stir to combine. Cook for 15 to 20 minutes, until the liquid released from the spinach has cooked off and the béchamel and vegetables have a thick, creamy consistency. Turn off the heat and add more salt to taste. Use a fine Microplane to zest the bright yellow outer layer of the lemon into the pan and stir to combine. Transfer the creamed spinach to a medium bowl to serve.

Grilled Broccolini and Scallions

Serves 4

Broccolini is a hybrid of broccoli and gai lan, or Chinese broccoli. Ten years ago, it was a rare and exotic new vegetable; today, it's in every supermarket, all year long, which makes this something you can make year-round, and also at the last minute, without a trip to the farmers' market. For this preparation, the broccolini and scallions are cooked quickly on a hot grill and tossed in an astringent lemony, mustardy vinaigrette. The broccolini really soaks up the vinaigrette. It makes a great accompaniment to the rich meat dishes at Chi Spacca; we serve it with Roasted Lamb Rack with Dried Persian Lime Tahini (page 193). I often order it, along with Moorish Lamb Shoulder Chops with Mint Yogurt (page 196), whenever I come into the restaurant to eat.

You will need a large platter to serve the vegetables.

To make the vinaigrette, combine the shallot, lemon juice, garlic, vinegar, mustard, salt, and a few turns of pepper in a small bowl. Gradually add the extra-virgin olive oil, whisking constantly.

To prepare the broccolini, trim and discard the dry stem ends of the broccolini; do this one at a time because each stalk will need to be trimmed at a different place.

Put the broccolini in a large bowl, drizzle with 2 tablespoons of the olive oil, sprinkle with 1 teaspoon of the salt, and toss to coat the broccolini with the oil and salt.

Trim and discard the root ends of the scallions and place them in a separate, large bowl. Drizzle with the remaining 2 tablespoons olive oil, sprinkle with the remaining ½ teaspoon salt, and toss to coat the scallions with the oil and salt.

Prepare a hot fire in a charcoal grill. (Alternatively, preheat a grill pan over high heat. Cooking method and times will be the same.)

Lay the scallions on the grill, along with as much of the broccolini as will fit in a single layer with space between the vegetables. (Depending on the size of your grill, you may need to cook the broccolini in batches. If you

For the Vinaigrette

2 tablespoons peeled and minced shallot

2 tablespoons fresh lemon juice

1 tablespoon finely chopped garlic

2 teaspoons champagne vinegar

1 teaspoon Dijon mustard

½ teaspoon kosher salt

Fresh coarsely ground black pepper

¼ cup extra-virgin olive oil

For the Broccolini

2 bunches broccolini (about 1 pound)

¼ cup olive oil

1½ teaspoons kosher salt, plus more to taste

2 bunches large scallions

are using a grill pan, you will definitely need to cook it in batches.) Cook the broccolini and scallions for about 5 minutes, using tongs to turn them often to prevent them from burning and so they cook evenly, until they are charred in places and the broccolini has softened slightly but is still crunchy. Remove the scallions and broccolini from the grill or grill pan and return it to the bowl you tossed the scallions in. If you are working in batches, cook the remaining broccolini in the same way and add it to the bowl with the first batch. Drizzle ¼ cup of the vinaigrette over the broccolini and scallions and toss to coat them with the vinaigrette. Add more salt to taste.

To serve, lay the broccolini and scallions on a large platter and drizzle with the vinaigrette left in the bowl.

Dario's Tuscan White Beans

Serves 4 to 6

These simple white beans are typical of those served at just about every trattoria in Tuscany. If you order beans in Dario Cecchini's steak house, the waiter walks around the table and ladles them into individual bowls for each guest. Then another waiter follows and, with a grand flourish, from about four feet above the table, sprinkles Dario's signature salt into the bowl. They have bottles of red wine vinegar and good Tuscan olive oil on the table, and they encourage you to dress your beans to your liking. It is a lot of fanfare for a bowl of beans, but it just goes to show how much the beans mean to them. And when you taste how delicious they are, I think you'll agree. One of the things I love about ordering beans in Italy is that they're always cooked properly, until they are creamy inside. Here, all too often chefs choose to cook beans until they are al dente; or, as I would say, "undercooked." Serve these beans in a big bowl with individual bowls as well as with olive oil, vinegar, and Dario Salt (page 19) so that people can serve and season for themselves. Plan ahead to make these because the beans need to soak for at least eight hours before you cook them.

You will need a large bowl and 4 to 6 smaller individual bowls to serve the beans.

Put the beans in a large bowl, cover them with water and soak overnight or for at least 8 hours. Drain the beans.

To cook the beans, put them in a large pot, add enough water to cover by 1½ to 2 inches, and stir in the extra-virgin olive oil. Add the onion, carrot, celery, garlic, sage, and rosemary and bring to a boil over high heat. Reduce the heat to medium-low to maintain a gentle simmer. Simmer the beans for about 2 hours, until they are tender and creamy, not chalky or al dente but also not falling apart, stirring occasionally and adding more water to the pot as needed to keep the beans covered at all times. Skim off and discard any foam that rises to the top while the beans are cooking. To test the beans for doneness, press one bean between your fingers; if it is creamy and silky, it's done. Turn off the heat.

For Cooking the Beans

1 pound dried cannellini beans (about 2 cups)

½ cup extra-virgin olive oil

1 large yellow Spanish onion, peeled and halved, root to tip

1 carrot, halved horizontally

1 celery stalk, halved horizontally

1 head garlic, unpeeled and halved through the middle

6 fresh sage sprigs

6 fresh rosemary sprigs

Remove the carrot, celery, and onion and eat or discard them. (I like to season them with olive oil and salt and snack on them.) Remove and discard the sage and rosemary. Remove the garlic, squeeze it out of the skins into the beans, and stir to combine; discard the skins.

To serve, transfer the beans to a large bowl and serve with a ladle. Serve with bottles of the finishing-quality olive oil and vinegar, and a bowl of the Dario salt on the table for each guest to use to finish their beans. For each 1 cup of beans and liquid, I suggest using 1 tablespoon olive oil, 1 teaspoon vinegar, and ½ teaspoon Dario salt.

For Serving

1 cup finishing-quality extra-virgin olive oil

¼ cup red wine vinegar

¼ cup Dario Salt (page 19)

Classic Vichy Carrots

Serves 4

Carrots are a wonderful, reliable vegetable. I don't think I've ever cooked a carrot that wasn't sweet and flavorful, whereas I've gone an entire season without serving beets because I couldn't find any that tasted good. There is no gray area for me in cooking carrots. I either roast them over such high heat that they char, or I treat them very delicately so they retain their bright colors and shapes. This recipe falls into the second category. It is one of my favorite applications for carrots, and one of the first things I learned to cook when I was in school at the Cordon Bleu: a classic French technique of cooking carrots in water, butter, and a small amount of sugar, so that when the water reduces, the butter and sugar glaze the carrots. The finished carrots are bright orange, with a concentrated, sweet flavor that is enhanced by the butter. Supposedly, Vichy carrots must be made with volcanic mineral water from the French town of Vichy. I am not a superstitious cook; I think any sparkling water will do the trick. In fact, it probably doesn't have to be mineral water, but I don't want to deviate too far from the traditional recipe since I gave these carrots the name.

You will need a medium bowl to serve the carrots.

Trim and peel the carrots and discard the trimmings or reserve them to make stock. Cut the carrots at an angle into 1-inch segments.

Melt the butter in a large sauté pan over medium heat. Add the carrots and toss to coat them with the butter. Add the sparkling water, sugar, and salt and cook the carrots for 8 to 10 minutes, until they are tender when pierced with a sharp knife and the liquid has reduced to a glaze to coat the carrots. (If the carrots are cooked before the liquid is reduced to a glaze, remove the carrots with a slotted spoon and continue to cook the liquid until it thickens. Return the carrots to the saucepan and stir to coat them with the glaze.) Turn off the heat, add the lemon juice, Aleppo pepper, and chives and stir to combine.

To serve, transfer the carrots to a medium bowl.

1½ pounds large carrots

4 tablespoons (½ stick) unsalted butter

1½ cups Vichy sparkling mineral water (or any bottled sparkling water)

1 tablespoon sugar

½ teaspoon kosher salt

1 tablespoon fresh lemon juice

½ teaspoon Aleppo pepper (or another smoky chile powder, such as sweet smoked paprika)

2 tablespoons finely chopped fresh chives (about 10 sprigs)

Celeriac Purée

Serves 4

Also called celery root, celeriac is a type of celery cultivated for its root. This purée is like the celery version of mashed potatoes. It is a must with the Moroccan-Braised Lamb Shanks with Pistachio Gremolata (page 204) and, in fact, would be a great complement to any preparation of lamb or other braised meats.

Both black and white unhulled toasted sesame seeds are sold as "roasted sesame seeds" in shaker canisters in the Japanese section of supermarkets. If you can't find them, use the more widely available hulled white sesame seeds and toast them in a small skillet over medium heat for 1 to 2 minutes, until they're toasted and fragrant.

You will need a medium bowl to serve the purée.

Heat the olive oil in a large sauté pan over medium-high heat until the oil is almost smoking and slides easily in the pan. Add the celeriac, sprinkle it with the salt, and cook until the celeriac is golden brown on all sides, about 15 minutes, turning to cook the celeriac all over. Add the milk, garlic, thyme, and sesame seeds and let the milk come to a simmer. Reduce the heat to medium-low to maintain a gentle simmer for about 15 minutes, until the celeriac is tender when pierced with a sharp knife. Turn off the heat and set aside to cool for at least 10 minutes. Remove and discard the thyme sprigs.

Transfer the celeriac, garlic, and milk to the bowl of a food processor fitted with a metal blade and purée until smooth.

Place a mesh strainer over a medium bowl and pass the purée through the strainer, pushing it through with a rubber spatula. Add more salt to taste.

To serve, transfer the celeriac purée to a medium bowl.

2 tablespoons olive oil

1½ pounds whole celeriac, peeled and cut into 1-inch cubes

1 teaspoon kosher salt, plus more to taste

2 cups whole milk

5 large garlic cloves, peeled

2 fresh thyme sprigs

1 tablespoon unhulled roasted sesame seeds (preferably black sesame seeds; or hulled white sesame seeds, lightly toasted)

Butterscotch Budino, Family Style   319

Lattice-Topped Slab Pies for Spring or Summer   321

Apple Quince Streusel Slab Pie   327

Banana Cream Slab Pie with Caramel Sauce and Bittersweet Chocolate Shavings   331

Buckwheat Maple Cake with Fresh Figs   336

Lemon Posset with Strawberries and Aged Balsamic   339

Pear Rosemary Tart with Chestnut Crust   341

Meyer Lemon Kumquat Tart with Rye–Cream Cheese Crust   344

Key Lime Cheesecake with Passion Fruit Caramel   348

Dario's Olive Oil Cake with Rosemary and Pine Nuts   352

Raspberry Jam Bars with Pistachio Crumble   355

Dolci

We keep a short, sweet menu of desserts at Chi Spacca, simply plated and ideal for serving family style at home. The recipes in this chapter, all seasonally inspired, make larger desserts than you'll be able to finish after a Chi Spacca meal. But whoever said they wish they didn't have leftover pie?

Butterscotch Budino, Family Style

Serves 6 to 8

I published my butterscotch budino recipe almost ten years ago in *The Mozza Cookbook,* but I decided to include a recipe for it in this book for a couple of reasons. First, it's everyone's favorite. The *budino* (which is Italian for "pudding") started out as a dessert at Pizzeria Mozza, but after many customer requests, we started serving it at Chi Spacca, where it is our best-selling dessert. The second and more important reason this recipe is here is because it is a new, easier-to-follow recipe that ensures you will succeed. At the restaurants we serve the budino in individual glasses, but in this recipe, it is served family style, with pretty mounds of whipped cream on top.

You will need a 12- × 7-inch oval ceramic baking dish (or another baking dish with a 12-cup capacity) to make and serve the budino.

To make the budino, place a mesh strainer in an oval ceramic (or another 12-cup-capacity) baking dish and set them aside.

Combine the egg yolks, whole eggs, and cornstarch in a medium bowl and whisk until no lumps remain.

Combine the dark brown sugar, kosher salt, and ½ cup water in a large stainless-steel saucepan and cook over high heat until the sugar melts and begins to boil. Continue boiling the sugar for 6 to 8 minutes, tilting and swirling the pan occasionally so it cooks evenly, until the sugar is lavalike and smoke is rising from the entire surface of the pan; you will also begin to see small black spots indicating that the sugar is just beginning to burn. Turn off the heat and add the cream and milk. (The sugar will harden and seize after you add the liquid; don't worry, it will dissolve.) Warm over medium-low heat, stirring constantly, until the sugar melts into the cream, about 5 minutes. Increase the heat to medium-high and cook until the mixture begins to simmer around the edges. Turn off the heat. Gradually add 1 cup or ladleful of the hot cream-sugar mixture to the bowl with the eggs, stirring constantly with the whisk to prevent the hot cream from cooking the eggs. Add another cup or ladleful of the hot cream, stirring constantly. Gradually add the contents of the →

For the Budino

3 extra-large egg yolks

2 extra-large eggs

¼ cup cornstarch

1½ cups lightly packed dark brown sugar

1½ teaspoons kosher salt

3 cups heavy cream

1½ cups whole milk

5 tablespoons unsalted butter

2 tablespoons Scotch whiskey

For the Caramel Sauce

1 cup heavy cream

1 vanilla bean

4 tablespoons (½ stick) unsalted butter

1 cup granulated sugar

¼ cup light corn syrup

bowl back to the saucepan with the remaining cream mixture, stirring as you add it. Cook the budino mixture over medium heat, stirring constantly, until it has thickened to the consistency of pudding, about 2 minutes. Remove the budino from the heat. Add the butter and whiskey and stir to melt the butter and combine. Pour the budino through the strainer into the baking dish and refrigerate, uncovered, for about 4 hours, to chill and set. If you are making the budino in advance, remove it from the refrigerator, cover the dish with plastic wrap, and return it to the refrigerator.

To make the caramel sauce, pour the cream into a medium saucepan. Split the vanilla bean in half lengthwise with a paring knife. Scrape the seeds from the bean and add the seeds and bean to the saucepan with the cream. Heat the cream over high heat until it begins to bubble around the edges. Turn off the heat, add the butter, and stir until it melts.

Combine the granulated sugar, corn syrup, and ¼ cup water in a large stainless-steel saucepan and cook over medium-high heat for about 8 minutes, until the caramel is a medium amber color, swirling the pan so the sugar cooks evenly and brushing down the sides of the pan with a wet pastry brush to remove any sugar granules. Remove the caramel from the heat. Add the cream and butter mixture, taking care because the hot caramel will steam and bubble when you add it, stirring with a whisk until the sauce is smooth. Turn off the heat and set aside until you are ready to pour the sauce over the budino. If the sauce cools and thickens, warm it over medium-low heat until it is easily pourable.

To make the whipped cream, put a large bowl and a wire whisk in the freezer for at least 10 minutes to chill. Remove the bowl and whisk from the freezer and pour the cream into the bowl. Whip the cream with the whisk until it thickens to soft peaks; when you lift the whisk out of the cream and turn it upside down, the peak of the cream will flop over. Add the crème fraîche and beat to return the cream to soft peaks.

To serve, remove the budino from the refrigerator and remove and discard the plastic wrap if you used it. Pour the caramel sauce over the budino and tilt the dish so the caramel flows to cover, leaving the edges of the budino exposed. Sprinkle the sea salt in whole flakes over the caramel sauce. Using a large spoon, dollop the whipped cream in waves over the budino, leaving space between the dollops for the caramel sauce to peek through.

For the Whipped Cream
3 cups heavy cream
1 cup crème fraîche
(or sour cream)

For Serving
1 teaspoon flaky sea salt

Lattice-Topped Slab Pies
for Spring or Summer

Serves 6 to 12

Let me first say that I love the name "slab pie," which refers to a pie formed in a sheet pan rather than a pie pan, so it's rectangular. Dahlia Narvaez, the longtime executive pastry chef at all of the Mozza Restaurant Group restaurants, brought me the idea for slab pie. She showed me a picture she'd seen in a cookbook and asked if she could try making one for the restaurants. It was such a creative and original presentation—literally, a *slab* of pie—I was all for it. Because it's made in a sheet pan, it makes a large quantity, so it's the perfect option for feeding a crowd; it has become our go-to dessert for events. When we're serving family-style meals, we put the whole slab in the center of the table for guests to dig into. The butter for the crust needs to be frozen for at least an hour before making the dough, so plan for that. A slab pie is shallower than a conventional pie, so there is less filling and more crust, which makes it even more inviting for a scoop of vanilla gelato or ice cream.

We change our slab pies with the seasons. This recipe is for the spring and summer versions. The springtime option is strawberry rhubarb pie, a classic combination. The summer option can be made with any combination of ripe, juicy, in-season stone fruit (so-named for the fact that they have a "stone," or pit, in the center), including peaches, nectarines, plums, or apricots; and fresh berries. We also serve Apple Quince Streusel Slab Pie (page 327) in the fall, and in the winter, Banana Cream Slab Pie with Caramel Sauce and Bittersweet Chocolate Shavings (page 331).

You can buy crystallized sugar (also called sanding sugar) at cooking and baking supply stores.

You will need a quarter sheet pan (9 × 13 inches) to make and serve the slab pie.

To make the springtime strawberry rhubarb filling, trim and discard the ends of the rhubarb and cut the stalks into 3-inch pieces. Remove and discard the hulls from the strawberries and cut the strawberries in half.

Put the granulated sugar in a large saucepan, add ¼ cup water, and stir to combine. Split the vanilla bean in half lengthwise with a paring knife. Scrape the seeds from the bean and add the seeds and bean to the saucepan. Bring the sugar mixture to a boil over medium–high heat, →

Spring: Strawberry Rhubarb Filling

3 pounds rhubarb

3 pints strawberries

1 cup granulated sugar

1 vanilla bean

½ cup brandy

swirling the pan so the sugar cooks evenly and brushing down the sides of the pan with a wet pastry brush to remove any sugar granules. Reduce the heat to medium-low and cook the sugar for 3 to 4 minutes, tilting and swirling the pan, until it is a medium amber color. Turn off the heat and add the rhubarb, taking care because the sugar mixture will bubble furiously and may splatter. (The sugar will seize and harden when you add the rhubarb. Don't worry, it will melt when you warm it in the next step.) Add the brandy.

Cook the caramel over medium heat, stirring until the seized sugar has melted and coats the rhubarb. Reduce the heat to medium-low and cook, stirring occasionally, until the rhubarb is tender but still holds its shape, 10 to 15 minutes. Turn off the heat, add the strawberries, and stir gently to combine. Transfer the filling to a baking dish or bowl and cool to room temperature. Remove and discard the vanilla bean. Cover with plastic wrap and refrigerate the filling for at least 2 hours to chill.

To make the summertime stone fruit and mixed berry filling, cut the stone fruit in half and remove and discard the pits. Cut each half into quarters.

Put the granulated sugar in a large saucepan, add ¼ cup water, and stir to combine. Split the vanilla bean in half lengthwise with a paring knife. Scrape the seeds from the bean and add the seeds and bean to the saucepan. Bring the sugar mixture to a boil over medium-high heat, swirling the pan so the sugar cooks evenly and brushing down the sides of the pan with a wet pastry brush to remove any sugar granules. Reduce the heat to medium-low and cook the sugar for 3 to 4 minutes, tilting and swirling the pan, until it is a medium amber color. Turn off the heat and add the stone fruit, taking care because the sugar mixture will bubble furiously and may splatter. (The sugar will seize and harden when you add the fruit. Don't worry, it will melt when you warm it in the next step.) Add the brandy.

Cook the caramel over medium heat, stirring until the seized sugar melts and coats the fruit. Reduce the heat to medium-low and cook, stirring occasionally, until the fruit is tender but still holds its shape, 10 to 15 minutes. Turn off the heat, add the berries, and stir gently to combine. Place a large strainer over a large bowl and strain the fruit so the liquid strains into the bowl. Remove and discard the vanilla bean and transfer the fruit to a bowl or baking dish. Pour the reserved →

Summer: Stone Fruit and Mixed Berry Filling

4 pounds fresh ripe stone fruit (peaches, plums, nectarines, apricots, or an assortment)

1 cup granulated sugar

1 vanilla bean

½ cup brandy

2 cups fresh berries (blueberries, blackberries, raspberries, boysenberries, or an assortment)

2 tablespoons cornstarch

For the Dough and Lining the Pie Pan

¼ cup heavy cream

¼ cup plus 2 tablespoons cold water

4 cups unbleached all-purpose flour, plus more for dusting

1 tablespoon plus 1 teaspoon kosher salt

1 pound (4 sticks) unsalted butter, cut into 1-inch cubes and frozen for at least 1 hour, plus more for buttering the pan

For Finishing and Serving

¼ cup whole milk

¼ cup crystallized sugar (or granulated sugar)

Vanilla gelato or ice cream (optional)

liquid into a small saucepan. Add the cornstarch and bring to a boil over medium heat, whisking constantly. Pour the liquid over the fruit and set aside to cool to room temperature. Cover with plastic wrap and refrigerate the filling for at least 2 hours to chill.

To make the dough and line the pie pan, whisk the cream and water together in a small bowl.

Combine the flour and salt in the bowl of a stand mixer. Fit the mixer with the paddle attachment and mix on low speed to distribute the salt. Add the butter and mix on low speed until the flour and butter come together into pea-size clumps. Add the cream and water and mix on low speed until the dough comes together. Lightly dust a large flat work surface with flour and transfer the dough to the floured surface. Gather the dough together into a ball, cut it in half, and pat it into two (2-inch-thick) blocks. Wrap each block separately in plastic wrap and place them in the refrigerator to chill until the dough is firm, about 2 hours.

Butter the bottom and sides of a quarter sheet pan, lightly dust it with flour, and tap out the excess.

Lightly dust a large work surface with flour. Remove one block of dough from the refrigerator, unwrap it, and place it on the floured surface. Cut the dough into large chunks and pound each chunk with a rolling pin to soften the dough. Bring the chunks together into a ball and gently knead until the dough is malleable. Pat the dough into a 2-inch-thick block. Dust the dough and rolling pin lightly with flour and roll the dough into a ⅛-inch-thick (at least 13- × 16-inch) rectangle, dusting the dough, rolling pin, and work surface with flour as needed.

Loosely roll the dough around the pin and lower it over the prepared pan, centering it so the dough hangs evenly over the edges of the pan. Working your way around the pan, lift the edge of the dough with one hand and let it drop down into the pan. At the same time, with your other hand, dip the flat side of the knuckle of your index finger in flour and use it to gently press the dough against the edges and into the creases of the pan to create straight, not sloping sides. (Don't stretch the dough to fit in the pan or it will shrink when it is baked.) Using kitchen shears, trim the dough so there is ¾ inch overhanging all around; discard the scraps. Dock the bottom of the piecrust with the tines of a fork and place it in the refrigerator to chill until the dough is firm, about 1 hour.

To begin making the lattice, line a large baking sheet with parchment paper. Lightly dust your work surface with additional flour. Remove the second block of dough from the refrigerator, unwrap it, and place it on the floured surface. Cut the dough into large chunks and pound each chunk with a rolling pin to soften the dough. Bring the chunks together into a ball and gently knead until the dough is malleable. Pat the dough into a 2-inch-thick block. Dust the dough and rolling pin lightly with flour and roll it into a ⅛-inch-thick (at least 13- × 16-inch) rectangle, dusting the dough, rolling pin, and work surface with flour as needed.

Trim the dough to create even edges all around and discard the scraps. With the long edge of the dough parallel to the counter, use a ruler and knife or pastry cutter to cut 14 (1-inch) strips across the length of the dough; discard the scraps. Turn a baking sheet upside down, line it with parchment paper, and dust the paper lightly with flour. Lay the dough strips on the baking sheet and place them in the refrigerator to chill until the dough is firm, about 30 minutes.

Remove the dough strips from the refrigerator to begin to weave a lattice top. Slide the parchment with the dough strips off the baking sheet and line the back of the baking sheet with another sheet of parchment. Dust the parchment with flour.

Lay 7 of the dough strips diagonally on the back of the baking sheet, leaving ¾ inch between each strip. Fold every other strip back like you're opening the page of a book and lay one of the remaining strips of dough diagonally on top of those that are still lying flat. Return the folded-back strips to their original position. Fold back the strips that you didn't fold the first time and lay another strip of dough across those that are lying flat, leaving ¾ inch from the first strip you added. Return the folded strips to their original position; you will begin to see the creation of a diamond-shaped basket-weave pattern. Continue folding back alternating strips of dough and adding more strips until you have woven them all in to form a lattice. Place the lattice in the refrigerator to chill until the dough is firm, about 30 minutes.

Remove the piecrust and filling from the refrigerator and scrape the filling onto the crust, making sure to get all the sugary ingredients out of the bowl, and smooth out the filling. Remove the lattice from the refrigerator and gently slide it off the parchment paper onto the pie, →

centering it. Trim the dough so both the strips and the bottom crust are overhanging the edge of the pan by ½ inch; discard the scraps. Lightly dust your fingers with flour and roll the edges of the dough tightly toward the center of the pan to create a smooth rolled lip around the edge of the pan. To crimp the pie, press the thumb of your dominant hand on the edge of the dough, pointing toward the center of the pie, and pinch around it with the thumb and forefinger of your nondominant hand to create a scallop shape. Continue, "leapfrogging" your fingers around the perimeter of the pie to create a scalloped edge. Place the pie in the refrigerator to chill until the dough is firm, about 1 hour.

Adjust the oven rack to the center position and preheat the oven to 400°F.

To finish and serve the pie, remove it from the refrigerator. Pour the milk into a small bowl and brush it over the entire surface of the pie, including the lattice and the crimped edges. Sprinkle the pie with the crystallized sugar and place it on a large baking sheet to catch the juices that may bubble over.

Bake the pie in the oven for 55 to 65 minutes, until it is a deep golden brown and the fruit is bubbling, rotating the baking sheet from front to back halfway through that time for even browning. Remove the baking sheet from the oven. Serve the pie with vanilla gelato or ice cream, if you like.

Apple Quince Streusel Slab Pie

Serves 6 to 12

This pie is made with a combination of apples and quinces, which gives it more layers of flavor than if it were simply an apple pie. Quince is a relative of the apple, but with a bumpy shape, a downy layer on the outside, and a unique, perfume-y scent. They have a short season: When you go to the farmers' market and see quinces, you know it's fall. You have to cook quinces before eating them, otherwise it is like biting into a raw potato. There are many varieties of apples that hold their shape when baked; I suggest you use a mix, which will give you an assortment of different flavors and textures and make for a more interesting pie. Granny Smith are the most readily available variety of baking apple, but some other baking apples to look for include Gala, Honeycrisp, Braeburn, Gravenstein, and Jonathan. If you can't find quinces, double the amount of apple filling in this recipe.

This pie is topped with crunchy streusel, which is not only delicious, it is also very easy to make. If you wanted to skip the more labor-intensive Lattice-Crusted Slab Pies for Spring or Summer (page 321), use the strawberry rhubarb or stone fruit and mixed berry fillings in place of the apple quince filling in this recipe.

You will need a quarter sheet pan (9 × 13 inches) to make and serve the slab pie.

To prepare the apples, put them in a large roasting pan. Add the granulated sugar and toss to coat the apples with the sugar. Cover with plastic wrap and set aside at room temperature for 1 hour (or refrigerate overnight) to allow the sugar to break down the apples and for the apples to begin to release their juices.

To prepare the quinces, combine the white wine, granulated sugar, cinnamon stick, star anise, clove, and orange peel in a medium saucepan. Add 1 cup water and bring the liquid to a boil over high heat. Cut a round of parchment paper slightly larger than the pot. Add the quinces and lay the parchment paper on the surface of the liquid to keep the fruit submerged. Return the liquid to a boil, reduce the heat to medium-low to maintain a steady simmer, and simmer the quinces until they are tender, about 1 hour. Turn off the heat and let the quinces cool in the poaching →

For the Apples

2 pounds tart baking apples (see headnote for a list of varieties), peeled, cored, and cut into 1-inch cubes

½ cup granulated sugar

4 tablespoons (½ stick) unsalted butter

1 vanilla bean

¼ cup fresh apple cider (or apple juice)

3 tablespoons lightly packed dark brown sugar

1 tablespoon cornstarch

liquid. If you are refrigerating the apples overnight, also refrigerate the quinces, covered, overnight.

Adjust the oven rack to the center position and preheat the oven to 300°F. (If you are doubling the apple filling instead of making quinces, adjust the oven racks so one is in the top third of the oven and the other is in the bottom third.)

Put the butter in a medium saucepan to begin to make brown butter. Split the vanilla bean in half lengthwise with a paring knife. Scrape the seeds from the bean and add the seeds and bean to the saucepan. Melt the butter over medium heat and cook it for about 10 minutes, swirling the pan occasionally so the butter browns evenly, until the foam has subsided and the butter is coffee colored with a toasted aroma. Turn off the heat and scrape the bottom to release the solids. Remove and discard the vanilla bean. If you refrigerated the apples, remove them from the refrigerator; remove and discard the plastic wrap. Drizzle the brown butter over the apples. Add the apple cider, brown sugar, cornstarch, nutmeg, and cinnamon to the roasting pan and stir to combine. Spread the apples out evenly over the surface of the pan. If you are doubling the apples, spread half of them over the surface of a second roasting pan or a large baking sheet.

Roast the apples in the oven for 25 to 35 minutes, stirring them every 10 minutes so they cook evenly, until the apples are tender but not falling apart. Remove the apples from the oven and set aside to cool to room temperature.

If you refrigerated the quinces, remove them from the refrigerator; remove and discard the plastic wrap. Place a mesh strainer over a medium bowl and strain the quinces. Remove and discard the cinnamon stick, star anise, clove, and orange peel. Add the quinces and ¼ cup of the strained liquid to the baking sheet with the apples and fold them together; discard the remaining juice. (If you are making the filling with only apples, combine the apples on one baking sheet.) Cover the baking sheet and refrigerate the filling for at least 2 hours, until it is chilled.

To make the dough and line the pie pan, whisk the cream and water together in a small bowl.

Combine the flour and salt in the bowl of a stand mixer. Fit the mixer with the paddle attachment and mix on low speed to distribute the salt.

1 teaspoon freshly grated nutmeg (grated with a fine Microplane or a nutmeg grater from a whole nutmeg)

¼ teaspoon ground cinnamon

For the Quinces

3 cups dry white wine

1½ cups granulated sugar

1 cinnamon stick

1 star anise

1 whole clove

1 strip of orange peel (peeled with a vegetable peeler)

2 quinces (1½ pounds), peeled, cored, and cut into 1-inch cubes

For the Dough and Lining the Pie Pan

2 tablespoons heavy cream

3 tablespoons cold water

2 cups unbleached all-purpose flour, plus more for dusting

2 teaspoons kosher salt

½ pound (2 sticks) unsalted butter, cut into 1-inch cubes and frozen for at least 1 hour, plus more for buttering the pan

For the Streusel Topping

½ cup plus 2 tablespoons unbleached all-purpose flour

½ cup plus 2 tablespoons granulated sugar

¼ teaspoon ground cinnamon

10 tablespoons (1¼ sticks) unsalted butter, cold

½ cup plus 2 tablespoons rolled oats

Add the butter and mix on low speed until the flour and butter come together into pea-size clumps. Add the cream and water and mix on low speed until the dough comes together. Lightly dust a large flat work surface with flour and transfer the dough to the floured surface. Gather the dough together into a ball, cut it in half, and pat it into a 2-inch-thick block. Wrap the block in plastic wrap and place it in the refrigerator to chill until the dough is firm, about 2 hours.

Butter the bottom and sides of a quarter sheet pan, lightly dust it with flour, and tap out the excess.

Lightly dust a large flat work surface with flour. Remove the dough from the refrigerator, unwrap it, and place it on the floured surface. Cut the dough into large chunks and pound each chunk with a rolling pin to soften the dough. Bring the chunks together into a ball and gently knead until the dough is malleable. Pat the dough into a 2-inch-thick block. Dust the dough and rolling pin lightly with flour and roll it into a ⅛-inch-thick (at least 13- × 16-inch) rectangle, dusting the dough, rolling pin, and work surface with flour as needed.

Loosely roll the dough around the pin and lower it over the prepared pan, centering it so the dough hangs evenly over the edges of the pan. Working your way around the pan, lift the edge of the dough with one hand and let it drop down into the pan. At the same time, with your other hand, dip the flat side of the knuckle of your index finger in flour and use it to gently press the dough against the edges and into the creases of the pan to create straight, not sloping sides. (Don't stretch the dough to fit in the pan or it will shrink when it is baked.) Using kitchen shears, trim the dough so there is ¾ inch overhanging all around; discard the scraps. Roll the edge of the dough under itself to create a thick lip that rests on the edge of the baking sheet. To crimp the pie, press the thumb of your dominant hand on the edge of the dough and pinch around it with the thumb and forefinger of your nondominant hand to create a scallop shape; continue, "leapfrogging" your fingers around the perimeter of the pie to create a scalloped edge. Dock the bottom of the piecrust all over with the tines of a fork and place it in the refrigerator to chill until the dough is firm, about 1 hour.

To make the streusel topping, combine the flour, granulated sugar, and cinnamon in the bowl of a stand mixer. Fit the mixer with a paddle →

For Serving
Vanilla gelato or ice cream (optional)

attachment and mix on low speed to distribute the sugar and cinnamon. Add the butter and mix on low speed until the flour and butter come together into pea-size clumps. Remove the bowl from the stand. Add the oats and mix them in with your hands to distribute the oats and form clumps of topping. Place the topping in the refrigerator to chill, about 30 minutes.

Remove the piecrust, filling, and topping from the refrigerator and scrape the filling into the crust, making sure to get all the sugary ingredients out of the bowl, and smooth out the filling. Scatter the topping evenly over the filling and refrigerate until the topping is firm.

Adjust the oven rack to the center position and preheat the oven to 400°F.

Place the pie on a large baking sheet to catch the juices that may bubble over and bake the pie in the oven for 55 to 65 minutes, until it is a deep golden brown and the fruit is bubbling, rotating the baking sheet from front to back halfway through that time for even browning. Remove the baking sheet from the oven. Serve the pie with vanilla gelato or ice cream, if you like.

Banana Cream Slab Pie with Caramel Sauce and Bittersweet Chocolate Shavings

Serves 6 to 12

Banana cream pie is an American classic. We dress up this version with caramel sauce and dark chocolate shavings. Our staff love it; they're so happy when they see this pie, left over from service the night before, at family meal.

The piecrust is "blind baked" for this pie, meaning it is baked before the filling is added. This method is used when making pies where the filling is not baked, like this one, or where the filling requires less baking time than the crust.

You will need a quarter sheet pan (9 × 13 inches) to make and serve the slab pie. You will also need pie weights (or dried rice or beans) to blind bake the crust, and a large pastry bag and a large star tip; we use an Ateco #8.

To make the dough and line the pie pan, whisk the cream and water together in a small bowl.

Combine the flour and salt in the bowl of a stand mixer. Fit the mixer with the paddle attachment and mix on low speed to distribute the salt. Add the butter and mix on low speed until the flour and butter come together into pea-size clumps. Add the cream and water and mix on low speed until the dough comes together. Lightly dust a large flat work surface with flour and transfer the dough to the floured surface. Gather the dough together into a ball, cut it in half, and pat it into a 2-inch-thick block. Wrap the block in plastic wrap and place it in the refrigerator to chill until the dough is firm, about 2 hours.

Butter the bottom and sides of a quarter sheet pan, lightly dust it with flour, and tap out the excess.

Lightly dust a large flat work surface with flour. Remove the dough from the refrigerator, unwrap it, and place it on the floured surface. Cut the dough into large chunks and pound each chunk with a rolling pin to soften the dough. Bring the chunks together into a ball and gently knead until the dough is malleable. Pat the dough into a 2-inch-thick block. →

For the Dough and Lining the Pie Pan

2 tablespoons heavy cream

3 tablespoons cold water

2 cups unbleached all-purpose flour, plus more for dusting

2 teaspoons kosher salt

½ pound (2 sticks) unsalted butter, cut into 1-inch cubes and frozen for at least 1 hour, plus more for buttering the pan

Nonstick cooking spray

For the Pastry Cream

10 extra-large egg yolks

1 cup granulated sugar

¼ cup cornstarch

¼ cup unbleached all-purpose flour

Dust the dough and rolling pin lightly with flour and roll it into a ⅛-inch-thick (at least 13- × 16-inch) rectangle, dusting the dough, rolling pin, and work surface with flour as needed.

Loosely roll the dough around the pin and lower it over the prepared pan, centering it so the dough hangs evenly over the edges of the pan. Working your way around the pan, lift the edge of the dough with one hand and let it drop down into the pan. At the same time, with your other hand, dip the flat side of the knuckle of your index finger in flour and use it to gently press the dough against the edges and into the creases of the pan to create straight, not sloping sides. (Don't stretch the dough to fit in the pan or it will shrink when it is baked.) Using kitchen shears, trim the dough so there is ¾ inch overhanging all around; discard the scraps. Roll the edge of the dough under itself to create a thick lip that rests on the edge of the baking sheet. To crimp the pie, press the thumb of your dominant hand on the edge of the dough and pinch around it with the thumb and forefinger of your nondominant hand to create a scallop shape; continue, "leapfrogging" your fingers around the perimeter of the pie to create a scalloped edge. Dock the bottom of the piecrust all over with the tines of a fork and place the piecrust in the refrigerator to chill until the dough is firm, about 1 hour.

Adjust the oven rack to the center position and preheat the oven to 350°F.

Remove the piecrust from the refrigerator. Spray a piece of parchment on one side with nonstick cooking spray and lay it, sprayed side down, on the piecrust. Fill the crust with pie weights (or dry rice or dried beans).

Bake the piecrust in the oven for 40 minutes. Remove the crust from the oven. Spoon out the pie weights, remove and discard the parchment paper, and return the crust to the oven to bake for an additional 15 to 20 minutes, until the crust is fully cooked and golden brown. (Set the weights aside to cool to room temperature, then put them away to use again for the same purpose.) Remove the piecrust from the oven and set it aside to cool to room temperature.

To make the pastry cream, combine the egg yolks and granulated sugar in the bowl of a stand mixer. Fit the mixer with the whisk attachment and beat on high speed until the yolks and sugar are very thick, pale yellow, and form a ribbon when the whisk is lifted from the bowl. Remove the bowl from the stand. Sift in the cornstarch and flour and whisk to combine.

4 cups whole milk
2 vanilla beans

For the Whipped Cream
4 cups heavy cream
¼ cup confectioners' sugar
1 tablespoon cornstarch
½ teaspoon pure vanilla extract

For the Caramel Sauce
1 cup heavy cream
1 vanilla bean
4 tablespoons (½ stick) unsalted butter
1 cup granulated sugar
¼ cup light corn syrup

For Assembling and Serving the Pie
10 ripe bananas
A small block of bittersweet chocolate for shaving

Put the milk in a medium stainless-steel saucepan. Split the vanilla beans in half with a paring knife. Scrape the seeds from the beans and add the seeds and beans to the saucepan with the milk. Bring the milk to a boil over high heat and turn off the heat. Gradually add 1 cup or ladleful of the hot milk to the bowl with the eggs, stirring constantly with a whisk to prevent the hot milk from cooking the eggs. Add another cup or ladleful of milk, stirring constantly. Gradually add the contents of the bowl back to the saucepan with the remaining milk, stirring as you add it. Cook the milk and eggs over medium heat, stirring constantly, until the mixture has thickened and bubbles in the center. Turn off the heat.

Place a mesh strainer over a medium bowl and pass the pastry cream through the strainer, using a rubber spatula to push it through. Cover the pastry cream with plastic wrap, pressing the plastic against the surface of the cream to prevent a skin from forming. Refrigerate the pastry cream until it is chilled, about 2 hours.

To make the whipped cream, combine 2 cups of the cream, the confectioners' sugar, and the cornstarch in a medium saucepan and cook over medium-high heat, stirring constantly with a whisk, for about 10 minutes, until it has thickened to the consistency of a loose pudding. Turn off the heat and scrape the cream mixture into a small bowl. (If there are dark bits on the side of your pot, leave them there rather than scraping them into the bowl.) Refrigerate the cream until it is chilled, about 1 hour. Remove it from the refrigerator and stir in the vanilla.

Put the bowl and whisk attachment of a stand mixer in the freezer for at least 10 minutes to chill. Remove the bowl and whisk from the freezer and pour the remaining 2 cups cream into the bowl. Put the mixer on the stand, fit the mixer with the whisk attachment, and beat the cream on medium-high speed until it forms soft peaks, 2 to 3 minutes; when you lift the whisk out of the cream and turn it upside down, the peak of the cream will flop over. With the mixer running on medium-high speed, add the cornstarch-cream mixture in a steady stream and mix for 1 to 2 minutes until stiff peaks form. Cover the bowl and place it in the refrigerator to chill until you're ready to decorate the pie.

To make the caramel sauce, pour the cream into a medium saucepan. Split the vanilla bean in half lengthwise with a paring knife. Scrape the seeds from the bean and add the seeds and bean to the saucepan with →

the cream. Heat the cream over high heat until it begins to bubble around the edges. Turn off the heat, add the butter, and stir until it melts.

Combine the granulated sugar, corn syrup, and ¼ cup water in a large heavy-bottomed saucepan and cook over medium-high heat for about 8 minutes, until the caramel is a medium amber color, swirling the pan so the sugar cooks evenly and brushing down the sides of the pan with a wet pastry brush to remove any sugar granules. Remove the caramel from the heat. Add the cream and butter mixture, taking care because the hot caramel will steam and bubble when you add it, stirring with a whisk until the sauce is smooth. Turn off the heat and set aside until you're ready to serve the pie. If the sauce cools before you're ready to use it, warm it over medium-low heat, stirring occasionally.

To assemble the pie, remove the pastry cream from the refrigerator and uncover the bowl. Spoon ¾ cup of the pastry cream into the center of the piecrust and use an offset spatula to spread it evenly over the bottom of the crust. Peel the bananas and slice them ½ inch thick. Lay one-third of the banana slices on the pastry cream in a single layer, making sure they are all touching but not overlapping. Spoon 1½ cups of the pastry cream over the bananas and use the offset spatula to spread it out toward the edges. Create another even layer with another third of the banana slices. Spoon the remaining pastry cream on the bananas and use the spatula to spread it to the edges. Lay the remaining banana slices on top of the pie, creating a third even layer of bananas.

Fit a large pastry bag with a large star tip. Remove the whipped cream from the refrigerator. Spoon the whipped cream into the bag and push it toward the tip. Twist the top of the bag until it puts enough pressure on the whipped cream that it squeezes out of the bottom of the bag. Holding the top of the bag with one hand and steering the tip with the other, pipe large rosettes to cover the surface of the pie, leaving a little bit of space between each rosette; refill the pastry bag as needed. Place it in the refrigerator until you're ready to serve it.

To serve, if you refrigerated the pie, remove it from the refrigerator. Shave the chocolate with a sharp knife to fall directly onto the pie. Serve with the warm caramel sauce on the side.

Buckwheat Maple Cake with Fresh Figs

Serves 6 to 8

There is a movement right now among bakers of using alternative flours, not necessarily for health purposes, but as a means of adding flavor to baked goods, and that is what I did here, using buckwheat flour. Despite the name, buckwheat is not in the wheat family, and in fact, it is gluten-free. Buckwheat flour has an unusual mushroom-ish color and an assertive, toasty flavor. The buckwheat flour, along with the maple sugar it is sweetened with and the olive oil, give this cake a deep color and rich, earthy flavor. It is topped with black Mission figs, a summer delicacy in Southern California. If you can't find Mission figs, any fresh figs will work. You'll want to make this cake in late summer and early fall, when figs are in season.

You will need a 14- × 5-inch (or similar-size) rectangular fluted tart pan with a removable bottom to make this. (The precise dimensions of the pan will vary from brand to brand.)

You will need a large rectangular platter to serve this cake.

Adjust the oven rack to the center position and preheat the oven to 325°F.

Spread the pistachios on a baking sheet and toast them in the oven for about 6 minutes, until they're lightly browned and fragrant, shaking the baking sheet and rotating it from front to back halfway through that time so the nuts brown evenly. Remove the baking sheet from the oven and set aside until the pistachios are cool enough to touch. Roughly chop them.

Increase the oven temperature to 350°F.

Butter the bottom and sides of a rectangular fluted tart pan and place the pan on a baking sheet.

Put the butter in a medium saucepan to begin to make brown butter and melt it over medium heat, swirling the pan occasionally so the butter cooks evenly, until the foam that develops has subsided and the butter is coffee colored and has a toasted aroma, about 10 minutes. Turn off the heat and scrape the bottom to release the solids. Set aside to cool slightly.

¼ cup shelled pistachios

8 tablespoons (1 stick) unsalted butter, plus more for buttering the tart pan

1½ cups plus 2 tablespoons maple sugar

½ cup almond meal (almond flour)

¼ cup plus 2 tablespoons buckwheat flour

Heaping ½ teaspoon kosher salt

½ cup plus 2 tablespoons extra-large egg whites

¼ cup olive oil

6 fresh figs (preferably black Mission figs)

2 tablespoons granulated sugar

Put the maple sugar, almond meal, buckwheat flour, and salt in a large bowl and whisk to combine. Make a well in the center of the ingredients and pour the egg whites, olive oil, and brown butter into the well. Whisk the wet and dry ingredients together until they form a smooth batter. Cut off and discard the stems and cut the figs in half lengthwise. Scrape the batter into the prepared tart pan. Lay the fig halves, cut sides up, in a single row down the center of the cake. Sprinkle the granulated sugar evenly over the batter and figs.

Bake the cake for 40 to 45 minutes, until the edges are golden brown, rotating the baking sheet from front to back halfway through that time for even browning. Remove the cake from the oven and set aside until it is cool enough to touch. Push up on the bottom of the tart pan to remove the outside rim. Transfer the cake, still on the bottom tin, onto a large serving platter.

While the tart is cooling, put the cream in a small bowl and sift in the confectioners' sugar to make a glaze, and whisk until the glaze is smooth, adding more cream as necessary for a drizzling consistency. Brush the top of the cake with the glaze and sprinkle with the chopped pistachios.

1 tablespoon heavy cream, plus more as needed

3 tablespoons confectioners' sugar (not packed)

Lemon Posset with Strawberries and Aged Balsamic

Serves 6 to 8

Posset is a traditional British dessert made with just three ingredients: cream, sugar, and (for lemon posset) lemon. It is made by heating cream with sugar and then adding lemon juice. The mixture is poured into a baking dish and refrigerated. The acidity in the lemon causes the cream to "set" to a custard-like consistency. What's incredible is that this happens by itself, as a reaction of the cream and lemon, without the addition of the gelatin used to set panna cotta or the egg yolks used to set custard. Posset is brand-new to my repertoire. I discovered it when I went with Ryan and Dahlia to London to do a pop-up for a week. When we weren't working, we were eating our way around the city, and it seemed like everywhere we went, we saw lemon posset on the menu. None of us had heard of it, so of course, we ordered it. And we loved it.

When I got back from London, I put two of our pastry cooks, Shiri Nagar and Cecily Feng, on the case of making a delicious, creamy lemon posset, and they succeeded. As much as we love Meyer lemons, we couldn't use them for this dish. Meyer lemons are less acidic than regular lemons, and they don't have enough acidity to set the posset. But if you use regular lemons, this recipe is foolproof.

Part of the beauty of posset is in its simplicity, so it seemed unfaithful to tradition to dress it up too much. This version is served family style, topped with fresh strawberries and drizzled with aged balsamic vinegar. Strawberries dressed in balsamic is a classic Italian combination, often served along with vanilla gelato, sometimes with cracked black pepper. Adding that combination to this simple cream dessert was a natural choice.

You need a quality, syrupy, aged balsamic vinegar to make this. Look for those labeled *balsamico condimento* ("balsamic condiment"). *Condimento* is a fraction of the cost of *aceto balsamico tradizionale* ("traditional balsamic"), but it has the same viscous consistency and a lot of the same complex acidity and sweetness. A good way to know you're getting the quality you want is to gauge the viscosity: it should be so thick that it coats the inside of the glass when you turn the bottle. Another good indicator is the price: *condimento* is generally in the $30 to $50 range, where *tradizionale* is closer to $200. It is not *inexpensive,* but you don't want to drizzle a salad dressing–quality balsamic vinegar on your dessert.

You will need a 12- × 7-inch oval ceramic baking dish (or another baking dish with a 12-cup capacity) to make and serve the posset. →

To make the posset, combine the cream and sugar in a medium stainless-steel saucepan and warm them over medium heat until the cream comes to a boil, about 10 minutes. Reduce the heat to low and simmer for 1 minute, stirring constantly. Turn off the heat. Using a fine Microplane, zest the bright yellow outer layer of the lemons into the pan. Cut one of the lemons in half and juice it; add ⅓ cup of the juice to the cream and stir to combine. (Reserve the second lemon to juice another time.)

Pour the posset into an oval ceramic (or another 12-cup-capacity) baking dish and refrigerate, uncovered, overnight, or for at least 4 hours, until it is chilled.

To serve, remove and discard the hulls from the strawberries. Adjust the blade of a mandoline to slice ⅛ inch thick. Slice 2 slices lengthwise from a strawberry and check their thickness; you want the slices just thick enough that they don't fall apart. If they are too thick, adjust the mandoline to slice thinner. If they are so thin that they don't hold their shape, adjust the blade to slice thicker. Slice the remaining strawberries lengthwise to fall directly onto the posset. Just before serving, drizzle the balsamic vinegar in a thin thread over the strawberries.

For the Posset

2½ cups heavy cream

1 cup sugar

2 lemons

For Serving

1 pint strawberries

Aged, syrupy balsamic vinegar

Pear Rosemary Tart
with Chestnut Crust

Serves 8 to 10

One of the first desserts I learned how to make was a classic, French pear frangipane tart. This is a contemporary version of that recipe, although I didn't start out with that idea in mind. We had chestnut flour in the kitchen from chestnut gnocchi we were making in the Osteria, and our pastry chef, Marisa Takenaka, was inspired to make a dessert with it. Marisa is Japanese, and in Japan they use chestnut purée in many desserts, so she wanted to do the same with chestnut flour. Chestnut flour has a delicious, subtle flavor, but the texture can be challenging. However, after a few tries, we created a delicious crust with a combination of chestnut and white flours. When I started thinking about what to combine with it, pears came to mind since both chestnuts and pears are wintery foods. We made many versions of this tart, tweaking things along the way, until we created something that looks very similar to the classic. But in utilizing this alternative flour and drizzling it with chestnut honey, we've made it actually very contemporary.

Chestnut honey is referred to as a "savory honey" because of its unusual, almost savory flavor, which is truly unique and difficult to describe; it is more often than not served with cheese. You can find chestnut honey at specialty food shops or cheese stores. If you can't find it, don't let that deter you from making this tart; just serve it without the honey. Be warned: a little goes a long way with chestnut honey; you and your guests will want to drizzle it in very thin threads. As much as it adds an unusual layer of flavor to a dessert such as this, it can also kill it if you add too much. Also, I should note that a scoop of vanilla gelato or ice cream would not be a bad idea with this tart. Warren pears are my preferred pears to work with: they're creamy, juicy, and flavorful. If you can't find them, look for Comice, D'Anjou, or Bartlett.

You will need an 11-inch round fluted tart pan with a removable bottom to make this.

You will need a large round platter to serve this tart.

To make the dough, whisk the egg yolks and cream together in a small bowl.

Combine the all-purpose flour, chestnut flour, sugar, and rosemary in the bowl of a stand mixer. Fit the mixer with the paddle attachment and mix on low speed to combine. Add the butter and mix on low speed until the dry ingredients and butter come together into pea-size clumps. Turn →

For the Dough

2 extra-large egg yolks

¼ cup heavy cream

1¾ cups unbleached all-purpose flour, plus more for dusting

1 cup chestnut flour

off the mixer, add the egg yolks and cream, and mix on low speed until the dough comes together. Lightly dust a large flat work surface with flour and transfer the dough to the floured work surface. Gather the dough into a ball and pat it into a 2-inch-thick disk. Wrap the dough in plastic wrap and place it in the refrigerator to chill until the dough is firm, about 2 hours.

Lightly dust a large flat work surface with flour. Remove the dough from the refrigerator, unwrap it, and place it on the floured surface. Cut the dough into large chunks and pound each chunk with a rolling pin to soften the dough. Bring the chunks together into a ball and gently knead until the dough is malleable. Pat the dough into a 2-inch-thick disk. Dust the dough and rolling pin lightly with flour and roll it into a ⅛-inch-thick (at least 12-inch) round, dusting the dough, rolling pin, and work surface as needed to keep it from sticking.

Loosely roll the dough around the pin and lower it over an 11-inch fluted tart pan with a removable bottom, centering it so the dough hangs evenly over the edges of the pan. To fit the dough into the pan, lift the edges of the dough and let the dough drop into the creases of the pan rather than stretching it to fit. (If you stretch the dough to fit, it will shrink when it is baked.) As you are lifting the dough, dip the knuckle of your index finger in flour and use it to gently press the dough against the edges and into the creases of the pan so it has straight, not sloping sides. Trim the dough so it is even with the edge of the pan; discard the scraps. Dock the bottom of the tart shell all over with the tines of a fork and place it in the refrigerator to chill until the dough is firm, about 2 hours.

To make the batter, combine the butter, almond paste, and sugar in the bowl of a stand mixer. Fit the mixer with the paddle attachment and mix on medium speed until the ingredients are combined and the mixture is smooth. Stop the mixer, add one of the eggs, and mix on medium speed to thoroughly combine. Stop to scrape down the sides of the mixer bowl, add the second egg and the almond meal, and mix to thoroughly combine.

To finish and bake the tart, adjust the oven rack to the center position and preheat the oven to 350°F.

½ cup sugar

2 tablespoons chopped fresh rosemary leaves

½ pound (2 sticks) unsalted butter, cut into 1-inch cubes and frozen for at least 1 hour

For the Batter

10 tablespoons (1¼ sticks) unsalted butter, softened at room temperature

4 ounces (½ cup) almond paste

½ cup sugar

2 extra-large eggs

½ cup plus 1 tablespoon almond meal (almond flour)

For Finishing

4 ripe but firm pears (such as Warren, Comice, D'Anjou, or Bartlett)

2 fresh rosemary sprigs

3 tablespoons sugar

Chestnut honey (or another savory honey)

Remove the tart shell from the refrigerator. Scrape the batter into the tart shell and smooth out the filling. Place one pear on a cutting board and cut 4 slabs off the core so you are left with a straight-sided core; discard the core and repeat with the remaining pears. Slice the pears horizontally ⅛ inch thick. Working with one slice at a time, lay the pears with the rounded, skin sides of the slices facing the crust to form a ring around the perimeter of the pan. Lay another row of slices, overlapping the first row, and continue, working your way inward, until you have covered the entire crust. Tear tufts of rosemary from the sprigs and stick them into the batter between the pears, around the edges of the tart. Sprinkle the sugar evenly over the surface and place the tart on a baking sheet.

Bake the tart in the oven for 28 to 35 minutes, until the edges of the tart are golden brown and the center is set and not wet looking, rotating the baking sheet from front to back halfway through that time for even browning. Remove the tart from the oven and set it aside until it is cool enough to touch. Push up on the bottom of the tart to remove the outside rim. Transfer the tart, still on the bottom tin, onto a large platter. Serve with the honey on the side for people to drizzle on their slices.

Meyer Lemon Kumquat Tart
with Rye–Cream Cheese Crust

Serves 8 to 10

Our pastry sous-chef, Marisa Takenaka, came up with this twist on a classic shaker pie, a custard-based pie that traditionally contains thin slices of lemon. In this version, Marisa replaces standard lemons with two special types of California citrus: kumquats and Meyer lemons. I love the texture of biting into the cooked citrus peel and how the sweetness of the custardy filling balances the peel's bitterness.

Meyer lemons are a hybrid of citron (a type of citrus with a thick peel) and a mandarin orange. They are similar in flavor to lemons, but sweeter and not as acidic. In Southern California we chefs and home cooks love our Meyer lemons, but what the younger generations don't know is that for a long time, until Alice Waters made Meyer lemons fashionable, they were taken for granted. If you had a lemon tree in your yard, it was most likely a Meyer lemon tree, and nobody cared. The East Coast lagged behind in their affinity for Meyer lemons, and when they did discover them, they were unable to buy them for a long time. Now Meyer lemons are widely available, and adored coast to coast. I love them, especially in desserts. What makes them particularly well suited for this pie is that they don't have as much white, bitter pith as regular lemons do. Since you slice the lemon, including the peel, it's nice not to have that touch of bitterness. That said, you can substitute regular lemons if Meyer lemons aren't available.

Rye flour adds another layer of flavor to the buttery crust for this tart, and it also gives it a pretty and an unusual color. We roll this dough out, fold it, and roll it out again repeatedly, a process that produces a flakiness that you would not ordinarily get with a dough made with rye. Before rolling out the crust, we press ridges across the length of the dough; this method is helpful when you need to roll dough to a large size while maintaining an even thickness and shape.

You will need an 11-inch round fluted tart pan with a removable bottom to make this.

You will need a large round platter to serve the tart.

To make the dough, put the butter, cream cheese, and salt in the bowl of a stand mixer. Fit the mixer with the paddle attachment and beat on medium speed until the mixture is light and fluffy, stopping to scrape down the sides of the bowl as necessary. Add the all-purpose flour and rye flour and mix on low speed for 2 to 3 minutes, until the dough is smooth. (Don't be alarmed: your mixer might seem to struggle when mixing this dough.)

Lightly dust a large flat work surface with flour and transfer the dough to the floured surface. Gather the dough together and pat it into a 2-inch-thick block. Wrap the block tightly in plastic wrap and refrigerate to chill until the dough is firm, about 2 hours.

Lightly dust your work surface with flour. Remove the block of dough from the refrigerator, unwrap it, and place it on the floured surface. Cut the dough into large chunks and pound each chunk with a rolling pin to soften the dough. Bring the chunks together into a ball and gently knead until the dough is malleable. Pat the dough into a 2-inch-thick block. Dust the dough and rolling pin lightly with flour. With the rolling pin parallel to the counter's edge, gently press 5 or 6 ridges across the surface of the dough. Roll the dough over the ridges to smooth them out and lengthen the dough and continue to roll out to an 8- × 20-inch rectangle with the short side parallel to the counter's edge, dusting the counter, dough, and rolling pin, and pulling at the edges of the dough periodically to keep them squared off. Fold the bottom edge of the dough one-third of the way toward the top and fold the top edge to meet the bottom edge, as if you were folding a letter, making sure the edges of the dough are aligned with each other. (This is called a letter fold.) Wrap the dough in plastic wrap and place it in the refrigerator for at least 30 minutes and as long as 1 hour to relax the dough; relaxing the dough will make it easier to roll out again, which you will do in the next step.

Remove the dough from the refrigerator, unwrap it, and return it to the flour-dusted work surface with the open long edge facing right. Dust the top of the dough and the rolling pin lightly with flour and create ridges down the length of the dough like you did previously. Gently roll the pin over the ridges, smoothing out the ridges and lengthening the dough in the process. Roll the dough out into a 10- × 24-inch rectangle with the short side parallel to the counter's edge, dusting the counter, dough, →

For the Crust

1 pound (4 sticks) unsalted butter, cut into 1-inch cubes and frozen for at least 1 hour, plus more for buttering the tart pan

1 pound cream cheese, cut into 1-inch cubes, cold

1½ teaspoons kosher salt

2 cups unbleached all-purpose flour, plus more for dusting

2 cups rye flour

For the Filling

4 Meyer lemons

1 heaping cup kumquats (5 to 8 kumquats)

2 cups granulated sugar

4 extra-large eggs

½ teaspoon kosher salt

For Finishing the Tart

1 extra-large egg white

2 tablespoons crystallized sugar (or granulated sugar)

and rolling pin as needed and pulling at the edges of the dough to keep them squared off. Make a second letter fold, folding the bottom edge of the dough one-third of the way toward the top and folding the top edge to meet the bottom edge. Wrap the dough in plastic wrap and refrigerate for 30 minutes to 1 hour to relax the dough.

Butter the bottom and sides of a fluted tart pan with a removable bottom.

Lightly dust your work surface with flour. Remove the dough from the refrigerator, unwrap it, and place it on the floured surface. Cut the dough in half, rewrap one half, and return it to the refrigerator. Place the other half on the floured surface and pat it into a 2-inch-thick disk. Dust the dough and rolling pin lightly with flour and roll the dough into a ⅛-inch-thick round (at least 14 inches in diameter), dusting the dough, rolling pin, and work surface with flour as needed.

Gently fold the dough in half and place it on top of the tart pan, centering it. Gently unfold the dough so it flops over the pan. To fit the dough into the pan, lift the edges of the dough and let it drop into the creases of the pan, rather than stretching it to fit. (If you stretch the dough to fit, it will shrink when it is baked.) As you are lifting the dough, dip the knuckle of your index finger in flour and use it to gently press the dough against the edges and into the creases of the pan so it has straight, not sloping sides. Using kitchen shears, trim the dough so there is ½ inch of dough overhanging all the way around; discard the scraps. Place the tart shell in the refrigerator to chill while you make the filling.

Line a large baking sheet with parchment paper. Lightly dust your work surface with flour. Remove the second block of dough from the refrigerator, unwrap it, and place the dough on the floured surface. Pound the other half of dough with a rolling pin to soften it until it is malleable. Dust the dough and rolling pin lightly with flour and roll the dough into a ⅛-inch-thick round (at least 14 inches in diameter), dusting the dough, rolling pin, and work surface as needed to keep it from sticking. Place the dough on the prepared baking sheet and place it in the refrigerator to chill while you make the filling.

To make the filling, adjust the blade of a mandoline to slice ⅛ inch thick. Slice off and discard the tops of the lemons to create a flat surface on each lemon. Thinly slice the lemons on the mandoline, discarding the end slice of each lemon. Thinly slice the kumquats into coins, discarding the top and bottom slices. Remove and discard the seeds from the lemon and kumquat slices and put the slices in a large bowl. Add the granulated sugar and toss to coat the citrus with the sugar. Set aside at room temperature for about 1 hour to allow the sugar to soften the citrus peels.

Whisk the eggs and salt together in a medium bowl and pour into the bowl with the citrus. Fold the eggs in with the citrus to evenly distribute the ingredients.

Remove the tart shell from the refrigerator and scrape the filling into the shell, making sure to get all the sugary ingredients out of the bowl, and smooth out the filling.

Remove the sheet of dough from the refrigerator. Roll the dough onto a rolling pin and rest it over the tart, centering it. Unroll the dough so it falls onto the tart and adjust it as needed. Trim the top sheet of dough so it's even with the bottom sheet. Using the tines of a fork at a 45-degree angle, press the top and bottom edges of the crust together, forcefully sweeping the fork toward you to seal the pie closed and cut the dough in one motion; discard the scraps. Cut 4 slashes in the crust, cutting all the way through to the filling in a starlike pattern, making sure the cuts don't touch one another, which would create a big hole in the crust.

Place the tart in the refrigerator to chill for at least 1 hour and as long as 1 day.

Adjust the oven rack to the center position and preheat the oven to 350°F.

Remove the tart from the refrigerator. Whisk the egg white in a small bowl and brush it onto the surface of the tart. Sprinkle the tart with the crystallized sugar and place the tart on a baking sheet.

Bake the tart in the oven for 1 hour to 1 hour 10 minutes, until the crust is golden brown, rotating the baking sheet from front to back halfway through that time for even browning. Remove the tart from the oven and set it aside until it is cool enough to touch. Push up on the bottom of the tart pan to remove the outside rim. Transfer the tart, still on the bottom tin, onto a large platter.

Key Lime Cheesecake
with Passion Fruit Caramel

Serves 8 to 10

I have always been a fan of Key lime pie, but I never made it a part of my repertoire because a true Key lime pie must be made with one ingredient that you'll never find in my cupboard: sweetened condensed milk. This cheesecake shows off the delicious flavor of Key limes, but it gets its silky, creamy texture from cream cheese and crème fraîche instead of canned milk. Key limes are more acidic and flavorful than Persian limes, the standard limes you see in American grocery stores. They're often sold in bags in regular grocery stores (also called California limes and Mexican limes, they're smaller and sometimes yellower in color) and are widely available in Hispanic grocery stores. If you can't find them, use whatever limes you can find; the cheesecake will still be delicious. The cheesecake is baked in a buttery coconut *pâte sucrée,* or "sugar crust." The dough is rolled out into a sheet, baked, and then you press a cake ring (bottomless tart ring) down onto it to cut the dough to the precise dimension of the ring, as if you were cutting (baked) cookie dough with a giant cookie cutter except you leave the cutter in place. The dough shrinks when baked so if we were to cut it before baking it, the crust would be smaller than the ring and the cheesecake filling would spill out of the bottom.

I love passion fruits, and since they come into season at the same time Key limes do, I use them to make a caramel sauce to serve with this pie. The small black seeds from the fresh passion fruits dot this caramel; it's really pretty.

You will need a 10-inch-diameter, 3-inch-high cake ring to make this. (A cake ring is a bottomless ring that, when placed on a baking sheet, acts as a cake pan.)

You will need a large round platter to serve the cheesecake.

To make the dough, whisk the egg yolks and cream together in a small bowl.

Combine the flour and sugar in the bowl of a stand mixer. Fit the mixer with the paddle attachment and mix on low speed to combine. Add the butter and mix on medium speed until the dry ingredients and butter come together into pea-size clumps. Turn off the mixer, add the egg yolks and cream, and mix on low speed until the dough comes together. Add the coconut and mix to combine. Lightly dust a large flat work surface

For the Dough

2 extra-large egg yolks

¼ cup heavy cream

2¾ cups unbleached all-purpose flour

½ cup sugar, plus more for dusting

with flour and transfer the dough to the floured surface. Gather the dough together into a ball and pat it into a 2-inch-thick disk. Wrap the dough in plastic wrap and place it in the refrigerator to chill until the dough is firm, about 2 hours.

Adjust the oven rack to the center position and preheat the oven to 325°F. Line a large baking sheet with parchment paper.

Lightly dust a large flat work surface with flour. Remove the dough from the refrigerator, unwrap it, and place it on the floured surface. Cut the dough into large chunks and pound each chunk with a rolling pin to soften the dough. Bring the chunks together into a ball and gently knead until the dough is malleable. Pat the dough into a 2-inch-thick disk. Dust the dough and rolling pin lightly with flour and roll it into a ⅛-inch-thick (at least 12-inch) round, dusting the dough, rolling pin, and work surface as needed to keep it from sticking. Lay the sheet of dough on the baking sheet and dock it all over with the tines of a fork.

Place the baking sheet in the oven to bake the crust for 18 to 20 minutes, until it is lightly browned, rotating the baking sheet from front to back halfway through that time for even browning. Remove the baking sheet from the oven.

While the dough is baking, butter the bottom and sides of a 10-inch cake ring.

Push the cake ring onto the baked crust, pressing the ring so it cuts all the way through the crust to the baking sheet. Leave the ring in place and set the baking sheet with the crust aside to cool to room temperature. Pull away the trimmings and put them in a bowl to snack on.

Reduce the oven temperature to 275°F.

To make the filling, combine the cream cheese, sugar, and lime zest in the bowl of a stand mixer. Fit the mixer with the paddle attachment and mix on medium-high speed until the mixture is completely smooth and fluffy, about 5 minutes, stopping to scrape down the sides of the bowl as needed. Stop the mixer, add one of the eggs, and mix on medium speed to thoroughly combine. Add the rest of the eggs, one at a time, stopping to scrape down the sides of the bowl between additions. Stop the mixer, add the crème fraîche and lime juice, and mix to combine. Turn off the mixer. Scrape the filling into the cake ring and smooth it out. →

½ pound (2 sticks) unsalted butter, cut into 1-inch cubes and frozen for at least 1 hour, plus more for buttering the cake ring

2 tablespoons shredded unsweetened coconut

For the Filling

18 ounces cream cheese, softened at room temperature

1 cup sugar

2 tablespoons lime zest (zesting only the bright green outer layer from about 3 limes; preferably Key limes)

4 extra-large eggs

2 cups crème fraîche

¼ cup lime juice (preferably from Key limes)

For the Topping

1 cup crème fraîche

1 extra-large egg yolk

2 tablespoons sugar

For the Caramel

18 ripe passion fruits

2 cups plus 2 tablespoons sugar

1 tablespoon corn syrup

For the Whipped Cream

3 cups heavy cream

1 cup crème fraîche (or sour cream)

Bake the cheesecake for 40 to 45 minutes, until it is set; the filling will be slightly wobbly in the very center when you jiggle the pan. Remove the cheesecake from the oven and set it aside to cool for 10 to 15 minutes, so that it cools enough that the topping doesn't melt when you add it in the next step.

To make the topping, while the cheesecake is cooling, whisk the crème fraîche and egg yolk in a small bowl. Pour the topping evenly over the cheesecake and sprinkle with the sugar.

Return the cheesecake to the oven to bake for 10 to 15 minutes, until the topping is set and looks glossy and baked onto the cheesecake. Remove the cheesecake from the oven and set it aside to cool to room temperature. Refrigerate the cheesecake, still on the baking sheet, for about 4 hours, to chill and set.

To make the caramel, cut the passion fruits in half lengthwise. Scoop the pulp and seeds out of the skins (which are more like shells) with a spoon and put them in a medium bowl. Discard the skins. Pass the pulp and seeds through a mesh strainer into a glass measuring cup. Measure out 1 cup of the juice and ½ cup of the seeds. Discard the remaining seeds and drink the remaining juice.

Combine the sugar, corn syrup, and ⅓ cup water in a medium saucepan and stir to combine. Bring the liquid to a boil over medium-high heat, swirling the pan so the sugar cooks evenly and brushing down the sides of the pan with a wet pastry brush to remove any sugar granules. Reduce the heat to medium and cook the caramel, tilting and swirling the pan, until it is a medium amber color, 3 to 5 minutes. Turn off the heat and add the passion fruit juice, taking care because the sugar mixture will bubble furiously and may splatter. (The sugar will seize and harden when you add the passion fruit. Don't worry; it will melt when you warm it.) Cook the caramel over medium heat for a minute or two until the seized sugar has melted. Turn off the heat and stir in the passion fruit seeds. Just before serving, transfer the caramel to a small pretty bowl for serving.

To make the whipped cream, put a large bowl and a wire whisk in the freezer for at least 10 minutes to chill. Remove the bowl and whisk from the freezer and pour the cream into the bowl. Whip the cream with the whisk until it thickens to soft peaks; when you lift the whisk out of the cream and turn it upside down, the peak of the cream will flop. Add the crème fraîche and beat to return the cream to soft peaks. Transfer the whipped cream to a medium pretty bowl for serving.

To serve, if the caramel sauce has cooled, warm it over low heat until it's a smooth, drizzling consistency.

Remove the baking sheet from the refrigerator and carefully slide the cake off the parchment paper onto a large platter. Dip a paring knife in hot water and run it around the inside edge of the cake ring to separate the cheesecake from the ring, wiping off the knife and dipping it in hot water as needed. Carefully lift the ring off the cake.

Serve chilled, with whipped cream and warmed passion fruit caramel sauce in bowls on the side. For neat, clean slices, use a long sharp knife dipped in hot water to cut the cheesecake.

Dario's Olive Oil Cake
with Rosemary and Pine Nuts

Serves 10 to 12

Throughout this book I have often talked about what a butcher would do in a given scenario. But instead of thinking about what a butcher *would* do, here is what a butcher, specifically Dario Cecchini, *does* do: he makes an olive oil cake, cuts it up, and serves it stacked high to guests who have just eaten a huge meal of meat. This is his recipe, which Dario's wife, Kim Wicks, was kind enough to share with me.

Italian leavening is available from online sources and in Italian grocery stores. If you can't find it, use equal parts baking powder and baking soda.

You will need a 10-inch angel food cake pan to make this.

You will need a large round platter or cake stand to serve this cake.

Bring the raisins and vin santo to a simmer in a very small saucepan over high heat. Turn off the heat and set aside for at least 30 minutes and as long as overnight, so the raisins can absorb the wine.

Adjust the oven rack to the center position and preheat the oven to 325°F.

Spread the pine nuts out on a baking sheet and toast them in the oven for 8 to 10 minutes, until they are fragrant and toasted, shaking the baking sheet and rotating it from front to back halfway through that time so the nuts brown evenly. Remove the pine nuts from the oven and set them aside to cool to room temperature.

Increase the oven temperature to 400°F. Oil the 10-inch angel food cake pan generously with olive oil and dust it lightly with flour.

Leaving the peels attached, lay the orange halves flat sides down and slice ¼ inch thick. Turn the oranges and slice ¼ inch thick again to form ¼-inch cubes.

Put the eggs, leavening, and ½ cup plus 2 tablespoons of the granulated sugar in the bowl of a stand mixer. Fit the mixer with the whisk attachment and mix over medium-high speed until the mixture thickens, 3 to

½ cup plump raisins (preferably flame raisins; about 5 ounces)

¼ cup plus 2 tablespoons vin santo (or another sweet dessert wine)

⅓ cup pine nuts

½ cup plus 1 tablespoon extra-virgin olive oil, plus more for the pan

1¾ cups unbleached all-purpose flour, plus more for dusting

1½ navel oranges, halved through the stems (not peeled), seeds removed and discarded

2 large eggs

2 teaspoons Italian leavening (such as Benchmate or Paneangeli; or 1 teaspoon baking soda plus 1 teaspoon baking powder)

4 minutes. Gradually add the olive oil by pouring it down the side of the bowl in a slow, steady stream and mix until the batter is emulsified. Reduce the mixer speed to low. Add one-third of the flour and mix until it is no longer visible, about 2 minutes. Add one-third of the raisins and mix just to incorporate them. Stop the mixer and scrape down the sides of the bowl. Repeat two more times, mixing in one-third of the flour at a time, then one-third of the raisins at a time, stopping to scrape down the sides of the bowl between additions, until all of the flour and all of the raisins have been incorporated. Turn off the mixer and remove the bowl from the stand. Add the chopped oranges and use a rubber spatula to gently fold them into the batter. Set the batter aside to rest for 10 minutes. Scrape the batter into the prepared cake pan and scatter the pine nuts over the top. Sprinkle the cake with the remaining ¼ cup granulated sugar. Tear tufts of rosemary from the sprigs and stick the tufts into the batter, distributing them over the surface of the cake in an attractive way.

Bake the cake for 10 minutes. Rotate the cake, lower the oven temperature to 325°F, and bake for another 30 to 35 minutes, until the cake is golden brown and a toothpick inserted comes out clean, rotating the cake from front to back once during that time so it browns evenly. Remove the cake from the oven and set it aside to cool.

To serve, run a knife or offset spatula around the inside of the pan to release the cake from the pan and put a large plate over the pan. Swiftly flip the cake and the plate to invert the cake onto the plate. Invert the cake again onto a large platter or cake stand. Pour the confectioners' sugar into a mesh strainer and tap the strainer over the cake to dust it lightly with the sugar. Serve the cake with a knife for guests to cut and serve themselves.

¾ cup plus 2 tablespoons granulated sugar

2 fresh rosemary sprigs

¼ cup confectioners' sugar

Raspberry Jam Bars
with Pistachio Crumble

Makes 12 or more bars, depending on how you cut them

A few years ago, Dahlia Narvaez and I were asked by the Pistachio Board to teach a baking class using pistachios, in China. My mind immediately went to one of my favorite pastries that I was making at the time, a jam-filled breakfast bar. I tweaked the bar to work with pistachios, and I ended up liking the new one better than the original. This is that improved recipe. The bars are equally great for breakfast, as an afternoon snack, or for dessert. They have a shortbread crust, and they're buttery, salty, and not too sweet—a totally addictive combination. The recipe makes more topping than you will need because it is constructed around one egg. Bake it on its own and sprinkle it over yogurt or ice cream.

You will need a large platter or a cake stand to serve these bars.

To make the topping, put the flour, pistachios, granulated sugar, baking powder, and salt in the bowl of a food processor fitted with a metal blade and pulse to a coarse-meal consistency. Add the butter and pulse until the butter and flour come together into pea-size clumps; don't mix it so much that the topping comes together into a homogenous dough. Transfer the topping to a large bowl. Add the egg and mix it into the crumb mixture with your hands; the topping will be crumbly and uneven. Cover the bowl and chill the topping until you're ready to use it.

To make the dough and bake the crust, adjust the oven rack to the center position and preheat the oven to 350°F.

Combine the flour, pistachios, granulated sugar, brown sugar, cornstarch, and salt in the bowl of the food processor. Add the butter and pulse until the dough comes together.

Lay a 12- × 16-inch sheet of parchment paper on your work surface and dust it lightly with flour. Place the dough on the floured paper and pat it into a 2-inch-thick block. Dust the dough and rolling pin lightly with flour and roll it into a 10- × 16-inch rectangle, dusting the dough and work surface with flour as needed to keep it from sticking. Transfer →

For the Topping

2½ cups unbleached
all-purpose flour

1 cup shelled pistachios

½ cup plus 2 tablespoons
granulated sugar

1¼ teaspoons baking powder

1 teaspoon kosher salt

10 tablespoons (1¼ sticks)
cold unsalted butter

1 extra-large egg, lightly beaten

For the Dough

4 cups unbleached all-purpose
flour, plus more for dusting

1 cup shelled pistachios

½ cup granulated sugar

½ cup lightly packed light
brown sugar

½ cup cornstarch

the parchment with the dough to a large baking sheet. Dock the dough with the tines of a fork.

Bake the dough for 20 to 25 minutes, until it is light golden brown, rotating the baking sheet from front to bank halfway through that time for even browning. Remove the crust from the oven and set it aside to cool to room temperature.

Spoon the jam onto the crust and use an offset spatula or the back of the spoon to spread it to the edges in an even layer. Measure out 2 cups of the topping and drop it in uneven chunks over the jam.

Return the baking sheet to the oven and bake the pastry for 30 to 40 minutes, until the topping is golden brown, rotating the baking sheet from front to back halfway through that time for even browning. Remove the baking sheet from the oven and set it aside to cool. Slide the parchment paper onto a cutting board and use a serrated knife to trim about ½ to 1 inch off the edges of the pastry to create an even, exposed edge. (The trimmings are yours to snack on.) Use the knife to cut the pastry into bars.

1 teaspoon kosher salt

1 pound (4 sticks) unsalted butter, cut into 1-inch cubes and frozen for at least 1 hour

2 cups raspberry jam

Sources

EQUIPMENT

Italy Professional Tinned Copper Pizza Pan
www.amazon.com

Ceramic Mortar
Fantes Kitchen Shop
www.fantes.com

Steel Mesh Glove
www.amazon.com
(many brands available)

MAIL-ORDER MEATS

Flannery Beef
www.flannerybeef.com
Unusually marbled and flavorful, California-raised Holstein beef. Chi Spacca's source for bistecca Fiorentina.

Heritage Foods
www.heritagefoods.com
Chi Spacca's source for heritage pork; they sell all types of meat, including lamb, poultry, and game.

Creekstone Farms
www.creekstonefarms.com
Grass-fed, corn-finished beef, heritage pork.

Pat LaFrieda Meats
www.lafrieda.com
Quality beef, heritage pork, domestic lamb, poultry, and game.

Snake River Farms
www.snakeriverfarms.com
Wagyu beef, dry-aged beef, heritage pork.

DeBragga
www.debragga.com
Beef, heritage pork, domestic
lamb, poultry.

Meat the Butchers
www.meatthebutchers.com
Beef, heritage pork, domestic
lamb, poultry.

Marx Foods
www.marxfoods.com
Grain-fed veal.

Salami Companies
Salumi
https://salumicuredmeats.com/
Producers of house-cured salami
and other cured meats.

Nduja Artisans Salumeria
www.ndujaartisans.com
Specializing in Italian cured
meats of all types: coppa,
culatello, speck, and salami, but
most famous for their n'duja.

Creminelli Fine Meats
www.creminelli.com
Best known for salami, but they
also make sliced meats like
prosciutto and coppa.
Also available at specialty food
stores.

Fra' Mani Handcrafted Foods
www.framani.com
Chef Paul Bertolli's company that
makes salami, pancetta, sausages,
cooked ham, and mortadella.
Also available at specialty food
stores.

Olympia Provisions
www.olympiaprovisions.com
Producers of salami and select
deli meats.

La Quercia
www.laquercia.us
Producers of prosciutto, pancetta,
lardo, and salami. Also available
at specialty food stores.

SPICES

Kalustyan's
http://foodsofnations.com/
For spices and spice blends.

SOS Chefs
https://sos-chefs.com/
For spices and spice blends.

La Boîte
http://laboiteny.com/
For spices, spice blends,
and fennel pollen.

**The Reluctant Trading
Experiment**
https://reluctanttrading.com/
For Tellicherry peppercorns,
spices, spice blends,
and sea salt.

Jacobsen Salt Co.
https://jacobsensalt.com/
For domestically produced flaky
sea salt.

Acknowledgments
by Ryan DeNicola

I cannot imagine what this book would look like without Carolynn Carreño. She guided us in every stage to ensure all bases were covered. Whether it was taking our words and turning them into something readable, or testing recipes for accuracy, she did fantastic work. I will never look at a cookbook the same way because of Carolynn's guidance.

The sous-chef at Chi Spacca, Joe Tagorda, has been a rock who made Chi Spacca run smoothly while we wrote this book. His hard work and dedication make books like this possible.

Hilario Cruz Molina and Miguel Zavala are the hidden gems of Chi Spacca. They helped develop many of the recipes in this book and have been instrumental in the quality of food at Chi Spacca since the doors opened.

The beautiful desserts in this book are due to the talents of our pastry chef, Dahlia Narvaez, and her sous-chef, Marissa Takenaka. They developed and tested all of our desserts, with the help of Shiri Nagar and Cecily Feng.

The diversity of the recipes in this book is due, in part, to the help of the other restaurants on "the corner." Liz Hong and Herbie Yuen gave us support in testing and developing many of the recipes.

Anna Nguyen is responsible for the gorgeous salads featured in this book. Anna is the reason this meat-focused cookbook has so many salads.

I constantly relied on the help of many cooks and sous-chefs on the corner, especially Hayley Porter, Ben Giron, and Francis Chua. They helped test and develop numerous dishes.

When I started as sous-chef at Chi Spacca, the chef at that time, Chad Colby, told me he was going to teach me every part of his job. He did just that, and was instrumental in the early years of Chi Spacca. Many of his dishes are featured in this book.

While many cooks and friends tested recipes, Heather Fogarty was indispensable in the outcome of the recipes. She tested most of the recipes in her home and provided text photos almost every night to show us how they turned out. The food in this book would taste very different without Heather.

We spent many hours in the dining room of Chi Spacca, where Ricardo Martinez and Nathalie Urbina made us feel comfortable with their hospitality.

The photographer, Ed Anderson, and food stylist, Valerie Aikman-Smith, embraced our rustic style and made our food look so beautiful throughout the book.

Cassandra J. Pappas did fantastic work designing the cookbook, with help on jacket design from Kelly Blair. They made this book beautiful from cover to cover.

Nancy's agent, Janis Donnaud, is the reason this book came about in the first place. Our editors, Peter Gethers and Tom Pold, found all of our mistakes, of which there were many!

Kate Green, Nancy's assistant, and her administrative help kept us organized: Kate called, copied, printed, e-mailed, and shipped throughout the whole process.

Michael Krikorian, our corner security and psychiatrist, kept us calm during every part of this book.

My parents, Dr. Gregg and Mary DeNicola, not only gave me guidance throughout the process, but also kept Chi Spacca open by being our best customers! My beautiful girlfriend, Zoe Stathopoulos, supported me and kept me on track in life.

Our regulars at Chi Spacca, of whom there are many, were our guinea pigs, trying new dishes, and they have kept Chi Spacca's doors open from the beginning.

Last and most of all, Nancy Silverton, my mentor and inspiration. Even when I think a dish is perfect, Nancy shows me ways to take it to the next level. She is making me a better cook every day and with every dish we create together.

Index

(Page references in *italics* refer to photographs of finished dishes.)

Aioli, 118–19, 230
  making by hand, 104–5
  Sweet Sherry and Garlic, 236–7
amberjack, 221
  Collars, Roasted, with Labneh,
    Zhug, and Radish Salad, *220,*
    221–3
anchovy(ies):
  Bagna Cauda Yogurt, *270,* 271–2
  by-product of curing in salt
    (colatura di alici), 249
  Cetara, and Butter on Toast, 62, *63*
  Crushed Lemon Bagna Cauda,
    278
  Lemon Salsa Rustica, 172–3
  Puntarella and Cauliflower Salad
    with Bagna Cauda, Soft-Cooked
    Eggs and, *86,* 87–9
  Roasted Lipstick Peppers with
    Mint, Pecorino Toscano and,
    66–7
  Spacca Caesar with Fried Parsley,
    Orange Zest, Bagna Cauda
    Croutons and, 101–3
angel hair pasta, in Fideus a la
  Catalana with Sweet Sherry and
  Garlic Aioli, 236–7

Angus beef, 130
Antica Macelleria Cecchini, Panzano,
  Chianti, Italy, 19
antipasto platter (*tagliere*), 36
  Butcher's Pâté, 52–4
  Chianti "Tuna," 56–7
  Duck Rillettes, *92,* 93–4
  how to build, 37
  Marinated Olives with Garlic and
    Fresh Pecorino, 64
  N'duja, 58
  Pane Tostato, 55
  Pork Tenderloin Pistachio Pâté, *48,*
    49–51
  Taralli, 46–7
  Whipped Lardo, 59
  see also pickle(d)(s)
Apple Cider Syrup, 187
Apple Quince Streusel Slab Pie,
  327–30
Armenian-Style Lamb Ribs with
  Jajik, 198–9
Artichokes, Roasted, Shaved Spring
  Vegetable Salad with Dill and
  (Insalata Primavera), 96–7
Asian cuisines and flavors, recipes
  inspired by, 4

Chrysanthemum Greens with
  Kumquats and Duck Rillettes
  Toasts, *92,* 93–5
Grilled Porcini-Rubbed Short Ribs
  with Salsa Verde and Scallions,
  140, 141–2
Lacquered Duck with Honey-
  Balsamic Glaze and Crispy Black
  Rice, *207,* 208–11
Roasted Amberjack Collars with
  Labneh, Zhug, and Radish Salad,
  220, 221–3
asparagus:
  al Cartoccio with Butter, Mint, and
    Parmesan, *284,* 285–6
  Insalata Primavera: Shaved Spring
    Vegetable Salad with Roasted
    Artichokes and Dill, 96–7
avocado(s):
  BLTA Salad with Aioli and Herb
    Bread Crumbs, 118–20
  Grains and Seeds Salad with
    Escarole, Bacon, Egg, Horseradish
    Dressing and, 121–5, *122*
  Pinkerton, with Pea Shoots,
    Toasted Pine Nuts, and
    Prosciutto, *80,* 81–2

avocado(s) *(continued)*:
  and Watercress Salad with Pears and Gorgonzola Vinaigrette, 90–1

bacon:
  BLTA Salad with Aioli and Herb Bread Crumbs, 118–20
  Rancho Beans, Chris Feldmeier's, 302–3
  Scallion Topping (for steak), *160*, 161–2
  Vinaigrette, 77–8
Bagna Cauda, 87–8
  Croutons, Spacca Caesar with Fried Parsley, Anchovies, Orange Zest and, 101–3
  Crushed Lemon, 278
  Puntarella and Cauliflower Salad with Anchovies, Soft-Cooked Eggs and, *86*, 87–9
  Yogurt, *270*, 271–2
balsamic (vinegar), 339
  Honey Glaze, 210, 211
Banana Cream Slab Pie with Caramel Sauce and Bittersweet Chocolate Shavings, 331–4, *335*
Barber, Dan, 291
Barbuto, New York, 183
Bars, Raspberry Jam, with Pistachio Crumble, *354*, 355–6
Bastianich, Joe, 7
beans:
  Rancho, Chris Feldmeier's, 302–3
  White, Tuscan, Dario's, 312–13
Béchamel Sauce, 308
beef, 133–62
  Aged, Trimmings, Yorkshire Pudding with, 304–5
  Bistecca Fiorentina, *133*, 134–5
  Brisket, Braised, with Salsa Verde and Horseradish Crème Fraîche, 156–8
  Carne Cruda, Osteria Style, 136–7
  Carne Cruda, "Tartufo Povero," *138*, 139
  cattle breeds and, 130
  Cheek and Bone Marrow Pie, *148*, 149–55
  dry-aged, 131

grades of, 131
  Pepper Steak "Dal Rae," *160*, 161–2
  Ryan's tutorial, 130–1
  Short Ribs, Grilled Porcini-Rubbed, with Salsa Verde and Scallions, *140*, 141–2
  Standing Rib Roast, APL Style, 143–4, *145*
  trimmings, in Pane Tostato with Bistecca Drippings, *60*, 61
  Tri-Tip, Coffee-Rubbed Grilled, 146–7
beets:
  Misticanza: Shaved Vegetable Salad with Radicchio and Sherry Dijon Vinaigrette, 106–7
  Roasted, with Chicories, Yogurt, and Lemon Zest, 115–16, *117*
berry(ies):
  Mixed, and Stone Fruit Filling for Lattice-Topped Slab Pie, 323–4
  see also strawberry(ies)
Bertolli, Paul, 6
Bistecca Fiorentina, *133*, 134–5
black bass, in Mischiato Potente: Mixed Pasta and Seafood Stew, *248*, 249–51
black pepper, 16–17
Black Rice, Crispy, *207*, 208–11
BLTA Salad with Aioli and Herb Bread Crumbs, 118–20
Boulettes Larder, San Francisco, 113
Brackett, Sylvan, 93
branzino:
  Fried Whole, with Pickled Cherry Peppers and Charred Scallions, *252*, 253–5
  Mischiato Potente: Mixed Pasta and Seafood Stew, *248*, 249–51
  alla Piastra with Wilted Soft Herbs, *224*, 225–6
bread:
  Crumbs, Bagna Cauda, 87–8
  Crumbs, Gremolata, 276
  Crumbs, Herb, 77–8, 118
  Focaccia di Recco (*focaccia col formaggio*, or focaccia with cheese), *38*, 39–45

Yorkshire Pudding with Aged Beef Trimmings, 304–5
  see also croutons; toast(s)
brining meat, 169, 170, 177
briquettes, 29
Brisket, Braised, with Salsa Verde and Horseradish Crème Fraîche, 156–8
Broccolini and Scallions, Grilled, 310–11
brown butter:
  Jus, 166–7
  Lemon Sauce, 244
  Orange Glaze, 266
Bruno, Mimmo, 40
Buckwheat Maple Cake with Fresh Figs, 336–7
Budino, Butterscotch, Family Style, *318*, 319–20
Burrata and Stone Fruit Salad with Mizuna and Sweet Peppers, 126–7
butcher's cut (*segreto*), use of term, 129, 172
butcher shops, 10
Butcher's Pâté, 52–4
butter:
  Brown, Jus, 166–7
  Brown, Lemon, 244
  Brown, Orange Glaze, 266
  Remoulade (Herb), 233–4, *235*
butter curlers, 62
Butter Lettuce and Herb Salad with Lemon Dijon Vinaigrette, 110–11
Butterscotch Budino, Family Style, *318*, 319–20

cabbage:
  Roasted, with Bagna Cauda Yogurt and Crunchy Grains, *270*, 271–3
  Roasted, with Toasted Caraway Vinaigrette, 274–5
Caesar:
  dressing, making by hand, 104–5
  with Fried Parsley, Anchovies, Orange Zest, and Bagna Cauda Croutons, 101–3

cakes:
    Buckwheat Maple, with Fresh Figs, 336–7
    Olive Oil, with Rosemary and Pine Nuts, Dario's, 352–3
Calabrian chile(s):
    N'duja, 58
    Salsa, 201, 202
Calabrian cuisine:
    Baked Mussels and Clams with N'duja and Aioli, and Toast for Dipping, 230–1
    N'duja, 58
Calamari, Fried, alla Piccata, 227–8, *229*
Candied Pecans, 83–4
cannellini, in Dario's Tuscan White Beans, 312–13
capers:
    Fried, 184
    Fried Garlic and, 136–7
caramel:
    Passion Fruit, Key Lime Cheesecake with, 348–51
    Sauce, *318*, 319–20, 332, 333–4
Caraway, Toasted, Vinaigrette, 274
carne, see beef; lamb; meat; pork
carne cruda (Italian for "raw meat"):
    Osteria Style, 136–7
    "Tartufo Povero," *138*, 139
carrots:
    Vichy, Classic, 314
    Whole Roasted, with Cracked Coriander and Cumin and Dill Yogurt, 283
Carr's Ciderhouse Cider Syrup, 187
Castelfranco:
    and Persimmon Salad with Candied Pecans, Parmesan, and Fruit-and-Nut Toasts, 83–5
    Roasted Beets with Chicories, Yogurt, and Lemon Zest, 115–16, *117*
Castelvetrano olive(s):
    Braised Lamb Necks with Preserved Lemon and, *190*, 191–2
    and Charred Lemon Salmoriglio, *256*, 257–9

cast-iron skillet on oven floor, to replicate intense heat from wood-burning oven, 14–15
cauliflower:
    Giardiniera, 73
    Pickles, Turmeric, 69
    and Puntarella Salad with Bagna Cauda, Anchovies, and Soft-Cooked Eggs, *86*, 87–9
    Wedges, Roasted, with Crushed Lemon Bagna Cauda, 278–9
    Whole Roasted, with Green Garlic Crème Fraîche and Sunflower Seed Crumble, 262–3
cavolo nero, in Braised Greens, 297
Cecchini, Dario, 5–6, 19, 52, 56, 293, 312, 352
Celeriac Purée, 315
celery:
    Insalata Inverno: Shaved Winter Vegetable Salad with Parmesan and Olio Nuovo, 98, *99*–100
    Leaf and Grains Garnish, *270*, 272
Cetara Anchovies and Butter on Toast, 62, *63*
charcoal-fired grills, 28–32
    fuels for, 28–9
    see also grilling on wood- or charcoal-fired grill
charcuterie, 6–7
    how to build an antipasto platter (or *tagliere*) with, 37
Cheesecake, Key Lime, with Passion Fruit Caramel, 348–51
Chestnut Crust, Pear Rosemary Tart with, 341–3
Chianti "Tuna," 56–7
chicken:
    Pollo alla Diavolo on Toast, 216–17
    Salad, Indian-Spiced, with Mixed Lettuces, Walnuts, and Preserved Lemon Vinaigrette, *112*, 113–14
    Stock, 149–50, 159
Chickpea Purée, Whole Roasted Eggplant with Zhug and, 267–9
Chicories, Roasted Beets with Yogurt, Lemon Zest and, 115–16, *117*

chile(s):
    Calabrian, in N'duja, 58
    Calabrian, Salsa, 201, 202
    chipotle, 187, 221
    Zhug, 222, 267, 268
chimney, starting charcoal fire with, 30
Chino Family Farm, San Diego County, 265, 298
chipotle chiles, 187, 221
Chi Spacca:
    origins and history of, 4–7
    spirit of Italian butcher as inspiration at, 3, 5–9
    style of cooking at, 3–4
    wood-fired cooking as focus at, 7
Chive Vinaigrette, 246
Chrysanthemum Greens with Kumquats and Duck Rillettes Toasts, *92*, 93–5
Chua, Francis, 204, 208
Cimarusti, Michael, 239
Citrus, Plate of, with Olio Nuovo and Fresh Mint, 306–7
citrus zesters, 14
clams:
    Fideus a la Catalana with Sweet Sherry and Garlic Aioli, 236–7
    and Mussels, Baked, with N'duja and Aioli, and Toast for Dipping, 230–1
coffee and spice grinders, 12, 17
Coffee Rub, 146
colatura di alici, 249
Colby, Chad, 6–7, 81, 180, 298
condiments:
    Green Garlic Crème Fraîche, 263
    Horseradish Crème Fraîche, 158
    N'duja, 58
    Preserved Lemons, 23
    Remoulade (Herb) Butter, 233–4, *235*
    see also dressings; garnishes; pickle(d)(s); sauces; spice blends
contorni, see side dishes
Corn, Creamed Summer, 298
Cream Cheese–Rye Crust, Meyer Lemon Kumquat Tart with, 344–7

crème fraîche:
  Green Garlic, 263
  Horseradish, 158
crescenza (also called stracchino),
    in Focaccia di Recco (*focaccia
    col formaggio*, or focaccia with
    cheese), *38, 39–45*
croutons:
  Bagna Cauda, Spacca Caesar with
    Fried Parsley, Anchovies, Orange
    Zest and, 101–3
  Olive Bread, Heirloom Tomato
    Panzanella with Feta Yogurt and,
    108–9
cucina povera, or "poverty cooking,"
    249
cucumber:
  Persian, in Feta Yogurt, 109
  Persian, in Jajik, 198–9
  Pickles, 72

Dal Rae Restaurant, Pico Rivera, Los
    Angeles, 161
Dario Salt, 19
Dates, Warm, with Sea Salt, 65
deep-fry thermometers, 13
Del Posto, New York, 227
DeNicola, Ryan, 4, 10, 24, 146, 175,
    177, 204, 212, 221, 233, 236, 246,
    265, 287, 339
  Chi Spacca grilling class, 27–33
  meat tutorial, 130–2
desserts (*dolci*), 8, 9, 316–56
  Buckwheat Maple Cake with Fresh
    Figs, 336–7
  Butterscotch Budino, Family Style,
    318, 319–20
  Key Lime Cheesecake with Passion
    Fruit Caramel, 348–51
  Lemon Posset with Strawberries
    and Aged Balsamic, *338,*
    339–40
  Meyer Lemon Kumquat Tart
    with Rye–Cream Cheese Crust,
    344–7
  Olive Oil Cake with Rosemary and
    Pine Nuts, Dario's, 352–3
  Pear Rosemary Tart with Chestnut
    Crust, 341–3

Raspberry Jam Bars with Pistachio
    Crumble, *354, 355–6*
  see also pies, slab
Dill Yogurt, 283
direct and indirect heat, 31–2
Di Stefano Cheese, 40
dolci, see desserts; pies, slab
Dragan, 90
dressings:
  Caesar, 102–3
  Caesar, making by hand, 104–5
  Horseradish, 121–3
  see also Aioli; Vinaigrette
duck:
  Lacquered, with Honey-Balsamic
    Glaze and Crispy Black Rice,
    207, 208–11
  Rillettes Toasts, Chrysanthemum
    Greens with Kumquats and, *92,*
    93–5
Dukkah, Pistachio-Hazelnut, *290,*
    291–2

egg(s):
  Grains and Seeds Salad with
    Escarole, Avocado, Bacon,
    Horseradish Dressing and, 121–5,
    122
  Grated, Little Gems with Herb
    Bread Crumbs, Bacon Vinaigrette
    and, *76,* 77–9
  Soft-Cooked, Puntarella and
    Cauliflower Salad with Bagna
    Cauda, Anchovies and, *86,* 87–9
Eggplant, Whole Roasted, with
    Chickpea Purée and Zhug,
    267–9
electric fire starters, 29–30
equipment, 11–14
  online sources for, 357
escarole:
  "blanched," 101, 113, 121
  Braised Greens, 297
  Grains and Seeds Salad
    with Avocado, Bacon, Egg,
    Horseradish Dressing and, 121–5,
    122
  Indian-Spiced Chicken Salad with
    Mixed Lettuces, Walnuts, and

Preserved Lemon Vinaigrette,
    112, 113–14
  Spacca Caesar with Fried Parsley,
    Anchovies, Orange Zest, and
    Bagna Cauda Croutons, 101–3

family-style, multi-course feasts,
    6–7
farmers' markets, 10–11
farro, in Grains and Seeds Salad with
    Escarole, Avocado, Bacon, Egg,
    and Horseradish Dressing, 121–5,
    122
Feldmeier, Chris, 146, 302
Feng, Cecily, 339
fennel:
  Insalata Inverno: Shaved Winter
    Vegetable Salad with Parmesan
    and Olio Nuovo, *98,* 99–100
  Insalata Primavera: Shaved Spring
    Vegetable Salad with Roasted
    Artichokes and Dill, 96–7
  Pickled, 70
  pollen, 163, 169, 177
  Rub, 20
  Salad, *248,* 250
  Whole Roasted, with Salsa Verde
    and Gremolata Bread Crumbs,
    276–7
Fernald, Anya, 301
Feta Yogurt, Heirloom Tomato
    Panzanella with Olive Bread
    Croutons and, 108–9
Fideus a la Catalana with Sweet
    Sherry and Garlic Aioli, 236–7
Figs, Fresh, Buckwheat Maple Cake
    with, 336–7
finger foods, *see spuntini* (Italian
    word for "snacks")
fire starters, electric, 29–30
fish and seafood (*pesce*), 218–59
  Amberjack Collars, Roasted, with
    Labneh, Zhug, and Radish Salad,
    220, 221–3
  Branzino, Fried Whole, with
    Pickled Cherry Peppers and
    Charred Scallions, *252,* 253–5
  Branzino alla Piastra with Wilted
    Soft Herbs, *224,* 225–6

Calamari, Fried, alla Piccata, 227–8, *229*
Fideus a la Catalana with Sweet Sherry and Garlic Aioli, 236–7
Fish Stock, 232
Lobster Potpie, *238*, 239–42
Mischiato Potente: Mixed Pasta and Seafood Stew, *248*, 249–51
Mussels and Clams, Baked, with N'duja and Aioli, and Toast for Dipping, 230–1
Salmon Steaks, Roasted, with Remoulade Butter, 233–4, *235*
Salt-Baked Fish with Green Olive and Charred Lemon Salmoriglio, *256*, 257–9
Skate Wing with Braised Leeks, Brown Butter, and Capers, 243–5
Yellowtail, Roasted, with Spring or Summer Vegetables, 246–7
see also anchovy(ies)
fishmongers, 10
Flannery, Brian, 130
Focaccia di Recco (*focaccia col formaggio,* or *focaccia with cheese*), *38*, 39–45
making Taralli with scraps of dough from, 46–7
food processors, mini, 13–14
464 Magnolia, Marin County, 163
French cuisine, recipes inspired by, 4
Little Gems with Herb Bread Crumbs, Bacon Vinaigrette, and Grated Egg, *76*, 77–9

Garam Masala, 21
garlic:
Fried Capers and, 136–7
Green, Crème Fraîche, 263
Mashed Potatoes, 299
mayonnaise, *see* Aioli
garnishes:
Bacon-Scallion Topping, *160*, 161–2
Candied Pecans, 83–4
Fried Capers, 184
Fried Garlic and Capers, 136–7
Fried Parsley, 102
Fried Rosemary, 213, *214*
Fried Sage, 164, 178

Grains and Celery Leaf, *270*, 272
Gremolata Bread Crumbs, 276
Herb Bread Crumbs, 77–8, 118
Pistachio Gremolata, 205
Pistachio-Hazelnut Dukkah, *290*, 291–2
Sunflower Seed Crumble, 263
gas grills:
indirect and direct heat in, 32
limitations of, 27–8
Giardiniera, 73
Giron, Ben, 246, 271
glazes:
Honey-Balsamic, 210, 211
Orange–Brown Butter, 266
Gorgonzola Vinaigrette, 90–1
grains:
and Celery Leaf Garnish, *270*, 272
and Seeds Salad with Escarole, Avocado, Bacon, Egg, and Horseradish Dressing, 121–5, *122*
green bean(s):
Charred Beans with Mustard Vinaigrette, 246–7
Pickles, Spicy, 71
Greens, Braised, 297
gremolata:
Bread Crumbs, 276
Pistachio, 205
Grilled Broccolini and Scallions, 310–11
grilled meats:
Bistecca Fiorentina, *133*, 134–5
Lamb Sausage Coils with Onion and Peppers, *200*, 201–3
Lamb Shoulder Chops, Moorish, with Mint Yogurt, 196–7
Pork-and-Veal Meatballs with Fresh Ricotta and Braised Greens, *174*, 175–6
Pork Chop, Tomahawk, with Fennel Pollen, *168*, 169–71
Pork Shoulder Blade Chops with Chipotle and Apple Cider Syrup, *186*, 187–8
Short Ribs, Porcini-Rubbed, with Salsa Verde and Scallions, *140*, 141–2
Tri-Tip, Coffee-Rubbed, 146–7

grilling on wood- or charcoal-fired grill, 27–33
basic kettle grill for, 28
at Chi Spacca, 7, 27
cleaning grill before, 29
controlling flames and, 33
direct and indirect heat in, 31–2
fuels for, 28–9
lighting fire for, 29–31
tips for, 32–3
grills, gas, limitations of, 27–8
grocery stores, fruits and vegetables at, 11
guanciale:
Charred Sugar Snap Peas with Yogurt, Lemon Zest and, 287–8, *289*
Fideus a la Catalana with Sweet Sherry and Garlic Aioli, 236–7

hanger steak, 136
Carne Cruda, Osteria Style, 136–7
Carne Cruda, "Tartufo Povero," *138*, 139
hardwood, grilling with, 28
see also grilling on wood- or charcoal-fired grill
hardwood charcoal (also known as lump charcoal), 28–9
see also grilling on wood- or charcoal-fired grill
hazelnut(s):
Milk-Braised Veal Breast with, 163–5
Pistachio Dukkah, *290*, 291–2
herb(s):
Bread Crumbs, 77–8, 118
and Butter Lettuce Salad with Lemon Dijon Vinaigrette, 110–11
Dario Salt, 19
Remoulade Butter, 233–4, *235*
Salsa Verde, 142, 157, 276
Wilted Soft, Branzino alla Piastra with, *224*, 225–6
Zhug, 222, 267, 268
Holstein cows, 130
Honey-Balsamic Glaze, 210, 211

Honeynut Squash, Roasted, with
    Pistachio-Hazelnut Dukkah, *290*,
    291–2
Hong, Liz, 141
horseradish:
    Atomic, 156
    Crème Fraîche, 156, 158
    Dressing, 121–3
Huntington Meats, 201

Indian (cuisine and flavors):
    Garam Masala, 21
    -Spiced Chicken Salad with Mixed
        Lettuces, Walnuts, and Preserved
        Lemon Vinaigrette, *112*, 113–14
indirect and direct heat, 31–2
ingredient-themed dinners, 7, 180
insalate, see salads
Israeli cuisine, recipes inspired by, 4
    Asparagus al Cartoccio with Butter,
        Mint, and Parmesan, *284*, 285–6
    Roasted Beets with Chicories,
        Yogurt, and Lemon Zest, 115–16,
        117
    Whole Roasted Cauliflower with
        Green Garlic Crème Fraîche and
        Sunflower Seed Crumble, 262–3
    Whole Roasted Eggplant with
        Chickpea Purée and Zhug,
        267–9
Italian cuisine, recipes inspired by,
    3–4
    Baked Mussels and Clams with
        N'duja and Aioli, and Toast for
        Dipping, 230–1
    Baked Potatoes with Whipped
        Lardo, Dario's, 293
    Bistecca Fiorentina, *133*,
        134–5
    Braised Lamb Necks with
        Castelvetrano Olives and
        Preserved Lemon, *190*, 191–2
    Branzino alla Piastra with Wilted
        Soft Herbs, *224*, 225–6
    Focaccia di Recco (*focaccia col
        formaggio*, or focaccia with
        cheese), *38*, 39–45
    Fried Calamari alla Piccata, 227–8,
        229

Grilled Pork-and-Veal Meatballs
    with Fresh Ricotta and Braised
    Greens, *174*, 175–6
Heirloom Tomato Panzanella with
    Olive Bread Croutons and Feta
    Yogurt, 108–9
Milk-Braised Veal Breast with
    Hazelnuts, 163–5
Mischiato Potente: Mixed Pasta
    and Seafood Stew, *248*, 249–51
Pancetta-Wrapped Rabbit with
    Braised Greens, 212–15
Parmesan Soufflé with Ragù
    Bolognese, 180–2
Pollo alla Diavolo on Toast, 216–17
Pork al Latte with Fennel Pollen
    and Crispy Sage, 177–9
Pork Tonnato with Crispy Capers,
    183–5
Roasted Ricotta-Stuffed Squash
    Blossoms with Tomato
    Vinaigrette, *294*, 295–6
Salt-Baked Fish with Green Olive
    and Charred Lemon Salmoriglio,
    256, 257–9
spirit of Italian butcher and, 3, 5–8
Tuscan White Beans, Dario's,
    312–13
see also spuntini (Italian word for
    "snacks")
Izakaya Rintaro, San Francisco, 93

Jajik, 198–9
Japanese cuisine, recipes inspired by:
    Chrysanthemum Greens with
        Kumquats and Duck Rillettes
        Toasts, *92*, 93–5
    Roasted Amberjack Collars with
        Labneh, Zhug, and Radish Salad,
        220, 221–3
Jar, Los Angeles, 156
Jus, Brown Butter, 166–7

kale, Tuscan, in Braised Greens, 297
kanpachi, *see* amberjack
Key Lime Cheesecake with Passion
    Fruit Caramel, 348–51
Kim, Jenee, 141
Kobe beef, 130

Krikorian, Michael, 198
kumquat(s):
    Chrysanthemum Greens with,
        and Duck Rillettes Toasts, *92*,
        93–5
    Meyer Lemon Tart with Rye–Cream
        Cheese Crust, 344–7

Labneh, Roasted Amberjack Collars
    with Zhug, Radish Salad and,
    220, 221–3
lamb, 189–206
    Necks, Braised, with Castelvetrano
        Olives and Preserved Lemon, *190*,
        191–2
    Rack, Roasted, with Dried Persian
        Lime Tahini and Grilled
        Broccolini and Scallions, 193–5,
        194
    Ribs, Armenian-Style, with Jajik,
        198–9
    Ryan's tutorial, 132
    Sausage Coils, Grilled, with Onion
        and Peppers, *200*, 201–3
    Shanks, Moroccan-Braised,
        with Pistachio Gremolata and
        Celeriac Purée, 204–6
    Shoulder Chops, Moorish, with
        Mint Yogurt, 196–7
Lang, Adam Perry, 143
lardo:
    Asador Potatoes, *300*, 301
    Whipped, 59
Lattice-Topped Slab Pies for Spring
    or Summer, 321–6, *322*
    Stone Fruit and Mixed Berry
        Filling for, 323–4
    Strawberry Rhubarb Filling for,
        321–3
Lawry's, Los Angeles, 304, 308
Leeks, Braised, 243–4
lemon(s):
    Anchovy Salsa Rustica, 172–3
    Brown Butter, 244
    Charred, and Green Olive
        Salmoriglio, *256*, 257–9
    Crushed, Bagna Cauda, 278
    Dijon Vinaigrette, 110
    Gremolata Bread Crumbs, 276

Meyer, Kumquat Tart with Rye–
  Cream Cheese Crust, 344–7
Posset with Strawberries and Aged
  Balsamic, *338*, 339–40
Preserved, 23
Preserved, Vinaigrette, 113–14
lettuce(s):
  BLTA Salad with Aioli and Herb
    Bread Crumbs, 118–20
  Butter, and Herb Salad with
    Lemon Dijon Vinaigrette, 110
  Little Gems with Herb Bread
    Crumbs, Bacon Vinaigrette, and
    Grated Egg, *76*, 77–9
  Mixed, Indian-Spiced Chicken
    Salad with, and Walnuts and
    Preserved Lemon Vinaigrette,
    112, 113–14
lime:
  Dried Persian, Tahini (marinade),
    193–5
  Key, Cheesecake with Passion Fruit
    Caramel, 348–51
Lipstick Peppers, Roasted, with
    Anchovies, Mint, and Pecorino
    Toscano, 66–7
Little Gem(s) (lettuce):
  with Herb Bread Crumbs, Bacon
    Vinaigrette, and Grated Egg, *76*,
    77–9
  Indian-Spiced Chicken Salad with
    Mixed Lettuces, Walnuts, and
    Preserved Lemon Vinaigrette,
    112, 113–14
Lobster Potpie, *238*, 239–42

mandolines, 12–13
Maple Buckwheat Cake with Fresh
    Figs, 336–7
marrow bones, in Beef Cheek and
    Bone Marrow Pie, *148*, 149–55
Mascarpone, Whole Roasted
    Sweet Potatoes with Orange–
    Brown Butter Glaze and, *264*,
    265–6
mayonnaise, garlic, *see* Aioli
meat (*carne*), 128–217
  bringing to room temperature
    before grilling, 32

brining, 169, 170, 177
cured, in antipasto platter,
    36, 37
mail-order, sources for, 357–8
resting, before cutting into, 33
Ryan's tutorial, 130–2
seasoning before grilling, 32–3
using the whole animal and,
    6–7
  see also beef; chicken; duck; lamb;
    pork; rabbit
Meatballs, Grilled Pork-and-Veal,
    with Fresh Ricotta and Braised
    Greens, *174*, 175–6
meat thermometers, 13, 33
Meyer Lemon Kumquat Tart with
    Rye–Cream Cheese Crust,
    344–7
Michael's, Santa Monica, 77
Michail, Debbie, 193
Microplane, 11, 14
Middle Eastern cuisine and flavors,
    recipes inspired by, 4
  Pistachio-Hazelnut Dukkah, *290*,
    291–2
  Roasted Amberjack Collars with
    Labneh, Zhug, and Radish Salad,
    220, 221–3
  Roasted Lamb Rack with Dried
    Persian Lime Tahini and Grilled
    Broccolini and Scallions, 193–5,
    194
  Za'atar, 25
  Zhug, 222, 267, 268
Middle Park Hotel, Melbourne,
    Australia, 149
Milk-Braised Veal Breast with
    Hazelnuts, 163–5
Miller, Bobby, 163
mini food processors, 13–14
Mint Yogurt, 196–7
Mischiato Potente: Mixed Pasta and
    Seafood Stew, *248*, 249–51
Misticanza: Shaved Vegetable Salad
    with Radicchio and Sherry Dijon
    Vinaigrette, 106–7
Mizuna, Burrata and Stone Fruit
    Salad with Sweet Peppers and,
    126–7

Molina, Matt, 6, 180
Moorish Lamb Shoulder Chops with
    Mint Yogurt, 196–7
Moroccan-Braised Lamb Shanks
    with Pistachio Gremolata and
    Celeriac Purée, 204–6
mortar and pestle, 11–12, 17
mushrooms:
  Carne Cruda, "Tartufo Povero," *138*,
    139
  Porcini Rub, 22
  portobello, in Insalata Inverno:
    Shaved Winter Vegetable Salad
    with Parmesan and Olio Nuovo,
    98, 99–100
  see also Porcini Rub(bed)
mussels:
  and Clams, Baked, with N'duja
    and Aioli, and Toast for Dipping,
    230–1
  Fideus a la Catalana with Sweet
    Sherry and Garlic Aioli, 236–7
mustard:
  Dijon, Lemon Vinaigrette, 110
  Dijon, Sherry Vinaigrette, 106
  Vinaigrette, 246

Nagar, Shiri, 339
Narvaez, Dahlia, 304, 321, 339, 355
N'duja, 58
nectarines, in Burrata and Stone
    Fruit Salad with Mizuna and
    Sweet Peppers, 126–7
New York steaks, in Pepper Steak
    "Dal Rae," *160*, 161–2
Nguyen, Anna, 83
North Abraxass, Tel Aviv, 115, 285
North African cuisine and flavors,
    recipes inspired by:
  Braised Lamb Necks with
    Castelvetrano Olives and
    Preserved Lemon, *190*, 191–2
  Moorish Lamb Shoulder Chops
    with Mint Yogurt, 196–7
  Moroccan-Braised Lamb Shanks
    with Pistachio Gremolata and
    Celeriac Purée, 204–6
  Preserved Lemons, 23
  Ras el Hanout, 24

Officina della Bistecca, Panzano, Chianti, Italy, 5–6, 293

oil, starting charcoal fire with, 30–1

olive(s):
Bread Croutons, Heirloom Tomato Panzanella with Feta Yogurt and, 108–9
Castelvetrano, Braised Lamb Necks with Preserved Lemon and, *190*, 191–2
Green, and Charred Lemon Salmoriglio, *256*, 257–9
Marinated, with Garlic and Fresh Pecorino, 64

olive oil, 17–18
Cake with Rosemary and Pine Nuts, Dario's, 352–3

Oliveto, Berkeley, 6

onion(s):
braised in apple cider vinegar, *186*, 188
Grilled Lamb Sausage Coils with Peppers and, *200*, 201–3
jarred cocktail, 90

Orange–Brown Butter Glaze, 266

Ottolenghi, Yotam, 4

ovens, wood-burning, replicating intense heat from, 14–15

Ozersky, Josh, 143

Pancetta-Wrapped Rabbit with Braised Greens, 212–15

Pane Tostato, 55
with Bistecca Drippings, *60*, 61

Panzanella, Heirloom Tomato, with Olive Bread Croutons and Feta Yogurt, 108–9

parchment: Asparagus al Cartoccio with Butter, Mint, and Parmesan, *284*, 285–6

Parks BBQ, Los Angeles, 141

Parmesan:
Shaved Winter Vegetable Salad with Olio Nuovo and (Insalata Inverno), *98*, 99–100
Soufflé with Ragù Bolognese, 180–2

parsley:
Fried, 102
Gremolata Bread Crumbs, 276

Parsnips, Roasted, with Chestnut Honey, Garlic, and Thyme, *280*, 281–2

Passion Fruit Caramel, Key Lime Cheesecake with, 348–51

pasta:
angel hair, in Fideus a la Catalana with Sweet Sherry and Garlic Aioli, 236–7
Mischiato Potente: Mixed Pasta and Seafood Stew, *248*, 249–51

Pastry Cream, 331–3

pâtés:
Butcher's, 52–4
Pork Tenderloin Pistachio, *48*, 49–51

pear(s):
Rosemary Tart with Chestnut Crust, 341–3
Watercress and Avocado Salad with Gorgonzola Vinaigrette and, 90–1

Pea Shoots, Pinkerton Avocados with Toasted Pine Nuts, Prosciutto and, *80*, 81–2

Pecans, Candied, 83–4

Pecorino, Fresh, Marinated Olives with Garlic and, 64

Pecorino Toscano, Roasted Lipstick Peppers with Mint, Anchovies and, 66–7

Pepe, Franco, 175, 249

pepper(corns) (black), 16–17
Steak "Dal Rae," *160*, 161–2

peppers:
baby bell, in Giardiniera, 73
Cherry, Pickled, *252*, 253
Grilled Lamb Sausage Coils with Onion and, *200*, 201–3
Lipstick, Roasted, with Anchovies, Mint, and Pecorino Toscano, 66–7
Sweet, Burrata and Stone Fruit Salad with Mizuna and, 126–7
see also chile(s)

Persimmon and Castelfranco Salad with Candied Pecans, Parmesan, and Fruit-and-Nut Toasts, 83–5

pesce, see fish and seafood

Piccata Sauce, 227–8

pickle(d)(s), 68–73

Cherry Peppers, *252*, 253
Cucumber, 72
Fennel, 70
Giardiniera, 73
Green Bean, Spicy, 71
Turmeric Cauliflower, 69

Pie, Beef Cheek and Bone Marrow, *148*, 149–55

Piedmontese cuisine:
Milk-Braised Veal Breast with Hazelnuts, 163–5
Pork Tonnato with Crispy Capers, 183–5

pies, slab:
Apple Quince Streusel, 327–30
Banana Cream, with Caramel Sauce and Bittersweet Chocolate Shavings, 331–4, *335*
Lattice-Topped, for Spring or Summer, 321–6, *322*
Stone Fruit and Mixed Berry Filling for, 323–4
Strawberry Rhubarb Filling for, 321–3

pig-themed dinners, 6–7, 180

pine nuts:
Olive Oil Cake with Rosemary and, Dario's, 352–3
Toasted, Pinkerton Avocados with Pea Shoots, Prosciutto and, *80*, 81–2

Pinkerton Avocados with Pea Shoots, Toasted Pine Nuts, and Prosciutto, *80*, 81–2

pistachio:
Crumble, Raspberry Jam Bars with, *354*, 355–6
Gremolata, 205
Hazelnut Dukkah, *290*, 291–2
Pork Tenderloin Pâté, *48*, 49–51

plating instructions, 9–10

plums, in Burrata and Stone Fruit Salad with Mizuna and Sweet Peppers, 126–7

Pollo alla Diavolo on Toast, 216–17

Porcini Rub(bed), 22
Double-Bone Veal Chops with Roasted Onions and Brown Butter Jus, 166–7

Short Ribs, Grilled, with Salsa
Verde and Scallions, *140*,
141–2
pork, 169–88
brining, 169, 170, 177
fatback, in Whipped Lardo, 59
fatback and belly, in N'duja, 58
fatback and pig parts, in Butcher's
Pâté, 52–4
ground, in Parmesan Soufflé with
Ragù Bolognese, 180–2
heritage breeds, 49, 132, 172, 183
al Latte with Fennel Pollen and
Crispy Sage, 177–9
Ryan's tutorial, 132
shoulder, in Chianti "Tuna," 56–7
Shoulder Blade Chops with
Chipotle and Apple Cider Syrup,
186, 187–8
Tenderloin, Segreto Style, with
Lemon-Anchovy Salsa Rustica,
172–3
Tenderloin Pistachio Pâté, *48*,
49–51
Tomahawk Chop, Grilled, with
Fennel Pollen, *168*, 169–71
Tonnato with Crispy Capers, 183–5
using the whole pig and, 6–7
-and-Veal Meatballs, Grilled,
with Fresh Ricotta and Braised
Greens, *174*, 175–6
see also bacon; guanciale
pork-themed dinners, 6–7, 180
Porter, Hayley, 225
porterhouse steak, in Bistecca
Fiorentina, *133*, 134–5
portobello mushrooms, in Insalata
Inverno: Shaved Winter Vegetable
Salad with Parmesan and Olio
Nuovo, *98*, 99–100
Posset, Lemon, with Strawberries
and Aged Balsamic, *338*,
339–40
potatoes:
Baked, with Whipped Lardo,
Dario's, 293
Garlic Mashed, 299
Lardo Asador, *300*, 301
Potpie, Lobster, *238*, 239–42

Preserved Lemon(s), 23
Vinaigrette, 113–14
Prosciutto, Pinkerton Avocados with
Pea Shoots, Toasted Pine Nuts
and, *80*, 81–2
Puglia, Taralli from, 46–7
Puntarella and Cauliflower Salad
with Bagna Cauda, Anchovies,
and Soft-Cooked Eggs, *86*,
87–9

Quince Apple Streusel Slab Pie,
327–30
Quinoa, in Grains and Seeds Salad
with Escarole, Avocado, Bacon,
Egg, and Horseradish Dressing,
121–5, *122*

rabbit:
Pancetta-Wrapped, with Braised
Greens, 212–15
radicchio:
Shaved Vegetable Salad with,
and Sherry Dijon Vinaigrette
(Misticanza), 106–7
see also Castelfranco
radish(es):
Misticanza: Shaved Vegetable
Salad with Radicchio and Sherry
Dijon Vinaigrette, 106–7
Salad, 222–3
Ragù Bolognese, Parmesan Soufflé
with, 180–2
Rancho Beans, Chris Feldmeier's,
302–3
Ras el Hanout, 24
Raspberry Jam Bars with Pistachio
Crumble, *354*, 355–6
Reichl, Ruth, 39, 187
Remoulade Butter, 233–4, *235*
resting grilled meat before cutting
into, 33
Rhubarb Strawberry Filling for
Lattice-Topped Slab Pie, 321–3
Rib Roast, Standing, APL Style,
143–4, *145*
rice:
Black, Crispy, *207*, 208–11
see also wild rice

ricotta:
Fresh, Grilled Pork-and-Veal
Meatballs with Braised Greens
and, *174*, 175–6
-Stuffed Squash Blossoms, Roasted,
with Tomato Vinaigrette, *294*,
295–6
Rillettes, Duck, Toasts,
Chrysanthemum Greens with
Kumquats and, *92*, 93–5
Ristorante Manuelina, Recco, Italy,
39, 40
Robuchon, Joël, 299
rosemary:
Fried, 213, 214
Olive Oil Cake with Pine Nuts and,
Dario's, 352–3
Pear Tart with Chestnut Crust,
341–3
Rothfeld, Steven, 262
rubs:
Coffee, 146
Fennel, 20
Porcini, 22
Rye Cream Cheese Crust, Meyer
Lemon Kumquat Tart with,
344–7

Sage, Fried, 164, 178
salads (*insalate*), 8, 9, 74–127
Beets, Roasted, with Chicories,
Yogurt, and Lemon Zest, 115–16,
117
BLTA, with Aioli and Herb Bread
Crumbs, 118–20
Burrata and Stone Fruit, with
Mizuna and Sweet Peppers,
126–7
Butter Lettuce and Herb, with
Lemon Dijon Vinaigrette, 110–11
Caesar, with Fried Parsley,
Anchovies, Orange Zest, and
Bagna Cauda Croutons, 101–3
Castelfranco and Persimmon, with
Candied Pecans, Parmesan, and
Fruit-and-Nut Toasts, 83–5
Chrysanthemum Greens with
Kumquats and Duck Rillettes
Toasts, *92*, 93–5

salads (*insalate*) (*continued*)
  Fennel, *248*, 250
  Grains and Seeds, with Escarole, Avocado, Bacon, Egg, and Horseradish Dressing, 121–5, *122*
  Heirloom Tomato Panzanella with Olive Bread Croutons and Feta Yogurt, 108–9
  Indian-Spiced Chicken, with Mixed Lettuces, Walnuts, and Preserved Lemon Vinaigrette, *112*, 113–14
  Insalata Inverno: Shaved Winter Vegetable Salad with Parmesan and Olio Nuovo, *98*, 99–100
  Insalata Primavera: Shaved Spring Vegetable Salad with Roasted Artichokes and Dill, 96–7
  Little Gems with Herb Bread Crumbs, Bacon Vinaigrette, and Grated Egg, *76*, 77–9
  Misticanza: Shaved Vegetable Salad with Radicchio and Sherry Dijon Vinaigrette, 106–7
  Pinkerton Avocados with Pea Shoots, Toasted Pine Nuts, and Prosciutto, *80*, 81–2
  Puntarella and Cauliflower, with Bagna Cauda, Anchovies, and Soft-Cooked Eggs, *86*, 87–9
  Radish, 222–3
  Watercress and Avocado, with Pears and Gorgonzola Vinaigrette, 90–1
Salmon Steaks, Roasted, with Remoulade Butter, 233–4, *235*
Salmoriglio, Green Olive and Charred Lemon, *256*, 257–9
salsas:
  Calabrian Chile, 201, 202
  Green Olive and Charred Lemon Salmoriglio, *256*, 257–9
  Lemon-Anchovy, Rustica, 172–3
Salsa Verde, 142, 157, 276
salt, 17
  -Baked Fish with Green Olive and Charred Lemon Salmoriglio, *256*, 257–9

Dario, 19
  kosher, rock sea, and flaky sea, 17
Salumi Nights, 7
Santa Maria barbecue, 146
Sasso, Anthony, 236
sauces:
  Béchamel, 308
  Caramel, *318*, 319–20, 332, 333–4
  Dill Yogurt, 283
  Jajik, 198–9
  Lemon Brown Butter, 244
  Mint Yogurt, 196–7
  Piccata, 227–8
  Tonnato, 183–5
  Zhug, 222, 267, 268
  see also Aioli; Bagna Cauda
Sausage Coils, Grilled Lamb, with Onion and Peppers, *200*, 201–3
scallion(s):
  Bacon Topping (for steak), *160*, 161–2
  Charred, and Pickled Cherry Peppers, *252*, 253–4
  Grilled Broccolini and, 310–11
Scuola di Pizza, 5–7
sea bass, in Mischiato Potente: Mixed Pasta and Seafood Stew, *248*, 249–51
seafood, *see* fish and seafood (*pesce*)
seafood shops, 10
seasonality, 11
seasonings:
  black pepper, 16–17
  Dario Salt, 19
  salt, 17
  see also spice blends
Seeds, Grains and, Salad with Escarole, Avocado, Bacon, Egg, and Horseradish Dressing, 121–5, *122*
segreto (butcher's cut), use of term, 129, 172
shaved vegetable salads:
  with Radicchio and Sherry Dijon Vinaigrette (Misticanza), 106–7
  Spring, with Roasted Artichokes and Dill (Insalata Primavera), 96–7

  Winter, with Parmesan and Olio Nuovo (Insalata Inverno), *98*, 99–100
sherry:
  Dijon Vinaigrette, 106
  Sweet, and Garlic Aioli, 236–7
shopping:
  from butcher, fishmongers, and farmers, 10–11
  online sources, 357–8
Short Ribs, Grilled Porcini-Rubbed, with Salsa Verde and Scallions, *140*, 141–2
Sicilian flavors, in Braised Lamb Necks with Castelvetrano Olives and Preserved Lemon, *190*, 191–2
side dishes (*contorni*), 8, 9, 260–315
  Asparagus al Cartoccio with Butter, Mint, and Parmesan, *284*, 285–6
  Beans, Charred, with Mustard Vinaigrette, 246–7
  Beans, Rancho, Chris Feldmeier's, 302–3
  Black Rice, Crispy, *207*, 208–11
  Broccolini and Scallions, Grilled, 310–11
  Cabbage, Roasted, with Bagna Cauda Yogurt and Crunchy Grains, *270*, 271–3
  Cabbage, Roasted, with Toasted Caraway Vinaigrette, 274–5
  Carrots, Classic Vichy, 314
  Carrots, Whole Roasted, with Cracked Coriander and Cumin and Dill Yogurt, 283
  Cauliflower, Whole Roasted, with Green Garlic Crème Fraîche and Sunflower Seed Crumble, 262–3
  Cauliflower Wedges, Roasted, with Crushed Lemon Bagna Cauda, 278–9
  Celeriac Purée, 315
  Citrus, Plate of, with Olio Nuovo and Fresh Mint, 306–7
  Corn, Creamed Summer, 298
  Eggplant, Whole Roasted, with Chickpea Purée and Zhug, 267–9

Fennel, Whole Roasted, with Salsa Verde and Gremolata Bread Crumbs, 276–7

Greens, Braised, 297

Honeynut Squash, Roasted, with Pistachio-Hazelnut Dukkah, *290*, 291–2

Leeks, Braised, 243–4

Parsnips, Roasted, with Chestnut Honey, Garlic, and Thyme, *280*, 281–2

Potatoes, Dario's Baked, with Whipped Lardo, 293

Potatoes, Garlic Mashed, 299

Potatoes, Lardo Asador, *300*, 301

Snap Peas with Chive Vinaigrette, 246

Spinach, Creamed, 308–9

Squash Blossoms, Roasted Ricotta-Stuffed, with Tomato Vinaigrette, *294*, 295–6

Sugar Snap Peas, Charred, with Yogurt, Guanciale, and Lemon Zest, 287–8, *289*

Sweet Potatoes, Whole Roasted, with Orange–Brown Butter Glaze and Mascarpone, *264*, 265–6

White Beans, Tuscan, Dario's, 312–13

Yorkshire Pudding with Aged Beef Trimmings, 304–5

Skate Wing with Braised Leeks, Brown Butter, and Capers, 243–5

slab pies, *see* pies, slab

snacks, *see* spuntini (Italian word for "snacks")

Snap Peas with Chive Vinaigrette, 246

Soufflé, Parmesan, with Ragù Bolognese, 180–2

Spanish Fideus a la Catalana with Sweet Sherry and Garlic Aioli, 236–7

spice blends:
  Dario Salt, 19
  Fennel Rub, 20
  Garam Masala, 21
  Ras el Hanout, 24
  Za'atar, 25

spice grinders, 12, 17

spices:
  black pepper, 16–17
  online sources for, 358

Spinach, Creamed, 308–9

spreads:
  N'duja, 58
  Whipped Lardo, 59

spring vegetable(s):
  Salad with Roasted Artichokes and Dill (Insalata Primavera), 96–7
  Snap Peas with Chive Vinaigrette, 246

spuntini (Italian word for "snacks"), 9, 34–73
  antipasto platter (or *tagliere*), how to build, *36*, 37
  Butcher's Pâté, 52–4
  Cetara Anchovies and Butter on Toast, 62, *63*
  Chianti "Tuna," 56–7
  Dates, Warm, with Sea Salt, 65
  Focaccia di Recco (*focaccia col formaggio*, or focaccia with cheese), *38*, 39–45
  Lardo, Whipped, 59
  Lipstick Peppers, Roasted, with Anchovies, Mint, and Pecorino Toscano, 66–7
  N'duja, 58
  Olives, Marinated, with Garlic and Fresh Pecorino, 64
  Pane Tostato, 55
  Pane Tostato with Bistecca Drippings, *60*, 61
  Pork Tenderloin Pistachio Pâté, *48*, 49–51
  Taralli, 46–7
  see also pickle(d)(s)

Squash, Honeynut, Roasted, with Pistachio-Hazelnut Dukkah, *290*, 291–2

Squash Blossoms, Roasted Ricotta-Stuffed, with Tomato Vinaigrette, *294*, 295–6

Standing Rib Roast, APL Style, 143–4, *145*

starters, *see* spuntini (Italian word for "snacks")

stock:
  Chicken, 149–50, 159
  Fish, 232

stone fruit:
  and Burrata Salad with Mizuna and Sweet Peppers, 126–7
  and Mixed Berry Filling, for Lattice-Topped Slab Pie, 323–4

stracchino (also called crescenza), in Focaccia di Recco (*focaccia col formaggio*, or focaccia with cheese), *38*, 39–45

strawberry(ies):
  Lemon Posset with, and Aged Balsamic, *338*, 339–40
  Rhubarb Filling for Lattice-Topped Slab Pie, 321–3
  Streusel Slab Pie, Apple Quince, 327–30

striped bass, in Mischiato Potente: Mixed Pasta and Seafood Stew, *248*, 249–51

Sugar Snap Peas, Charred, with Yogurt, Guanciale, and Lemon Zest, 287–8, *289*

Summer Vegetables: Charred Beans with Mustard Vinaigrette, 246–7

Sunflower Seed Crumble, 263

Sweet Potatoes, Whole Roasted, with Orange–Brown Butter Glaze and Mascarpone, *264*, 265–6

Swiss chard, in Braised Greens, 297

Syrup, Apple Cider, 187

tagliere, *see* antipasto platter

Tagorda, Joe, 257

tahini:
  Chickpea Purée, 267–8
  Dried Persian Lime (marinade), 193–5

Takenaka, Marisa, 341, 344

Taralli, 46–7

tarts:
  Meyer Lemon Kumquat, with Rye–Cream Cheese Crust, 344–7
  Pear Rosemary, with Chestnut Crust, 341–3

Tellicherry peppercorns, 16

thermometers:
  deep-fry, 13
  meat, 13, 33
Thollaug, Cameron, 99
thyme, in Za'atar, 25
toast(s):
  Carne Cruda, Osteria Style, 136–7
  Cetara Anchovies and Butter on, 62, *63*
  Duck Rillettes, Chrysanthemum Greens with Kumquats and, *92*, 93–5
  Pane Tostato, 55
  Pane Tostato with Bistecca Drippings, *60*, 61
  Pollo alla Diavolo on, 216–17
tomato:
  BLTA Salad with Aioli and Herb Bread Crumbs, 118–20
  Heirloom, Panzanella with Olive Bread Croutons and Feta Yogurt, 108–9
  Vinaigrette, *294*, 295
Tonnato, Pork, with Crispy Capers, 183–5
tools, 11–14
  online sources for, 357
Tracht, Suzanne, 156
Tri-Tip, Coffee-Rubbed Grilled, 146–7
Tuna, Poached, in Pork Tonnato with Crispy Capers, 183–5
Turmeric Cauliflower Pickles, 69
turnips, in Misticanza: Shaved Vegetable Salad with Radicchio and Sherry Dijon Vinaigrette, 106–7
Tuscan cuisine and flavors, recipes inspired by:
  Bistecca Fiorentina, *133*, 134–5

Chianti "Tuna," 56–7
Salt, Dario's, 19
White Beans, Dario's, 312–13
two-burner cast-iron griddle/grill pans:
  on oven floor, 15
  on stovetop, 28

veal:
  Breast, Milk-Braised, with Hazelnuts, 163–5
  Chops, Porcini-Rubbed Double-Bone, with Roasted Onions and Brown Butter Jus, 166–7
  ground, in Parmesan Soufflé with Ragù Bolognese, 180–2
  -and-Pork Meatballs, Grilled, with Fresh Ricotta and Braised Greens, *174*, 175–6
  Ryan's tutorial, 131
Vinaigrette, 94, 115, 126, 310
  Bacon, 77–8
  Caraway, Toasted, 274
  Chive, 246
  Gorgonzola, 90–1
  Lemon Dijon, 110
  Mustard, 246
  Preserved Lemon, 113–14
  Sherry Dijon, 106
  Tomato, *294*, 295

Wagyu beef, 130
watercress:
  and Avocado Salad with Pears and Gorgonzola Vinaigrette, 90–1
  BLTA Salad with Aioli and Herb Bread Crumbs, 118–20
Waxman, Jonathan, 77, 183
Whipped Cream, *318*, 320, 332, 333, 349, 351

Whipped Lardo, 59
White Beans, Tuscan, Dario's, 312–13
Wicks, Kim, 19, 352
wild rice:
  Grains and Celery Leaf Garnish, *270*, 272
  Grains and Seeds Salad with Escarole, Avocado, Bacon, Egg, and Horseradish Dressing, 121–5, *122*
Willinger, Faith, 19, 249
Winter Vegetable Salad with Parmesan and Olio Nuovo (Insalata Inverno), *98*, 99–100
wood-fired grills, 28–33
  at Chi Spacca, 7, 27
  fuels for, 28
  see also grilling on wood- or charcoal-fired grill

Yellowtail, Roasted, with Spring or Summer Vegetables, 246–7
yogurt:
  Bagna Cauda, *270*, 271–2
  Dill, 283
  Feta, Heirloom Tomato Panzanella with Olive Bread Croutons and, 108–9
  Jajik, 198–9
  Labneh, 221–2
  Mint, 196–7
  Roasted Beets with Chicories, Lemon Zest and, 115–16, *117*
Yorkshire Pudding with Aged Beef Trimmings, 304–5
Yuen, Herbie, 308

Za'atar, 25
Zhug, 222, 267, 268
Ziman, Jess, 253

A NOTE ABOUT THE AUTHORS

Nancy Silverton is the co-owner of Osteria Mozza (which was awarded a Michelin Star in 2019), Pizzeria Mozza, Chi Spacca, and Mozza2Go, in Los Angeles and Newport Beach, California. She is the founder of the La Brea Bakery and is the only person ever to be awarded both the Outstanding Chef and Outstanding Pastry Chef awards from the James Beard Foundation. In 2014, Silverton was listed as one of the Most Innovative Women in Food and Drink by both *Fortune* and *Food & Wine* magazines, and in 2017, she was profiled in an episode of Netflix's award-winning docu-series *Chef's Table*. Silverton is the author of ten cookbooks, including *Mozza at Home, The Mozza Cookbook, A Twist of the Wrist, Nancy Silverton's Sandwich Book, Nancy Silverton's Pastries from the La Brea Bakery* (recipient of a 2000 *Food & Wine* Best Cookbook Award), *Nancy Silverton's Breads from the La Brea Bakery,* and *Desserts*. She is planning to open two new restaurants, an Italian steakhouse in the Hollywood Roosevelt Hotel called The Barish—named after her ancestors, who were cattle ranchers in Saskatchewan, Canada, during the early twentieth century—and Pizzette in Culver City.

Ryan DeNicola, a graduate of the Culinary Institute of America in Hyde Park, New York, is the executive chef of Chi Spacca in Los Angeles. Ryan began cooking as a child, inspired by his grandmother and father. He worked in kitchens across the country, but has found most inspiration from working in Los Angeles at the kitchens of Son of a Gun, Michael's, and Pizzeria Mozza. Ryan was named to Zagat's 30 Under 30 list in 2015 after taking the reins of Chi Spacca at age twenty-seven.

Carolynn Carreño is a writer whose essays and feature stories have been published in *The New York Times Magazine, Saveur, Gourmet, Bon Appétit, Food & Wine, Playboy, Tu Ciudad,* the *Los Angeles Times,* and the *Los Angeles Times Magazine,* among other publications. She is the author or co-author of more than fifteen books and is currently working on a memoir, *Cooking My Way to Mexican,* about food and family. She lives in San Diego and Mexico City.